The Game of t

The Game of the Name

INTRODUCING LOGIC, LANGUAGE,
AND MIND

Gregory McCulloch

CLARENDON PRESS · OXFORD
1989

Oxford University Press, Walton Street, Oxford OX2 6DP
Oxford New York Toronto
Delhi Bombay Calcutta Madras Karachi
Petaling Jaya Singapore Hong Kong Tokyo
Nairobi Dar es Salaam Cape Town
Melbourne Auckland
and associated companies in
Berlin Ibadan

Oxford is a trade mark of Oxford University Press

Published in the United States
by Oxford University Press, New York

British Library Cataloguing in Publication Data
McCulloch, Gregory
The game of the name: introducing logic, language
and mind.
1. Language. Philosophical perspectives
I. Title
401
ISBN 0-19-875087-0
ISBN 0-19-875086-2 (pbk.)

Library of Congress Cataloging in Publication Data
McCulloch, Gregory.
The game of the name: introducing logic, language, and mind/
Gregory McCulloch.
Bibliography: p.   Includes index.
1. Analysis (Philosophy)   2. Cognitive science.   I. Title.
B808.5.M43   1989   146'.4-dc19   88-37246
ISBN 0-19-875087-0
ISBN 0-19-875086-2 (pbk.)

Typeset by Joshua Associates Limited, Oxford
Printed and bound in
Great Britain by Biddles Ltd.
Guildford and King's Lynn

For Ros

Preface

This book is an introduction to central aspects of contemporary philosophy. It started life in 1978 as an undergraduate dissertation on John McDowell's insufficiently celebrated paper 'On the Sense and Reference of a Proper Name'. Then, as now, that paper seemed to me to concentrate into one vivid issue many of the major concerns of twentieth-century philosophy. At length the undergraduate dissertation grew into an Oxford B. Phil. thesis, which in turn was expanded, under McDowell's supervision, and awarded the D. Phil. in 1983. This book is the latest member of that series, although not one sentence even of its immediate predecessor remains.

The reason for this abrupt discontinuity has already been given: the book is intended primarily to introduce undergraduates to the major philosophical concerns on which McDowell's paper focuses so vividly. These concerns are almost exclusively to do with language and logic, on the one hand, and mind, on the other, and thus with the organizing notion, meaning. Of course, anyone who knows anything about modern philosophy will probably know that it has had these rather exclusive concerns for the best part of the present century. But the obsession with meaning has been refocused and, if anything, intensified of late by the growth of, and partial invasion of philosophy by, the discipline called 'cognitive science'. This development gives rise to mixed feelings. On the one hand, there is no doubt that philosophy, at least in English-speaking circles, has been enjoying something of a renaissance since, say, the mid-1960s. It needs little imagination or expertise to appreciate the qualitative improvement in resourcefulness, depth, focus, and professionalism shown by the average post-1970 philosophical book or article over its counterpart of the 1950s: and a chief reason for this, it seems to me, is the presence of fall-out from the re-emergence of the 'computer model' of the mind. But on the other side of the matter is an increasing problem. The new mind/language/computers 'interface' philosophy is helping to generate a vast secondary literature of technical and pseudo-technical material, much of it presupposing highly specific and contentious answers to profound philosophical questions which usually receive, at best, a cursory mention. Thus new students who wish to work into this contemporary material have a serious problem. They realize they have to know a bit about modern logic, and rather more about its attendant metaphysics and about the elements of materialism in the philosophy of mind. And they certainly receive the impression from much modern literature that some grand synthesis has taken place which somehow incorporates all that is best in these three fields. What, in my experience, they are unlikely to find much explicit help with is the original shape and nature of the material that has allegedly been thus synthesized. But without this they are helpless.

So I have attempted to provide such help here. I have assumed the small familiarity with elementary symbolic logic which the usual introductory course makes available, the general awareness of the problems, aims, and methods of analytic philosophy which one or two years of undergraduate studies would provide, and little else besides. My hope is that by working through this book the student will gain the sort of orientation that an entry into central contemporary debate requires: a sense of where the 'interface' philosophy has come from, and thus a feel for the typical philosophical concerns and alternatives that its background dictates.

I should, however, admit here to a certain somewhat ulterior motive. Despite my admiration for much recent work on language, mind, and logic, I am rather sceptical about the 'interface' philosophy, and doubt whether much of it is even on the right lines: certainly I do not suppose, as some of its more enthusiastic proponents seem to do, that it is only a matter of time before someone gets all the details right and we can stop worrying about mind and language. Thus, as well as being intended to serve as an introduction to the background of contemporary debate, this book is also partly intended to inculcate in the reader the right sort of philosophical attitude to its subject-matter. Philosophy flourishes best when people come together to cultivate the art and skills of good thinking: it degenerates into useless scholasticism, deservedly scorned by those in other walks of life, when its practitioners consider themselves to be the guardians and perpetrators of an overarching and all-powerful body of doctrine. In my view, too many contributions to the aforementioned secondary literature are barely philosophical at all, but instead read like popularizing sketches towards an adumbration of a prolegomenon for any future naturalistic metaphysic. But producing work like this is every bit as bad as looking for one's philosophy in the *Oxford English Dictionary*, and equally to be avoided.

I have been aware of three of the particular vices to which a book of the present kind is prey. First, one should not merely attempt to produce a bland or even-handed conspectus of even the main possible positions in the field. Apart from the fact that such an enterprise would be virtually impossible in the present case due to sheer size and complexity, such handbooks can at best inform: whereas philosophy students should be encouraged to think for themselves as early as possible. But second, neither should the author of an introduction set out to defend rigorously and in detail one particular position in the field. Such an effort can exemplify the best of philosophical rigour and commitment to argumentation, and perhaps even inspire similar things in some readers. But it is perhaps more likely to bemuse or intimidate, to engender a sense of powerlessness and an ultimate disinclination to reason things out. Finally, of course, one should not merely discuss in a piecemeal and disconnected fashion whatever aspects of the contemporary scene one happens to find most interesting at the time. Some kind of unifying theme is required.

I have principally tried to avoid these three vices by a policy of ruthless suppression. For unity, I have taken one particular issue— that of the Proper Name—and pursued it through the various regions of logic, language, and mind with which I am concerned, barely glancing at any other phenomenon. What will emerge, I hope, is that the Proper Name is as good a peg as any on which the relevant topics may be hung. To avoid blandness I have written from one particular, and not exactly orthodox, perspective on how the matters with which I am concerned should hang together: and I have tried to make this perspective defensible and reasonable. However, I have not tried to have the last word on things, and have certainly not defended my orientation against all comers, or followed up the possible lines of development to any significant degree. Worse, as the more experienced reader will quickly realize, I have not skimped on quietly suppressing complications when I deemed this to be necessary. I make no apologies for any of this. The business of the teacher of philosophy, above all, is to inspire discussion and a move towards understanding, to provoke reasoned debate in the context of a moderate knowledgeability. This is what I have tried to do.

I am grateful to a number of people for various kinds of help. Michael Lockwood supervised the B.Phil. thesis and John McDowell, besides supervising the D.Phil version, encouraged me to turn it into a book. Robert Black, Harold Noonan, Peter Smith, and Tim Williamson commented on large portions of earlier drafts of the material, suggesting numerous improvements and generally forcing me to produce a better work than I could otherwise have done. An exchange of letters and articles with Peter Carruthers helped me to become clearer about what I wanted to say in chapter 6. Thanks are also due to Roger Gallie, Jonathan Harrison, Roger Montague, and Sir Maurice Shock. A special mention is due to Nick Measor, who over the years, first as tutor and then as colleague and friend, helped me in more ways than I could possibly now remember. But above all I am grateful to Rosalind McCulloch, without whose continued faith and support all would have been in vain, and to whom I dedicate this book with love and admiration.

G.W.McC

University of Nottingham
December 1987

Contents

Bibliographical Note

Since this is an introductory text I have not attempted anything like comprehensiveness in the citation of references. Rather I have appended to each chapter a fairly short bibliography of works which are either too important to be missed from any list, or especially helpful in orienting the reader on a specific topic. Textual references to major historical sources, notably the works of Frege and Russell, and to works frequently mentioned, are by title, occasionally abbreviated in a manner explained at the relevant time. Other textual references are by authorial surname, with date of publication if appropriate (e.g. QUINE (1940)). In all cases, details are to be found in the Further Reading section at the end of the appropriate chapter, and also in the main Bibliography.

List of Abbreviations

Books and articles

NN	*Naming and Necessity* (Kripke (1980))
OD	'On Denoting' (Russell (1905))
OR	'On Referring' (Strawson (1950))
PB	'A Puzzle About Belief' (Kripke (1979))
PLA	'The Philosophy of Logical Atomism' (Russell (1918b))
RDD	'Reference and Definite Descriptions' (Donnellan (1966))
VR	*The Varieties of Reference* (Evans (1982))

(for full details see Bibliography)

Journals

A	*Analysis*
BBS	*Behavioural and Brain Sciences*
PAS	*Proceedings of the Aristotelian Society*
PQ	*Philosophical Quarterly*
PR	*Philosophical Review*
S	*Synthèse*

Propositions (in order of appearance)

(Def∀) '$\forall x(Gx)$' is T if and only if the function G ... yields T for each argument of the domain.

(Def ∃) '$\exists x(Gx)$' is T if and only if the function G ... yields T for at least one argument of the domain.

(RTD) 'the G is H' = '$\exists x(\forall y(Gy \leftrightarrow x = y) \,\&\, Hx)$'

(DefI) '$Ix(Gx, Hx)$' is T if and only if (i) the function G ... yields T for just one argument of the domain, and (ii) the function H ... yields T for that same argument.

(DQ) Treat descriptions quantificationally

(NQ) Treat natural names quantificationally

(ND) Treat natural names as descriptions

(LL) (Leibniz's Law)

    FROM Ga

    AND $a = b$

    INFER Gb

(PA) (Russell's *Principle of Acquaintance*) 'You cannot name anything you are not acquainted with.'

(RP) (*Russell's Particularism*) 'In every atomic fact [simplest imaginable fact] there is one component which is naturally expressed by a verb. This . . . is a relation. . . . Atomic facts contain, besides the relation, the terms of the relation. . . . These . . . I define as "particulars". Only particulars can be named.'

(Def ◇) '◇ *P*' is T (at @) if and only if '*P*' is T at at least one possible world.

(Def□) '□ *P*' is T (at @) if and only if '*P*' is T at all possible worlds.

(Def ◇ *) an object *x* of @'s domain yields T (at @) for any function ◇ *G* . . . if and only if *x* yields T for *G* . . . at at least one possible world.

(Def□*) an object *x* of @'s domain yields T (at @) for any function □ *G* . . . if and only if *x* yields T for *G* . . . at all possible worlds.

(IND) A natural name '*N*' as used by speaker *S* abbreviates the description which *S* would offer in reply to 'Who/What is *N*?'

Introduction

ISSUES

This book is intended to introduce the reader to some central issues in contemporary philosophy. More specifically, it deals with topics in the philosophies of mind, language, and logic. More specifically still, it is a book about proper names. The link between these themes needs to be briefly explained.

That contemporary philosophers should be concerned with the mind is not surprising. Questions about minds, regarding how they fit into and interact with the world at large, are perhaps the oldest and most intractable philosophical issues of all. Some of them, moreover, become particularly pressing in the context of 'scientific' viewpoints: and contemporary philosophy is dominated by such viewpoints. That language should then be a focus is also hardly surprising. We ourselves are paradigm cases of beings with minds, and our use of language is central to our psychological mode of being. And once language is in the picture, logic cannot be far behind, since the logical analysis of linguistic structures is a crucial part of any understanding of how they work. In any case, philosophers have always been concerned with logic—logic being the study of what comprises a certain type of goodness in argument and reasoning, and philosophers being above all professionals in these two domains, how could things be otherwise?

BACKGROUND

There are, however, more specific and partly historical reasons why these stock philosophical interests should arrange themselves in the way that informs this book. Logic as a proper developing science came of age just over a hundred years ago, particularly in the work of Gottlob Frege. Frege set out to systematize the type of reasoning typically used by mathematicians, and his general use of examples indicate also an interest in the language used by scientists when going about their serious information-gathering business. So successful was his attempt that it would not have been surprising had it alone encouraged philosophers to concentrate more and more on these typical uses of language. But the reception of Frege's work was influenced by a growing concentration by philosophers on the idea that science is the major, or even only, source of genuine knowledge of the overall nature of things. As a result, traditional philosophical and metaphysical work has come to be invaded by, and considered to overlap with, more specialized concerns to do with the elements of logic and language as considered in a scientific context. Not that these matters could ever be pursued in complete isolation from each other: but twentieth-century philosophy in English-speaking countries has certainly brought off a characteristic and distinctive synthesis.

Such general links with the philosophy of mind which immediately arise in this context were further strengthened by Frege's specific orientation. Part of his achievement was to devise a new symbolism to help formulate his logical insights. But he was concerned too with questions about the ways in which thinkers—the users of linguistic argument—understand the words and symbols used. This was partly because he considered the logic of his own time to be hopelessly on the wrong track owing to its mistaken conception of how mind and language are related. He therefore made efforts explicitly to embed his logical theses in what he believed to be a more adequate conception of mind and thought. And this moved his concerns into a wider arena: the philosophies of mind and language generally. In any case, one cannot do logic without involving such matters, at least implicitly. Arguments are, after all, usually propounded in ordinary language, and if logic could tell us nothing about these arguments then it would not be worth bothering with. The very least that a logical symbolism like Frege's should be capable of, then, is expressing, accurately enough for reasoning purposes, the arguments whose goodness and badness we are most interested in—the ones we are likely to use. But assessing a symbolism's adequacy in this way presupposes some grasp of *what it is* for a stretch of reasoning to 'give accurate expression to' the thoughts involved in the argument: and this is the business of the philosophy of language.

For these and other reasons one simply cannot claim to have a proper acquaintance with contemporary English-language philosophy unless one has some detailed appreciation of how the broad currents just mentioned have come together: and the main aim of this book is to provide the reader with the necessary perspective.

WHY NAMES?

A philosopher of language once said that proper names are 'pegs on which to hang descriptions'. This was intended as a view about how names contribute to logically significant discourse, and as such we shall encounter it in the final chapter. However, as a description of how I have organized the materials of this book the claim is most apt. This brings us to a final question: Why should proper names figure at the centre of a book about the aforementioned topics? The main reason again goes back to Frege. His central logical insight involves naming and attendant notions, as we shall see. So given Frege's subsequent importance this is a natural issue to focus on. There is, furthermore, a rich and illuminating literature on the subject—and this book, after all, is an introduction to the philosophy which gave rise to that literature. Finally, we live in a world of particular things: material objects, places, persons, institutions. These are the things which we characteristically name; for Frege they are all *objects*, basic extralinguistic entities on which he built his logic; and they are also central among the things we think and reason about. We thus arrive back at the philosophy of mind. For the question, How can thoughts be *about* things in the world?, is one of its most fundamental concerns.

PLAN

Chapter 1 is concerned with the logical background to the issues that concern us. First Frege's basic logical ideas are described in plain outline, and it is then explained why proper names are such a central issue given the Fregean starting-point. Chapter 2 sets out Russell's version of these Fregean ideas, and explains some of the reasons that led him to reject Frege's specific proposals about names and related expressions. Chapter 3 deepens this Russellian attack on Frege by unearthing the views about knowledge and meaning that underlie it: and although it is argued that Russell's extreme views on these matters are untenable, it is also shown that there is a serious charge against Frege which survives this anti-Russellian conclusion. In respect of this outstanding matter Strawson's diagnosis of a mistake that Russell allegedly makes when opposing Frege on names, etc., is described, and it is set out in more detail how one might develop the Fregean theory further. But we find that no progress is to be made beyond this point until the matter of *meaning* is clarified. Chapter 4 concerns an influential attack on Russell initiated by Kripke's work on 'modal' logics, that is logics containing words like 'necessarily' and 'possibly'. The outlines of Kripke's work are accordingly sketched, but it is concluded at length that the 'modal' argument fails—or, at least, rests upon a 'non-modal' background. By now the matter of meaning is pressing, and in chapter 5 we turn to this: first describing, in plain outline, Frege's theory of meaning (*Sinn*) and its relationship to the logical theory described in chapter 1. The remainder of the chapter treats the notion of meaning in a more general context, and a 'third person' approach to the phenomenon, based on common-sense or 'Intentional' psychology, is defended. The rest of the book is then concerned with the problems left outstanding from chapters 1–4, with the intention that the intervening discussion of meaning will have made them easier to deal with. In chapter 6 an account of demonstratives (expressions like 'this', 'that', etc.) is given and defended, whose principal feature is that uses of such expressions have no *Sinn*—so are in this sense meaningless—unless they actually refer to an object. Theories like this are widely rejected on the strength of some apparently formidable arguments taken from the philosophy of mind, and the second half of the chapter is given over to a direct confrontation with these arguments. The thesis of *externalism* in the philosophy of mind is defended in the teeth of the Cartesian thesis of *internalism* which, it is shown, underlies the aforementioned arguments. This brings us to chapter 7, where Russell is more or less upheld, after a struggle, against Strawson on the question of definite descriptions (expressions like 'the tallest woman', 'the present king of France', etc.). A crucial matter here is that Russell's notorious importation of epistemology into logic and language is, after a fashion, upheld: more or less as Russell said, you cannot name anything you are not acquainted with. This leads on to chapter 8 and proper names themselves. Another batch of Kripkean objections to Russell's proposals are considered, and it is conceded that Russellian 'description' theories of names face a number of serious problems. But after a discussion of the sort of alternative treatment suggested by Kripke's work it emerges that this alternative *also* faces a number of serious problems. Indeed, in a sense, they are the very same problems as those faced by the Russellian approach. I conclude, somewhat tentatively, that the best approach to names in the face of these difficulties would probably incorporate elements from both treatments.

1

Frege: The Background

I SEMANTICS

It was Frege's innovations in the foundations of logic which brought philosophers to focus so intently on proper names and related notions. Consequently, we begin by reminding the reader of enough of the basic ideas of modern logic to make the initial moves in the debate intelligible. In these opening sections the accent is on straightforward, non-technical exposition of what are in fact Frege's leading logical ideas, with very little by way of criticism and qualification, or formal development. Other important aspects of Frege's work, which more properly belong to the philosophies of language and mind rather than to logic, will be discussed in chapter 5.

Frege's most striking innovation was his treatment of the generality expressed by words like 'all', 'everything', 'nothing', 'some', etc. Generality had always been of interest to logicians in the sense that the most systematic and central part of traditional logic was concerned with the interrelations between general propositions, as in inferences like:

All dogs are mammals

All mammals are animals   So, all dogs are animals.[1]

But there is a sense in which even this central part of logic was not very adequately understood before Frege. Broadly speaking, the logician's interests range from the purely descriptive to the definitional or elucidatory. The descriptive task is essentially classificatory or taxonomic, since it involves sorting arguments into good and bad ones. The task of providing definitions and elucidations involves *semantics*: and it was the semantics of generality which was not very well understood before Frege. Roughly speaking, semantics concerns the meaning, or significance, of language: but to say this is not to say very much, since all sorts of features and functions of language can be considered as aspects of its meaningfulness. For instance, language serves to conjure up ideas and feelings, to incite people to action, to oil the wheels of interpersonal exchange, to convey pieces of information, and so on. Logicians, however, are typically concerned with aspects of one rather restricted, though undeniably important, function of language, and with a small number of concepts intended to elucidate these aspects. The function is that of using language to argue and reason, which normally involves starting off with one or more premisses or assertions and then drawing one or more conclusions from them. As remarked above, part of the logician's task is then to sort arguments into the good and the bad. But this immediately raises the question, what *makes* an argument good or bad?—and addressing this question is one of the central tasks of semantics. Essential to the idea of the goodness of an argument is that of *truth*: classically, a good deductive argument is one whose conclusion *must be* true if its premisses are. So one can attempt to elucidate what it means to say that a conclusion *must be* true if certain premisses are. But one may also enquire into the notion of truth itself, and attempt to give an elucidation and/or definition of it. One very important subsidiary idea, whichever of these two projects is undertaken, is that whether or not a proposition is true depends partly upon its internal constitution: the words it comprises and the way in which these words are joined together. Consequently, the semantic enterprise characteristically involves the logician in attributing to words and other structurally relevant features of propositions certain *logical powers* or *semantic values*, which are conceived of as those properties of the expressions, etc. which help to determine whether or not the propositions in which they appear are true. And this in turn is supposed to help answer our question, what it is about a valid argument that *makes it* valid? That is, an adequate attribution of semantic values is supposed not only to show what it is about propositions that make them true or otherwise, but also to show why certain propositions have to be true if certain others are.

All of this will become clearer as we work through specific examples in the following sections, where we focus on Frege's account of semantic value: his account of the logical structure of language, and of the logical or semantic powers of the elements of this structure. Frege's views here focus on the links between language and the world. For it can hardly be denied that a concern with truth is also a concern with the relationship between language and its subject-matter.

We are interested in truth because we are interested in what the world is like: truths tell us, precisely, how things are with the world. And this suggests the following idea, which is at the heart of Frege's (and hence subsequent) semantics: an expression's semantic power is to be explained in terms of the fact that the expression *represents* or *stands for* some or other extralinguistic entity, or item in the world. That is, different expressions or sorts of expressions are said to represent different entities or sorts of entities, and this is supposed to account for the variety in the expressions' logical behaviour, as when they appear in arguments. Part of the greatness of Frege's achievement resides in the precision and power of his interpretation of this idea. As we shall soon see, proper names slip into this story with an immediate, and arguably ineliminable, centrality: but before this can be explained we must have before us the fundamental logical ideas which Frege introduced on the basis of the approach to semantics just mentioned.

2 ARITHMETICAL LANGUAGE

Frege's logic grew out of his semantic analysis of simple arithmetical language. His view of arithmetic will seem rather odd, at least to some readers, and it is certainly controversial. However, as we shall see in §6, one does not have to accept it even if one accepts the Fregean approach to logic which grew out of it. On the other hand, starting off with the arithmetical ideas certainly makes the logical ones easier to grasp: so I suggest that the reader take on board the material of the present section with as many pinches of salt as that requires.

Suppose we start with the basic numerals '1', '2', '3', ..., and with signs for elementary arithmetical operations—say, '+', '−', '×', '÷'. And we allow that these two kinds of sign can be combined in the usual ways to make complex arithmetical expressions, such as '3 + 4', '45 − 8', '6 × 105', etc. Frege proposed the following account of the arithmetical meaning or significance of these three different kinds of expression. First, we are to suppose that the subject-matter of arithmetic partly consists of a stock or *domain* of numbers. Numbers are to be thought of as real, though abstract (non-material) *objects*: they are as much a part of the Universe as, say, sticks and stones, and are not merely 'concepts' or ideas in people's minds. Nor are they material things such as marks on paper: they are abstract objects which, said Frege, are indicated by (some of) these marks—for instance, numerals like '1', '2', and '3'. That is, these basic numerals stand for, or represent, one or other member of the domain of numbers, or arithmetical objects. Thus '1' represents the number one, '2' represents the number two, and so on. And such a fact, according to Frege, constitutes the arithmetical meaning or significance of these basic numerals.

Similarly, said Frege, the complex expressions like '3 + 4' also represent numbers. For instance, '3 + 4' represents the number seven, '45 − 8' represents the number thirty-seven, and so on (in general: perform the operation suggested by the complex expression, and the solution is the number represented).

That takes care of the first two types of arithmetical expression: and on the basis of these two proposals Frege then proceeded to give his semantic account of the third kind of expression mentioned above, namely, the operator symbols '+', '−', etc. The trick depends on noticing that the complex expressions exhibit arithmetically significant patterns. Thus

$$3 + 4 \qquad 7 + 4 \qquad 33 + 61 \qquad \text{and} \qquad 98 + 2$$

exhibit the following pattern: they each consist of a numeral, followed by '+', followed by another numeral. This pattern we may exemplify thus:

$$`\ldots + - - -\,',$$

with the gaps '. . .' and '− − −' marking the places where numerals have to be inserted in order to form a complex arithmetical expression. Now, just as Frege took it that numerals and complex arithmetical expressions represent real extralinguistic things—numbers—so he took the *patterns* also to represent something real (though again abstract). These things he called *functions*, and he considered them to be complementary to, but fundamentally different from, objects. The essence of these simple arithmetical functions, for Frege, consisted in their capacity to 'take' one or more numbers and 'yield' a corresponding number. Thus the function represented by '. . . + − − −' takes a pair of numbers (or the same one twice over) and then yields their sum: for instance, it takes three and four and yields seven. Similarly, the function represented by '. . . × − − −' also takes a pair of numbers (or the same one twice over), and then yields their product: and so on. Think of a function as a sort of abstract machine or processor which needs to be fed with certain things, like numbers, and which duly extrudes others. In Frege's terminology a function takes *arguments* and yields *values*. And he characterizes their 'need' to take arguments by calling them 'unsaturated', or 'in need of completion': and the idea here is that if one 'saturates' or 'completes' a function with argument(s), then values result. The point now is that if you specify what value a certain function will yield for each possible combination of arguments it can take, the contribution of the corresponding pattern to the significance of the discourse will have been explained. Once it is grasped, say, that '... + – – –' represents a function which yields the sum of any pair of numbers, the arithmetical significance of the operator '+' is also grasped.

These are the core ideas of Frege's semantic analysis of language. We start off with some primitive signs (in the present case, the basic numerals) which are said to stand for extralinguistic entities (numbers). We are also shown ways of combining these simple signs with each other to produce complex signs (e.g. '3 + 4') which are also said to stand for extralinguistic entities (numbers again). Finally, by recognizing the patterns exhibited by the complex expressions we can elucidate the workings of the signs like '+'. We do this by stipulating how the assignments of semantic values to the complex expressions are determined on the basis of the initial assignments to the primitive ones. In this way, the arithmetical significance of the expression-forming operators like '+' is systematically explained. In Frege's terms, what one is explaining is the semantic nature or power of the operator by way of a definition of the function it represents or stands for. Thus the arithmetical power of '... + – – –', as we said, resides in its standing for a function which yields the sum of any two numbers which it may take.[2]

It is important to keep constantly in view a fundamental distinction we have been observing, which was mentioned briefly at the end of § 1. This is the distinction between linguistic expressions and what the expressions are said to represent or stand for. Thus we have already distinguished between numerals, which are linguistic expressions like '1', '2', '3', . . ., and numbers, like the numbers one, two three, . . ., which for Frege are abstract extralinguistic objects. Similarly, we have distinguished between functions, which for Frege are also abstract constituents of extralinguistic reality, and the expressions which signify them: we have used '... + – – –', '... × – – –', and so on, for this purpose. (From now on, we shall call these expressions *functors*, and we shall adopt the following convention. Instead of writing the long-winded 'the function represented by "... + – – –"', we shall simply write 'the function ... + – – –', underlining the material which actually serves to represent the function in question.) The *general* distinction between words and what they signify is important, and not especially controversial: one must obviously distinguish between, say, a word like 'London'—samples of which can be found all over the world, and which can be repeated, deleted, made of red ink, and so on—and the great city on the Thames of which the word is the name. Frege simply made the same distinction between bits of *arithmetical* language and the abstract arithmetical items which, according to him, they signify. Now there is evidently a significant difference between the commonsensical view that London (the city) is an entity which exists in the extralinguistic world, and the rather more specialized view that the number one, though abstract, is also an item in extralinguistic reality: and Frege's stance on this matter is perhaps the most controversial aspect of his view of mathematics generally. However, the correctness of this *mathematical* stance is one thing, and the idea that one should distinguish between words and what they signify is something else— something which cannot seriously be disputed in general, and which is of the utmost importance to modern work in semantics.[3]

Equally general in application, and equally relevant to our concerns, is Frege's object/function distinction itself, and we shall pass directly to his seminal applications of it to the realm of logic. This will serve both to fix the idea more firmly and to introduce our specific subject-matter.

3 TRUTH FUNCTIONS

Frege applied his ideas to certain basic logical words which operate on propositions to produce new propositions, and which appear in characteristic types of argument. What grew out of this was the systematic truth-table treatment of the propositional calculus familiar from elementary logic textbooks (it will be convenient to explain Frege's ideas with the hindsight which these developments provide). Frege took the usual logician's assumption that each proposition is either true or false (but not both), and expressed it thus: each proposition stands for an object, either the True (T) or the False (F) (but not both). T and F, like numbers, are supposed to be objects in the extralinguistic realm (for reasons that will become apparent, we shall call them *truth-values*). So, if we start out with a stock of propositions, such as 'London is a city', 'The Thames is a river', etc., we are to assign each one a value: either T or F. Suppose we also have the conjunction 'and', with the help of which we can make complex propositions like 'London is a city and the Thames is a river'. These complex propositions too are to be assigned either T or F, and Frege then suggested that a functional analysis of 'and' could be given. His essential move was to see complex propositions such as 'London is a city and the Thames is a river', or 'Paris is in France and cheese is expensive', as exhibiting the common pattern exemplified by

'... & – – –'

(writing '&' for 'and', and this time letting '...' and '– – –' mark places for propositions). Frege's idea was that one should treat this pattern as a functor which represents *a function from truth-values to truth-values*. It then remains to give a specification of what this function yields for any particular combination of values taken, and the logical role of 'and' will have been accounted for in a general way. That is precisely what the familiar truth-tables do: that for '... & – – –', for instance, lays down that a complex proposition such as 'London is a city and the Thames is a river' will be assigned T if both conjoined propositions are, and will otherwise be assigned F. The other familiar logical words (e.g. 'if', 'or', 'not') are defined in an analogous way.

The crucial thing to notice here is the parallel with the treatment of arithmetical language described in §2. Just as Frege explained the significance of arithmetical operators like '+' with the help of the object/function distinction, so too did he explain that of the logical words like 'and'. The underlying explanation is in each case of the same type. In each case we have a basic stock or domain of objects, signified by certain expressions (simple or complex), and a selection of functions, whch are signified by functors (discernible patterns in the complex expressions), and which take objects of the domain as arguments, and yield values. One difference concerns the sizes of the domains: there are infinitely many numbers but only two truth-values (although it is possible to generalize the basic idea and end up with a 'many-valued' logic, i.e. a logic with extra truth-values in addition to T and F). Another difference is that the theory of truth-functions helps one formulate simple and rigorous accounts of logical notions like validity, and mechanical ways to check, for example, whether certain arguments are valid. For instance, the definition of the function '... & – – –' yields an account of why an argument like

London is a city and the Thames is a river;

So, London is a city,

is valid. As the truth-table shows, the premiss cannot be true unless both components are, in which case the conclusion—which just is one of these components—will be true too. So there is no assignment of truth-values under which the premiss is T and the conclusion F: so the conclusion *has* to be T if the premiss is.

4 PREDICATE CALCULUS

So much for the first important application to logic of Frege's object/ function idea. We now turn to the predicate calculus, which contains the rigorous logic of generality that he made possible. As we noted in §1, the core of traditional logic was concerned with generalizations about types of thing—such things as animals, dogs, mammals, etc. The interest was in propositions about *all* animals, *some* mammals, *every* dog, etc. (see the example in §1). Frege, however, proceeded by first focusing on propositions about *individual* animals, mammals, dogs, etc. And as in the cases already considered, but this time somewhat more plausibly, he called these individuals *objects*, and assumed that in making the relevant generalizations we intend to be speaking about a domain or stock of such objects. Thus, in Frege's view, the proposition

Bryan Ferry is a man

is a proposition about the object Bryan Ferry, and the words 'Bryan Ferry' comprise a *Proper Name* of that object. Frege understood Proper Names to be expressions which represent particular given objects of the domain, just as he considered numerals to represent particular given numbers (thus numerals *are* Proper Names—of numbers—given Frege's view of arithmetical reality). This paves the way for an object/function analysis of propositions about individual objects in our domain of discourse. For the propositions

Bryan Ferry is a man

Mick Jagger is a man

Raquel Welch is a man

exhibit a pattern which we can exemplify thus:

'. . . is a man',

where '. . .' marks a place for a Proper Name of an object. Further-more, not only do our three propositions exhibit a common pattern, but each is either T or F (the first two T, the last one F). So we can consider the pattern, by analogy with the other cases described in the foregoing sections, as a functor which represents *a function from objects to truth-values*. Such functions are a species of what we shall call *first-level functions*, for reasons which will emerge in the following section. As before, it helps to think of these functions as abstract machines or processors which, when fed with a certain thing from the relevant domain, extrude something else. In this case we have a type of function which takes an object such as an individual man or woman (or dog or . . .) and yields a truth-value—either T or F. And we can easily specify what value such a function will yield for a given argument: the function . . . is a man, for instance, yields T if it is fed with an object which is a man, and F if it is fed with an object which is not a man.[4]

Notice again the parallels with other cases. Just as Frege took '. . . + – – –' to represent a function from numbers to numbers, and '. . . & – – –' to represent a function from truth-values to truth-values, so he took '. . . is a man' to represent a function from objects to truth-values. Once again we have two types of expression, simple and complex (e.g. 'Bryan Ferry', 'Mick Jagger is a man'), to which assignments are made (in this case, of objects and truth-values respectively), and elucidations, trading on the function idea, of how the assignments to the complex expressions are determined by the assignments to the simple ones. In this way, Frege attempted to account for the logical or semantic powers of predicative phrases such as 'is a man', 'walks', 'is larger than', etc. by way of the definitions of the first-level functions that he considered these expressions to stand for. Note too the appearance for the first time of Proper Names, explicitly so-called, that is, expressions understood to represent single given objects of the domain (for reasons that will emerge in §11, I always use capital letters when speaking of Frege's category of Proper Names).

5 GENERALITY

Having thus developed the idea of the first-level function in order to account for predicative phrases, Frege applied it to give his celebrated account of generality. He took as fundamental the general word (quantifier) 'everything', and suggested ways in which propositions containing other quantifiers such as 'all', 'some', 'every', etc. might be re-expressed or recast so that 'everything' is the only quantifier remaining. For instance, he proposed 'Everything, if it is a man, is mortal' for 'All men are mortal', 'Any man is mortal', etc.: and he suggested 'It is not the case that everything, if it is an animal, is not furry' for 'Some animals are furry'. As the reader will recall, being able to effect such recastings is now part of the stock-in-trade of the elementary logic student.

The recastings all involve propositions which are 'about everything', that is, propositions of the form 'Everything is so and so'.[5] The crucial points which Frege exploited then are (a) that these general propositions are to be assigned either T or F, and (b) that 'everything', in such propositions, occupies a place which could be occupied by a Proper Name: see, for instance, the pairs

>Stonehenge is material
>
>Everything is material

and

>Stonehenge, if it is material, occupies space
>
>Everything, if it is material, occupies space.

Given these two points, Frege was able to go for the patterns discernible in general propositions and propose a functional analysis of how their truth-values are determined. Since the quantifiers stand where Proper Names can stand, it follows that a proposition starting with a quantifier can be regarded as made up of the quantifier and a first-level functor (because the first-level functors we have considered are simply defined as the patterns which are exemplified by removing a Proper Name from a proposition). Frege called the function represented by a functor in such a quantified proposition the *corresponding function* of the quantifier in question. Thus the corresponding functions in our two displayed propositions are

>the function . . . is material

and

>the function . . ., if it is material, occupies space.

Now, Frege had already shown how to define this sort of first-level function: one merely stipulates which arguments it yields T for, and which it yields F for. His insight then was to appeal to these accounts of first-level functions in order to give a semantic account of the quantifiers themselves: a proposition beginning with 'everything' *is to be assigned T if the corresponding function yields T for each argument of the relevant domain, and is otherwise to be assigned F.* In other words,

(DefGen) 'Everything is so and so' is *T* if and only if the function ... is so and so yields *T* for each argument of the domain.

So, for example, we have it that 'Everything is a man' is T if and only if the function ... is a man yields T for each argument—that is, for each object of the domain. In this case, of course, we get an F. For, although our corresponding function yields T for many arguments— Bryan Ferry, Mick Jagger, Rod Stewart ...—there are many more in our domain of discourse for which it yields an F (although a single one, say Raquel Welch, would do nicely). Thus, by (DefGen), 'Everything is a man' comes out F.

On this simple idea rests the whole modern development of logic: there is a sense in which logic as a properly systematic branch of knowledge did not really exist before its introduction. The most dramatic illustration of the idea's power resides in its treatment of propositions involving multiple generality, that is propositions in which two or more quantifiers interact, such as

(1) Everything is connected to everything.

Before Frege's time there had been no fully satisfactory and suitably general semantic account of such propositions. This meant, in effect, that a properly general understanding of quantifiers was simply not available. Amazingly, the simple idea enshrined in (DefGen) is itself sufficient to fill this gap. The secret is to treat the different occurrences of quantifiers in propositions expressing multiple generality as *nested*, and thus to deal with them one at a time by repeated applications of (DefGen). Here the recognition of first-level functors is absolutely crucial: for instance, corresponding to the first occurrence of 'everything' in our proposition (1) is the first-level functor

... is connected to everything.

So (DefGen) immediately gives the result that the original proposition (1) is T if and only if the function '... is connected to everything' yields T for each argument, that is for each object of the domain. For illustrative purposes let us suppose that our domain consists of the three objects *a*, *b*, and *c* (for what is involved where indefinitely or infinitely large domains are intended see §§ 9 and 10). Now what is it for each of these objects to give T at that function? Well, we know that *if* the proposition '*a* is connected to everything' is T, then *a* yields T at the function . . . is connected to everything. Thus, if *each* such proposition is T, so is our proposition (1). So the proposition (1) is T (relative to our chosen three-object domain) if all the propositions

(1.1) *a* is connected to everything

(1.2) *b* is connected to everything

(1.3) *c* is connected to everything

are T. But what is it for all *these* propositions to be T? Here we refer back again to (DefGen): '*a* is connected to everything', for instance, is T if and only if the function *a* is connected to – – – yields T for each argument. So, we ask again: what is it for each object to yield T at this function? Here we know that if '*a* is connected to *a*' is T, then *a* indeed yields T at the function *a* is connected to . . . . Similarly if '*a* is connected to *b*' is T, then *b* also yields T at this function. So, putting all this together, we can say that (1.1) is T if the following propositions are T:

(1.1a) *a* is connected to *a*

(1.1b) *a* is connected to *b*

(1.1c) *a* is connected to *c*.

By exactly parallel reasoning we can then establish that proposition (1.2) is T if the following are T:

(1.2a) *b* is connected to *a*

(1.2b) *b* is connected to *b*

(1.2c) *b* is connected to *c*

and similarly for (1.3). Thus we have it eventually that the original proposition (1) is T if the nine following propositions are all T:

a is connected to *a*

a is connected to *b*

a is connected to *c*

b is connected to *a*

b is connected to *b*

b is connected to *c*

c is connected to a

c is connected to b

c is connected to c.

And what is it for each of these to be T? Here at last we appeal to the definition of the two-place function . . . is connected to – – –: this will yield T for a pair of objects such as a and b if and only if a is connected to b.

In this way the Fregean account of the truth or otherwise of our original proposition (1) proceeds in steps: in assessing the proposition we cross back and forth between (DefGen) and propositions involving first-level functors like '. . . is connected to everything', 'a is connected to – – –', etc. And, because we at no time need to consider more than one quantifier with its corresponding functor, (DefGen) suffices, in the context of the rest of the Fregean machinery, to account for the occurrence of every quantifier, no matter how many there may be in the proposition in question.

Notice how crucial Frege's object/function analysis is to the account of generality: the definition (DefGen) itself presupposes the account of first-level functors which Frege provided, and the style of analysis is appealed to repeatedly in the sort of stepwise procedure just described.[6] Notice too the apparent reliance on the notion of a Proper Name, and in two ways. First, at least when considering propositions involving multiple generality, cross-reference back to (DefGen) seems to require the presence of Proper Names like 'a' for sample objects from the domain. And second, the crucial bottom-line identification of our first-level functors itself seems to rest upon the recognition of Proper Names, since these functors are defined as a pattern recognizable in a proposition containing a Proper Name. Here, then, is the first intimation of the importance of Proper Names in the context of Fregean logic: although, as we shall soon see, the truth of the matter here is not straightforward.

6 BEDEUTUNG AND SINN

In each of the three cases we considered in §§ 3–5—truth-functions, predicates, and, finally, quantifiers—Frege's analysis in terms of object and function furnished the basis of subsequent logical and semantic work, yielding, for instance, the first properly comprehensive theory of generality, including elucidations and definitions of validity and related notions. More than this, Frege was partly responsible for shifting the attention of philosophers on to the philosophies of logic and language; and much of this attention, of course, is still there. In so doing, Frege also set the scene for the philosophical debates over various aspects of naming and related matters which are our main business, and the very basic sketch of his semantics has been laid out because these debates cannot be understood properly unless this standard background is fresh in the mind.

We have sketched the fundamentals of Frege's theory of semantic value: what he himself came to call his theory of *Bedeutung*. He took on this ordinary German word and gave it a technical purpose when he came to introduce another, complementary, notion which he called *Sinn*. As we have seen, the *Bedeutung* (reference) of an expression is an extralinguistic correlate, which is supposed by Frege to help account for the expression's logical behaviour. *Sinn* (sense) was introduced later when Frege considered in more detail how his logical doctrines should be placed in a more general philosophical context, and it is intended to be that property of an expression in virtue of which the expression is 'grasped' or understood by those who use the language. For, as was remarked in the Introduction, Frege made an effort to embed his logic in a broader theory of how mind and language interact in the making of significant statements, and it was while doing this that he found it necessary to distinguish *Sinn* from *Bedeutung*: in effect, he came to the conclusion that understanding or grasping even the logical significance of an expression cannot consist merely in knowing or understanding what its *Bedeutung* is. These difficult matters will be addressed in chapters 5 and 6.[7]

Frege explained his theory of *Bedeutung* in the course of developing a new calculus, different in symbol but not in spirit from the calculi explained in modern presentations of elementary symbolic logic. It will help now if we ourselves introduce some symbols, and also some further refinement of the Fregean account of generality as so far explained. For arbitrary proposition-forming first-level functors we shall write 'G ...', 'H ...', etc., with '...' as before marking a place for a quantifier or Proper Name (most of the points to be made will only require recognition of one-place functors (see § 5): but, where appropriate, the notation will be extended in obvious ways, with 'R ..., – – –', for instance, serving as an arbitrary two-place functor). For arbitrary Proper Names we shall use 'a', 'b', 'c' ..., and for 'everything' we shall write '$\forall x$'. We adopt the rule that in attaching a quantifier to a functor to form an arbitrary quantified proposition the gap in the functor will be filled thus: '$\forall x(Gx)$', and so on. Thus, we can distinguish where necessary between, say, '$\forall x(Rxx)$', which would serve for a proposition like

Everything is connected to itself,

and '$\forall x(R\ldots,x)$', which would serve for a functor like

... is connected to everything.

Sample arbitrary propositions will be, for example, 'Ga', 'Gb', 'Hc', '$\forall x(Gx)$', '$\forall x(Hx)$', etc. (DefGen) becomes

(Def $\forall$) '$\forall x(Gx)$' is T if and only if the function $G\ldots$ yields T for each argument of the domain.

Now Frege, we have seen, treated 'everything' as basic and suggested ways of recasting propositions containing other quantifiers so that this was the only one remaining. Consequently, his symbolism only obtained one quantifier, his version of '$\forall x$'. But it is helpful to have another to hand. Frege recast 'something' as 'at least one thing' and then defined this in terms of 'everything' and 'not'. Writing '$\exists x$' for 'at least one thing' and '$-$' for 'not', we put his stipulation thus:

$$\exists x(Gx)' = {}^{\backprime}-\forall x(-Gx)'$$

(i.e. 'something is a crow' = 'at least one thing is a crow' = 'not everything is not a crow'). But one does not have to proceed in quite this way. One can introduce '$\exists x$' as a primitive quantifier itself and give it its own Fregean treatment, as in

(Def $\exists$) '$\exists x(Gx)$' is T if and only if the function $G\ldots$ yields T for at least one argument of the domain.

In so doing one could, indeed, thereby do without (Def $\forall$), since '$\forall x$' can itself be defined in terms of the primitive '$\exists x$' (and '$-$') as follows:

$$\forall x(Gx)' = {}^{\backprime}-\exists x(-Gx)'$$

('everything is a crow' = 'not (even) at least one thing is not a crow'). Ease and elegance in the semantics are best served if only one of (Def $\forall$) or (Def $\exists$) is used. Readability in the calculus, then, is facilitated by the introduction of the other quantifier by the appropriate definition. Later, in §17, we shall see that other primitive quantifiers can be introduced as required.

Although the ideas we have set out form the basis of modern work in the areas that concern us, various details of Frege's particular approach are more or less controversial: and some of them do not need to detain us further. As we noted in § 2, although Frege's logical doctrines grew out of his analysis of arithmetical language, it is possible to accept these doctrines without explicitly endorsing his specific views about arithmetical reality. As I hope the intervening sections have borne out, Frege's explanations of truth-functions, etc. are sufficiently clear in themselves for this to be possible. So, acceptance of the fundamental object/function distinction by no means requires acceptance of specific views about what objects and functions there actually are, and we need not accept or examine Frege's perhaps surprising view that numerals signify real but abstract extralinguistic objects. In the main we shall be concerned with the application of Frege's ideas to discourse about uncontroversial, concrete items such as animals, stones, pieces of furniture, etc.: and we shall accept, with a minimum of argument, the anyway commonsensical view that these things certainly do belong to extralinguistic reality (see §§ 24–5). The crucial ideas which we shall carry forward are (a) the Fregean account of generality, and (b) the idea of the Proper Name, that is an expression whose logical or semantic role is explained in terms of the fact that it stands for a given object: and so I turn now without more ado to the relationships between these two ideas.[8]

7 PROPER NAMES AND QUANTIFIERS

We noted in passing (§ 4) that Frege makes use of the idea of Proper Names—i.e. expressions which represent particular objects—when explaining the application of his object/function analysis to the logic of generality, and that Proper Names therefore figure somehow in the Fregean treatment of generality, and hence at the basis of the standard modern approach to logic. This appearance was strengthened by the discussion of multiple generality in § 5: and the matter will now be put into sharper focus. We shall then be in a position to see why Proper Names have been and need to be discussed in depth, given the context of the Fregean apparatus. Three issues, and their interrelations, will bulk large in what is to come. The issues are

(1) the fundamental Fregean distinction between quantifiers and Proper Names;

(2) the role played by Proper Names and associated ideas in Fregean treatments of generality;

(3) the bearing of Frege's views about Proper Names on our own understanding of the proper names and related expressions of natural languages like English.

Issues 1 and 3 come up in the discussion of how Frege's ideas may be applied to arguments and other fragments of natural language. Issue 2 is more narrowly logico-semantic, but it has had enormous influence, for instance on the discussion of the other two issues. I take up these three issues in turn.

Frege's distinction between object and function is his most important distinction of all. A function's essence consists in the fact that it takes certain things and yields certain others, in the way explained above. Objects, on the other hand, have no such role. This distinction is to be respected even when the functions concerned are not functions which take objects as arguments. For instance, and crucially in the present discussion, second-level functions, which are represented by quantifiers (see § 5), must be distinguished from objects, which are represented by Proper Names. Correspondingly, quantifiers and Proper Names themselves must be sharply distinguished. It is true that they share a grammatical feature, in that both combine with certain first-level functors to make propositions. But at the semantic level they are drastically different (Russell's theory of descriptions, which trades on the difference, has been called 'a paradigm of philosophy'—see chapter 2). The most glaring difference between them is this. For Frege, a Proper Name is an expression which is assigned an object as its semantic value: it is in virtue of its standing for that particular object that the logical role of the expression is to be explained. Given this, the semantic treatment of a Proper Name makes a very specific presupposition—namely, a presupposition about the existence or 'availability' of the particular object in question. Without this it is unclear, to say the least, how 'the' object could be assigned to the Proper Name. As we shall see in some detail, this fact about Proper Names gives rise to some serious logical and philosophical problems, so that the very idea of applying standard Fregean treatments to stretches of ordinary language is thereby put in question. Things are otherwise, on the other hand, where the Fregean account of quantifiers is concerned. This account proceeds, we have seen, by way of specifications of second-level functions (as in (Def ∀) and (Def ∃)): and although these specifications make somewhat studious and non-committal mention of objects (as in 'yields T for each argument in the domain'), there is no mention or invocation of any one specific object, as there is in the treatment of Proper Names. It is true that there have to *be objects* if the standard Fregean apparatus is to be employed—as we saw in § 5, one must begin by stipulating a domain of objects over which one is generalizing—and we shall see that this fact has important links (albeit subtle ones) with the issue of Proper Names. But the important difference between quantifiers and Proper Names remains, just because accounting for an expression of the latter type requires the existence of a specific, given object, rather than just a more or less generally specified range of objects. We shall mark this difference by saying that Proper Names, unlike quantifiers, are *object-invoking*, and that a treatment of a given expression as a Proper Name itself *invokes the object* which is to be the *Bedeutung* of that expression. Thus we shall say that a treatment of 'Bryan Ferry' as a Proper Name invokes Bryan Ferry, that very man, himself.

8 THE COMMITMENT CLAIM

We turn now to the second issue mentioned at the beginning of § 7; that of the role played by Proper Names in Fregean accounts of generality. The precise nature of such conceptual links as may exist between Proper Names and Fregean quantifiers is a somewhat delicate matter, and it will need some careful explanation. However, we shall see that one must at least accept that there *could be* Proper Names if the Fregean treatment of generality is to be adopted. It follows from this that any problems there may be with the idea of the Proper Name are, more or less directly, problems for the whole Fregean quantifier apparatus. Hence one very important reason for discussing them; although there are others, of course: see chapters 6–8.

In § 5 it was explained how the Fregean treatment handled propositions involving multiple generality such as 'Everything is connected to everything'. At various points in the explanation, we appealed to propositions like 'a is connected to everything', 'b is connected to a', etc., working with the assumption that we could specify members of our domain by use of the Proper Names 'a', 'b', etc. And, on the face of it, such use of Proper Names is indispensable. For a crucial part of the whole account comes after we apply (Def ∀) to the original proposition: this leaves us asking whether the function

... *is connected to everything* yields T for each object. But this, we saw, in turn involves further applications of the rule (Def ∀) (in order, of course, to account for the contribution of the second occurrence of 'everything'). And these applications need further propositions to work on, since (Def ∀) is a rule about the truth or otherwise of propositions: hence, in asking whether each object yields T at the function . . . is connected to everything, we resorted to the subsidiary propositions '*a* is connected to everything', '*b* is connected to everything', etc. Thus it seems that, if the Fregean account is to be applied across the board, we certainly need to appeal to Proper Names of objects in our chosen domain.

But then, arguably, this conclusion can be strengthened to the claim that one cannot apply the Fregean apparatus *at all* without the appeal to Proper Names. According to (Def ∀), recall,

(1) $\forall x(Gx)$

is T if and only if

(2) the function $\underline{G \ldots}$ yields T for each argument of the domain.

(See §§ 5, 6.) But consider now the following claim, and its relation to (2):

(3) each proposition formed by writing a Proper Name of an object of the domain in the slot of '$G \ldots$' is T.

On the face of it, claims (2) and (3) amount practically to the same thing. One can make the essential point in the following way. '$\forall x(Gx)$' involves a corresponding function which we represent by '$G \ldots$', and is T if and only if each *saturation* or *completion* is T. Now, this last notion can be understood in either of two ways. Speaking of extralinguistic reality, we can say that the funct*ion* is completed when it is fed an appropriate argument (in this case an object). Speaking of expressions, we can say that a funct*or* is completed when it is made into a proposition by being combined with an appropriate expression (in this case a Proper Name). Whichever way we speak, it is correct to talk of obtaining T (or F) on completion, since this will just be the value of the corresponding function for the given object—or, in other words, what the resulting proposition is assigned. Thus it would seem that one may speak indifferently either of the value of the function $\underline{G \ldots}$ for the object a, or of the value assigned to the proposition 'Ga'. Since the first way of speaking invokes the fundamental Fregean object/function analysis, appealed to in the treatment of generality, and the latter involves the idea of the Proper Name, the net result seems to be that adopting the treatment of generality as good as commits one to recognizing Proper Names. Thus we seem at this point to have our demonstration of the importance of Proper Names to the modern logical tradition. From (Def ∀) we can see that the Fregean account of (1) appeals to (2). If it is true that (2) is tantamount to (3), then the account of (1) as good as appeals to (3): and this seems to mean that any incoherence in (3), or in the very idea of having Proper Names, would infect (2) and thereby threaten to undermine the account of (1)—that is, threaten to undermine (Def ∀) and, therefore, Fregean accounts of generality.

So, the claim is that in adopting the Fregean treatment as enshrined in (Def ∀), etc. one as good as commits oneself to the idea of the Proper Name. Call this the *Commitment Claim*. Is it true?

9 THE NAMELESS

A good way to approach this question is by considering an evident absurdity in accounts of the universal quantifier which are based on (3). For, consider: arguments often concern indefinitely large or even infinite domains of things which are all or mostly Nameless. And in such cases the mooted account of (1) in terms of (3) yields some strange results. Thus, suppose there are just ten tigers: Arnold, Brett, Clive, and their seven Nameless friends. Then the argument

> Arnold, Brett, and Clive are tame tigers
> So, all tigers are tame

would be a valid argument on a treatment that takes (3) as basic. Given that Arnold, Brett, and Clive are the only tigers with Proper Names, the truth of the premiss will suffice for the truth of the conclusion, since every proposition 'if *a* is a tiger then *a* is tame' will be T. But this could furnish an unhappy demonstration of the inadequacy of the treatment based on (3), since we are supposed to be able to rely on our valid arguments: and the tameness of the Named three hardly guarantees that of their friends. Moreover, a treatment which took (2) as basic would do rather better, since it would only deliver T for the conclusion if *all* the seven Nameless tigers, as well as our Named three, yielded T at the function if . . . is a tiger, then . . . is tame. And this is *not* something which is guaranteed by the truth of the premiss.

Such a case clearly demonstrates the lack of equivalence between (2) and (3): and now think of all the possible arguments about stars, trees, grains of sand, donkeys, and all the other enormous domains of mostly Nameless objects. How *could* it be right to say, as a proponent of the Commitment Claim would, that adoption of the basic Fregean treatment as good as commits one to the idea of the Proper Name? Surely we can understand what it means to say that each object in the domain of donkeys yields T at the function . . . is vegetarian, without supposing, what is manifestly false, that every donkey has a Proper Name. So what does it matter whether *any* donkey has a Proper Name, or even whether we recognize the category of Proper Names at all?

In §2 we remarked briefly that a proposition is a declarative sentence as used with an understood meaning or interpretation. What the above examples help to show is that the semantic or logical power of a proposition can outstrip the expressive resources of the language to which it belongs. If one says, of a group of donkeys, that they are all vegetarian, then it certainly follows from what one has said that each individual member of that group is a vegetarian: for if just one of them is omnivorous or worse, the original claim is false. This is self-evident. However—and here is the crucial point—it is a purely accidental or contingent matter whether one has the linguistic or other resources to spell out these implications of what is said: for instance, to say of an individual donkey alone that it is vegetarian one needs a Proper Name, or a word like 'this', or, perhaps, some non-linguistic means of picking it out, like a pointing gesture or whatever. And such devices might simply not be part of one's language or linguistic repertoire. The essential point here is quite general, and is frequently encountered by philosophers (among many others): one often finds onself trying to draw from a view some novel or unremarked consequence for which adequate linguistic expression is lacking in the language being used. This is one reason for 'borrowings' from other languages, and for the use of technical terms, jargon, and neologisms. In introducing such terms one, in effect, *extends the language*; one produces a new word or phrase which is intended to express something previously not expressible within the language in question, even though it may follow from things which are so expressible.

This familiar idea immediately suggests how we might restore the

Commitment Claim in the face of the Nameless. Instead of (3), we should say

> (4) any proposition formed by writing a Proper Name of an object of the domain, *whether already available or newly introduced*, in the slot of '*G* . . .', is T.

This would keep the tigers at bay, for if we were to start introducing Proper Names for all the Nameless tigers in the above example we should eventually get a false proposition if there are any non-tame ones, and this (by the new account (4)) would falsify 'All tigers are tame'. Adoption of (4) would also make invalid the argument:

> Arnold, Brett, and Clive are tame tigers
> So, all tigers are tame

—as we know it must be, since we never had any intention of moving from premiss to conclusion in the first place.

In some such way as this the flagrant inadequacy of (3) can be made good, and the Commitment Claim can now be reinstated. In effect, the claim now amounts to the idea that if one is prepared to use (2) to account for the truth of (1) then one should also be prepared to use (4) for the same purpose, since so to do only involves a commitment to the idea of *extending one's language* by the introduction of Proper Names in order to express things which manifestly follow from things already expressible within it. This claim will now be upheld.[9]

10 THE VERY IDEA OF NAMING

It is certainly true that there are broadly Fregean logics which do not explicitly recognize the category of Proper Names (see QUINE (1940)), and the main reasons for this non-recognition will be introduced in chapters 2 and 3. But such logics do not, by failing to recognize the category of Proper Names, thereby refute the Commitment Claim. For this is merely the claim that *if* a Fregean understanding of the quantifiers is employed, *then* there can be no objection in principle to the introduction of Proper Names into the language in question. But even this claim may look dubious to many readers, given that many modern semantic treatments of generality do not so much as mention the idea of the Proper Name, even when explaining the application of their versions of (Def ∀), etc. to propositions involving multiple generality, and even though they follow Frege in all essentials. So in what sense *precisely* are they 'committed' to Proper Names?

The appeal in (4) to *potential* Proper Names—to the idea that our rule for '∀x' should draw not just on our actual stock of Proper Names (if there is one), but on the idea that we could just add them as required—brings out clearly the following 'picture' of what a Fregean understanding of generality commits us to. Set over against our propositions there is a range or domain of objects, perhaps infinitely large, which the propositions can be 'about'. In particular, our quantified propositions such as 'All tigers are tame' are generalizations about the objects in the domain, and their truth or falsity depends on how things happen to be among these objects. The idea enshrined in (4) is that of a sort of imaginary procedure in which one would go through the domain, picking out each object in turn and (if necessary) giving it a Proper Name. This would make possible the formation of the propositions of the form 'if *a* is a tiger, then *a* is tame', with '*a*' a Proper Name, all of which would need to be T if the original generalization is to be T. But to say that a particular proposition 'if *a* is a tiger, then *a* is tame' is T is, by Fregean lights, to say that the object Named by '*a*' gives T when presented to the function if . . . is a tiger, then . . . is tame. Thus it is clear that what is appealed to overall is not so much the *existence* of Proper Names as the mere possibility of their introduction, so that the explicit appeal to Proper Names enshrined in both (3) and (4) is strictly redundant. The crucial appeal is to the idea that the objects of the domain can each be 'taken', notionally to be sure, and 'presented' to the relevant first-level function. Giving the objects Proper Names is at best an optional extra: one can always rest content with (2), and just say that '∀x (if x is a tiger, then x is tame)' is T if and only if each object, taken on its own, yields T when presented to the function if . . . is a tiger, then . . . is tame. Nevertheless, it is plain that the 'optional extra' involves no new sort of logical or semantic commitment: *if* the idea of 'presenting' an individual object to a function is appealed to, *then* there can hardly be an objection to idea of it having or being given a Proper Name. What is in effect a commitment to the idea that individual objects can be 'invoked' would already have been made.

Now standard modern treatments explain the conditions for truth of a quantified proposition '∀x (Gx)' in the following way. First, what is in effect the corresponding functor of the quantifier is isolated and called an 'open sentence': in the present case, this would be written '*Gx*'. There is then introduced the idea of 'assigning' an object as the 'interpretation' of the 'free variable' (namely, the 'x') of the open sentence. Next is introduced the idea of truth-relative-to-an-interpretation—that is, the open sentence 'Gx' is said to be either true or false relative to the assignment of a given object to the variable. The proposition '$\forall x(Gx)$' is then said to be (simply) true if and only if 'Gx' is *true relative to all interpretations*. But this procedure materially differs in no relevant respect from accounts based on (4) which explicitly employ the idea of the Proper Name. First, the idea of assigning an object as the interpretation of the free variable in 'Gx' is quite clearly of a piece with 'presenting' that object to the function $G \ldots$, to the extent that, in both cases, the object itself is invoked, and the semantic result is held to turn crucially on this invocation. It is true that the former procedure appears to be neutral on the questions whether open sentences stand for functions: but this is a different matter (see §6). Thus it is plain that as far as the treatment of quantification over objects is concerned, the modern approach described above does not materially differ from approaches based on (2). But since, as we saw in the previous paragraph, the essential semantic commitments of (2) do not materially differ from those of (4), it is difficult to see how those prepared to employ the modern notion could object in principle to the enrichment of their language by the introduction of Proper Names. And this result is all the proponent of the Commitment Claim needs.

Second, the application of the modern treatment to cases of multiple generality is also not materially different from the one described in §5 which explicitly employed Proper Names. To evaluate for truth or falsity in the modern style a multiply quantified proposition such as '$\forall x \forall y(Rxy)$' one first must isolate the open sentence '$\forall y(Rxy)$'. If this is true relative to all interpretations then the original proposition is simply true. Suppose, then, we assign a certain object to the 'x' in '$\forall y(Rxy)$'. In order to determine whether we have truth here we now have to reapply the procedure for the remaining quantifier: so, *keeping the interpretation of the* 'x' *fixed*, we ask whether 'Rxy' is true relative to all interpretations. It is necessary to keep fixed the given object as interpretation for 'x', since the aim is to see whether *it* stands in the relation $R \ldots, - - -$ to each argument. But then the point on which proponents of the Commitment Claim can rest their case is simply that 'fixing' a given object as the interpretation of 'x' is just the same as pretending, for the sake of the evaluation of 'Rxy' relative to all interpretations, that

'x' is a (temporary) Proper Name of the given object. There just cannot be any difference in principle between evaluating relative to all interpretations 'Ray', with 'a' a Proper name of a given object, and doing the same with 'Rxy' on the understanding that that same object is 'fixed' as the interpretation of 'x'.

In sum, we seem to be left with a more-or-less direct conceptual link between Fregean treatments of generality and the idea of the Proper Name. This is because at least the *introduction* of Proper Names ought always to be a notional option given a Fregean approach to generality. If we help ourselves to the idea of objects being 'taken' one by one and 'presented' to functions, or 'assigned' to open sentences, then we thereby help ourselves to the idea that these objects could be given Proper Names. No extra conceptual machinery seems to be involved.[10] We just could not grasp what it means for, say, a given object to be 'assigned' to a free variable unless we could also grasp the idea of that variable serving as a (temporary) Proper Name for that object. On the other hand, if we cannot just help ourselves to the first idea, then the whole approach breaks down. So there is this much of a link: *Fregean accounts of generality are tenable if and only if Proper Naming is*. Both ideas involve the notion that we can isolate and maintain contact with, 'in thought', the individual objects over which we generalize. And for this reason our main focus throughout will be on what it is to reason and think about objects in this way, and, in focusing thus, we shall at the same time be investigating a crucial, primitive idea of the Fregean apparatus.

II PROPER NAMES AND CANDIDATE PROPER NAMES

We come at last to the third issue mentioned in § 7; the relationship between what Frege called Proper Names, and those expressions of natural languages which we call proper names (hereafter 'natural names'). This may look straightforward; aren't they just the same thing?

The following line of thought might make one think so. Frege needs certain first-level functors for his definitions of the quantifiers, and these functors are in a sense correlative with Proper Names. Thus, suppose we have a stretch of language which is or can be formed into one or more arguments, some of which trade upon the logic of 'everything' or 'something' as used to make generalizations about objects. Applying a Fregean analysis to the discourse will require us to isolate its first-level functors: '. . . is a man', '. . . is mortal', and so on. But as likely as not this will itself require isolation of some Proper Names. These will be the expressions (if any) other than the quantifiers which make propositions when written in the slots of the functors. So, isolating the functors will amount to isolating Proper Names. This is certainly how Frege proceeds:

Statements in general . . . can be imagined to be split up into two parts; one complete in itself, and the other in need of supplementation . . . Thus, e.g., we split up the sentence

'Caesar conquered Gaul'

into 'Caesar' and 'conquered Gaul'. The second part is 'unsaturated'—it contains an empty place; only when this place is filled up with a proper name does a complete sense appear (*Function and Concept*, p. 31).

Here he clearly invokes our intuitive or pre-theoretical analyses of the propositions in question. We just do seem to have an understanding of our own language whereby it slices, among other ways, into expressions that stand for particular objects, and others which combine with them to make propositions. Frege's semantics just helps itself to this understanding, for instance in passages like the one just cited. Is this not completely straightforward?

Actually, this is a far from straightforward issue, as much of what follows will elaborately demonstrate. The bald truth is that Proper Names are Fregean animals, and it is an open question whether they can serve as replacements for or proxies of certain expressions that we are wont to use in our ordinary reasoning (hereafter 'candidate Proper Names', or just 'Candidates'). It is one thing to say, as the proponent of the Commitment Claim does, that adopting the Fregean approach commits one to the very idea of the Proper Name—that is, to the idea that one could in principle introduce Proper Names into one's language. And it is quite another to say, as for instance Frege does in the above passage, that certain expressions of natural language can *themselves* be regarded as Proper Names. As we shall see in the next chapter, it is possible, even given a broadly Fregean approach, to offer treatments of natural names such as 'Caesar' under which they are not considered to be Proper Names. Whether or not such treatments are required, and whether they can be successfully carried through, are among the principal questions we shall be addressing.

One further indication that caution is required here is provided by the fact that Frege also proposed to treat expressions like 'the centre of gravity of the solar system', 'the highest prime number', 'the teacher of Alexander' (hereafter '(definite) descriptions'), as Proper Names; and we certainly do not call *these* proper names. And, again, Frege seemed to want to apply Proper-Name treatments to expressions like 'I', 'he', 'that', etc. (demonstratives and indexicals—see chapter 6): and, although we shall see that there certainly is a lot to be said for this, the fact remains that the proposal to group this heterogeneous category with natural names and definite descriptions is no mere recapitulation of natural-language grammatical or logical classifications.

The essential point behind all this is that, strictly speaking, Frege intended his ideas to apply to reasoning conducted in a new calculus designed for the task—in symbols like those that elementary logic students are forced to manipulate. In Frege's hands these systems of symbols were to be understood as new languages in which such things as mathematical reasoning could be conducted. Such calculi have very simple and sensible grammars, designed with the Fregean semantics in mind, so that for any given formula of the calculus it is a straightforward matter to apply the Fregean rules in the course of, for example, checking arguments for validity. Consequently, links with *natural-language* arguments, their messy grammar and all, are somewhat indirect. Students have to learn to *rewrite* their messy arguments into the nice notation: and one of the first things they then discover is that the match with the new symbolizations can be a bit rough and ready, as with 'if' and the material conditional, or 'some' and the existential quantifier. It is then incumbent on the proponent of the calculus either to deny or explain away the apparent mismatch, or, failing that, to claim that the mismatch *is irrelevant for the purposes to hand*. Thus, on the one hand, we have our ordinary-language propositions of which, as native speakers, we have a pretty firm grasp; and on the other, we have sentences of calculus (or word-salad)[11] which we take to convey what we want to say, at least accurately enough for the reasoning purposes at hand. Clearly, a Fregean Proper Name is, strictly speaking, an element of a Fregean calculus or of a word-salad constructed with such a calculus in mind: whereas natural names and other Candidates are part of natural language as found on the streets. Of course, the Fregean category is not accidentally called what it is. As has already been remarked, Frege was influenced by the apparent facts that we can and do use words to speak of individual objects, and that we call at least some of these words proper names. The intention then is that the semantics

and logical properties of propositions of calculus which contain
Proper Names will be close enough to those of the corresponding
propositions containing Candidates for the title of Frege's category
to be appropriate. But this is a substantive thesis about the semantic
character of natural languages, a mildly empirical hypothesis to the
effect that, *at least for standard reasoning purposes*, certain natural
expressions can be replaced by or considered to be Proper Names.
And the situation here is analogous to one in which a possibly
inexact translation of a word from, say, English into French is
proposed in a certain context precisely because, given the purposes
of that context, the possible inexactness just does not matter. The
crucial point is that it has to be *shown* that differences do not matter
in the specific cases. And, as we shall start to see in the following
chapter, this is not always an easy thing to do when faced with the
proposal to treat this or that stretch of reasoning as though it
contains Proper Names.[12]

12 THEORY OF MEANING

The remarks of the previous section are relatively innocent. But it
has to be acknowledged that much recent discussion of our issues
has a rather different focus. As we have presented them, Fregean
semantic ideas belong to the theory of formal symbolic logic, and
only impinge on the nature or structure of natural language to the
extent that they are supposed to give us precise or rigorous ways of
conducting at least some of our ordinary reasoning, and also to
provide insight into such notions as logical consequence. However,
there is a somewhat distinct 'anthropological' enterprise of accounting for, or explaining, the actual given nature of natural languages:
and this—the 'theory of meaning'—also involves the application of
Fregean semantic ideas. On the one hand, there are the nice artificial
Fregean calculi, with their simple grammars and explicit semantics.
On the other there is, for example, English, which even in straight
information-carrying uses is grammatically wayward and semantically mysterious (if not incoherent, as Frege thought). Perhaps the
major preoccupation of analytic philosophy this century has been
the desire to cast light on the natural with the help of the artificial: to
come to understand better the workings of the former by applying
the techniques and insights that went into the invention of the latter.
And this sort of enterprise gives another lever on our overall
concern. Instead of merely asking whether natural names (and other

Candidates) can be considered as Proper Names for this or that purpose, we can ask: Are these expressions as it were *naturally occurring* Fregean Proper Names; do they, as they *actually* behave, resemble the corresponding elements of the calculi as they behave? Thus, we shall sometimes be concerned not only with pragmatic questions of whether this or that proposed Fregean treatment of a stretch of reasoning is adequate for the given purposes, but also with more complex questions about whether Fregean semantics provides a good paradigm for explaining how the actual natural bits of discourse work, semantically speaking.

In this regard it helps sometimes to distinguish between offering a *paraphrase* (adequate for the reasoning purposes at hand), and giving a *semantic representation* (in a logically or semantically 'perspicuous notation'). But for many purposes this distinction is irrelevant to the point at issue, and I shall normally speak merely (as I have done so far) of a *treatment*, say of a proposition or of a type of natural-language expression. The idea of a paraphrase I shall take to be clear enough to require no more explanation than has already been given. We just do normally know pretty well what we need to say for a given purpose, and are likewise usually competent to judge whether or not this or that stipulated phrasing into another language or calculus will do. The 'semantic representation' idea is rather less straightforward. However, the basic thought is that propositions of natural language have (or sometimes have) a more or less determinate logical or semantic structure which it is the business of the theorist of meaning to uncover and display. For various reasons, though, this structure is deemed not to be always evident from the associated grammar or syntax, so that in order to expose the semantic structure the theorists must embark on a process of 'tidying up' the language whose structure they are out to reveal (and it cannot be denied that natural languages are riddled with redundancy, and stylistic and other quirks). As often as not, largely because of the centrality of Frege's ideas, this means offering propositions of a Fregean calculus (or word-salads constructed therefrom) and then claiming that they not only convey the import of (i.e. translate) the original, but also display ('represent') its semantic nature in a less misleading ('perspicuous') form.

The (important) general idea of meaning will be considered in chapter 5, although there is no attempt there to provide anything like a comprehensive 'theory' of it. For the rest, it would take too long, and would anyway not, I think, be very fruitful, to examine in detail all the reasons why philosophers have concerned themselves with the theory of meaning. It sometimes seems that many philosophers so engaged have anyway forgotten them. But this much is true and appropriate: the concern with meaning should have as its goal a sort of generalized self-understanding. Since our use of language is a central part of our distinctive mode of being, and since reasoning and information-gathering are (or have increasingly become) salient components of this central part, it is entirely appropriate that philosophy should be concerned to understand the Reasoning Mind, and that this concern should have a linguistic focus, and hence confront the matter of meaning. We may not exactly *be* what we say (or think we say), and the world may not be the way we say it is. But we tend to think that that is the way it is: and all of this is a very large part of what we are. This ought to be enough to get the philosopher started on issues to do with language and meaning. So we shall certainly be pursuing questions taken from the theory of meaning, not to the death but at times with vigour. However, the general line I shall promote is that while meaning itself is philosophically important, the construction of more and more accurate systems of semantic representation is not.[13]

13 A SPRINGBOARD FOR ENQUIRY

Given the Fregean background sketched in §§ 1–6, our next concern was to discover the extent to which the idea of the Proper Name is a fundamental and ineliminable component of the Fregean approach. We saw that although it is natural explicitly to use the notion when explaining the quantifiers one need not proceed in this way even if one adopts the basic Fregean approach (§§ 8–9). However, it seems that Fregean approaches are bound up with Proper Names at least to this extent: if the Fregean account of generality is viable, then it ought to be possible, at least in principle, to *introduce* Proper Names into the language concerned (§ 10). Thus, any problem for the idea of Naming is a problem for Fregean logic, and therefore (more or less directly) with much recent work in the philosophies of logic, language, and mind. So we can test the Fregean framework by investigating the idea of the Proper Name, and how it might be deployed in practice.

In this connection we can be guided by the fact that Frege, mostly by way of example and application, suggested Candidates from natural language for treatment as Proper Names: for example, natural names, descriptions, demonstratives. So we can usefully explore the adequacy of the Fregean approach by seeing whether we could conduct normal reasoning involving these natural expressions in a medium (calculus or word-salad) where the expressions are replaced by or regarded as Proper Names: and in so doing we shall be investigating a crucial way in which the 'Fregean revolution' has made its impact on the subsequent philosophical tradition.

But questioning the adequacy of paraphrases becomes, at the limit, an investigation into whether Fregean semantics is a useful paradigm in terms of which the actual semantic structure of natural languages can be explained. So we can also ask: Are there any *naturally occurring* Proper Names, and if so which are they? Such meaning-theoretic questions have their point, and will also be pursued in what follows.

Further Reading

Frege explains the ideas introduced in this chapter in *Function and Concept* and 'On Concept and Object', both of which are to be found in: *Translations from the Philosophical Writings of Gottlob Frege*, eds. P. T. Geach and M. Black (Oxford, 1960). He initially introduced his logical system in his *Begriffsschrift*, parts of which are reprinted ibid. The whole work, along with some relevant later material, is translated by T. W. Bynum as *Conceptual Notation and Other Articles* (Oxford, 1972). For a final complete exposition of his mature system see *The Basic Laws of Arithmetic*, tr. M. Furth (Berkeley and Los Angeles, 1964), pp. 33–51.

The standard work on Frege is M. Dummett, *Frege: Philosophy of Language* (London, 1973). This is, indeed, by far the best general philosophical work on logic and language available, and, although very difficult in places, it amply repays repeated consultation. In connection with the present chapter, see especially chapters 1–4. For a sustained defence of Fregean styles of logical analysis in the face of traditional and contemporary alternatives see P. Geach, *Reference and Generality* (Ithaca, 1962). A useful collection of papers on Frege is C. Wright (ed.), *Frege: Tradition and Influence* (Oxford, 1984), and an excellent discussion of Frege's views on mathematical reality (§ 2) is C. Wright, *Frege's Conception of Numbers as Objects* (Aberdeen, 1983).

For the seminal papers largely responsible for the 'meaning-assignment explosion' mentioned in § 12 see D. Davidson, *Inquiries into Truth and Interpretation* (Oxford 1984). Two useful works in this field are M. Platts, *Ways of Meaning* (London, 1979), and M. Davies, *Meaning, Quantification and Modality* (London, 1980). See esp. Platts (1979), chaps. 1 and 2, and Davies (1980), Pt. I. Davidson's proposals are also the subject of the papers collected in G. Evans and J. McDowell (eds.), *Truth and Meaning* (Oxford, 1976).

For a Fregean logic without Proper Names (§ 10) see W. V. Quine, *Mathematical Logic* (Cambridge, Mass., 1940), §§ 26–7. For the Commitment Claim (§§ 8–10) as it bears on non-Fregean logics see F. Sommers, *The Logic of Natural Language* (Oxford, 1982), chaps. 1–3, 11, and G. McCulloch, 'Frege, Sommers, Singular Reference', *PQ* 34 (1984); repr. in Wright (1984). For the Commitment Claim itself see Dummett (1973), pp. 14–19.

NOTES

1. By 'proposition' is meant a declarative sentence as used with a fixed meaning or interpretation: and by 'word' or 'expression' is meant a logically significant component of such a sentence. For a discussion of these matters see chaps. 3, 5, and 6.

2. The treatment immediately generalizes: once the basic treatment of an operator like '+' is available, this suffices for propositions of arbitrary complexity. Thus, a proposition like '$(3 \times 4) + (7 - 2)$' exhibits the familiar '$\ldots + - - -$' pattern, the only difference from the basic case being that the gaps are occupied by complex expressions rather than by numerals. But once the numbers signified by these complex expressions are given, they serve as arguments to the function represented by '$\ldots + - - -$' in the normal way. Notice that Frege's general approach dispenses with the initially plausible idea that the components of a proposition make their contribution to the overall significance in a manner which reflects their linear ordering: this is, indeed, one of the more striking aspects of the idea that one must recognize 'patterns' in propositions. For example, the fact that '3' is the first arithmetical expression in '$(3 \times 4) + (7 - 2)$' is not reflected in the Fregean account of the complex expression's arithmetical significance. Rather, on Frege's approach, the first thing one must note is the central occurrence of '+', and the overall pattern which groups around it. For more on these matters, see chap. 4, §§ 33–5.

3. A related distinction is that between *use* and *mention*. Where expression E stands for extralinguistic item I, we distinguish between using E to speak about I, and speaking about, or mentioning, E itself. In the first proposition below, the two names are *used* to speak of the cities in question. In the second, the names are *mentioned*.

    London has fewer hills than Edinburgh.

    'London' has fewer letters than 'Edinburgh'.

    Of course, in mentioning an expression one uses another one: in the second proposition above, the names of our cities appear enclosed in quotation marks. It is convenient to treat the whole of such an expression (i.e. name + quotes) as though it is itself *a name of an expression*. Thus consider the following (true) propositions:

- (a) London is a city
- (b) 'London' is a name of a city
- (c) ''London'' is a name of a name of a city

etc.

4. '. . . is a man' is a *one-place* functor, since it represents a function which only requires one object as argument: in this it is analogous to 'not . . .' (which represents a function which only requires *one* truth-value in order to yield another), and '. . .²' (which stands for the square function, a function which only requires one argument (e.g. the number two) in order to yield another (in this case, of course, the number four)). But obviously these are special cases. By analogy with '. . . and – – –' or '. . . + – – –', which represent functions needing two arguments (or the same one twice over), first-level functors can be *two-place* ('. . . is larger than – – –'): and then the series continues ('. . . is between – – – and ' ' '' is *three-place*; '. . . is nearer to – – – than ' ' ' is to : : :' is *four-place*, etc.). An *n*-place functor represents a function that requires *n* arguments (not necessarily distinct) to produce a value.

5. That is, the recastings result either in propositions of the 'Everything is so and so' form, or in propositions of the 'it is not the case that everything, etc.' form. But the treatment of the latter type of proposition is accommodated by Frege's treatment of the former once the truth-table for 'not' is to hand. For we know from this table that 'It is not the case that *P*' is T if and only if *P* is F. It follows that, once the embedded material can be accounted for, the whole negated proposition is also accommodated. For parallel reasons, Frege's treatment of the basic case also suffices for embeddings of quantifiers in complexes like 'Everything is so and so, and something is this or that', once the truth-tables of 'and', etc. are to hand. For what happens when one quantifier is embedded by another, as in, say, 'Everyone loves someone', see the end of the present section.

6. Indeed, quantifiers themselves can be regarded as standing for functions, namely, *second-level functions* which take first-level functions as argument and yield T or F as value. That is,

>   Everything is fat

and

>   Everything is thin

exhibit the common pattern

>   Everything . . .,

where '...' now holds a place for a first-level functor. Then (DefGen) simply defines the (second-level) function represented by the above pattern, just as, say, the appropriate truth-table defines the function represented by the pattern '... & – – –'. Of course, one can go on to discern functors which stand for functions of an even higher level: for instance, a function which yielded T or F as value for a second level function as argument would be a third-level function. It would be a useful exercise for the reader to try to identify one.

7. A welter of technical terms have been introduced to cover distinctions more or less like those marked by Frege's distinction between *Sinn* and *Bedeutung*. Since the exact nature of the distinction(s) posited often varies in all sorts of ways, for all sorts of theoretical reasons, and, in particular, often involves departures from Frege, it is perilous to read too much into such parallels as there are. However, roughly speaking, this is how the terms line up:

Bedeutung-*like notions*	*Sinn*-*like notions*
Meaning (capital 'M')	meaning (small 'm')
reference/referent	sense
extension	intension
semantic value/role	cognitive value/role
designation/denotation	connotation
nominatum	content

8. Although cottoning on to the use of the basic object/function distinction is crucial to a grasp of the elements of Fregean logic, it is at least arguable that the Fregean claim that functors stand for functions, which are as much a part of extralinguistic reality as any object, is dispensable metaphor. For notice that the 'nature' of a function is normally explained by a rule or table (e.g. (Def∀) or a truth-table): such things are supposed to explain the semantic role of the appropriate *functor* by characterizing the *function* it allegedly represents. But, it can be asked, why bring the function in at all: why not just say that the rules, etc. simply describe the semantic role or power of the functor directly; what extra work does the function do? And there certainly does seem to be a contrast here with the explanation of Proper Names, at least where this proceeds by way of assignments of concrete objects like Bryan Ferry. The invocation of an extralinguistic entity seems clearly to have a literal point and utility which can seem to be lacking in the treatment of functors: consider, for instance, the resort to the extremely meta-phorical idea that a function is a sort of abstract machine or processor. However, the issues raised by this, although important, are too far off our main subject to be gone into, and I shall not consider them. In what follows I shall continue to speak, where it is convenient, of functions, leaving it open whether this is merely an eliminable manner of speaking.

For more on this type of point see chap. 5, § 46, and chap. 6, § 59. See also DUMMETT (1973) chap. 7 and WRIGHT (1983).

9. Note that I have been cautious and only claimed that *if* one adopts the Fregean type of approach exemplified by (2) *then* one should also be prepared to use (4), and hence commit oneself to the idea of the Proper Name. But it may be thought, given the argument of the present section, that such caution is out of place: surely, whatever one's analysis of generality, the truth of 'Everything *G*'s' entails that any given individual thing *G*'s—and what is to prevent the introduction of Proper Names in order to give expression to such entailments? Now I think the thought behind this query is correct, in that commitment to a general claim about a range of objects involves commitment to specific claims about individuals in the range. The problem is, however, that one could make the general claim in a language to which it is *grammatically* impossible to add Proper Names: this appears to be the case, for example, with pre-Fregean traditional term logics, which have no analogue of the first-level functor, and hence no analogue of the sort of gap in a proposition which a Proper Name needs to occupy. See SOMMERS (1982) and MCCULLOCH (1984).

10. Note that there is something metaphorical, not only in the Fregean idea that objects can be 'presented' to functions (or 'assigned' to open sentences), but also in my claim that one could in principle thereby introduce Proper Names of objects in the domain. Clearly, it would be impossible to Name objects if we could not find them, or if they kept running away! Thus one has to see the metaphorical characterizations as attempts to spell out the kind of picture or model which is involved in a particular semantic view: and this is reflected in the final formulation of the Commitment Claim in the text, where it is claimed that Fregean accounts of generality 'are tenable' if and only if Proper Naming is. However, in any concrete case, where the idea is to gather evidence for or refutation of some quantified claim, the way to proceed is by 'tracking down' this or that individual object, and determining, in some appropriate way, whether the open sentence is true relative to *it* (or whether *it* yields T at the corresponding function). And in such a situation one surely would also be able to Name the object if one so desired. (All of this leaves it wide open just what is to count as 'tracking down' an object, and this will presumably vary according to what sort of object is in question: contrast donkeys with, for instance, numbers as construed by Frege. Some of these matters will be raised later in chaps. 6 and 7.)

11. Of course, once the symbolizing trick has been learned one can relax, and just use enough abbreviation and/or symbolization to suit present convenience. This is to construct *word-salads*: fragments of no-one's language that use elements from two or more (the open sentence '*x* is a tiger' is an example). The basic point remains, however: in so far as a fragment of word-salad contains constructions drawn from formal

calculi, the question of its match with the ordinary language propositions it is held to rephrase must arise.

12. Some readers may have noticed that when introducing symbols in §6 I
did not proceed in Frege's manner, by setting up a whole artificial
language and providing interpretations or translations for its predicates,
etc. Rather, I presented certain formulae ('schemata') as abbreviations
or representations of 'arbitrary' propositions, etc., merely casting them
in a form that resembled the formulae of a logical calculus. For many
purposes this difference of approach is immaterial: and that includes the
purpose of making the present point. Exactly the same issues are raised
by the two questions (i) Does this proposition of this artificial language
adequately translate, for given reasoning purposes, this proposition of
natural language? and (ii) Can this proposition of natural language be
fairly abbreviated or represented (for given reasoning purposes) by this
schema, whose structure or syntax is to be understood in the obvious
way by reference to artificial calculi?

13. It should be noted that 'theory of meaning' is used by philosophers in a
number of ways. In its broadest sense 'the theory of meaning' just means
the general branch of study whose concern is to elucidate the notion of
meaning itself. But, more narrowly, one can offer a theory of meaning
for an entire language—attempt to state, for each expression of the
language, what its meaning is. Let us call this a *meaning assignment*
theory. One can then approach the general issue of meaning as follows:
attempt to state what general form must be taken by *any* meaning-
assignment theory of any language. This is a favourite pastime of some
philosophers, who are usually motivated by the idea that imposing
general 'constraints' on the enterprise of meaning-assignment is a good
way, if not the only way, of elucidating the metaphysical nature of
meaning itself (i.e. of giving a general 'theory' of the sort of thing
meaning is): see esp. DAVIDSON (1984). Finally, one can forsake some of
the generality of these approaches, and merely offer proposals or
'theories' about the nature of the meaning had by specific types of
expression of natural language. This was the standard approach
adopted by philosophical logicians before the meaning-assignment and
meaning-assignment-constraining explosion was ignited in the late
1960s. And it is the approach I shall cleave to in what is to come. My
reason for this is the belief that focusing on specific cases affords a
livelier initial appreciation of the issues concerned than does a plunge
into the midst of grander designs. What we shall say makes presuppositions about and has implications for many of the issues
addressed by grand designers. But my belief is that this itself will be
clearer from a more humble perspective, so that those grounded in what
is to come will be equipped thereby to do their own designing on a
grander scale if they so wish.

2
Russell: The Basic Problem

14 ENTER RUSSELL

Frege's seminal work made its initial impact somewhat indirectly, through the writings of a few contemporary logicians and mathematicians whom he influenced. Prominent among these were Russell and Whitehead, whose *Principia Mathematica* became the standard locus of the new logic. Russell had made earlier attempts to formulate a logic of generality, and he had produced a theory of a more or less traditional, and thus not wholly satisfactory, nature. But a turning-point came with his 1905 paper 'On Denoting' (OD), where he rather opaquely set forth the elements of a Fregean treatment. This paper, despite the opacity, has become a touchstone for the debates that have subsequently raged over Frege's notion of the Proper Name, so I proceed now to lay out the leading themes of OD, and their debts to and bearing on Fregean ideas.

By far the most important point here, as far as we are concerned, is that Russell was exercised in OD by what he took to be a number of serious defects in Proper-Name treatments of descriptions: and he later generalized his criticisms to cover the case of natural names and some other Candidates. So one major task before us is that of coming to grips with the substance of these criticisms. However, the import of OD is by no means merely negative, for it also contains Russell's celebrated theory of descriptions, with which he proposed to *solve* the problems he had unearthed whilst retaining the substance of a Fregean semantic approach.[1] Moreover, Russell also later suggested how his alternative treatment of descriptions could be applied to the cases involving other Candidates, in order to solve the problems which he claimed to have found with Proper-Name treatments of these expressions. So another important task now before us is that of explaining Russell's theories of descriptions and natural names.

15 RUSSELL ON DENOTING

In OD Russell is concerned, he tells us, with *denoting phrases*, of which he gives examples: 'By a "denoting phrase" I mean a phrase such as any one of the following: a man, every man, all men, the present King of England, the present King of France . . .' (OD, p. 41). With the exception of the last two expressions, these are examples of the quantifiers treated by Frege: and Russell goes on to reproduce, in all essentials, that same Fregean treatment. The exceptions indicate Russell's proposal, which it is our main business to explain, that descriptions be treated along with the quantifiers: and this marks a fundamental departure from Frege who, as was noted in chapter 1, treated descriptions as Proper Names.

Russell says that a denoting phrase may be recognized by its 'form' (OD, p. 41). He does not pause to explain, but what he seems to have in mind is this. A denoting phrase is anything which yields a proposition when joined with what he calls a 'propositional function' (with the exception of natural names, perhaps; these are barely considered in OD). Propositional functions turn out to be similar to what we called first-level functors in chapter 1. Russell writes 'I use "$C(x)$" to mean a [propositional function]': later he gives 'C(everything)', 'C(nothing)', 'C(something)' as examples of things which could be either true or false, i.e. propositions. Clearly, '$C(x)$' is here doing much the same service as our 'G . . .', etc. of chapter 1. Note a difference: what we called a funct*or* Russell calls a funct*ion*. But his presentation and intentions concerning the difference between expressions and what they signify are neither clear nor consistent, and it will not profit us to try to straighten them out. Nothing will be lost if we silently interpret Russell's '$C(x)$' in the manner extended to our own 'G . . .'.[2]

Armed with this essentially Fregean grammatical analysis, Russell goes on to give an essentially Fregean semantics for the quantifiers. To be more accurate, he presents a nightmarish list of clauses of which the following are examples:

(1) C(everything) means '$C(x)$ is always true'
(2) 'C(a man)' means 'It is false that "$C(x)$ and x is human" is always false'.

(See OD, pp. 42–3.) However, the basic intention is straightforward enough. Most of Russell's messy clauses are his suggestions for recasting different sorts of quantified propositions so that they will all succumb to a common treatment. In recasting, he proceeds, more or less, in what has become the standard Fregean manner learned by logic students (see § 5). The common treatment is supposed to pivot on (1). Russell says that 'the notion "$C(x)$ is always true" is taken as ultimate and indefinable, and the others [*namely quantifiers*] are defined by means of it' (OD, p. 42; but compare (2)!).[3]

Recall that we are treating '$C(x)$' as Russell's way of writing a first-level functor. By '$C(x)$ is always true', furthermore, he means what we, adopting his notation, would put like this:

'$C(x)$' represents a function which yields T for each argument of the domain.

Given this, Russell's (1) becomes:

'C (everything)' means 'the function $\underline{C(x)}$ yields T for each argument of the domain':

and this is clearly tantamount to our (Def ∀).[4]

So far, this is pure (or better, impure) Frege. But then Russell makes his abrupt departure over the treatment of descriptions: 'It remains to interpret phrases containing "the". These are by far the most interesting and difficult of denoting phrases' (OD, p. 44). Pausing only to quibble over usage, Russell plunges straight on with the paradigm of philosophy. It has an inauspicious beginning: Russell says that '"the father of Charles II was executed" becomes: "It is not always false of x that x begat Charles II and that x was executed and that 'if y begat Charles II, y is identical with x' is always true of y"' (ibid.).

As he then notes, this may seem a somewhat incredible interpretation; and before stating it in a more perspicuous form we must start to appreciate some of Russell's reasons for offering it.

16 DESCRIPTIONS: THE BASIC PROBLEM

The interpretation is Russell's response to what he saw as a number of fatal defects in Frege's proposal to treat descriptions as Proper Names: and the one that will concern us most arises as follows. A Proper Name, recall, is an expression whose semantic power derives from the fact that it stands for a given object. Thus, Frege's proposal was that a proposition containing a description, say 'the father of Charles II was executed', should be treated as something with the semantic character of 'Ga', with the Proper Name 'a' serving for the description and 'G' for the rest.[5] Such a proposition is T if the signified function yields T for the object referred to by 'a', and F if the function yields F for that object. One gets to the heart of Russell's objection by reflecting as follows. It is routine to formulate descriptions which pick out no object at all: for example, 'the present king of France', 'the largest number', 'the dragon which does not take its meals with Denis Thatcher'. And it is routine to formulate descriptions which pick out too many objects: for example, 'the woman who married Richard Burton', 'the number larger than four million', 'the unemployed Briton'. Then suppose we make a proposition with such an expression: say

(1) The present king of France is bald

or

(2) The unemployed Briton knows it is for the best.

According to Frege, what we have here are Proper Names in the slots of first-level functors: propositions which will be T or F depending on what the signified functions yield when presented with the relevant objects. But which objects? There is no present king of France, and there are very many unemployed Britons.[6] As a result, the proposed Fregean treatment of (1) and (2) evidently cannot be applied, since it appeals to conditions which just do not obtain. And the essential source of the problem is this: Proper Names are *object-invoking* (see § 7), and in the case of the 'failed' descriptions in propositions like (1) and (2) *there just is no appropriate object to be invoked*. This—the vulnerability of Proper-Name treatments to the fact that the world may not oblige with the object they wish to invoke—is what I call the *Basic Problem* (for Proper Name treatments).

Now the rest of the present book is given over to setting out the various ramifications of the Basic Problem, and to evaluating their force. But it can be seen, even given just the material already to hand, that Russell here puts his finger on a serious matter. First, consider the thing from the point of view of the logicians who take themselves to be offering logically adequate paraphrases, into Frege-inspired symbolism, of propositions like (1) and (2) (compare § 12). On the face of it they cannot even do this much in cases involving failed descriptions. Thus, consider a piece of reasoning such as:

The present king of France is bald
So, there is at least one thing which is bald.

This is evidently a valid argument, in that *if* the premiss is true, then the conclusion has to be. So the very least that the logician must do is to show how the truth of the premiss would necessitate or guarantee the truth of the conclusion. This involves describing what it would be for the premiss to be true, in such a way that one could read off, with the help of the associated semantic treatment of the other expressions involved, the fact that any circumstance in which the premiss is true is also a circumstance in which the conclusion is true. Now, if the description can be treated as a Proper Name, and 'there is at least one thing which ...' is treated in the standard way as '$\exists x$', this business is straightforward. From the definition of a Proper Name, we know that our premiss will be T just when the object assigned to the description is bald, that is, just when that object yields T at the function ... is bald. But, of course, in the circumstance of an object—any object—yielding T at that function, we can see immediately, given the normal Fregean treatment of '$\exists x$', that the conclusion would be T also. For this treatment, recall, is contained in:

(Def$\exists$) '$\exists x(Gx)$' is T if and only if the function G ... yields T for at least one argument of the domain.

So, if the object assigned to 'the present king of France' yields T at the function ... is bald, obviously at least one argument does, so (by (Def$\exists$)) our conclusion would be guaranteed to be T. This is all very straightforward—until we recall the Basic Problem that there is no object in the domain which answers to the description![7]

Now Frege, it goes without saying, was aware of the Basic Problem, and he had seen it as a defect in natural language that it allowed failed descriptions to be formulated. On the face of it this response looks rather odd: should he not have said that it is a defect in his logic that it cannot cope with the offending propositions? However, Frege proposed to get around the Basic Problem by stipulating that failed descriptions should be assigned some arbitrary object, say the number zero, to serve as semantic value: and this would ensure that the propositions containing them could be assigned a truth value. For presumably the function ... is bald yields F for the number zero; or perhaps we can just stipulate that it shall. But either way, if zero *were* bald, then at least one object—zero—would yield T at the function ... is bald, so the conclusion then would also be T, and the validity of our argument would be accounted for. This is just one of a variety of technical manœuvres which are designed to ensure that the argument above comes out valid, and, for reasons which will be explained in chapter 3, such manœuvres—odd as they may initially look—cannot easily be faulted in their own terms: cannot easily be faulted, that is, as technical solutions to a technical problem.

Russell, however, did not consider that such suggestions got to the bottom of the matter, and we shall eventually see that he was right here: there is an aspect of the Basic Problem which is not removed at all by the sorts of technical manœuvre just described. Some initial feel for the source of Russell's dissatisfaction can be had by reflecting on the use to which semantic ideas are put by theorists of meaning (compare § 12). Roughly speaking, the aim of such theorists is to account for the actual nature and behaviour of natural language expressions such as our descriptions, for instance by representing their semantic structure with the help of Frege-inspired symbolism. But because of the Basic Problem, any attempt to follow Frege and treat failed descriptions as Proper Names immediately faces the sort of difficulty already described, with the result that no coherent account of propositions containing them would have been given. However, from the point of view of the meaning-theorist's enterprise, there is an evident problem in reaching for the logician's technical solution of supplying some arbitrary object as semantic value. For a semantic representation which has it that the proposition 'The present King of France is bald' is not about a man, or someone who rules France, but instead concerns some arbitrary object like zero, has surely lost all contact with linguistic reality. It is as clear as anything could be that any normal assertion of this proposition could not sensibly be treated as a remark about zero or any other such arbitrarily chosen object. Of course, given the facts, there is an obvious sense in which the remark would not be about any King either—even if this had been the intention of the speaker— and to this extent there is a first-rate mystery about what sort of meaning the remark would have: a mystery which it will take us a long time to unravel. But, plainly, it is certainly going to take a lot of persuasion to convince us that the 'zero option' is even remotely plausible here. Hence, it is clear that Russell is on to something: it is very odd that what purports to be a powerful and general logical theory can either offer no treatment of, or at best responds merely with an arbitrary assignment of semantic values to, apparently perfectly intelligible English propositions, which are as capable as any others of being used in argument and reasoning. And it was this that provided Russell with one major reason to introduce his alternative theory of descriptions.[8]

But what exactly *is* Russell's theory?

17 RUSSELL ON DESCRIPTIONS

In a nutshell, Russell's theory of descriptions is simply an alternative treatment of propositions containing description which is explicitly designed to avoid the Basic Problem (and the other problems with Proper-Name treatments which are explained later in this chapter). Stripped of the nightmarish qualities that attend its first appearance, the theory is simple enough, and amounts to a proposal for recasting propositions containing descriptions into ones which instead contain the basic quantifiers 'everything' and 'something', and other logical particles. In OD, we saw Russell recast the proposition

(1) The father of Charles II was beheaded

into the daunting form

> It is not always false of x that x begat Charles II and that x was executed and that 'if y begat Charles II, y is identical with x' is always true of y.

A rather clearer statement of what Russell was after is given by:

> not everything failed to beget Charles II; and any begettor of Charles II is the same as any other; and whatever begat Charles II was executed.

The basis of both formulations is the thought that a proposition 'the G is H' is true if and only if

(i) at least one thing is G
(ii) at most one thing is G
(iii) whatever is G is H.

Russell's paraphrase, and the clearer one just offered, are T if and only if conditions (i)–(iii) hold, which means that they are T if and only if 'The G is H' is T. In precisely this sense the paraphrases thus yield a semantic treatment of propositions containing descriptions without invoking an object for the description to stand for. In symbols, and with the '∃' quantifier to hand, conditions (i)–(iii) are captured by

(RTD) 'the G is H' = '$\exists x(\forall y(Gy \leftrightarrow x = y)\ \&\ Hx)$':

and this definition introduces the general form which Russell subsequently came to give for propositions containing descriptions. Here the absolutely crucial point is that no appeal has to be made to the idea that descriptions are Proper Names, *one does not need to invoke an object* in accounting for a description, and the Basic Problem simply does not arise. For instance,

The present king of France is bald

would be treated by Russell as:

$$\exists x(\forall y(Ky \leftrightarrow x = y) \,\&\, Bx),$$

and this happens to be F since nothing yields T at the function:

$$\underline{\forall y(Ky \leftrightarrow \ldots = y) \,\&\, B \ldots)}.$$

But if something *did* yield T at this function, then our proposition would be T: and the cardinal point is that this account of what would make the proposition true does not invoke an object as semantic value of the description.[9]

Thus, the key feature of Russell's treatment is that it is *quantificational*, that is, descriptions are treated by way of the apparatus for generality: 'the', in effect, is defined in terms of 'everything' and/or 'some', and so semantically it is handled by whichever of the clauses (Def∀) and (Def∃) is taken as primitive. Given this, one could actually go further and treat 'the' itself as a basic quantifier, as in:

(Def*I*)   '*Ix*(*Gx, Hx*)' is T if and only if (i) the function $\underline{G \ldots}$ yields T for just one argument of the domain, and (ii) the function $\underline{H \ldots}$ yields T for that same argument.

Under this treatment (1), say, is first recast so as to contain the functors '... begat Charles II' and '... was executed' ('*G* ..., *H* ...'), and the new quantifier '*Ix*' is then introduced to serve for 'the', so that the symbolization of 'the *G* is *H*' comes out as '*Ix*(*Gx, Hx*)'. This can be plugged into (Def*I*) and a truth-value determined. Once again, the 'denoting phrases' of the form 'the so and so' are treated, like all the others considered by Russell, by way of Fregean quantifier rules. No single object which uniquely satisfies 'so and so' has to be invoked as the thing represented by the description. If the description represents anything at all it is a (second-level) function from first-level functions to truth-values (see §5); and a clause like (Def*I*) specifies the nature of this function. As before, the essential source of the original difficulty—that Proper Names are object invoking—is removed.

The power of Russell's response is obvious and unquestionable: a nasty-looking problem for an overall Fregean approach is avoided by an ingenious proposal using only materials already available within the approach. Furthermore, as we shall now see, quantificational accounts of Candidates can be appealed to in other areas in order to solve or avoid problems which afflict Proper-Name treatments. It is small wonder, therefore, that Russell's theory of descriptions, and variants of it, should have formed the basis of a widespread orthodoxy.

18 ENTER NATURAL NAMES

Astronomers used to think that a planet lurked inside the orbit of Mercury. They accordingly introduced the natural name 'Vulcan', and (no doubt) said things like:

(1) Vulcan is a hard planet to observe.

Now, Frege proposed that natural names are to be treated as Proper Names, so according to him the truth-value of (1) is to depend on what the function . . . is a hard planet to observe yields for the planet taken as argument. But the astronomers were wrong: there is no such planet, and this Fregean proposal therefore cannot be implemented.

Little stories like this suggest immediately that the Basic Problem is not just something that concerns descriptions: natural names, too, can fail to correspond to an appropriate object, so that there is nothing for a Proper-Name treatment to invoke (unless, of course, an arbitrary value like zero is assigned). Thus, although Russell said little about natural names in OD, he soon took to discussing the issue of empty or vacuous names, bringing to bear on it the same sorts of considerations he adduced in the case of descriptions.[10] Now, there are, we shall see, undeniable differences between natural names and descriptions: for instance, in the normal case, a natural name is only introduced when one wishes to employ a handy label for an object with which one is, in a sense that will have to be examined (chapters 7 and 8), familiar or acquainted. Hence, there is a sense in which natural names, unlike descriptions, are not so to speak *formulable on request*, so there is no obvious analogue in the case of names of the routine and legitimate formation of descriptions without an object that answers to them. Nevertheless, the fact remains that it is possible to introduce vacuous names in the normal run of things, and in all good faith, as our astronomers did, so it is possible for the Basic Problem to get a grip. Furthermore, it is certainly possible to introduce a natural name by *explicit* descriptive means; a certain type of person might, for instance, say 'Let's call the tallest woman in the world—whoever she is—"Longthighs"'. In such cases it is clear that the object to be invoked by a Proper-Name treatment of the natural name would have to be the object (if any) which answered the description. But then this yields a sense in which one *could* 'routinely and legitimately' introduce natural names without an object that answers to them. And even if, as seems to be the case (see §82), such descriptive introductions of names are rare outside of philosophy, we can easily imagine that this could have been otherwise. At least pending further investigation, therefore, it is justifiable to accept that the Basic Problem afflicts the Proper-Name treatment of natural names as much as that of descriptions, even if the ultimate force of the Problem is somewhat reduced in this case.

Given this, one might hope to find a response to the Basic Problem with natural names which is parallel to the one Russell offered for descriptions. And this is exactly what Russell produced. His response to the Basic Problem where descriptions are concerned proceeds on the basis of:

(DQ) Treat descriptions quantificationally—

this, as we saw in the previous section, is the key idea of his theory of descriptions. His response to the Basic Problem where natural names are concerned, in a nutshell, is then:

(NQ) Treat natural names quantificationally.

And, obviously enough, if (DQ) solves or avoids the Basic Problem where descriptions are concerned (NQ) will do the trick for natural names. But how can natural names be treated quantificationally? Here, we shall see, Russell has a lot to answer for. He introduced the subsidiary injunction:

(ND) Treat natural names as descriptions.

And this is the core of Russell's theory of natural names, and of those of many others who followed him. Once (ND) is to hand it combines with (DQ) to yield the effect of (NQ) and hence to secure the advantage, sought by Russell, of avoiding the Basic Problem for natural names. But (ND) may strike you as odd: how can one treat natural names as descriptions? Russell saw no problem:

The names that we commonly use, like 'Socrates', are really abbreviations for descriptions. ... When we use the word 'Socrates' we are really using a description. Our thought may be rendered by some such phrase as 'The master of Plato', or 'The philosopher who drank the hemlock', or 'The person whom logicians assert to be mortal', but we certainly do not use the name as a name in the proper sense of the word ('The Philosophy of Logical Atomism', p. 201; compare *Principia Mathematica*, pp. 31, 50).

The core idea expressed here is that one should always recast a proposition containing a natural name, replacing the name with a description that it can be taken to abbreviate, and then render *this* proposition into a form whereby the description gets a quantificational treatment. Thus one would go from, say:

Socrates was mortal

to, say:

The philosopher who drank the hemlock was mortal

and then to:

One and only one thing is a philosopher who drank hemlock, and whatever is a philosopher who drank hemlock was mortal

and then finally (using obvious symbolizations) to:

$$\exists x(\forall y(PwdHy \leftrightarrow x = y) \,\&\, Mx).$$

As such this could merely be a proposal about logically adequate paraphrases (compare § 11). However, Russell had more than this in mind, as is evinced by his use of the word 'really' in the above quote, and as his claims elsewhere to be exposing the genuine logical form of propositions testify. What seems to be afoot here is a meaning-theoretic claim (compare § 12), to the effect that natural names are synonymous with, in the manner of shortenings for or abbreviations of, quantificational descriptions. This highly influential view is extensively debated in recent philosophy and it will be considered in detail in chapters 4 and 8.

Where are we? We have now seen that Russell found a Basic Problem with Proper-Name treatments, both of descriptions and of natural names, which arises out of the fact that some of these expressions do not have an object which answers to them in the normal way. So he offered an alternative theory of descriptions, based on Fregean quantifier ideas (§ 17), and later extended this theory so that it could cope also with natural names. But the reader may well notice something odd here. Russell found problems with *failed* descriptions and *vacuous* natural names: but he responded with alternative theories apparently for *all* descriptions and *all* natural names. And this looks like over-reaction: why not merely replace the Proper-Name treatment in the problematic (failed or vacuous) cases only? At this point our plot thickens considerably. First, there are further applications of Russellian treatments in other striking cases where Proper-Name accounts of descriptions and natural names seem to founder: and second, there are deeper aspects of the Basic Problem which we have yet to uncover, and which themselves suggest that the Problem does not merely afflict the failed and vacuous cases. So the next task is to explain the further applications of Russell's theories of descriptions and of natural names, in order that we may see more clearly the shape of the Russellian orthodoxy which grew around them. Then we shall turn, in chapter 3, to the deeper aspects of the Basic Problem.

19 MODALITY

The further problems encountered by Proper-Name treatments come up when propositions containing certain important verbs and adverbs are considered. Chief among these are psychological verbs like 'believes', 'doubts', and 'wonders', which will be considered in the following section, and modal adverbs like 'necessarily' and 'possibly'. Part of the trouble in these cases is straightforward enough: if a Candidate in a proposition containing one of these words fails to refer to an object, then any attempt to treat the Candidate as a Proper Name will encounter the Basic Problem. However, there is an extra twist where psychological and modal contexts are concerned: Proper-Name treatments seem to run into difficulties *even when there is an object to serve as semantic value*. And for this reason one may feel tempted to extend quantificational treatments, which appear to avoid these difficulties, beyond the vacuous and failed cases we have already considered. Now it should be made clear at the outset that this conclusion is not, in fact, obligatory. As we shall see in chapters 4 and 6, the issues surrounding the modal and psychological contexts are rather more complex than might initially be supposed: and, in particular, one can be sympathetic to the Russellian response to the Basic Problem without having to accept that the problems we are about to describe lend further support to a quantificational treatment of descriptions and natural names. Nevertheless, it is a fact that many have been attracted to Russellian treatments of the Candidates just because of the way they seem to make possible, at a stroke, extremely neat solutions to a varied batch of thorny difficulties. So for this reason alone it is useful to consider these further applications of Russellian ideas.

The difficulties arise as follows. The value which a function yields for a certain object does not depend at all on what Name(s) (if any) the object may have (compare §§ 9–10). If a certain object gives, say, T at a certain function then that is, as it were, strictly a matter between the object and the function. For example, a rose yields T at the function . . . smells sweet even if it is unNamed and unregarded: and a person cannot avoid giving F at the function . . . is tall, dark, and handsome by deed poll—otherwise this book would not be listed under 'McCulloch'. Suppose then that an object x has two Proper Names, 'a' and 'b', which Names we can therefore describe as *co-referential*. Whether or not 'Ga' is T will depend on what x yields at the function G . . .: and whether or not 'Gb' is T will depend on *exactly the same thing*. So 'Ga' and 'Gb', therefore, are guaranteed to have the same truth-value. Hence, given the reasoning just outlined, it ought to be possible to endorse as valid the following deductive rule or procedure:

Leibniz's Law (*LL*)

> FROM Ga
> AND $a = b$
> INFER Gb

(where 'a' and 'b' are any Proper Names, and 'G . . .' is any first-level functor). For if we have '$a = b$', this must be because the two Names 'a' and 'b' are co-referential: in which case the propositions 'Ga' and 'Gb' are guaranteed to have the same truth-value. But this means in particular that when we have '$a = b$', substituting one Name for the other is guaranteed never to lead from T to anything but T: and this licenses (LL).

However, suppose we now say that two *Candidates* are co-referential if, on a Proper-Name treatment, they would each be assigned the same object as semantic value. The problem then, as we shall see, is that variations of truth-value like those ruled out by the above argument are precisely what occur when appearances of co-referential Candidates in propositions containing the modal and psychological words are considered. In other words, (LL) appears to fail when we have Candidates in these contexts. Given the convincing nature of the argument for (LL), it is then tempting to conclude that the Candidates cannot be treated as Proper Names.

Let us see how this all applies to specific cases. As will be explained in more detail in chapter 4, it is customary to treat the modal words as components of operators 'it is necessary that' and 'it is possible that', which take propositions to make propositions (compare 'not'), and to symbolize these operators as '□' and '◇' respectively. Now, as we shall also see in chapter 4, the exact interpretation of these modal notions is a delicate matter. However, a true proposition is said to be *necessarily true* if it is in some sense just *bound* to be true, and so *could not have been* false. Thus, plausible examples of propositions which are necessarily true are logical truths like '$P \leftrightarrow P$', and mathematical truths like '$2 + 3 = 5$'. Similarly, a false proposition is said to be *necessarily false* if it is bound to be false, or could not have been true: and equally plausible examples of propositions which are necessarily false are contradictory propositions like 'P & −P', or 'some squares are round'. This should be familiar enough.

Now, necessary falsehoods are propositions, we have said, which are just bound to be false. Given this, it is open to us to draw a contrast between necessary falsehoods and all other propositions— those which at least *could* be or have been true—and to call all members of this second class *possibly true* propositions. If this is done, all necessary truths will count as being possibly true (since they are not necessarily falsehoods): but there will be, besides, other examples of propositions which are possibly true. For example, non-necessary (contingent) propositions which actually happen to be true, but which could have been false, will also count as possibly true, for example, 'There are snakes in Wales'. And so will (contingent) propositions which actually happen to be false but which nevertheless could have been true, for example, 'There are snakes in Ireland'. Given this sort of division among propositions we can then explain the truth-values of propositions beginning with the operators '□' and '◇' as follows:

> '□P' is T if and only if 'P' is necessarily true,

and

> '◇P' is T if and only if 'P' is possibly true.

It then turns out that both:

$$\Box(2 + 3 = 5) \quad \text{and} \quad \Diamond(2 + 3 = 5)$$

come out as T, as do both:

$\diamondsuit$ (There are snakes in Wales)

and

$\diamondsuit$ (There are snakes in Ireland)

whereas both:

$\square$ (Some squares are round)

and

$\diamondsuit$ (Some squares are round)

come out F. In general: if 'P' is a necessary falsehood, then '$\square P$', '$\diamondsuit P$', and 'P' will all be F; if 'P' is a necessary truth, then '$\square P$', '$\diamondsuit P$', and 'P' will all be T; and if 'P' is neither a necessary truth nor a necessary falsehood (i.e. is contingent), then '$\square P$' will be F, '$\diamondsuit P$' will be T, and 'P' will be whatever it happens to be.

Consider now the proposition:

(1) The Queen of Scotland is not a Queen of Scotland.

This is, of course, F: worse, not only is it F, but it surely could not have been *other than* F—how could any Queen of Scotland fail to be a Queen of Scotland? Hence, it seems that (1) is necessarily false: hence, it is not possibly true. In other words:

(2) $\diamondsuit$ (The Queen of Scotland is not a Queen of Scotland)

is F. But now consider the proposition:

(3) The Queen of Australia is not a Queen of Scotland.

Like (1), this too is F, because it so happens that:

(4) The Queen of Scotland = the Queen of Australia.

However, although (3) is F, it certainly does not seem at all right to maintain that it *had* to be F, that is, could *not* have been T. For, surely (4) itself could have been F—for example, if Scotland had withdrawn from the United Kingdom in 1975. And, in such a circumstance (3) would then have been T, since the Queen of Australia *would not* have been a Queen of Scotland. Thus (3) did not have to be F—it could have been T—so it is possibly true. In other words:

(5) $\diamondsuit$ (The Queen of Australia is not a Queen of Scotland)

is T.

All of this seems reasonably straightforward. However, suppose now we make two assumptions:

(A1) '$\Diamond$ (... is not a Queen of Scotland)' stands for a function from objects to truth-values,

and

(B)   definite descriptions are to be treated as Proper Names.

(A1) is just an application to modalized propositions of the type of Fregean semantic analysis described in chapter 1: and (B) is just Frege's proposal for the treatment of descriptions.[11] Together, however, these assumptions lead straight to the sort of difficulties described at the beginning of this section. For, given (B), our two descriptions 'the Queen of Australia' and 'the Queen of Scotland' will each be assigned the very same object—Queen Elizabeth II of England—as semantic value. And, given (A1), the truth or falsity of both (2) and (5) will depend on exactly the same thing—namely, what Queen Elizabeth gives when presented to the function $\Diamond$ (... is not a Queen of Scotland). But then, of course, (2) and (5) are guaranteed to have the same truth value: yet—as we saw—*they have different ones*. For (2) is F and (5) is T. Furthermore, given the assumptions (A1) and (B) the inference:

(5), (3), therefore (2)

turns out to be an instance of (LL) (with the two descriptions as 'a' and 'b' and the functor mentioned in (A1) as 'G ...'). But the premisses here are T and the conclusion is F—so (LL) fails if we make the assumptions (A1) and (B)! Yet (LL), as we showed at the beginning of this section, cannot fail for Proper Names 'a' and 'b' and first-level functor 'G...'.

This outcome is clearly intolerable. Either the reasoning to the conclusion that (2) and (5) have different truth-values is faulty, or one or more of the assumptions (A1) and (B) must be given up. Admittedly, modal notions are rather unclear: nevertheless, it seems that the examples chosen are about as uncontentious as any examples could be, so that, if the modal notions are to have any application at all, the decision about (2) and (5) will have to stand. So, (A1) or (B) must go. Now, (B) has already given trouble: witness the discussion of the Basic Problem. Moreover, (A1) just looks like a straight application of a very basic Fregean idea. So, why not drop (B) and thereby extend Russell's quantificational treatment from the failed cases?

This seems immediately to give considerable relief from the troubles just described. For, if the descriptions are treated in Russell's quantificational manner, the above argument that (2) and (5) are guaranteed to have the same truth-value just cannot get started. For it begins from the assumption that the truth-value of these propositions will be determined by what Queen Elizabeth yields at the function $\diamond$ (... is not a Queen of Scotland): and this assumption is false if the descriptions are treated in a quantificational way. For, as we have already seen, quantifiers in a Fregean logic are not assigned objects as semantic values, but are instead treated as standing for second-level functions (see § 5). And there is no *obvious* reason why co-referential Candidates should have to stand for the same second-level function: on the contrary, the evident differences in truth-value between the likes of (2) and (5) seems to indicate otherwise, since these propositions furnish an example of a first-level function (that mentioned in (A1)) which would be taken on to T by one of the second-level functions, and on to F by the other. Moreover, if the Proper-Name treatment of the descriptions is abandoned, (LL) would no longer be relevant to the possibility of an inference from (5) and (3) to (2), so that the principle would not be threatened by the stated variations in truth-values between (5) and (2). For (LL), after all, is a principle concerning the intersubstitutability of *Proper Names*: and if the descriptions in our propositions are *not* treated as Proper Names, but are instead given a quantificational treatment, then (LL) simply does not apply in this case. Thus, a Russellian treatment of the descriptions seems to promise an avenue of escape from our difficulties.

Furthermore, all the above considerations seem to extend readily to the case of natural names, and Russell's treatment of natural names furnishes a corresponding promise of a solution. For example, not only is

(6) Hesperus is not the same planet as Hesperus

F: it is hard to see how it could ever be anything else, so that:

(7) $\diamond$ (Hesperus is not the same planet as Hesperus)

is also F. Now, it happens too that:

(8) Hesperus is not the same planet as Phosphorus

is F, since the names here are both names of the planet Venus. However, this fact was discovered by empirical means. So, given the natural assumption that whatever is discovered empirically could have turned out otherwise—and it certainly seems easy to envisage how the investigations of astronomers could have delivered the opposite verdict—it seems that (8) is possibly true, so that:

(9) $\Diamond$ (Hesperus is not the same planet as Phosphorus)

is T. But, of course, this evident difference in truth-value between (7) and (9) is ruled out if we make the assumptions:

(A2) '$\Diamond$ (Hesperus is not the same planet as . . .)' stands for a function from objects to truth-values

and:

(C) natural names are to be treated as Proper Names,

since these assumptions entail that the truth-values of (7) and (9) depend on what the function $\Diamond$ (Hesperus is not the same planet as . . .) yields when presented with the object Hesperus (which is Phosphorus): and this has to be the same in both cases. Furthermore, plainly, since we have:

(10) Hesperus = Phosphorus,

the inference:

(9), (10), therefore (7)

would furnish a counterexample to (LL), since the premises are T but the conclusion is F.

In this way still further encouragement to adopt a Russellian treatment of the Candidates is at hand, for reasons parallel to those given above when descriptions were considered. For, neither the above argument that (7) and (9) are (contrary to appearances) guaranteed to have the same truth-value, nor the claim that (9), (10), and (7) furnish a counterexample to (LL), would apply if (C) were dropped and replaced by the Russellian proposals

(ND) Treat natural names as descriptions,

and

(DQ) Treat descriptions quantificationally.

For the names would no longer be assigned objects as semantic value; and (LL), being a principle to do with the behaviour of Proper Names, would not be applicable to (9), (10), and (7).

Overall, then, Russell's theories of descriptions and natural names not only help one cope with the Basic Problem of failed descriptions and vacuous names, but they also seem to help one avoid the sorts of problems we have rehearsed in this section, which apply even when there *is* an object to be invoked as semantic value for certain Candidates. And this makes the Russellian approach look even more attractive—especially given the points to be made in the following section. However, as we have already said, there are complexities involved in the matters discussed in this section which tend to undermine the cogency of Russell's proposals: moreover, much depends on how exactly one deals with the semantics of a language enriched by the operators '□' and '◇', and we shall go on to see (chapter 4) that modern wisdom tends to find against Russell when this business is opened. But as a first shot the proposals have their obvious attractions, especially in the context of the other paradigmatic applications of the Russellian treatment.

20 PSYCHOLOGICAL CONSTRUCTIONS

Propositions containing psychological constructions like '... believes that – – –', '... supposes that – – –', '... wonders whether – – –', etc. present difficulties like the ones above to which Russellian approaches give promising initial answers. Questions about propositions like this, however, are particularly vexed, being linked to issues of fundamental importance in the philosophies of mind and language: and, once more, it can be doubted whether Russell's proposals are either required or satisfactory—although the issues raised here are not exactly analogous to those raised in the modal case. But, however this may be, the type of proposition concerned will receive detailed attention in chapters to come.

The psychological constructions in question take Proper Names or quantifiers in their first slot and propositions in their second one. What results are propositions that make a psychological statement, or report. Consider, for instance:

Thatcher believes that there is no alternative;

Someone supposes that the moon is made of green cheese;

The Queen of England wonders whether things will ever return to sanity.

Appearances of Candidates in the propositions which fill the second slot provide striking examples of the Basic Problem. For example, we are often ready with reports like:

(1) This detective believes that the murderer of Marilyn Monroe escaped in an aeroplane,

say, in the course of describing the detective's state of mind, perhaps with a view to explaining relevant behaviour. But beliefs can easily be mistaken, and, for example, in the case of (1) it could be that the detective is just wrong to suppose that there is a murderer of Marilyn Monroe. Yet it seems plain that even beliefs based upon mistakes are still beliefs, reportable like any other, so we evidently need to be ready with a semantic account of, for example (1), even if the detective is mistaken in the way suggested. In other words, quite regardless of whether Marilyn Monroe *was* murdered, it is surely possible for someone to believe that she was, and to infer from this and other beliefs the further thought that the murderer in question must have escaped in an aeroplane. In such a situation a proposition like (1) would then merely be a (true) report of this line of thought. However, the proposal for treating descriptions as Proper Names runs into trouble here for predictable reasons. If *no-one* murdered Marilyn Monroe then there is no appropriate object to yield T when presented to the function This detective believes that . . . escaped in an aeroplane: yet, as we have just seen, (1) could be T for all that.

What is more, we saw in §18 that astronomers said things like 'Vulcan is a hard planet to observe'. They were serious and honest workers, so surely:

(2) Those astronomers believed that Vulcan is a hard planet to observe

should be T. But it cannot be if 'Vulcan' is treated as a Proper Name and 'Those astronomers believed that . . . is a hard planet to observe' is a first-level functor: for the planet does not exist.

Notice too the particular absurdity which results in these cases from proposals to assign some arbitrary object such as zero to vacuous Proper Names. Given, as we said, that propositions like (1) and (2) are reports of the state of mind of whatever is referred to by the expression in the first slot, any proposed semantic treatment of these propositions ought to be, so to speak, *psychologically credible*: it ought to deliver a treatment of the proposition which accords with the psychological facts. But it is evident that neither (1) nor (2) can be seriously interpreted as reports of beliefs about zero, or about any other arbitrarily selected object. As we shall see further in chapters 5 and 6, this psychological dimension of our enterprise furnishes a powerful and somewhat independent lever on the matters arising out of the problem of Naming (because, roughly, talk of propositions and meaning, and talk of beliefs, are largely concerned with the same subject matter).

So far we have fairly straightforward exemplifications of Russell's Basic Problem. But, as in the case of modal contexts, worse follows: even Candidates which *do* correspond to objects give substitutivity problems. Thus, we certainly have it that:

(3) Most Anglo-Saxons believe that the Queen of England is the Queen of England.

Furthermore, it is also the case that:

(4) The Queen of England is the Queen of Australia.

Nevertheless, it is plain that there is no valid inference from (3) and (4) to:

(5) Most Anglo-Saxons believe that the Queen of England is the Queen of Australia.

For, in the first place, it would not be at all surprising to learn that (5), unlike (3) and (4), is in fact false simply because large numbers of Anglo-Saxons simply do not realize that Australia has a Queen. But even if this is not the case it is plain that the truth of (3) and (4) alone could not *guarantee* that of (5). For example, there could be a widespread misapprehension among Anglo-Saxons, deliberately fostered by certain newspapers and magazines, that someone other than Elizabeth II of England—for example, Ms Pamela Stephenson— was in fact the Queen of Australia. (5) would then simply misrepresent the psychological facts, and would therefore be F, despite the fact that (3) and (4) were T.

However, the problem here, predictably enough, is that (3) and (5) are guaranteed to have the same truth-value given the natural assumptions:

(A3) 'Most Anglo-Saxons believe that the Queen of England is . . .' stands for a first-level function,

and

(B) definite descriptions are to be treated as Proper Names.[12]

Given (A3), the truth value of any proposition formed by writing a Proper Name in the slot of 'Most Anglo-Saxons believe that the Queen of England is . . .' will turn on what the represented function yields for the Named object. Given (B), the object in the case of each of our samples (3) and (5) would be Elizabeth II. So, assumptions (A3) and (B) guarantee that (3) and (5) will get the same value: contrary to the evident fact that they need not.

What is more:

(6)   Even when there was no evidence that Hesperus = Phosphorus, most astronomers believed that Hesperus = Hesperus

is a fair bet. And, of course, we have

(7)   Hesperus = Phosphorus.

However, the prospects are decidedly dim for:

(8)   Even when there was no evidence that Hesperus = Phosphorus, most astronomers believed that Hesperus = Phosphorus.

This is surely F—one certainly hopes so. But, as before, if we assume:

(A4) 'Even when there was no evidence that Hesperus = Phosphorus, most astronomers believed that Hesperus = . . .' stands for a function from objects to truth-values,

and

(C)   natural names are to be treated as Proper Names

then (6) and (8) are guaranteed to have the same truth-value (whichever value Hesperus, that is Phosphorus, gives when presented to the appropriate function).

Notice further the predictable apparent violations of (LL). In the face of the assumptions (A3), (A4), (B), and (C), the inferences:

      (3), (4), therefore (5)

and

      (6), (7), therefore (8)

will have T premises and F conclusions, despite being instances of the principle.

The attractiveness of Russellian solutions to all of these problems should once more be evident. For instance, if descriptions and natural names are not treated as Proper Names, then the root problem is avoided. The failure of the description in:

(1) This detective believes that the murderer of Marilyn Monroe escaped in an aeroplane,

or of the name in:

(2) Those astronomers believed that Vulcan is a hard planet to observe

would be neither here nor there, since the Russellian accounts of such expressions does not assume that they must have objects to refer to. Furthermore, since the Russellian explanations of the truth-values of (3), (5), (6), and (8) will not proceed by speaking of what happens when a referred-to object is presented to the appropriate function, the argument that these pairs of propositions must have the same value loses its force. And finally, of course, once quantificational treatments are offered for the Candidates in all the above propositions, the two displayed inferences will not be instances of (LL), and so the relevant variations in truth-values will not provide counterexamples to the principle.

As in the modal case, however, the issues here depend precisely upon what the semantic treatment is given of a language containing the new constructions: and, as before, but for rather different reasons, we shall see that Russell's handling of the matter was not entirely correct. Nevertheless, the initial plausibility of his suggestions is undeniable, and it consequently should be clear enough why Russell's views on descriptions and natural names have exercised such a grip on logicians and philosophers of language. With Russell's proposals on descriptions and natural names in place, the problems described in the present chapter all seem to be dealt with at a stroke: and it is hard to think of a stronger reason for accepting a pair of semantic proposals. Certainly, it is no surprise that Russell's views on descriptions and natural names should have become widely accepted and imitated.

Despite this, we shall see that most aspects of the Russellian orthodoxy have been hotly disputed: and we shall also see that certain aspects of it must be rejected. We start in the next chapter by reviewing Russell's overall strategy as described above, and noting its principal weakness. This will then lead us to further Russellian arguments against Proper-Name treatments, involving the deeper aspects of the Basic Problem mentioned in § 18, and from there to the prospects for a Fregean counter-attack.

Further Reading

For Russell's initial attack on Frege's theory of descriptions, and formulations of his quantificational alternative, see 'On Denoting', *Mind*, 14 (1905); repr. in *Logic and Knowledge*, ed. R. Marsh (London, 1956) (page refs. are to this version). This is a collection of some of Russell's most important articles, which are usually cited from this source. See also B. Russell and A. Whitehead, *Principia Mathematica*, vol. i (Cambridge, 1910), esp. Introd., chap. 3. For Russell's original traditional theory of generality, see his *The Principles of Mathematics* (London, 1903), chap. 5.

An excellent work on Russell is R. M. Sainsbury, *Russell* (London, 1979), chaps. 2–5. For helpful discussion of descriptions see G. Evans, *The Varieties of Reference*, ed. J. McDowell (Oxford, 1982), §2.4, and also M. Dummett, *Frege: Philosophy of Language* (London, 1973), pp. 161–8.

For a clear and entertaining discussion of the issue of non-existent objects (§ 16) see 'On What There Is', W. V. Quine, *From a Logical Point of View* (Cambridge, Mass., 1953), chap. 1. 'Reference and Modality', chap. 8 of this important work, is an early and influential discussion of the problems raised by modal and psychological constructions (§§ 19–20). See also the excellent papers in P. T. Geach, *Logic Matters* (Oxford, 1972), Pt. IV. For the 'I' quantifier (§ 17) see Evans (1982), pp. 57 ff.; Dummett (1973), pp. 160–71; and M. Davies *Meaning, Quantification and Modality* (London, 1980), pp. 151–2.

NOTES

1. Another OD criticism of Frege concerns the notion of *Sinn*, which, Russell implies, involves 'an inextricable tangle' (p. 50). There is certainly an inextricable tangle in the relevant passages of OD: but we shall continue to ignore the matter of *Sinn* altogether for the time being. As remarked in § 6, it will start to intrude in §§ 26–31, and will ultimately be of prime importance (from chap. 5).

2. It should be noted in passing that there is another use for 'propositional function', according to which it is understood to be a function from, say, an object to a *proposition* (rather than to a truth-value). Furthermore, Russell occasionally said that the propositions are *expressions* ('The Philosophy of Logical Atomism', p. 185); and it is clear that this would help to blur the distinction between functions and functors (see *Principia Mathematica*, pp. 14–15).

3. Note too the astonishing way in which Russell treats 'man' and 'human' as interchangeable: he even goes so far as to analyse 'I met a man' as ' "I met x, and x is human" is not always false' (OD, p. 43). Not even the

usual drivel about 'the generic sense of "man"' could be deployed to accommodate this.

4. To be sure, Russell seems to posit a synonymy by using 'means'. But if we replace 'means' with its implication 'is true if and only if' (and look to our using and mentioning) then, to all intents and purposes, we get (Def∀).

5. Of course, Frege might well treat a description as *syntactically* (i.e. grammatically) complex, since it is possible to view the pattern exemplified by 'the father of . . .' as a type of first-level functor which represents a function from objects to objects (see §43 below). Thus a more perspicuous symbolization for our proposition would be something like '$G(f(b))$', with 'f . . .' representing the function the father of . . ., and 'b' serving for 'Charles II'. But as far as the present semantic point is concerned, this syntactic complexity is irrelevant, since the description ('$f(b)$'), when treated as a Proper Name, is assigned an object as semantic value.

6. Of course, one can formulate perfectly acceptable *plural* descriptions in the latter type of case, such as 'the unemployed Britons', or 'the members of the Cabinet'. But our concern, here and elsewhere, is with singular descriptions—descriptions which can apply at most to one thing.

7. It is sometimes suggested that although, say, the present king of France does not exist, 'he' still in some sense has being, or 'subsists', and so can after all be invoked by a Proper-Name treatment. In OD Russell brusquely rejects Meinong's suggestion to this effect, and in general maintains that one should no more contemplate the 'being' of the non-existent in logic than one would in any other non-logical project or activity (pp. 45–7). And he is right here at least to this extent: the domain of objects which we standardly take ourselves to be talking about and interacting with, and which should therefore be invoked by semantic treatments of what we say, is intended to coincide with the world of our non-logical activities—that is, with the world of existing objects, or some part thereof; indeed, it is doubtful whether more than this *could* be intended.

8. Russell's own concerns tended to overlap the two enterprises just mentioned. That is, he not only sought a treatment of descriptions which would be adequate for reasoning or logical purposes, but he was also fond of saying that his solution to the Basic Problem helped one to expose the (genuine) 'logical form' of the corresponding English sentences containing descriptions, which he thereby deemed to have a 'misleading' grammatical structure. And this is precisely the sort of claim that the theorist of meaning would make.

9. Hence, Russell's claim (OD, p. 51) to be able to deal with a description without assigning it 'any significance on its own account'—by this he means that he posits no object as 'the meaning' of a description, but

shows instead how to recast propositions containing descriptions into quantificational form. Notice that one might retort that Russell *has* assigned descriptions a 'significance on their own account'—namely, a second-level function (see § 5): although this charge would not, of course, threaten Russell's claim to have solved the Basic Problem by avoiding the problematic attempt to invoke an object.

10. Actually, there are some differences of emphasis in Russell's treatment when he turns to natural names. He tended to discuss names from fiction or myth like 'Romulus', and tended also to lean more heavily on certain epistemological aspects of the Basic Problem which we shall introduce in chap. 3. As far as the matter of fiction is concerned, this raises complications, owing to the arguably special status of discourse in and about fiction, and is better left aside for special treatment (not to be offered in the present book). As for epistemology, Russell's is flawed (see §§ 24–5), even though his fundamental motivation is on the right lines: but this entire matter is fraught with difficulty, and will need extended treatment (see chaps. 6, 7, and 8).

11. It is vital here not to be misled into thinking that Frege himself subscribed to the likes of (A1). As it happens, he barely considered modality; moreover, for reasons that will only become fully clear in chap. 5, it is unlikely that he himself would have adopted claims like (A1) had he done so. The idea behind the discussion in the text is merely that it would be perfectly natural to adopt (A1) and its ilk if one were extending Fregean ideas to modal languages. For more on this matter see the parallel point in n. 12 below and chap. 4.

12. Again, be clear that the position described in the text is not Frege's own, but rather represents a natural extension of his ideas to sentences involving psychological constructions. As we shall see in chap. 5, Frege himself approached these matters by abandoning assumptions like (A3).

3

Russell: The Official View

21 INTENSIONALITY SUSPENDED

Russell's overall strategy as described in the previous chapter goes as follows. First, it is noted that failed descriptions and vacuous natural names do not submit very well, if at all, to Proper-Name treatments. Second, alternative Russellian treatments of these expressions, expressly designed to avoid the Basic Problem, are offered. Third, it is then noted that Proper-Name treatments even of *successful* descriptions and natural names meet problems when they occur mixed with modal and psychological constructions. Fourth, it then appears that the alternative Russellian treatments seem to avoid these problems too, so that, finally, one feels encouraged to conclude that Proper-Name treatments of descriptions and natural names are best avoided altogether, and the Russellian alternatives preferred. The outcome seems to be that no definite descriptions or natural names should be treated as Proper Names—and, as we shall see below, Russell also produced arguments designed to show that most occurrences of the other Candidates, demonstratives and indexicals, should also not be so treated. But before coming to that it will be instructive to see how Frege might defend his view that definite descriptions and natural names should be treated as Proper Names against the Russellian line of argument just described.

The easiest move to dispute is the one made at the third step. The key point here, recall, is that descriptions and natural names, when mixed with modal or psychological constructions, do not appear to obey the substitution principle (LL), even though it seems that Proper Names ought to do so. Thus, the natural conclusion to draw is that descriptions and natural names do not function as Proper Names in those contexts. However, there is an alternative diagnosis.

Why *should* Proper Names obey the substitution principle? The answer given in § 19 goes as follows: whether or not an object gives T at a function G ... is a matter, as we said, between the function and the object, and cannot turn on what, if anything, the object is *called*. So, where 'a' and 'b' are Proper Names of some one object x, the truth or otherwise of 'Ga' and 'Gb' both depend on exactly the same thing—namely, what x yields at the function G . . .. Thus, it seems guaranteed that co-referential Proper Names will be intersubstitutable without change of truth-value, and that, in particular, if we have 'Ga' and '$a = b$', we should be able to infer 'Gb'—which is to say that we should be able to endorse (LL). Since we seem to have counterexamples involving descriptions and natural names and the modal or psychological constructions, however, Russell immediately 'blames' the Proper-Name treatment of these Candidates. But the alternative diagnosis is to 'blame' the modal and psychological constructions themselves: perhaps they just do not submit to straightforward Fregean analysis, so that, for intance, it is just wrong to treat propositions like:

It is necessarily the case that Hesperus = Phosphorus,

or

Most Anglo-Saxons believe that Hesperus = Phosphorus,

as though they contain first-level functors of the standard 'G . . .' sort. That is, instead of giving up the assumptions:

(B) definite descriptions are to be treated as Proper Names,

and

(C) natural names are to be treated as Proper Names,

one might instead give up the assumptions (A1)–(A4) which all involved the root idea that Frege's basic object/function analysis is to be extended to propositions containing the modal and psychological words. To use the jargon, the idea here would be that the simple Fregean treatment is only to be deployed on *extensional* language, and that other treatments must be given to the non-extensional or *intensional* language which contains the modal and/ or psychological words. And, of course, if this is right, it is perhaps for *this* reason, rather than the one which Russell gives, that (LL) fails for these contexts.

Furthermore, there is a somewhat independent reason for taking this second line. Note that the two displayed propositions above themselves contain or embed a whole proposition ('Hesperus = Phosphorus'), so that it is possible to view them as containing the proposition-forming operators 'It is necessarily the case that . . .' and 'Most Anglo-Saxons believe that . . .', whose gaps need to be filled by a proposition. In this the operators are analogous to 'not', which also makes a proposition from a proposition. However, recall that the Fregean way with 'not' is to treat it as standing for a function from truth-values to truth-values, whose nature is specified in the standard truth-table. And the fact is that such a treatment simply is not available for the modal and psychological operators. For example, although

Stalin was a Georgian

is certainly T, we cannot infer from this fact alone whether either of

It is necessarily the case that Stalin was a Georgian

or

Most Anglo-Saxons believe that Stalin was a Georgian

is T or F: for it is clear that these further matters depend on more than the mere truth or falsity of the embedded proposition. Given this, we can see straight off that *some* extensional Fregean treatments of the sort introduced in chapter 1 just will not apply when the modal or psychological words are involved: one needs, at least, to modify or extend the basic logical and semantic treatments. And seeing this, we should consequently be suspicious of Russell's arguments which revolve around the substitution principle: for perhaps other aspects of Frege's extensional logic need to be modified also. So—pending further investigation into the semantics of intensional constructions—we should at least suspend judgement on Russell's arguments.[1]

This immediately weakens considerably the Russellian argument that *no* descriptions or natural names can be treated as Proper Names: pending the further investigation into intensional contexts, we are simply left with the Basic Problem, and Russell's proposals which arose out of his consideration of it. But, shorn of the extra support which they appear to derive from the substitutivity considerations, these proposals, as we noted in §18, look like overreaction: why not merely adopt Russell's treatment for the failed and vacuous cases, retaining the Proper Name treatment for all the rest? At this point we encounter the deeper aspects of the Basic Problem which were mentioned in §18. As we shall now see, the argument against Proper-Name treatments which starts off with the simple consideration of the Basic Problem can be made to take off in an alarming fashion, and it soon threatens the very idea of the Proper Name—and therefore, given the result of §10, threatens the whole

Fregean edifice. Having developed this line of argument, it will take us the rest of the book to put things completely back together again.

22 THE BASIC PROBLEM AGAIN: THE PROPOSITIONAL AND EPISTEMIC FACTORS

Our illustrations of the Basic Problem involved cases where we *know* that no unique object satisfies a description or answers to a natural name: we know that there is no unique present king of France, or unemployed Briton, or planet Vulcan. And this immediately suggests the idea that a quantificational treatment is only to be considered in such cases, and that Frege's Proper-Name treatment would be satisfactory in all the rest. Is there any reason, other than the suspended ones to do so with substitutivity, for going any further in a Russellian direction? Well, in the first place, there are many cases where we are just *agnostic* on the relevant issue, as in the case of a description of some object which is not known, but merely posited, to exist (e.g. 'the murderer of Marilyn Monroe', 'the virus that causes multiple sclerosis'). Something similar goes for at least some natural names: do we know whether Homer, or King Arthur, or Robin Hood, existed? And in such cases the Proper-Name treatment seems as questionable as in the failed and vacuous cases. *For a proposed treatment of some range of phenomena is only acceptable if there is no available rival treatment which, all things considered, is better.* In the present case, the phenomena comprise the evident facts that propositions like:

(1) The murderer of Marilyn Monroe escaped in an aeroplane

and

(2) King Arthur defeated the Saxons,

can be used in reasoning, and so have a logical or semantic nature, which we expect logicians to account for. And the rival theories are respectively the Proper-Name and Russellian treatments of these phenomena. Now, because we are agnostic with respect to the Candidates used in (1) and (2), we have to say that, for all we know, the Proper-Name treatment fails: for example, if Marilyn Monroe *wasn't* murdered, there is no appropriate object for the account to invoke, so it is in real danger of falling into the difficulties which Russell detects in the Proper-Name treatment of descriptions which are *known* to fail. We could, of course, stipulate that these

Candidates had better therefore be assigned some arbitrary object like zero if there is no more suitable object available (see § 16 above and § 30 below). Such a recourse, however, falls foul of the meaning-theoretic objection noted in § 16: how can it be right to suppose that (1), say, for all we know, may be about zero, or some other arbitrary object? But with Russell's alternative theory to hand, we do not even have to address this question: no such danger attends Russell's proposal, since the whole point of it is to get by without the problematic invocation. Given the italicized principle concerning competing treatments, therefore, a quantificational treatment of agnostic cases seems preferable if quantificational treatments are to be offered at all.

So, Russell's argument against Proper-Name treatments seems readily to extend from straightforward failed and vacuous cases to agnostic ones, where there is a genuine question, answer unknown, about whether an appropriate object exists. But now it is unclear, to say the least, what degree of confidence is required in order to rule out an agnostic stance with respect to some description or natural name we wish to treat—even assuming, what is hardly uncontentious, that 'degrees of confidence' can be adequately quantified. That is, the burden of the last paragraph is that a description or natural name is better not treated as a Proper Name if there is a chance, for all we know, that no appropriate object corresponds to it, since, if such a possibility is realized, a Proper-Name treatment will either not work at all or will be artificial. Alternatively, we might say that *no* expression should be treated as a Proper Name unless it is *guaranteed* to succeed in picking out the intended object: since without such a guarantee, the chance of failure surely remains. But this idea of seeking a guarantee about an object's existence looks distinctly unpromising: certainly as far as ordinary material objects are concerned, it is very unclear what could count as such a guarantee, as sceptics and their opponents tirelessly point out. So it might seem simpler at this point just to avoid these treacherous issues altogether by applying a Russellian treatment to *all* descriptions and natural names: in this way it might seem that we can secure our logic without having to worry too much about the rest of the world. Thus, we rather suddenly arrive, by a route not too dissimilar from one travelled by Russell (see § 24), at his conclusion that descriptions and natural names—all of them—should be treated quantificationally. And this time we have made no mention of the controversial facts involving intensionality. That is, simply as a result of the pressure deriving from the Basic Problem and the associated epistemological considerations just described, we seem to have a good reason for concluding that these Candidates had better *not* be treated as Proper Names.

These associated epistemological considerations involve two factors. On the one hand we have certain propositions containing Candidates which we expect to be dealt with by our semantics: call this the Propositional Factor. And on the other there is the worry whether agnosticism about the existence of the object to be invoked by Proper-Name accounts of these Candidates is reasonable: call this the Epistemic Factor. Together, these two factors seem to restrict the applicability of Proper-Name treatments. If we have a proposition like:

(1) The murderer of Marilyn Monroe escaped in an aeroplane,

then—as meaning-theorists—we know that our job is to account for the semantic nature or structure of this proposition. But, if we are also genuinely unsure as to whether there is an appropriate object answering to this Candidate, the proposal to treat it as a Proper Name is immediately put under pressure: to the extent that we are in doubt about the object, so too must we be in doubt about whether the treatment actually works.

Now there is a sense in which the original arguments based on failed and vacuous cases derived their fundamental thrust from these deeper considerations. For, clearly, cases of Candidates known to fail are just those in which we have the best possible reason for claiming that a Proper-Name treatment will not work: clear 'agnostic' cases like that of (1) are those where our reasons for suspicion are somewhat less powerful, but still evidently compelling. The problem then, for Proper-Name treatments, appears to be the difficulty of checking this epistemological line of thought once it has begun. So, in trying to get to the bottom of Russell's arguments, it will profit us to focus on the Propositional and Epistemic factors. First we shall consider Russell's own handling of the Epistemic Factor, and the suggestions he developed in consequence (§§ 24–5). Then we shall consider how a Proper-Name theorist might try to prevent the epistemological line of thought even from beginning, by manipulation of the Propositional Factor: this leads to a Fregean counter-attack, which will be described in § 30. The chapter will end on an impasse, to be resolved in chapters 5–8.

23 LOGICALLY PROPER NAMES

So far, the argument may still look like a fairly local affair concerning the treatment of Candidates within a Fregean setting. Although Frege, as we saw, wanted to treat both natural names and descriptions as Proper Names, so that the Russellian conclusion mooted in the previous section looks like bad news for him, the fact remains that Russell's own treatments, we saw, are essentially Fregean (§§ 17–18): his theory of descriptions, in particular, makes essential use of the Fregean quantifier apparatus. But, now recall: are we not supposed to be able, at least in principle, to *introduce* Proper Names in a Fregean setting (§ 10)? Yet the conclusion we have reached is that a description or natural name is better not treated as a Proper Name if there is a danger that no appropriate object corresponds to it: conversely, we said that *no* expression should be treated as a Proper Name unless it is *guaranteed* to succeed in picking out the intended object. But, are there, or could there be, such expressions? Indeed, are there, or could there be, such objects—objects, that is, whose existence is guaranteed for us in the appropriate fashion? And at this point it starts to look as though the Basic Problem is far from a local affair, since consideration of the factors underlying it seems to lead to the conclusion that we cannot have Proper Names *at all* unless we can guarantee for ourselves some appropriate objects (whatever exactly that means): and if we cannot have Proper Names we cannot have the Fregean apparatus either. Logic totters!

Now, not only, in this way, is the problem of introducing Proper Names just as much Russell's as it is Frege's, but Russell seemed to be aware of this, even if only subliminally. In § 18 we quoted him as saying that natural names are not 'name[s] in the proper sense of the word'. By this last phrase Russell just means Proper Names—he sometimes called them 'logically proper names'—and their role in his thought is intriguing. When addressing broad questions of logic he tended to slip into the Fregean way of treating natural names as Candidate Proper Names—only to retract when he remembered to add that, because of the Basic Problem, neither natural names *nor* descriptions could be happily so treated. But this is a difficult practice for Fregean logicians to maintain, since they will often, in demonstrating entailments or just giving examples, want to treat the result of presenting an object (specified or otherwise) to a certain function. As we saw in the discussion of this practice in §§ 9–10, it usually involves the introduction of open sentences in the style 'Gx', which are treated to all intents and purposes as though they are propositions of the standard Fregean '*Ga*' form: in effect, the '*x*', when it is imagined to be interpreted, is treated as an arbitrary Proper Name. Thus, a Fregean logician's normal practice enacts, at least by implication, the thought that it ought to be possible at least to *introduce* Proper Names into a language where the standard Fregean logic is being applied. And because of this Russell was in effect forced—like any other Fregean logician—to acquiesce in the doctrine that there are or could be genuine, i.e. logically Proper, Names.[2]

Russell consequently applied 'logically proper name' to precisely those expressions which *would* be treated as Proper Names when translated into the *Principia Mathematica* notation. If we assume for the moment that the Basic Problem rules out entirely Frege's proposal to treat natural names and descriptions as Proper Names, then this leaves such Candidates as demonstratives and indexicals—expressions like 'I', and those uses of 'he', 'this', 'that', etc. which pick out, in about the most basic way immediately imaginable, identifiable objects of reference. Could not these be genuine Proper Names? Well, the Basic Problem might not look very serious when applied to them. Unlike descriptions, demonstratives do not lend themselves easily to serious introduction in contexts where the existence of an appropriate object would normally be treated as problematic. Unlike natural names *and* descriptions, they are hardly, if ever, used in the perceptual absence of the object concerned. So demonstratives seem a good initial bet if Proper Names are what you want: one might, for example, adopt a *mixed strategy* towards the Candidates (see § 31), and treat names and descriptions in a quantificational manner, and demonstratives as Proper Names. And, in a sense, this was Russell's view for quite a long period: notoriously, he said that 'The only words one does use as names in the logical sense are words like "this" or "that"' ('The Philosophy of Logical Atomism' (PLA), p. 201). However, for reasons that will now be made clear, this Russellian doctrine is not quite what it seems, since Russell conjoined it with the view that only very special objects could be Named even by uses of demonstratives and indexicals. And ordinary material objects did not, for Russell, fall into this special category, for reasons that are very much to do with epistemological considerations like those discussed in the previous section. But this move, we shall see, takes Russell into a blind alley.

24 A RUSSELLIAN BLIND ALLEY:
THE OFFICIAL VIEW

Russell's epistemological views tended to be extreme, and this helped to lead him into the extreme position on Proper Names just mentioned. First, he subscribed to a *Principle of Acquaintance* (*PA*): 'you cannot name anything you are not acquainted with' (PLA, p. 201). This doctrine has a core of truth in it, although it takes some unpacking (see §§ 59–60, 71–2). But, as we shall see, it can be construed as a harmless claim to the effect that the thinking or reasoning mind works by being 'in contact' with certain elements which determine the nature of the thinking, and that the sort of contact involved has epistemological significance. In other words, given that thinking is standardly a conscious affair, the thinking mind typically just does know, or can 'survey', *what* it is thinking, where this 'what' is a complex of elements (a structured thought or whatever) whose elements too are known or surveyable. Or again, we can say that when one engages in conscious thinking or reasoning, one's subject-matter is in some sense 'transparent' or 'psychologically real' for one, is just there 'before the mind'. However, Russell also believed that the only things that one could really be acquainted with in the appropriate way were what he called 'particulars'—allegedly immediate contents of thought and experience which are 'given' to the mind—and the properties or universals that these particulars exemplify. And whatever, if anything, particulars are actually supposed to be, Russell was adamant that *material objects are not particulars*; so that material objects, for Russell, were not 'given' to the thinking mind, but rather had to be constructed in some way out of the particulars which were so given. Correspondingly, he said that while particulars would certainly be 'known by acquaintance', things like material objects could only be 'known by description' (see PLA, pp. 196 ff.). Call this *Russell's Particularism (RP)*.[3]

Now, suppose we have a use of a declarative sentence:

(1) This is white,

where 'this' is being used as a demonstrative which, to speak with the vulgar, is intended to pick out a piece of chalk x. (*PA*) and (*RP*) combine to make trouble for a straightforward Proper-Name account of (1). In the circumstances, the use of (1) results in a proposition of whose semantic nature we can reasonably ask for an account. But, according to (RP), the speaker is not acquainted with the piece of chalk x—because it is not a particular—so the speaker cannot, by (PA), Name it. Hence, an account of the use of (1) which incorporates a Proper-Name approach to 'this', and thus proceeds by trying to assign the object x to the demonstrative, simply *misrepresents the nature of the proposition produced*, by crediting the speaker with the ability to Name a material object—something which, according to Russell, the speaker cannot do. Thus he claims:

We say 'This is white'. If you agree that 'this is white', meaning the 'this' that you see, you are using 'this' as a proper name. But if you try to apprehend the proposition that I am expressing when I say 'This is white', you cannot do it. If you mean this piece of chalk as a physical object, then you are not using a proper name. It is only when you use 'this' quite strictly, to stand for an actual object of sense, that it is really a proper name (PLA, p. 201).

There is an obscurity in this passage, since it is unclear whether, by the phrase 'the proposition I am expressing', Russell means the proposition about the piece of chalk 'as a physical object', or just the proposition used by Russell to refer to *his* 'object of sense' (i.e. particular), which object will be different from the one referred to by the person Russell is addressing. But the overall idea is clear enough: one can Name one's 'objects of sense', but one cannot Name physical objects (which are not 'objects of sense'—recall (RP)), and so any proposition supposedly involving a Name of a physical object has to be given a different treatment.

We thus find Russell subscribing to two striking doctrines. One is to the effect that all discourse apparently about material objects is really about (or must be reinterpreted as being about) systems of particulars: 'The names that we commonly use, like "Socrates", are really abbreviations for descriptions; *not only that, but what they describe are not particulars but complicated systems of classes or series*' (PLA, p. 201, emphasis added). The other is the view that logically proper names are rather hard to come by, and can only ever apply to apprehended particulars, so that the possibilities for Proper Naming exist in a region drawn very close around the thinking subject: '. . . it [is] very difficult to get any instance of a name at all in the proper strict logical sense of the word' (ibid.). The upshot is what I shall call *Russell's Official View*. This is the view that nearly all Candidates—even demonstratives when the intended referent would normally be said to be a material object—are not to be treated as Proper Names, but must instead be construed as descriptions (if they are not descriptions already) and then given a quantificational treatment in the spirit of §17. And this is conjoined with the claim that only particulars—allegedly immediate objects of thought or consciousness—can be given Proper Names.

(PA) and (RP) obviously yield a very extreme interpretation of the Epistemic Factor which was introduced in §22: and Russell's approach here derives, in part, from his concern with epistemo-logical matters in general. For example, he was concerned, like other empiricists, with the evident 'gap' between 'the immediate contents of experience', on the one hand, and claims, purporting to be about 'the external world', which are based on them. One with such concerns cannot help but be dogged by the problems of scepticism: surely immediate experience could be just the way it is even if there were no external objects for the experiences to be about; despite how things seem, the world is not 'guaranteed' (compare §22). Russell was no exception here, and, given such concerns, (PA) implies that agnosticism is in order—and Proper-Name treatments therefore suspect—whenever the subject is not directly aware of the object allegedly spoken about. And (RP)—playing right into the hands of the sceptic, as it were—states that this will always be the case when the intention is to speak of a material object.

Because it is thus entwined with these larger epistemological issues, the Official View looks like a standard response to the standard sceptical problems that confronted Russell *qua* empiricist. On the one hand, there are propositions of sort S_1 evidently about a type of thing—in this case material objects. On the other hand, there are propositions of sort S_2 about another type of thing—in this case 'particulars'. Furthermore, the S_2 propositions concern matters which are in some way 'given', whereas the S_1 sort concern matters which 'go beyond' what is given, even though S_2 propositions are supposed to provide some kind of evidence or grounding for the truth of the others. But this encourages scepticism, which character-istically poses awkward questions about the nature and strength of the evidential links which are alleged to hold between propositions of the two sorts. Hence there are attempts at the following type of anti-sceptical response: someone tries to show how anything that we want to say using the S_1 sort of proposition—thereby exposing ourselves to sceptical questions—can as well be expressed in S_2 propositions instead, which—because they concern what is 'given'— are immune to sceptical attack.[4] Thus, the Official View, which has the look of just such a response, implies that instead of producing, say, the allegedly risky proposition:

(1) This is white,

with 'this' intended to pick out a material piece of chalk, one should produce something of the form:

(2) The G is white,

where 'G . . .', if it contains any Proper Names at all, will only contain Proper Names of particulars, of which the material piece of chalk is then alleged to be a 'complicated system of series or classes'. And, in general, any proposition 'Ga', with 'a' a Candidate which apparently applies to a material object, must be treated rather after the fashion '$\exists x (\forall y (- - -$', with all the purported reference to individual material objects removed. Then, because these Russellian paraphrases contain at most Proper Names of items which are guaranteed to exist (particulars are 'given'), even the extreme form of the Basic Problem is avoided, and at the same time the sceptic, apparently, is side-stepped.

However, although some of Russell's intentions seem to be fairly well captured by this line of thought, the overall view is just incoherent. Consider first: what sorts of things populate the domain of the quantifiers in the Russellian paraphrases such as (2)? Obviously one cannot coherently stipulate a domain of material objects in the normal way. So to do, in a Fregean setting, is to allow that it should at least be possible in principle to introduce Proper Names of elements of the domain (§10)—but the Russellian argument described at the beginning of this section is supposed to show, precisely, that material objects *cannot* be Named. So one immediately thinks of searching for some way of populating the domain with respectable 'surrogate' objects—perhaps the 'complicated systems of classes or series [of particulars]' mentioned by Russell in the passage quoted above. But how can this help? No matter *what* the members of the domain are conceived of as being, if one tries to allow that these members can verify a quantified proposition in the normal way, for instance by yielding a value at the quantifier's corresponding function, or by serving as the interpretation of a free variable, then, as we saw in §10, one cannot resist the idea that such members could in principle be Named. So Russell's suggestion here just does not work: if we can quantify over 'systems of particulars', then we can Name them. Hence, if material objects are considered to be such things, we can Name material objects too, and there must be something wrong with the argument, based on (PA) and (RP), to the effect that we *cannot* Name material objects.

This conclusion, to which I shall return below, indicates that Russell's anti-sceptical concerns, to reconstrue talk of material objects in terms of talk of particulars, cannot easily subserve the idea that Candidates ought to be given a quantificational treatment. And a moment's reflection shows that there is also a problem in the other direction: there is a clear sense in which Russell's Official View provides *no relief whatsoever* from the difficulties which prompt the anti-sceptical concerns. Crudely, the sceptic will try to exploit the fact that although it is 'given' that, say:

(3) I am acquainted with white-piece-of-chalkish particulars,

it does not follow that I know that:

(1) This is white,

where (1) is supposed to make reference to a piece of chalk. But, surely obviously, it is *no use whatsoever* to meet this attack merely with the proposal to rephrase (1) after the fashion:

(4) $\exists x (\forall y (y$ is a complicated system of particulars which includes *these* (now given to me), and ... $\leftrightarrow x = y) \& x$ is white).

For if the system ($=$ the piece of chalk, construed Russell's way) is supposed to contain as members particulars (or classes of series thereof) which are *not now* 'given', then (4) will 'go beyond' (3) in much the same way as (1) does (hence the dots), and so will *still be open to a kind of sceptical attack*. On the other hand, if (4) merely concerns the particulars mentioned in (3), then it will clearly have gone nowhere in treating (1). Either way, as I said, there is a sense in which the Official View seems to bring no relief from the sceptical problems that worried Russell.

Clearly, something has gone badly wrong somewhere. What, exactly?

25 OUT OF THE BLIND ALLEY: BACK TO THE BASIC PROBLEM

The essential problem here, I suggest, is that there are at least three different epistemological worries in play, and only one of them is really relevant to the discussion of Proper-Name treatments of ordinary-language Candidates.

The first worry is over the familiar question:

(A) How can we know that there are material objects at all?

which is particularly troublesome for those who take their cue from Descartes and suppose that we have no direct dealings with material objects, but must instead somehow infer their existence from the nature of experience. Russell was clearly bothered by some such question—although it is a delicate matter to what extent during the period under discussion he was held in thrall by the classical 'veil of perception' doctrine, according to which material objects are known to us, if at all, from 'behind' the experiences which represent them. But, however, this may be, it is clear that Russell's claim that material objects are nothing but complicated systems of classes or series of particulars might help with question (A). For we certainly know that there are particulars, and perhaps we can also be allowed, without too much sceptical challenge, to know that they cluster together in systems: after all, experience itself usually comprises a complex system of elements. In this context, (PA) and (RP) help to lay the foundation of what we unproblematically know about, and then the specific doctrine about objects attempts to build an answer to (A) on this foundation.

Given this view, however, we can surely be acquainted with material objects after all, despite the official denial contained in (RP). For, if we can be acquainted with particulars, and indeed with complex clusters of particulars which—according to the doctrine— are *parts* of material objects, then in *precisely this sense* we can also be acquainted with material objects: we are 'given' an object when we are 'given' some part of it. Thus, there is also a sense—even granted (PA)—in which we can, after all, Name material objects, even if they are systems of particulars. This point surfaced in the discussion of the Official View in the previous section, and I shall return to it below.

Suppose we grant that the above sort of response to (A) is successful. Nevertheless, it does not, by itself anyway, completely answer another sort of sceptical challenge:

(B) How can we know as many truths about material objects as we think we know?

For as we remarked earlier, our ordinary experience of material objects is subject to a 'limited showing' condition, in that we usually only experience small portions of what we take to be an object's whole career (we are only acquainted with some of the particulars of which, according to Russell, it consists). Thus we do not experience the tables and chairs claimed still to be present in otherwise empty rooms. Nor do we experience the unobservable particles which, we are told, are responsible for the observable features of such tables and chairs. Because of this, another batch of sceptical questions, as indicated by (B), can get started: how do we know the table and chairs remain in an otherwise empty room, how do we know there are unobservable particles, and so on. And merely claiming that material objects are systems of particulars which can be 'given' will not help here, since these new sceptical questions concern the nature and organization, as it were, of those elements of the system which we do not experience, and which are not, therefore, 'given'.

Naturally there are various ways of responding to these kinds of challenge. One way was indicated in the previous section: attempt to paraphrase S_1-type knowledge-claims apparently about material objects into S_2-type knowledge-claims that merely concern particulars. It is highly debatable, of course, whether any such reconstruction programme could be made to work: but one thing is clear. This is that the envisaged type of wholesale reinterpretation of ordinary knowledge-claims about material objects would need a great deal more than the mere proposal to reconstrue Candidates as quantificational descriptions containing, at most, Proper Names of particulars only. In the first place, many of the allegedly problematic S_1-type claims do not even contain Candidates—e.g. 'there are unobserved tables': and even when they do, as in 'there are unobserved tables *in the next room*', the treatment of the Candidate need not be relevant to the sceptical question. Moreover, as we noted in the previous section, even when sceptical doubt does focus on a Candidate, as in:

(1) This is white,

where (1) is supposed to give expression to a piece of knowledge about a confronted piece of chalk, it does not seem to help much merely to offer the proposal to rephrase (1) after the fashion:

(2) $\exists x (\forall y (y$ is a complicated system of particulars which includes *these* (now given to me) $\ldots \leftrightarrow x = y)$ & x is white).

For if the system (= the piece of chalk, construed Russell's way) is supposed to contain as members particulars (or classes or series thereof) which are *not now* 'given' (the dots represent these), then (2) will be in much the same sort of epistemological boat as (1) is, and so will *still be open to a kind of sceptical attack*. On the other hand, if (2) does not in this way allude to epistemologically troublesome matters, then it will clearly have gone nowhere in treating (1).

To the extent that Russell was concerned with sceptical questions like (B), it is thus evident that he simply did not take his anti-sceptical proposals far enough. If there genuinely is a serious problem about how we can know things about material objects, such as might be expressed in (1), then the correct solution to this is not to look for ways like (2) of re-expressing these propositions: ways, that is, which themselves mimic faithfully the epistemological commitments of the original propositions. What is needed is a complete reconstruction, starting at the beginning, of the relevant part of language, the interpretation of which just must not flirt with the sort of epistemo-logical commitments which allegedly make the original propositions problematic.

But, whether or not such a reconstruction is either required or possible, it is clear that confronting sceptical questions like (B) need not be the business of the logician or meaning-theorist concerned to account for the behaviour of Candidates. For at least one legitimate task here is that of giving a satisfactory account of the usual Candidate-containing propositions which we normally take our-selves to know. This is a job which is just there to be done in its own right, and it is then a further, difficult, and of course controversial question whether we can defend against sceptical attack our claims to know the sorts of proposition accounted for by the logician. So at this point, perhaps with sighs of relief, we can turn our backs on sceptical question (B).[5] But there remains the third type of sceptical question mentioned at the beginning of this section: this is the question:

(C) How can we know when we are genuinely encountering a material object?

Now this does seem to be relevant to the treatment of the Candidates—indeed, it is the sort of epistemological worry that we saw to underlie the Basic Problem (§ 22). Suppose we take ourselves to have answered (A) in something like Russell's manner: then, as we remarked, there is a sense in which we can be acquainted with objects (by being acquainted with their parts), and so a sense in which we can Name them. Moreover, this last conclusion is reinforced by what was said about question (B). In so far as we turn our backs on the idea that we should reconstruct talk of material objects so that it is no longer vulnerable to sceptical challenge, and instead concern ourselves with the semantic articulation of what the sceptic actually challenges, we have to accept that we can Name material objects—or we do if we adopt a Fregean approach. Indeed, it becomes a matter of relative indifference whether or not we consider objects to be systems of particulars, *à la* Russell, since the net result will be the same anyway: we can Name, and so be acquainted with, material objects. Thus we can at this point quietly forget about (*RP*) ((*PA*) will be examined in chapters 5–8). But all of this still leaves quite untouched the idea that, in clear agnostic cases at least, there is an acknowledged danger that Proper-Name treatments of Candidates fail for all we know, and that if they do fail, we shall have given no satisfactory account of the propositions in which these Candidates appear. This thought trades, not on scepticism, but on ordinary standards of what it is reasonable to doubt. Given this, and in the absence of some better understanding of when agnosticism is appropriate, this seems to mean that we have as yet no clear idea how to decide whether any given Candidate is to be treated as a Proper Name. But this is just to say that question (C) is relevant to the business of treating Candidates as Proper Names. For if we could be clearer about the answer to (C), we should be clearer about when a Proper-Name treatment of a Candidate is appropriate. Thus it seems that, even after those more or less irrelevant parts of Russell's Official View which derive from his concern with traditional scepticism have been excised, there remains a relevant challenge to Proper-Name treatments, linked to the Basic Problem and deriving from the Epistemic Factor, which has to be confronted if Fregean ideas are to be applied.

Nevertheless, the precise nature of the challenge, even (or perhaps especially) when it is disentangled from Russell's general epistemological concerns which we have been describing, remains obscure. The line of thought starts off in a more or less straightforward fashion: there does seem to be something strange about the idea that we should invoke, as logicians, objects which may well not exist for all we know. Hence the appeal of quantificational treatments of the likes of 'the murderer of Marilyn Monroe'. But where does all this lead to? Since we are turning our backs on the drastic attempts at anti-sceptical reconstruction that, partly at least, inspired Russell's Official View, there is no escape from the conclusion that material objects are, in principle anyway, Nameable. Yet how can we 'guarantee' the objects to make this possible? Certainly Russell's attempts at this, in the form of his responses to sceptical questions like (A) and (B), have been seen to be no use at all. And nothing else very obvious springs to mind: so perhaps we should look more closely at the original epistemological argument against Proper-Name treatments. Is it, after all, really cogent?

To this end, we turn now to a consideration of the Fregean counter-attack mentioned above, which concentrates on the Propositional Factor, and whose aim is to show that there is really no Basic Problem for Proper-Name treatments.

26 RUSSELL AND MEANING

The Fregean counter-attack was launched by Strawson in his influential 1950 article 'On Referring' (OR). The attack consists partly of some criticisms of Russell's theory of descriptions, partly of a defence of a Proper-Name approach to these expressions, and partly of a diagnosis of a deep flaw in Russell's main argument to the conclusion that there is a Basic Problem. Our principal concern now is with the diagnosis: the dispute over the correct treatment of descriptions will be considered in chapter 7.[6]

According to Russell, the Basic Problem arises because a proposition like:

(1) The present king of France is bald

cannot be treated satisfactorily by the view that descriptions are Proper Names, since this view invokes the object represented by the description: and there is no such object, unless something arbitrary is stipulated, in which case the root of the problem will still not have been dealt with. Now not only did Russell think that the semantics should give some account of the workings of (1), but he had a definite idea of what sort of results should flow. For instance, he said that (1) is 'certainly false', and expected any semantic account to deliver this result (OD, p. 53). He saw it as a further virtue of his own theory that this result was forthcoming: from (Def ∃) it is clear that Russell's rendition of (1), namely

$$\exists x (\forall y (Ky \leftrightarrow x = y) \mathbin{\&} Bx),$$

is F. But Strawson objects to this as follows:

... suppose someone were ... to say [(1)] to you with a perfectly serious air ... Would you say, 'That's untrue'? I think ... not. But suppose he went on to *ask* you whether you thought that what he had just said was true, or was false ... I think you would be inclined, with some hesitation, to say that you did not do either; that the question of whether or not his statement was true or false simply *did not arise*, because there was no such person as the king of France (OR, p. 12).

So we immediately seem to have a disagreement over whether propositions with failed descriptions, such as (1), are false (Russell) or not (Strawson), and thus, perhaps, an argument about the behaviour of descriptions in English. Put like this, however, the dispute is a blank mystery that undergraduates are sometimes encouraged to contemplate. Is this an argument about the correct use of 'false'? Would it help to conduct a survey to see if some consensus appears? Is it just that the English spoken around Cambridge in 1905 deviates from nice 1950 Oxford usage? Who cares?—to uncover the real issue we have to see how Russell deploys the notion of *meaning*: and this involves complexities, exploited by Strawson, which have so far been suppressed.

Although Russell himself attacked what he took to be Frege's particular conception of *Sinn*, he is often to be found interlarding his semantic considerations with observations about meaningfulness in general. A prominent example is the following test which he proposes for deciding whether a Candidate is a Proper Name:

Whenever the grammatical subject of a proposition can be supposed not to exist without rendering the proposition meaningless, it is plain that the grammatical subject is not a proper name i.e. not a name directly representing some object (*Principia Mathematica*, p. 66).

Plainly, Russell is here appealing to the two factors which underlie the Basic Problem: 'supposing' the 'grammatical subject' of a proposition not to exist is making play with agnosticism, or invoking the Epistemic Factor, whilst considering whether, given such a supposition, the proposition is 'meaningless' is a way of introducing the idea that a failed invocation of an object means that no semantic treatment would have been secured. This is the Propositional Factor. Russell's test can then be applied to our (1) to yield the result which he found so unsatisfactory:

now consider 'the [present] king of France is bald'. By [the thesis that descriptions are Proper Names] this ... ought to be about the denotation of the phrase 'the [present] king of France'. But this phrase . . . has certainly no denotation . . . Hence one would suppose that 'the [present] king of France is bald' ought to be nonsense; but it is not nonsense . . . (OD, p 46).

(By 'denotation' Russell means the object which satisfies the description.) Here the point is that we have the best possible reason for disbelieving in the existence of an object answering to the description in question, yet at the same time, according to Russell, we also know that (1) is 'not nonsense', and so should be given a semantic treatment. In other words, it must be the case that either:

(a) there is a unique king of France who is bald;

or

(b) there is a unique present king of France who is not bald;

or

(c) there is no unique present king of France.

If a Proper-Name treatment is offered, then given (a) (1) is T, given (b) (1) is F, and given (c), says Russell, *(1) is nonsense, or meaningless*. But the problem then, as Russell saw it, is that our proposition (1) is clearly meaningful, and that this is a datum which any semantics just has to accommodate. Indeed, merely to *call* (1) a proposition implies that something meaningful is in play, since as we said in chapter 1, a proposition is a declarative sentence as used with a fixed meaning or interpretation.

Nevertheless, it is in this style of argument that Strawson diagnoses a deep flaw: and the points he makes in this regard bear directly on the dispute over falsity mentioned at the beginning of this section.

27 STRAWSON'S DIAGNOSIS

Strawson brands the 'true, false, or meaningless' classification which Russell bases on the options (a)–(c) a 'bogus trichotomy'. In illustration, he (in effect) proposes a distinction between two kinds of meaning which a declarative sentence can have or express: on the one hand, the sentence's *significance*, and on the other, the *statement(s)* which the sentence may make. What are significant, says Strawson, are *sentences* considered merely as linguistic entities. What are candidates for truth and falsity are *statements* which issue from *uses* of these sentences. Thus consider:

(2) The present prime minister of the United Kingdom is a man.

This can be considered as a mere string of words which is capable of being used at different times to make different statements, some true and some false. For example, anyone using it in 1977 (call this utterance U) would have spoken truly. On the other hand, anyone using it in 1980 (utterance V) would have spoken falsely. in Strawson's terminology, U and V involve the one clearly significant *sentence* (2) and make two distinct *statements*, one a true statement about James Callaghan, the other a false one about Margaret Thatcher. However, a present-day utterance (W) of our sentence:

(1) The present king of France is bald

would make neither a true statement nor a false statement, according to Strawson, since there is no relevant king for it to make a true or false statement about. But, Strawson continues, it is just *confusion* to respond to this with the Russellian complaint that (1) would therefore be a piece of nonsense. For the *sentence used* is obviously a perfectly significant piece of English—unlike *real* pieces of nonsense such as ')e@u(9*&,. ~1:/a'—and so utterance W would be a use of a perfectly meaningful (= significant) *sentence*. What would be lacking would be a true or false *statement*. Thus, according to Strawson, Russell's argument as described above rests on a conflation of the quite distinct claims: (i) W makes no true or false statement, and (ii) sentence (1) lacks significance: a conflation that can hardly be avoided if just the one term, 'meaning' (or 'proposition'), is employed. And once this distinction is minded, says Strawson, the basic motivation for Russell's quantificational theory of descriptions—and of the other Candidates—vanishes. There is, says Strawson, no Basic Problem.

28 WAS RUSSELL JUST CONFUSED?

Now, as we shall see (§56), there is every reason to accept the principle of Strawson's distinction between significance and statement; so to this extent there can be no quarrel with the observation that there is something too hasty about the argument that deploys the 'bogus trichotomy'. For Russell shows no awareness of anything like the statement/significance distinction, but merely speaks, as we have so far done, of propositions, that is declarative sentences understood to have a certain given meaning or interpretation. And such a way of speaking, we have just seen, is potentially ambiguous since a declarative sentence can have more than one kind of meaning, and hence can be 'meaningless' in more than one way. Nevertheless, Strawson does not, with this diagnosis, get to the bottom of the matter.

To see this, consider again what Russell says about

(1) The present king of France is bald.

The essential strategy is to argue that although we may easily formulate a proposition like (1) (the Propositional Factor), we know that the description does not pick out an object (the Epistemic Factor), so that, unless it resorts to arbitrary assignments of semantic values, a Proper-Name treatment will not work. The question to ask here is: treatment of what? Note first that we again just called (1) a 'proposition', so that there is a potential ambiguity. However, since the declarative sentence written next to '(1)' is clearly not a piece of nonsense like ')e@u* 9*&,. ~1:/a', we can safely conclude that neither Russell nor Strawson would object to the idea that (1) is a proposition in the sense that it is a significant sentence. So far so good. However, as Strawson makes very plain, one would not look to things like the Proper-Name approach in order to give an account of this significance. As we have already noted, the significance of a sentence is something which, as it were, it carries around from use to use: so it is not appropriate to ask, for example, which given object is to be assigned to the description. Thus, semantic theories such as the Proper-Name treatment—or, indeed, Russell's quantificational treatment—are not really addressed to the question of significance at all but are, if anything, dependent upon it (since there can be no semantic account until there is a use of a significant sentence). Thus it is clear that Russell's complaint about the Proper-Name account's failure to deliver a treatment of (1) has to be pitched, to use Strawson's terminology, at the level of statements, if it is to be at all sensible. And, in effect, this is precisely how it is pitched, since Russell claims that the treatment he requires must show that (1)—or as he *should* have said, that a use of (1)—will be false (issue in a false statement) since the description fails (see §26).

It is wrong to see nothing but *confusion* on Russell's part here. For, as we saw in chapter 1, one proper concern of the logician or the meaning-theorist is to give semantic accounts of language as used in reasoning and the making of serious assertions: and there is little doubt that uses of (1) could figure in such things, even when France is a Republic. Hence, it is perfectly natural, and not at all confused, to expect semantic treatments of such uses to be forthcoming, and to claim that where they are not, the use of the sentence would simply be, from a logical point of view, the production of a 'meaningless noise'. And although Russell may be wrong to harbour this expectation, or wrong in the concrete semantic proposals that he made, alluding to his neglect of the significance/statement distinction cannot help with these matters. At best, it might help to show why he came to the wrong conclusions: but first, it has to be shown that he *did* come to the wrong conclusions.

Thus, we arrive back at the mysterious dispute over the falsity or otherwise of (uses of)

(1) The present King of France is bald

which was shelved in § 26. And what has emerged is that this is really a dispute about the kind of meaning (= statement) that such a use would convey. According to Russell, what would result is a false statement of the quantificational type delivered by his theory of descriptions. According to Strawson, neither a true nor a false statement would result. Who is right?

The reader will rightly complain that this question is scarcely less mysterious than the one it has just replaced. And it is a fact, as we shall see in chapters 6 and 7, that questions like this are extraordinarily difficult to get into proper focus, much less to settle. The immediate aim, then, is to get clearer on what this question involves.

29 WHAT CAN STRAWSON MEAN?

First we have to note a rather studied vagueness in Strawson's complaint against Russell's view of

(1) The present King of France is bald.

We know he rejects Russell's treatment (= semantic account) of (1) (of the statement that a use of (1) would make). But is this because Strawson thinks that *no* semantic treatment is required: or is it because he thinks that a *different* treatment is required? Relatedly, does Strawson hold that a use of (1) would make *no* statement (and therefore no true or false statement): or does he hold that it *would* make a statement, but not a statement that is either true or false (i.e. a neither-true-nor-false statement)? Some passages in Strawson's work suggest one interpretation, some suggest another. On the whole, however, it is likely that Strawson did not at the time distinguish very clearly between the alternatives, but that the view to the effect that *no* semantic treatment of a use of (1) would be required is much closer to what he meant to say.

Still, what do these options amount to? Arguably, there are *three* different options here, although only two of them are clearly versions of a Proper-Name approach, and we shall restrict attention to these. The odd one out is a version of the idea that (1) *does* make a statement—namely a statement that is neither true nor false—*of which a semantic treatment has to be given*. This proposal can be taken to imply that in order to treat (1) we need a *third truth-value*, something beyond or between F and T, which is what must be assigned, for example, to propositions involving failed descriptions. For if a sentence is in this sense taken to express something that can be put up for logical assessment it needs to be assigned a suitable semantic value so that its contribution to more complex expressions (for example, sentences formed with the help of truth-functions) can be worked out. And if we have neither T nor F, we need another. But this line of thought will not be pursued here, since it is rather remote both from Strawson's and our own main concerns.[7]

The remaining two views are these:

(a) that a use of (1) *would* make a statement, but a statement, unfortunately, *without any truth-value at all*;

and

(b) that a use of (1) would simply not make any statement.

Now, as we shall see in chapter 6, there can be important differences between views like these. Nevertheless, we can ignore these putative differences for present purposes. For, whichever view is adopted, the result is that the relevant use of (1) would not be given any *semantic* treatment, and so—in this sense—would just be 'written off' from the logical point of view. Given the rest of what Strawson says about the kinds of statements made by uses of sentences containing *successful* description, both (a) and (b) thus amount to Proper-Name approaches. So Strawson's counter-suggestion to Russell's theory of descriptions boils down to an invitation to acquiesce in the allegedly unsatisfactory Proper-Name account.

Now, we standardly use propositions like (1) in order to make serious assertions, perhaps as links in a chain of reasoning; and we also undoubtedly regard logic as an important, if not the *most* important, dimension of assessment of such utterances. Thus it seems that we have to regard this Strawsonian 'writing off' of the use of (1) as the claim that to use this proposition involves a very serious *misuse or malfunction of language*: otherwise it would be totally unacceptable—indeed barely intelligible—to refuse to offer a semantic treatment of the proposition. However, we can at least imagine serious attempts to use (1) in order to convey information, or draw a conclusion from some premises, where all the usual conditions for making intelligible and logically relevant remarks are met. So how can it be right to claim, as the proponent of (a) or (b) must claim, that language would be malfunctioning in such a situation? What could be the *point* of the claim that *no* logically relevant remark would have been made by such a use? It is precisely *this* that Russell is complaining about when he complains that Proper-Name accounts are prey to the Basic Problem: the charge is, precisely, that serious uses of (1) would be perfectly proper and legitimate contributions to intelligible discourse, and would thus be as much the business of the logician's as they could be, and so ought not to be 'written off' as (a) and (b) imply.

This aspect of Russell's point is perhaps even more vivid in 'agnostic' cases such as

(2) The murderer of Marilyn Monroe escaped in an aeroplane.

Given the conditions of ignorance under which we at present operate, it is not known whether the description in (2) succeeds. Thus, it is not known whether uses of the sentence would be 'written off' from the logical point of view, that is stigmatized as a kind of linguistic malfunctioning, by a Proper-Name treatment. Yet— Russell would say—we know *in advance* that (2) *just is* fit for proper, serious, and logically relevant use: how else—for example—could it guide the sayings and investigations of detectives and journalists? How can it, therefore, be remotely plausible to 'write off' such uses from a logical point of view?

Hence the basis of the mysterious dispute between Russell and Strawson over the type of statement, if any, made by uses of sentences containing failed descriptions—and thus the basis of the even more mysterious dispute over whether or not such uses should be assigned F—is this: Can it be right simply to 'write off' what are, to all appearances, perfectly legitimate attempts to *say something*, that is, apparently full-blooded contributions to linguistic exchange? Now it is clear that we do not as yet have the materials with which to answer such a question: much more needs to be said about the use of language, and about what is involved in calling something a 'full-blooded contribution to linguistic exchange'. However, it will help if at this point we give the outline of the kind of answer that Strawson could offer to the Russellian challenges just explained. This will at least show us what the options are between which we have eventually to choose.

30 THE FREGEAN COUNTER-ATTACK

We noted in §16 that one might consider the Basic Problem either as a problem for those interested in giving paraphrases into logically adequate notation for reasoning purposes, or as a problem for the meaning theorist: and we hinted that this latter way of looking at the problem is the more fundamental. This will now be borne out: we shall see how Strawson, *qua* logician, could hope to deal satisfactorily with the Basic Problem. But we shall also see how this leaves the meaning-theoretic aspect of the Problem untouched. Subsequently, therefore, our main focus will be on this matter.

Suppose we start off with the elements of a Fregean calculus along with suggestions for how the formulae of this calculus could be used to paraphrase (for reasoning purposes) bits of ordinary language, including the proposal to treat descriptions as Proper Names. Strawson's idea is that we can then give schematic explanations of the sorts of statements that these formulae could be used to make: that is, we give, among other things:

> *general directions* for [the use of descriptions] to refer to or mention particular things or persons,

and also

> *general directions* for [the use of sentences containing descriptions] in making true or false assertions [statements] (OR, p. 9).

Such Strawsonian 'general directions' would give the significance (compare §27) of the descriptions and formulae, and could consist of clauses like:

> an expression of the form 'the G' is to be assigned the object (if any) which is uniquely G

and

> a formula of the form 'The G is H' makes a true statement if the function $\underline{H} \ldots$ yields T for the object referred to by 'the G', and a false statement if that function yields F for that object.

Armed with such specifications we could then go on to treat the calculus along more or less Fregean lines, by giving standard semantic treatments of its elements, and by describing the valid transformations, etc. that would be allowed on our statement-making formulae.

What of the fact that it is quite a routine matter to form descriptions which correspond to no unique object? According to Strawson, any difficulty here would be removed 'at a stroke' by the doctrine of presupposition:

We are to imagine every rule of the logical system, when expressed in terms of truth and falsity, is preceded by the phrase 'Assuming that the statements concerned are either true or false, then . . .' (*Introduction to Logical Theory*, p. 176).

That is, our understanding of the rules of the calculus is to presuppose or assume that the transformations, etc. are always to be on formulae which express (true or false) statements: other formulae (e.g. those containing failed descriptions) are just not covered by the rules of the system, and so, in a sense, cannot make trouble for them.[8] In other words, we just imagine that empty Proper Names are 'banished from logic', and the propositions containing them 'written off' from the logical point of view. Then, for example, one might explain the goodness of a bit of reasoning from, say:

The *G* is *H*

to

There is an *H*

by noting that it is in accord with the rule:

'From *Ha* infer $\exists x(Hx)$'

which, *assuming it is used within the realm of true or false statements*, always leads to T when the premiss is T. And *this* fact, of course, is explained by the underlying Fregean semantics as enshrined in such things as the rule (Def∃).

However, suppose we descend from these abstract considerations of how our calculus is supposed to work, and consider instead an *actual* piece of reasoning of the form shown above which might be produced in a real situation. What if the description in the bit of reasoning fails, so that the premiss does not receive a truth-value? Here the Strawsonian proposal is along these lines: although uses of formulae containing this *particular* description would not *themselves* be given a semantic treatment, any reasoning of which they formed a part could still be assessed and classified from a logical point of view. For even if one or more formulae of the reasoning fails to receive a semantic interpretation it can still be said that *had* the necessary presuppositions of the reasoning been met, then it *would have* been valid or otherwise, depending on whether it conformed to a valid rule.

In this sort of way, one might hope to retain the simplicity of the basic Fregean Proper-Name account of descriptions, and to relegate the failures of which Russell made so much to the status of unfortunate mistakes on the part of individual reasoners, rather than see them as sources of difficulty in the semantics. In effect, this approach incorporates Frege's claim that it is a *fault* in natural language that it allows failed descriptions, etc. to be produced (compare § 17). For the idea here is that a properly rigorous Fregean calculus, along with the associated semantics, will yield a sort of ideal logical model of our ordinary reasoning: natural languages, that is, are supposed to conform to the Fregean paradigm, but it is allowed that they do not always succeed, and sometimes lapse into a sort of incoherence, as in the present sort of case where a description fails.[9]

As an approach to purely formal matters, this is more or less orthodox, and well understood: although there is certainly more to be said on the matter. However, we shall not pursue the formal questions any further. For it is clear that, from the *meaning-theoretic* point of view, this sort of proposal leaves the main outstanding issue untouched: or rather, it simply assumes that it has been settled against Russell. Anyone who adopts this line has to swallow the conclusion that serious utterances using failed descriptions, however intelligible and useful they may be, either do not make statements, or at best make statements which are to be 'written off' from the logical point of view (note that assigning such descriptions an arbitrary object like zero is a form of 'writing them off', since *any* assignment that keeps the formal side of things smooth will do). This is what divides the present treatment from Russell's which sees this outcome as a Basic Problem for the approach.

Pending further investigation, then, we are left with two opposing meaning-theoretic suggestions for dealing with uses of failed descriptions (and empty natural names, etc.). According to Russell, one should treat all such expressions in a quantificational way, and thereby avoid the problems that affect Proper-Name accounts.

According to Strawson, the failures are mere 'local' affairs which can be accommodated by Proper-Name approaches, in the way just described, at no cost to the overall attempt to base semantic representations on straightforward Fregean ideas. On the Russellian account, the problem sentences make (false) statements: on the Strawsonian, they do not make any—or they do not make any with logical import or consequence. And one can find this conclusion intolerable, not because of the confusion alleged by Strawson (§ 27), but because, like Russell, one can find it self-evident that the 'local' uses which employ failed descriptions, etc. still make false statements. Strawson's positive suggestion, in effect, is that there is no need to insist on this. The way forward must therefore involve an investigation into the notion of *statement* and its equivalents, if these rival claims are to be assessed. This is the real issue raised by a contemplation of the Basic Problem.

31 THE SHAPE OF THE ISSUE

Where does all of this leave us? We saw that Russell's attack on Proper-Name treatments of the Candidates derives extra support from the interaction of the Epistemic and Propositional factors (§ 22). We went on to see that Russell's own handling of the Epistemic factor is confused and unsatisfactory (§§ 24–5). However, the fact remains that rejecting Russell's particular epistemology is one thing, and that dealing with the epistemological argument that underlies the Basic Problem is something else. For even if we suppose that we just *can*, sometimes, Name material objects, this still leaves quite untouched the idea that, at least in 'agnostic' cases, there is a danger that Proper-Name treatments of Candidates fail for all we know, and that if they do fail, we shall have given no semantic treatment of the propositions in which these Candidates appear. And in the absence of some better understanding of when agnosticism is 'appropriate', this means that we have as yet no idea how to decide whether any given Candidate is to be treated as a Proper Name. The above discussion of Strawson and the Propositional Factor just underlines this conclusion, since it has brought home that the 'risk' run by a Proper-Name account is that of having to 'write off', as instances of a most serious kind of linguistic malfunction, what are to all appearances perfectly legitimate and intelligible uses of language.

And at this point the shape of the issue before us starts to emerge. On the one hand, we have a pressure, deriving from the fundamental Fregean apparatus, to recognize *some* Proper Names, or at least to make sense of the idea of such expressions. On the other hand, there is an opposing pressure, described at length in the foregoing sections, which is set up by consideration of the Basic Problem and its epistemological underpinnings. Thus we have powerful theoretical reasons for, and powerful reasons against, the introduction or recognition of Proper Names, the whole lot pivoting on the facts that (a) we start off wanting to give an account of certain propositions of our language, and (b) that Proper Name accounts apparently sometimes do not work satisfactorily, and sometimes seem susceptible to the risk that they may not work satisfactorily, for all we know. What has emerged is that *if* we are to proceed further, we need to know more about these pivotal facts. Crucially, what exactly is entailed by the idea that one may need to 'write off' apparently perfectly legitimate uses of language?

These are the matters that we have to address: and the way we shall proceed is as follows. Concerning each type of Candidate, we shall ask how sure we are that propositions containing such expressions are guaranteed to have a semantic structure which we need to account for. And we shall ask how reasonable it is to import agnostic doubts with respect to the object which a Proper-Name treatment would invoke. Moreover, whilst we have seen reason to reject the letter of Russell's Official View, we shall see that its spirit is still very much alive. For the spirit of the View is that we should distinguish among Candidates, on account of the epistemological factors underlying the Basic Problem, between those Candidates which can, and those which cannot, be treated as Proper Names. And this idea lives on, in some form or another, in most theories of the Candidates. For what is often adopted is just such a *mixed strategy* of offering different sorts of treatment of different sorts of Candidates. Of course, there are many possibilities here, given the initial list of Candidates (natural names, descriptions, demonstratives . . . (§ 11)). Thus, one may select among whole natural categories, for instance, treating natural names and demonstratives as Proper Names, descriptions otherwise. Or one may subdivide the natural categories, for instance, treating some descriptions as Proper Names, others otherwise: and/or similarly for natural names. And these approaches can be blended in various ways to produce different overall theories (see chapters 6–8).

However, in adopting a mixed strategy one has to confront one of the hardest tasks in the area. This is the task of offering some principled reason—*a demarcation criterion*—to support the favoured partiality: that is, one has to defend the division of Candidates into those which are, and those which are not, treated as Proper Names. For Russell, we have seen that the chief factor involved here was epistemological: he held that one can only Name things with which one is acquainted (§ 24). There is, as I have already hinted, a strand of unexceptionable truth in this view: but it is also the case that various other matters—logical, metaphysical, as well as epistemological—are also involved here in various combinations, and some of the issues are extremely difficult and controversial. It stands very much to Russell's credit that he should have forced philosophers to think long and hard about these matters in the ways that will be described. Russell's extreme views about Naming are at least cousins of views of high philosophical value, many of which are current even if unacknowledged: and we shall understand mind and language all the better if we appreciate this.

Further Reading

Russell explains his Official View in 'The Philosophy of Logical Atomism', which appears in *Logic and Knowledge*, ed. R. Marsh (London, 1956). Also in this collection is 'The Nature of Acquaintance'. For more on this epistemological strand in the Official View see 'Knowledge by Acquaintance and Knowledge by Description', which is chap. 10 of Russell's *Mysticism and Logic* (New York, 1918), and see also chap. 5 of his *The Problems of Philosophy* (London, 1912).

For an excellent discussion of Russell on acquaintance see R. M. Sainsbury, 'Russell on Acquaintance', in *Philosophers Ancient and Modern*, ed. G. Vesey (Cambridge, 1986), and for a modern attempt to make something of Russell's idea that naming has to be backed up by knowledge of the named object see G. Evans, *The Varieties of Reference*, ed. J. McDowell (Oxford, 1982), esp. chaps. 4 and 5.

Strawson's criticisms of Russell are to be found in 'On Referring', *Mind*, 59 (1950); repr. in P. F. Strawson, *Logico-Linguistic Papers* (London, 1971) (page refs. are to this repr.). See also Strawson's *Introduction to Logical Theory* (London, 1952), pp. 184–90. A clear discussion of these criticisms is to be found in R. M. Sainsbury, *Russell* (London, 1979) pp. 113–22. For a discussion of presupposition, mentioned in § 29, see chap. 2 of M. Dummett, *Truth and Other Enigmas* (London, 1978). For more on the issue between Strawson and Russell see the Further Reading for chap. 7.

The classical source for the epistemological matters raised in §25 is R. Descartes, *Meditations*, in *The Philosophical Writings of Descartes*, vol. 2, tr. J. Cottingham, *et al.* (Cambridge, 1985). For helpful discussion see 'Epistemology Naturalized', in W. V. Quine, *Ontological Relativity and Other Essays* (New York, 1969), and A. J. Ayer, *The Problem of Knowledge* (Harmondsworth, 1956).

NOTES

1. Indeed, the status of the Russellian arguments about intensional contexts is rather more dubious than the remarks in the text imply. For, analogous to (LL) there is the law for first-level functors to the effect that *coextensive* first-level functors—those which are true of just the same objects—may be intersubstituted without change of truth-value: thus, from '$-Ga$' and '$\forall x(Gx \leftrightarrow Hx)$' one can certainly derive '$-Ha$'. Yet, now consider, even though both:

   (1) $\Diamond$ (the tallest rational animal is not a featherless biped)

   and

   (2) $\forall x(x$ is a rational animal $\leftrightarrow x$ is a featherless biped)

   are T, it is equally evident that:

   (3) (the tallest rational animal is not a rational animal)

   is F. Yet, the inference (1)–(3) would have a very similar form to the law for first-level functors given the sorts of assumptions made in §§ 19–20. Moreover, it is clear that a similar 'counterexample' using psychological verbs could also be constructed. By reasoning parallel to that explained in those sections, then, Russell would have to conclude that predicates cannot be treated as first-level functors!

2. It should also be noted that Russell treated quantificational descriptions as 'dummy' Proper Names, by introducing the notation '$(1x)(Gx)$': such a dummy Name could then serve as proxy for the official Russellian:

   $$\exists x(\forall y(Gy \leftrightarrow x = y) \& \ldots x)'$$

   for many purposes (since both combine with an appropriate first-level functor to yield a proposition) (see *Principia Mathematica*, pp. 66–71). However, such dummy Names were not considered by Russell to be logically Proper Names simply because he took the quantificational paraphrase to give their essential semantic contribution: so they were not object-invoking.

3. It should be stressed that Russell continually changed his views, including the ones presently under discussion: furthermore, it is arguable that these very views were actually in a state of flux during the

period 1905–18 when the influential position on the Candidates was being worked out (see SAINSBURY (1986)). I shall ignore such matters, however, since they do not appear to be relevant to the points to be made.

4. This is a very common syndrome, of which typical examples are:

S_1 propositions are about:	S_2 propositions are about:	anti-sceptical response:
other minds	behaviour	behaviourism
objects	sense data	phenomenalism
theoretical entities	measuring instruments	instrumentalism

see AYER.

5. The difference between (A)-type and (B)-type questions is clearly explained in QUINE (1969a), pp. 69–78.

6. Although Strawson is in OR chiefly concerned with descriptions, it is possible (as indeed Strawson briefly indicates) to generalize both the attacks and Strawson's corresponding defence of Proper-Name views so that they apply equally to the cases of all Candidates. But the matters here are straightforward, so I shall tend to restrict attention to descriptions, and leave the reader to imagine the appropriate extensions.

7. There is *perhaps* an echo of this view in Strawson. For he appears to introduce a new semantic relation, *presupposition*, which is distinct from classical entailment but which, like entailment, holds between statements: 'a statement [A] presupposes a statement [B] if the truth of [B] is a precondition of the truth-or-falsity of [A]' (*Introduction to Logical Theory*, p. 175).

   Now, if a statement A entails a statement B, B is 'a necessary condition of the truth, simply, of [A]' (ibid.). On the usual understanding of this, which Strawson seems to endorse, one can therefore infer B from A and, by contraposition, infer $-A$ from $-B$ (for instance, 'Everything moves with the times' entails 'Oxford moves with the times': so we have it that 'Not everything moves with the times' can be derived from 'Oxford does not move with the times'). Things appear otherwise with presupposition: if A presupposes B then, whilst one can still infer B from A (since if A is T then B has to be), the converse fails. If we have $-B$, then A is neither T nor F, so assuming—as Strawson seems to do—that $-A$ will only be T if A is F, truth would not be preserved under contraposition. However, as we shall see below, there is a different interpretation of Strawson's notion of presupposition according to which it is not really the same sort of relation as entailment (compare n. 8).

8. Notice that on this interpretation *presupposition* is not a relation between sentences or statements, but is merely a guiding assumption

which one is supposed to make in using the logic to translate stretches of reasoning. It is not a logical relation, like entailment, in any sense.

9. This approach also makes it possible to defend the arbitrary assignment of zero, say, to otherwise failed Proper Names. The point here is that if a logician is to prove nice general results concerning this or that type of logic, or wishes to give rigorous definitions of notions such as logical consequence, it has to be *guaranteed* in some way that every formula dealt with receives a semantic value. In practice, then, one needs to adopt a method for stipulating that otherwise untreated expressions are automatically *given* one. And although, as Russell rightly pointed out, this is a technical trick, that itself is harmless given that the intention of such logicians is not to model precisely the actual behaviour of particular stretches of natural language, but rather to produce an 'ideal' system to which natural language is then alleged to approximate (well enough for reasoning purposes). The points at which 'arbitrary' assignments need to be made are then precisely those points at which natural language allegedly lapses from its ideal.

4
Kripke: The New Orthodoxy

In chapter 1 we described the Fregean background in terms of which the Proper-Names issue is best understood. In chapter 2 we described the Russellian position on descriptions and natural names around which, as we noted, a substantial orthodoxy grew. Then in chapter 3 we exposed the roots of the Russellian arguments, and indicated the questions which have to be decided if these matters are to be seen aright. But before proceeding directly to that business there is one more thing we have to do. Since around 1970 a new anti-Russellian (and, it is often alleged, anti-Fregean) orthodoxy concerning the treatment of names and other Candidates has arisen. By far the most influential factor here is Kripke's work on natural names and modal operators in *Naming and Necessity* (*NN*): and it would be pointless to try to move forward without first assimilating the elements of this new orthodoxy as there set out.

NN is a remarkable book, rich in philosophical content piled layer on layer. On the surface there is an attack on Russell's theory of natural names which deploys two arguments, one based on modality, the other on the nature of naming. Beneath these are metaphysical themes concerning the nature of necessity, the a priori, essentialism, scientific realism, the mind-body problem, and the existence of unicorns. Our concern in this chapter is with the first, modal argument against Russell: the second one will be considered in chapter 8. The other themes of *NN* will be largely ignored, except in so far as they bear directly on the issue of naming. This does not mean, however, that these other themes are of no importance: on the contrary, many of the issues raised by Kripke are of major and lasting philosophical significance.

The core of Russell's theory of natural names, recall, is the injunction

(NQ) Treat natural names quantificationally.

This he hoped to obtain from

(ND) Treat natural names as descriptions,

and

(DQ) Treat descriptions quantificationally

(see §18). Principally, Kripke attacks the crucial injunction (ND). He claims to offer semantic and other reasons for denying that natural names abbreviate descriptions. Kripke tells us that he came to these conclusions in the course of inventing his influential semantics for modal words like 'necessarily' and 'possibly'. And it is certainly true that *within this system* no equivalence between natural names and descriptions of the type required by Russell's theory is forthcoming. But whether or not *this* is an objection to Russell depends, for instance, on whether Kripke's overall treatment is better than some other which incorporates Russell's theory of natural names. This is the question we have to settle. In the present chapter, we shall see that, read in a certain innocent way, the modal argument is not at all decisive. However, it is interpreted by Kripke in the context of his modal semantics: and this gives rise to some further anti-Russellian reflections on the semantic characteristics of our target expressions. Kripke's semantic framework is accordingly described, and its implied views about natural names discussed. We shall ultimately find that no very convincing case against Russell (much less Frege) is forthcoming from these modal considerations, despite the appearance given by the modern orthodoxy that Kripke has engendered. But one crucial question concerning our 'access' to the objects we speak and think about is left dangling, and this is taken up again and developed in chapter 6. The issue of natural names then returns in chapter 8, where Kripke's other main line of argument against Russell is considered.

33 SCOPE

Students of elementary arithmetic soon learn that, say,

$$2 \times 3 - 7 = ?$$

is not an easy job to tackle. Do you multiply two by three, then subtract seven from the result, thus offering minus one as solution: or do you subtract seven from three, then multiply the result by two and offer minus eight? Well, this depends on what whoever set the problem expects, and without further guidance these expectations are not given. So it is important to have some method to distinguish the two tasks. One way is to use brackets, and thus to identify the above tasks as

$$(2 \times 3) - 7 \qquad \text{and} \qquad 2 \times (3 - 7)$$

respectively. Or, to avoid excessive uses of brackets, we could have a convention according to which the original problem is to subtract seven from three and then multiply, the other task being ruled out unless indicated explicitly by the use of brackets. Either will do, as long as things are clear.

Elementary logic students soon meet a closely parallel problem (the same problem, given Frege's views, as explained in chapter 1). Is

$$P \rightarrow Q \,\&\, R$$

a conditional whose consequent is a conjunction: or is it a conjunction, one of whose conjuncts is a conditional? Again, without some convention and/or extra symbolism, the matter remains undecided: thus we normally distinguish between

$$P \rightarrow (Q \,\&\, R) \qquad \text{and} \qquad (P \rightarrow Q) \,\&\, R.$$

There are more complicated logical examples: and these are what will concern us in what follows. For example, there is obviously an important logical difference between

not everything smokes

and

everything does not smoke.

The first merely denies the claim that everything smokes (one non-smoker would suffice to bear it out) whereas the second makes the riskier claim that *everything* is a non-smoker. This difference between our propositions turns, as in the simpler cases considered above, on the fact that the same vocabulary is combined in different ways: and these different manners of composition are reflected in the semantic accounts that a Fregean logic would give of the symbolization of the propositions. Our two propositions go into symbols as

$$-\forall x(Gx) \qquad \text{and} \qquad \forall x(- Gx)$$

respectively, and the crucial point then is that whereas '$\forall x - Gx$' is ready as it stands to be assessed by means of (Def$\forall$), and will be assigned T if and only if each object of our domain yields T when presented to the function $-G \ldots$, '$-\forall xGx$' is a negated proposition, and so we must go first to the truth table for '—'. This will tell us that the original proposition is T if and only if '$\forall xGx$' is F. So *now* we can turn to (Def$\forall$) to see whether '$\forall xGx$' is T or F. Whichever value we obtain, we assign the reverse value to '$-\forall xGx$'. The key difference between our two original propositions thus turns on the order in which the quantifier and the negation sign are *dealt with* (compare §5), and we express this by speaking of the *relative scope* of one operator with respect to another. In '$\forall x - Gx$' the quantifier, which must be treated first, has *wide scope* relative to the negation sign. In the other proposition, the reverse obtains. And at the bottom of this happy modern treatment we find Frege's idea of recognizing different 'patterns' in propositions (§2), since to say that an expression E has wide scope relative to expression E' is to say that the semantic appraisal of the whole must recognize a pattern corresponding to E before it gets to that corresponding to E' (see, for example, the discussion of multiple generality in §5).

Natural language abounds with declarative sentences which seem to need some such apparatus to guard against a related sort of ambiguity which we may call 'structural' ambiguity: that is, an ambiguity which arises out of the way in which the units of the sentence can be put together.[1] One possible example is the logician's favourite 'Everyone loves someone'. Is this saying that everyone loves *someone or other*, or is it saying that there is some *one* person whom everyone loves? (Compare 'Everyone loves someone—even if only their mother', with 'Everyone loves someone—namely Bob Hope'.) One of the strengths of modern logic is that it provides routinely for the removal of such possible ambiguities. In this case we get '$\forall x(\exists y(Rxy))$' and '$\exists x(\forall y(Ryx))$' respectively, so that each 'reading' of our one English sentence (i.e. each proposition it may be considered to be) gets its own unambiguous expression in the calculus, one of which must first be referred to (Def$\forall$), whilst the other must go first to (Def$\exists$). The notion of structurally ambiguous sentences will be considered again in §35.

Kripke's modal argument against Russell's (ND) involves the uncontentious sort of logical fact about scope that we have been describing. For just as scope considerations come up when quantifiers are mixed with negation, or with each other, so they seem to come up when *modal* words such as 'necessarily' and 'possibly' are used. For example, we can distinguish between the claims

(1) necessarily, everything is part of the Universe,

and

(2) everything is necessarily part of the Universe.

(1) is straightforward and seems true, saying only that the following is necessary: everything is part of the Universe. Since it is *impossible* to find an object that yields F for the function ... *is part of the Universe* (merely to find an object shows that it is such a part), the proposition 'everything is part of the Universe' *has* to be T: so it is necessary. Now (2) is of a type which we did not consider in our original discussion of modality, since it involves the use of a modal operator embedded within the scope of a quantifier: and one of Kripke's finest achievements has been to suggest how such puzzling propositions should be interpreted. His views here will be explained in §§ 36–7, but even without that explanation it is relatively easy to see that (2), unlike (1), is F. For it claims, in effect, that each thing is such that *it* is necessarily part of the Universe, and this seems F since lots of things exist only contingently. For example, the Moon is not a necessary part of the Universe, since the Moon might not have existed.

As with the previous cases, these points give no trouble in a formal setting, the two readings coming out as:

$$\Box(\forall x(Px)) \quad \text{and} \quad \forall x(\Box Px)$$

respectively (writing '$\Box$' for 'necessarily', as in § 19). But on the basis of matters like these, it is possible to launch a serious attack against Russell's theory of names. Let us see how.

34 SCOPE: NAMES AND DESCRIPTIONS

In OD Russell noted that scope phenomena would come up on his proposed treatment of descriptions (see OD, pp. 51 ff.). Recall that his usual rendition of 'The G is H' would be

(1) $\exists x(\forall y(Gy \leftrightarrow x = y) \ \& \ Hx)$.

This leaves room for scope considerations when we consider *negating* 'The G is H', since (1) can either be negated as a whole, to give

(2) $-\exists x(\forall y(Gy \leftrightarrow x = y) \ \& \ Hx)$,

or the negation can occur within the scope of the two quantifiers, as in

(3) $\exists x(\forall y(Gy \leftrightarrow x = y)\ \&\ -Hx).$[2]

Intuitively speaking, (2) denies 'The G is H' simply by denying that there is a unique object x which …, whereas (3) denies our proposition by allowing that there is such an object but denying that it is H.

Now, in a somewhat parallel fashion, descriptions also give rise to scope phenomena when mixed with '$\Box$' and '$\Diamond$'. Thus, suppose we have a proposition 'The G is H' and want to 'modalize' it by adding '$\Diamond$'. For example, the relevant original proposition might be

(4) The Queen of Australia is not a Queen of Australia.

Certainly on a quantificational approach we have a choice, corresponding to the two possible formalizations:

(5) $\Diamond\ (\exists x(\forall y(QoAy \leftrightarrow x = y)\ \&\ -QoAx))$

and

(6) $\exists x(\forall y(QoAy \leftrightarrow x = y)\ \&\ \Diamond -QoAx)).$

The initial proposition, (4), is itself F: not only that, it seems clear that it could not have been other than F. For how could this be true: a Queen is not a Queen? Thus (4) is not possibly true, and so (5) comes out F (compare § 19). What of (6)? This involves the use of a modal operator embedded within the scope of a quantifier, and is therefore less straightforward. Nevertheless, it is relatively easy to see that (6), unlike (5), is T. For what it says, in effect, is that the Queen of Australia—namely Queen Elizabeth II of England—*might not have been* Queen of Australia: that is, it says that she is only *contingently*, rather than *necessarily*, the Queen of Australia. And this seems clearly to be T: we can certainly quite easily imagine how Australia might have become a republic in 1945, and thus have severed all formal links with the English monarchy. And had this happened, of course, Queen Elizabeth II of England would *not* have been Queen of Australia.

The fact that scope phenomena occur when descriptions are mixed with negation and with modal operators is entirely predictable given a Russellian proposal to treat descriptions quantificationally, since we saw in the previous section that there is independent reason to suppose that scope phenomena arise when *quantifiers* are mixed with negation and modal operators. So the fact that scope choices arise when, for example, propositions like (4) are modalized may be taken to help confirm that Russell's treatment of descriptions answers to our usual understanding of them. But, now recall Russell's theory of natural names (§18). According to this treatment, natural names are quantificational, since they are to abbreviate descriptions which themselves are treated quantificationally. Given this, one would therefore expect that just as (4) admits of more than one modalization by the addition of '$\diamond$' to its symbolization, so too does

(7) Socrates did not drink the hemlock.

For, according to Russell (§18), (7) is to be recast as

(8) The philosopher who drank the hemlock did not drink the hemlock,

and (8), like (4), can be modalized with '$\diamond$' in different ways, yielding either

(9) $\diamond (\exists x(\forall y((Py \& DHy) \leftrightarrow x = y) \& -DHx))$

or

(10) $(\exists x(\forall y((Py \& DHy) \leftrightarrow x = y) \& \diamond -DHx))$.

And once again, as in the case of (5) and (6), we appear to have divergent truth-values. Since (8) seems necessarily false, (9) would have to come out F: whereas nothing seems easier than to imagine that the philosopher who drank the hemlock—namely, Socrates—might not have drunk the hemlock, for example, had his nerve failed him at the last moment; so that (10), it seems, should come out T.

So, in a nutshell, if Russell is right about natural names, there surely ought to be scope choices to make when the business of modalizing (7) with '$\diamond$' is contemplated. But an important part of Kripke's case is the claim that this is not so: unlike natural language propositions like (8), says Kripke, those like (7) *do not* give rise to these scope choices: so Russell's theory of natural names is incorrect. The argument here might be something like this: there are two ways of modalizing (8), but only one way of modalizing (7), so (7) and (8) are not synonymous. But they only differ in the fact that 'Socrates' appears in (7), whereas 'the philosopher who drank the hemlock' appears in (8): so *these* expressions are not synonymous. Clearly, if the same kind of argument could be run for the *general* case—i.e. for *any* name/description pair, then this would seem to be a powerful argument against Russell.

35 SCOPE CONVENTIONS

Now it may well seem far from obvious that English is the way that Kripke claims it to be. And, in my experience, most untutored speakers (for example, undergraduates new to the question) have *no* sharp views about the possibility of divergent modalizations of (7). This goes even when they know their basic Fregean logic, and is largely caused by the deep obscurity of modal notions. Moreover, it is a fact that the above argument about modalizations is reinforced, in Kripke's hands, by his own particular account of how names and descriptions are to be treated in a modal logic, which we shall discuss in §§ 38–9. Furthermore, there is something of a complexity in the notion of 'modalization' which will not really emerge fully until chapter 8, when Kripke's other main line of argument against Russell is considered. Nevertheless, Kripke does here seem to put his finger on to *some* kind of difference between names and descriptions: for there are other, similar examples. For instance, although it was true in 1949 that

    (1)   George VI is the English monarch,

and was also true then that

    (2)   Princess Elizabeth will become the English monarch,

it certainly was not true then that

    (3)   Princess Elizabeth will become George VI.

In other words, although (1) looks like an identity proposition, the name and description involved cannot be intersubstituted every-where without change of truth-value—witness (2) and (3)—and so therefore, it seems, cannot have the same meaning (compare § 19). What is more, of course, this example seems to show that if 'George VI' does have the same meaning as some description, this will have to be a description which could never yield a truth when substituted for the description in (2): for otherwise, the failure of the inference to (3) would show that this description did not, after all, mean the same as 'George VI'. But what sort of description could this be? Moreover, consider the difference between

    (4)   The English monarch used to be a man,

and

(5) Queen Elizabeth used to be a man.

(5) is not at all ambiguous, but straightforwardly states a falsehood. But (4) does seem to be (structurally) ambiguous, in that although it *can* be understood to say the same as (5), there is also an obvious sense in which (4) is T—it is made so by the fact that England has had kings—in which case (4), understood in this second way, does not say the same thing as (5), *despite the fact that*

(6) Queen Elizabeth is the English monarch.

In this last example we can think of 'temporalizing' as an analogue of 'modalizing', in that (4), say, could be symbolized as the result of applying the temporal operator 'It used to be the case that' to 'The English monarch is a man': and the main point then is that there is a scope option here. (Perhaps, similarly, (2) and (3) could be seen as the result of applying 'It will be the case that' to identity propositions.) Such examples, like the modal ones adduced by Kripke, seem to show that names and descriptions, even when they apply to the same objects, behave overall rather differently when they are mixed with certain kinds of operators on propositions, so that, in this sense, a name cannot be synonymous with a description. Indeed, given examples like our temporal ones, we might suppose that Kripke's whole point is that whereas:

(7) Socrates might have failed to drink the hemlock

is just unambiguously T,

(8) The philosopher who drank the hemlock might have failed to drink the hemlock

is (structurally) ambiguous, despite the fact that

(9) Socrates is the philosopher who drank the hemlock:

for (8) is T if the description is given wider scope than the 'might have', and F if the 'might have' is given the wider scope.

However, if this were *all* that Kripke meant, he would not be posing a real threat to Russell's (ND). For, as we shall now see, one can certainly introduce a new expression as an abbreviation for an existing one, but subject to the proviso that certain scope ambiguities which would arise for sentences containing the original are to be resolved in a determinate way where this new expression is concerned.

For example, we saw in § 33 that

$$2 \times 3 - 7 = ?$$

does not, by itself, represent an unambiguous task, so that some further device has to be used: for instance, we suggested either the use of brackets, or the adoption of a convention to the effect that, failing other indication, subtraction is to precede multiplication. But here is another way: we in general use brackets, so that no convention exists to tell us how to 'read' the specification above. But we then also introduce a symbol '★', which means the same as '×', *except that* '★', unlike '×', *is to be given maximum scope* in the likes of

$$2 \star 3 - 7 = ?$$

This is perfectly intelligible, even if rather strange. Given such a stipulation, it clearly follows that, say:

$$6 \times 8 = ?$$

and

$$6 \star 8 = ?$$

are the same tasks with the same solution. Nevertheless, whereas, given what we have just said:

$$2 \times 3 - 7 = ?$$

does not unambiguously specify one single task,

$$2 \star 3 - 7 = ?$$

certainly does: it specifies the task that we could also specify, if we were to use brackets, as

$$2 \times (3 - 7) = ?$$

In other words, we can say that '★' *is* an abbreviation for '×', but such that it is always to be given maximum scope.

But this sort of manœuvre immediately suggests a way in which Russell could hang on to (ND) *even given* the claim that names and descriptions behave differently in modal and other contexts (another will be mentioned in § 39). For, clearly, one could say that natural names, *unlike descriptions*, are always to be used 'on the understanding' or 'according to the convention' that they have maximum scope relative to operators like those we have been considering. If such a convention were in force then that would immediately explain the fact, mentioned above, that whereas (5) and (7) are (structurally) unambiguous, this is not the case for their respective partners (4) and (8). (5) and (7) would be unambiguous for exactly the same reason as is:

$$2 \star 3 - 7 = ?$$

namely, because of a scope convention. And (4) and (8) would be ambiguous for exactly the same reason as is

$$2 \times 3 - 7 = ?$$

namely, because of unresolved scope possibilities. But all of this would be compatible with the fact that each natural name is an abbreviation of some description, just as everything in the arithmetical case is compatible with the fact—which we laid down explicitly, after all—that '$\star$' abbreviates '$\times$'.

One might, of course, wonder whether any such scope convention is built into the use of names: and it is true that arguments for this conclusion do not readily spring to mind (but see § 78). It will certainly not do merely to point at the different scope behaviour of names and descriptions, since, as we shall see, Kripke offers an alternative diagnosis of these facts which is intended to rule out the suggestion just made. But, of course, by the same token, neither will it do for *Kripke* merely to point to the scope phenomena in order to argue for his favoured conclusion, for precisely the same reason: there is an alternative. Obviously we shall have to tread carefully on this issue. But however this may be, it is clear that, given the foregoing, there is not much in the scope considerations *as presently conceived* to trouble a Russellian. So let us turn without more ado to an account of Kripke's modal system, within which Kripke interprets the scope phenomena in a manner which is widely thought to give extra support to his anti-Russellian claims about natural names. First I explain the system, then the interpretation, then the anti-Russellian argument based on them.

36 KRIPKE'S POSSIBLE WORLDS

Kripke's views are formulated in the context of his 'possible-world' semantics for modality, the elements of which are as follows. Propositions like the ones we have been considering in this book are said to be either T or F, and the value assigned to a proposition depends upon how extralinguistic reality happens to be. Here we imagine the history of the Universe running its course and ourselves as trying to say what different aspects of this process are like: if we succeed we speak truly, if we fail we speak falsely (or perhaps sometimes say nothing true or false: see §29). Call the actual total run of events, past, present, and future, the *actual world* (@). The basic idea of Kripke's modal semantics is to think of @ as an entity, one *possible world*, and then to generalize.

The exact interpretation of this notion is a contentious matter, and there are various alternatives. Furthermore, even displaying enough of Kripke's system to make his anti-Russellian argument explicit involves a lengthy explanation: and even then I shall be ignoring certain tricky but fortunately irrelevant technicalities. But the fundamental idea, to which we ourselves have already appealed informally, is that of imagining or specifying, in enough detail for whatever purposes are to hand, an alternative course of history which *might have come about*. Thus, although, say, Socrates drank the hemlock, we can evidently make sense of the thought that this was only contingent; he didn't have to drink hemlock; he might not have. That is, we can imagine a possible situation or circumstance in which he did not. Whereas things are otherwise with 'no square is round'. Not only is this T, but we cannot imagine or conceive it as being any other way; we cannot imagine, that is, any possible situation or circumstance in which there is a round square. Possible world semantics involves taking this idea of possible circumstances or situations seriously, and trying to make the idea firm and rigorous enough to provide semantics for *modal logics*: that is logics enriched with operators like our '$\square$' and '$\diamondsuit$'.

Consider first the actual world, @. It exists all around us, and in that sense we know it quite intimately. But in another way it is partly unknown to us—we do not know everything about it. Thus, we can imagine ourselves, when trying to get the truth on this or that matter, as attempting always to come up with a better or more accurate specification of @, where the best specification of @ would be the sum total of truths about it. Now, consider the following sets of propositions which we might formulate about @: (i) simple predications[3] like:

Mick Jagger is a man;

(ii) complex propositions formed from members of (i) with the help of truth-functions, like

Mick Jagger is a man and London is a city

and (iii) quantifications on propositions in (i) and (ii) like

Something is a man

or

Something is such that Mick Jagger is a man and it is a city.

Each set consists of propositions about @, the actual world. Fregean logic, in effect, shows how the truth-values of the propositions of (ii) and (iii) are determined by the values assigned to the propositions of (i), so that once these latter values are given, the complex facts about @ which are stated by the truths in (ii) and (iii) are settled. For, clearly, if we have the truth-values of all our simple predications, then we can determine, by the use of truth-tables, a listing of the truths in (ii)—namely all those true propositions formed by the application of truth-functors to members of (i). Similarly, we can use (Def∀), etc. to determine the truths among our quantified propositions, and thereby start to compile the list of truths in (iii). Furthermore, we can then just keep on reapplying the rules in order to expand (ii) and (iii), determining the values of, for example, truth-functions of quantified propositions, quantifications on these more complex propositions, and so on. With respect to (ii) and (iii), as well as with respect to these expansions of them, we can say that (i) is *basic*: once these propositions (and their values) are given, the values of all the rest follow by the Fregean definitions, and hence the relevant complex truths are determined. Indeed, given the further idea that a member of (i) is F unless it appears among the truths of (i), we can rest content with the truths of (i) only. For, clearly, given the latest assumption, (i)'s truths will determine (i)'s falsehoods, and then the two lots, as before, will determine the values of the members of (ii) and (iii), expanded or otherwise.

We can thus, in this sense, at least say that the truths of (i) *partially determine* @: once these fundamental truths are given, the complex truths about @ in the sets (ii) and (iii), which need not be *all* the complex truths about @ (hence the 'partial'—see below), are themselves fixed, and cannot, as things are, turn out any other way. Thus we can, in this sense, ignore (ii) and (iii) for many purposes. Now, consider the Fregean conception of our most fundamental propositions, the truths in (i). These will comprise all our true simple predications:

Mick Jagger is a man

Raquel Welch is a woman

Red Rum is a horse

—and each of these is T, according to Frege, in virtue of the fact that the relevant objects Mick Jagger, etc. yield T when presented to the functions referred to by the basic functors '. . . is a man', etc. In other words, (i)'s truths are themselves determined by a domain of objects (i.e. those objects whose names appear in the propositions of (i)), and by the fact that each primitive functor stands for a function which 'divides' this domain into objects it yields T for, and objects it yields F for. So —given that (i)'s truths determine all of the values of the members of (i), which in turn determine the truths of (ii) and (iii), and thus at least partially determine @—we could say, finally, that the two stipulations,

(a) of a domain of objects,

and

(b) of a list, for each primitive functor, of which (if any) of those members of the domain yield *T* at the function to which it refers,

themselves at least partially determine @.

Call these stipulations the (*partial*) *blueprint of* @. Kripke's generalization then is simple: one can just imagine *changing* or *permuting* this blueprint, say, by adding or deleting objects and/or altering the list under one or more functors. Each of these altered specifications (new (partial) blueprints) will generate a class of truth-valued propositions analogous to those in the original (i) and will thus, thereby, generate new classes corresponding to (ii) and (iii). In exactly this way, a (partial) blueprint might be said to determine at least some of the (simple and complex) 'facts' about an *alternative possible world*. Just as @ is at least partially determined by its blueprint, so we can go on to say that at least some of the new blueprints (the 'permitted' ones) will at least partially determine *alternative possible worlds*: that is alternative complete courses of history.

Now for some qualifications. In the first place, since we do not imagine ourselves to have names of every object, nor knowledge of every simple property that an object can have, we do not suppose that our class (i) contains all the basic truths there are about @.

Hence even the totality of truths in classes (i)–(iii) does not exhaust the facts about @: hence our blueprint only *partially* determines @. For this reason, any permutation of @'s blueprint—say an alteration of the lists under some of the primitive functors—will only itself, normally, partially determine an alternative possible world. And normally when we imagine possible situations we do just give enough details for the purposes at hand—'suppose that Thatcher had resigned over the Westland affair'—and imagine that certain other, vaguely acknowledged, matters remain the way they are in @. Thus, we would suppose that most of the other characters and institutions involved in the Westland affair behaved, in the imagined circumstances, in much the same way as they did in @. Other matters we simply do not care about: we do not care what Thatcher had for breakfast on the morning of her imagined resignation, nor where she took herself off to afterwards, nor whether a crocodile drowned in a swamp near the Nile. Thus, in general, we should certainly distinguish between the abstract or formal idea of a possible world, as a complete domain of individuals all of whose simple properties are given, and our own partial and incomplete specifications of these worlds. But this need not worry us here, since even @ in this sense transcends our ability to specify it. From now on I shall omit the explicit qualification 'partial', and say for brevity that a (permissible) blueprint simply determines its possible world.

There are also some complications about permuting @'s blueprint in order to provide a blueprint of another possible world. For example, is it in order to *add* new objects, which do not exist (in @) but which might have existed? This question is obviously closely related to the question, briefly mentioned in § 16, whether there are, in some sense, objects which do not (actually) exist. But we shall not pursue that matter any further, and shall restrict ourselves to permutations which, at most, *delete* objects which exist in @. In other words, we shall assume both (a) that only existent objects occur in @'s domain, and (b) that no new objects can be stipulated to occur in another possible world's domain. There is a further matter. I mentioned above that only 'permitted' blueprints would specify a possible world. What does this mean? Well first, a permitted blueprint has to be *consistent* (otherwise it will define an *impossible* world). So, for instance, we should rule out a blueprint that is obtained from @'s simply by adding the stipulation that W. V. Quine should be assigned to the functor '... is more than six feet tall'. Although there is nothing impossible about the bare idea that Quine should have been more than six feet tall, Quine is actually rather shorter than this, so would already be entered under '. . . is less than six feet tall'. But it is impossible to be both more and less than six feet tall, so the envisaged blueprint would not define a *possible* world, and would not be permitted. (Of course, things would be otherwise if Quine were at the same time taken away from '. . . is less than six feet tall', but that would yield a different blueprint from the one initially envisaged.)

Second—though this is more contentious—one may want to restrict the number of permitted blueprints because of *essentialist scruples*. Some people think that objects have properties which are essential to their very being, in the somewhat abstract sense that it is absolutely impossible—no matter what other physical, etc. changes are made—for the objects to exist or to have existed without these properties. For example, Quine is both a human being and a philosopher. But while it seems clear that he could have existed without being a philosopher (for instance, if he had continued as a journalist at the *Grove Gazette*), it is less clear, to say the least, that he could have existed without being a human being. So perhaps he is *essentially human*: could Quine have been a teapot, or a poached egg, or a prime number, or a god? Presumably not: although the last case is at least debatable, and questions about essence are difficult and contested. But we do not need to pursue this matter, except to remark that *one* way of accommodating essentialist views is in terms of permitted blueprints. Where x is an object said to be essentially G, one would just not permit any blueprint which included x in the domain of objects but did not list x as giving T at the function referred to by 'G . . .' (see FORBES chaps. 5–7).

So, a permitted blueprint determines a possible world. That is, if you stipulate a domain of objects and distribute them among a set of primitive functors consistently and in accordance with such essentialist scruples as may be justified, you make available a description of a possible course of history, populated by the objects of the blueprint's domain, and characterized by the occurrences, etc. reported by the propositions generated by the listings under the functors. One of these, we have seen, is the actual course of history @. The others are courses of history which did not come about *but which might have*, at least in the sense that their descriptions are intelligible and consistent (relative to the aforementioned parameters). Note that a possible world, on this conception, is something whose properties are just stipulated: all that is needed is a 'given' domain of objects and a permitted assignment of these to the primitive functors. There is no question here of 'discovering' what a possible world is like, for instance by using a special sort of telescope. Once the blueprint is specified, any further 'discoveries' can be made by logical means alone.[4]

This idea—that possible worlds are things whose fundamental properties are just stipulated in the above fashion—will be discussed further in § 40. But the next task is to show how Kripke used his possible world apparatus to give his justly celebrated semantic interpretations of the modal words 'necessarily' and 'possibly'.

37 KRIPKE'S MODAL SEMANTICS

As was remarked in § 19, the words in question are treated as two operators ('$\Box$' and '$\Diamond$' respectively) which, like negation, take propositions to make propositions and can appear inside the scope of quantifiers and truth-functions applied to these propositions: thus we can go from, say:

$$Ga \quad \text{to} \quad \Diamond Ga, \quad \text{or} \quad \Box Ga,$$

and thence to, say:

$$\exists x(\Diamond Gx) \quad \forall x(\Box Gx), \quad \exists x(\Box Gx \,\&\, P), \text{etc.}$$

The task then is to show what determines the truth-values of the propositions containing the new operators: and this is where possible worlds come in.

There are two basic cases to consider for each operator: those where it works on a proposition (as in '$\Diamond Ga$'), and those where it appears in the corresponding functor of a quantifier (as in '$\forall x \Box Gx$'). The first cases are covered by:

(Def$\Diamond$) '$\Diamond P$' is T (at @) if and only if 'P' is T at at least one possible world;

and

(Def$\Box$) '$\Box P$' is T (at @) if and only if 'P' is T at all possible worlds.[5]

Thus consider the proposition

(1) Hitler invaded Scotland in 1940.

Happily this is actually F (i.e. is determined to be F by @'s blueprint). But it seems clear that one could start off with @'s blueprint and permissibly modify it in various relevant ways so as to end up with a blueprint of a world (W^*) which determines that (1) comes out T. Thus we say that although (1) is F at @, it is T *at W^**. This means that (1) is T at at least one possible world, so (by (Def◇)) it follows that

(2) ◇ (Hitler invaded Scotland in 1940)

is also actually T. Notice too that (1) is *not* T at *all* possible worlds (@, for instance, is a world at which it is F). So (by (Def□)) the proposition:

(3) □ (Hitler invaded Scotland in 1940)

is actually F.

Now the operators '□' and '◇' are intended to express some interesting concepts of necessity and possibility. And, although these are slippery notions, Kripke's definitions certainly seem to be on to something. Intuitively, it surely *might have been the case* that Hitler invaded Scotland in 1940; it is only contingent that he did not; his invasion was not, as it were, an absolute impossibility. So, in this sense, (1) expresses a possibility, and (2) should be actually T, just as Kripke's (Def◇) says it is. Furthermore, the basic notion used—that of a notionally possible alternative course of history, involving many of these same agents as actual history involved, but in different configurations—has evident intuitive appeal: how else are we to conceive of might-have-beens? Similarly, it is not true that Hitler *had to* invade Scotland in 1940; it was not, as it were, absolutely necessary for him to do this. So, in this sense, (1) does *not* express a necessity, and (3) should then be actually F—just as Kripke's (Def□) says it is. Once again, note the appeal: how else are we to conceive of what is necessary, or what *has to be*, except in terms of what *every* coherent course of history would contain?[6]

Having settled in the above ways how values are to be assigned to propositions beginning with our operators, occurrences of such propositions in larger truth-functions present no problem: that is the business of the truth-tables. This leaves us to account for cases where the operators occur inside the scope of quantifiers. This is equally straightforward. Here the operator forms part of a quantifier's corresponding functor, as in, for instance '$\forall x(\square Gx)$'. So given (Def∀), we can therefore say that our quantified sentence will be (actually) T if and only if each object of @'s domain yields T (at @) when presented to the function $\square G \ldots$. So, if we can say what it is for an object of @'s domain to give T at @ when presented to such a function, we shall have explained the semantics of the quantified proposition. We simply say:

(Def□*) an object x of @'s domain yields T (at @) for any function $□ \, \underline{G \ldots}$ if and only if x yields T for $\underline{G \ldots}$ at all possible worlds,

and

(Def◇*) an object x of @'s domain yields T (at @) for any function $◇ \, \underline{G \ldots}$ if and only if x yields T for $\underline{G \ldots}$ at at least one possible world.

Thus, what we say with, for example (Def◇ *) is that an actual object *might have been a police officer*, say, if and only if that object is a police officer at some possible world: that is, if and only if some permitted blueprint determines a simple predication wherein 'police officer' is truly predicated of that object. Again, the attractiveness of this is evident.

The literature on possible worlds is enormous and growing, and runs the whole gamut in respect of technical sophistication and metaphysical pretension. Moreover, Kripke's conception of possible worlds is not the only one in the market: others, for instance, seem committed to something more like the idea that worlds are to be discovered rather than stipulated ('telescope' approaches: see, especially, LEWIS (1986)). What is more, the sketch before us is neither exhaustive nor in any way rigorous or beautiful. However, it will suffice for the present purpose. This is to show how Kripke's positive views about natural names, and the corresponding criticisms of Russell, grow out of his possible world framework.

38 DESIGNATORS

In his applications of his apparatus to modal propositions of natural languages, Kripke calls natural names and descriptions *designators*. He attempts no elaborate definition, but his usage suggests that a designator is an expression whose semantic interpretation is effected by the assignment to it of an object. As such, designators are obviously rather like Proper Names, so that Kripke's *overall* proposal is to this extent similar to Frege's (recall that Frege considered natural names and descriptions to be Proper Names).[7] However, Kripke distinguishes among designators with the help of his possible-world semantics (here he departs from Frege, who barely mentioned modality). Designators, says Kripke, can be either *rigid* or *non-rigid*:

> a *rigid designator* stands for the same object at every possible world (at which it stands for anything at all),

whereas,

> a *non-rigid designator* stands for different objects at different possible worlds (compare *NN*, pp. 47 ff.).

If we assume that at least some descriptions are designators, then these provide clear examples of the non-rigid variety. For instance, 'the first boxer to knock down Muhammad Ali in a professional fight' designates the Englishman Henry Cooper at @—that is, Cooper was the first man in actual history to achieve the relevant distinction. However, we can well imagine a permitted reshuffle of @'s blueprint which has Cooper failing to connect with that famous left hook, but which leaves the course of all other fights involving Ali as they are in @, so giving a possible world *W'* at which the relevant distinction goes to Joe Frazier. Since Cooper and Frazier are different men, 'the first boxer to knock down Muhammad Ali in a professional fight' thereby stands for different men at different possible worlds, so by Kripke's definition this description is a non-rigid designator. Putting the main point another way, we can say that the semantic value of a non-rigid designator (and hence the above sort of description, according to Kripke) has to be *relativized* to possible worlds. We have already come across parallel examples of relativization of semantic value to possible world. For example, the proposition 'Quine is a philosopher' *happens* to be true—is T at @— but, because we can surely stipulate a possible world *W** at which Quine never even learned to read and write, but instead went into British politics, we say that the proposition is F at *W**. And something analogous has to be said about the functor '... is a philosopher': although it applies to Quine *at* @, it fails to apply to him *at* W*.

The identification of rigid designators is a rather more contentious matter, although the definition is as clear as that for non-rigid designators. However, Kripke's claim is that natural names (or most of them) are rigid: and the idea here is that there is no sense to be made of the proposal to alter @'s blueprint in such a way that, say, 'Henry Cooper' comes to stand for someone other than Henry

Cooper at any other possible world; although, of course, we can stipulate possible worlds *in* which someone else—say Lenny Bruce—is *called* 'Henry Cooper'. Now we shall have to look into such arguments as Kripke offers for this claim about natural names, but, assuming it is correct, there is an important contrast made out between this natural name and the description 'the first boxer, etc.'. At @ , both stand for the same man, Henry Cooper. But, at other possible worlds, they diverge. At some worlds (e.g. W') the description stands for someone other than Cooper: but this is not the case where the name is concerned, assuming it is a rigid designator. By the definition of this notion, if it stands for Cooper at @ then it stands for Cooper, if anyone, at every possible world, including W'. In other words, the semantic value of a rigid designator (and hence a natural name, according to Kripke) is *not* relativized to possible worlds.

This alleged difference between natural names and descriptions over the matter of relativization of semantic value to possible world is adduced by Kripke as an explanation of the scope phenomena mentioned in §§ 34–5. The point here, recall, was that while typical English declarative sentences of the form

(1) The G is necessarily H

can be 'read' in two ways, depending on whether the description is given wide or narrow scope relative to 'necessarily', things appear otherwise with declarative sentences like

(2) N is necessarily H,

where 'N' is a natural name. Given these two points, there is an apparent problem for Russell, since if natural names abbreviate descriptions, and declarative sentences with the form of (1) are structurally ambiguous, one would expect the same to go for propositions with the form of (2). But according to Kripke this is just not so. And the distinction among designators is supposed to explain this alleged fact. If the description in the likes of (1) is non-rigid, it stands for different objects at different possible worlds. This in turn explains the structural ambiguity, since we have to distinguish between

(DESCRIPTION WITH WIDE SCOPE) Saying, concerning the object which 'the G' stands for (at @), that it is H at each possible world W (where it exists),

and

(DESCRIPTION WITH NARROW SCOPE) Saying, concerning each possible world W, that the object (if any) which 'the G' stands for (at W) is H (at W)

(note the relativizations 'at @', 'at W', etc). Thus a wide-scope reading of 'The first boxer to knock down Muhammad Ali in a professional fight is necessarily left-handed' says, in effect, that Henry Cooper is left-handed at every possible world he exists at: whereas the narrow-scope version merely has it that at each possible world, whoever (if anyone) is the first, etc. *at that world*, is left-handed. Given the plausible assumption that being the first, etc. is no essential property of Cooper's, these are clearly different claims, and the difference can be put down to the fact that 'the first, etc.' stands for Cooper at @, but for different objects at other worlds, that is has a relativized semantic value.

If natural names are rigid, however, there can be no analogous divergence in their case: if 'Cooper' stands for Cooper (if anyone) at every possible world, there is no difference between (i) saying that whoever 'Cooper' stands for *at* @ is left-handed at some world W, and (ii) saying that whoever (if anyone) 'Cooper' stands for *at* W is left-handed at W. Hence, one would not expect a structural ambiguity to occur in propositions with the form of (2), and so Kripke's doctrine that natural names are rigid can be taken as an explanation of the fact, if it really is one, that there *is* no such structural ambiguity.

Now we saw that the scope phenomena by themselves are not much of a problem for Russell (see § 35). If the idea is merely that some explanation has to be given of the evident facts about scope behaviour, then, as we saw, it is open to Russell to accept these scope phenomena at face value and just explain them away in terms compatible with (ND). So we should ask some awkward questions with respect to any anti-Russellian use to which Kripke puts his distinction among designators. For instance, is Kripke making or assuming *some other claim* about natural names which Russell cannot accommodate? At length we shall see that there is *something* here to trouble Russell, or at least his Official View (§ 24): but it is not obviously a point about natural names—or not without a lot more argument, anyway—and it is, surprisingly enough, little or nothing to do with modality.

But first, let us consider Kripke's most direct anti-Russellian argument. The first shot goes like this:

(1) descriptions are non-rigid designators;
(2) natural names are rigid designators;

so,

(3) natural names and descriptions do not have the same semantic properties;

and the crucial point is that the conclusion (3) seems to be at odds with

(ND) Treat natural names as descriptions,

so that acceptance of (1) and (2) requires a rejection of Russell's theory. What are we to make of this?

39 NATURAL NAMES AND RIGID DESIGNATION

The first thing to note is that (1) is false, since some descriptions *are* rigid designators (if designators at all). One source of examples is mathematics, which gives rise to such descriptions as 'the sum of three and four'. At @ this description picks out seven. But are there any possible worlds at which it picks out anything *other* than seven? Well, it is very plausible to claim that mathematical truths are necessary: and if this is right, '$3 + 4 = 7$' will come out true at every possible world (by Kripke's definition (Def□)). But then it is hard to see how 'the sum of three and four' can pick out anything *other than* seven at a possible world, so that if it picks out anything at any possible world it will pick out seven. This makes it a rigid designator. In addition to this, it is easy to turn *any* description into a rigid designator as follows. As noted, 'the first boxer to knock down Muhammad Ali in a professional fight' stands for Henry Cooper at @. That is, Henry Cooper is the first boxer *at @* to knock down Muhammad Ali in a professional fight. So consider now the description 'the first boxer *at @*, etc.', and ask who it stands for at some arbitrary possible world W. It will at W stand for the boxer (if any) who uniquely satisfies '. . . is the first boxer *at @*, etc.'. But this is Cooper. So if Cooper exists in W the description will stand for him at that world. If he does not exist there it will stand for no one. So, at any possible world, our new description stands for Cooper if anyone; so it is rigid. More generally, any description 'the G' can be made rigid simply by the addition to it of a clause 'at W', where 'W' is the name of *any* possible world. For what happens in any possible world is fixed, so that any description modified in the stated way will keep the same object (if any) when considered with respect to any possible world.[8]

Kripke was aware of this, of course, and proposed rather briefly to distinguish between two different kinds of rigid designator: those which are rigid *de facto*, and those which are rigid *de jure*. And he said further that descriptions, where rigid, are merely rigid *de facto*, whereas natural names are always rigid *de jure*. This yields the following modification of argument (1)–(3):

(1*) descriptions are not *de jure* rigid designators;
(2*) natural names are *de jure* rigid designators;

so,

(3) natural names and descriptions do not have the same semantic properties.

The force of the entire modal argument thus seems, at this point, to rest on the new distinction and the grounds for making it in the proposed way. What does this involve?

Actually Kripke offers very little by way of explanation or justification of this manœuvre. But, intuitively speaking, the distinction appealed to is between expressions which, as it were, merely turn out (*de facto*) to be rigid, and those which are somehow legislated to be rigid, and which therefore belong to the category in some more interesting or intimate sense. At bottom, then, we seem to have an appeal to how we do (or perhaps should) understand natural names and descriptions: somehow this is supposed to make it manifest that natural names, unlike descriptions, are legislated or stipulated to be rigid (hence '*de jure*'). And if we come to see this, then we shall come to see that Kripke's explanation of the scope phenomena is superior to Russell's. However, this is surely rather odd, given that the very idea of rigidity is a technical notion introduced by Kripke himself in the course of expatiating on the modal apparatus of *NN*. What aspect of our understanding of natural names could this procedure reveal?

We go some way towards answering this question when we attend to the following claims, and others like them, which are scattered throughout *NN*:

. . . such terms as 'the winner' and 'the loser' don't designate the same object in all possible worlds. On the other hand, the term 'Nixon' is just a *name* of *this man*. When you ask whether it is necessary or contingent that Nixon won the election, you are asking ... whether ... *this man* [might] ... have lost the election (p. 41).

There is no reason why we cannot *stipulate* that, in talking about what would have happened to Nixon in a certain counterfactual situation, we are talking about what would have happened to *him* (p. 44).

It is *given* that the possible world contains *this man* ... We can point to the *man*, and ask what might have happened to *him*, had events been different (p. 46).

Don't ask: how can I identify this table in another possible world ...? I have the table in my hands, I can point to it, and when I ask whether *it* might have been in another room, I am talking, by definition, about *it* (pp. 52–3).

... we begin with the objects, which we *have* and can identify ... (p. 57).

... when we say counterfactually 'suppose Aristotle had never gone into philosophy ...', we need ... only mean, 'suppose that *that man* had never gone into philosophy ...' (p. 57).

The essential idea here appears to be as follows. Although both natural names and descriptions can be said to have objects which they stand for, there is a crucial difference in the way that these types of expression give us 'access' to the objects in question. In using a name the access is direct: the linguistic expression serves, as it were, as a mere proxy for the object itself, which is thereby 'given' to us as a subject of discourse (thus note Kripke's repeated uses of emphasized demonstratives in the above passages). Things are otherwise with descriptions. Although a successful description will enable us to speak of the described object, the access it provides to that object is indirect: presumably the idea is that the access is 'mediated' by the linguistic material which indicates which thing (if any) the description applies to.

What exactly is going on here? The point seems to be intimately related to the conception of possible world with which Kripke is working (see § 36). Recall that the essential points are that a possible world is determined once its blueprint has been specified, and that in specifying a blueprint one must

(a) stipulate the domain of objects which occupy the world,

and

(b) (permissibly) stipulate, for each primitive functor, which of these objects it applies to.

Kripke's idea seems to be that the first task, that of stipulating the objects for a blueprint, is something to be done with the help of natural names: giving a list of names *just is* the way to stipulate the objects concerned. That is, we are to imagine ourselves as having, by way of our natural names, a direct method for laying down which objects are to belong to a given possible world: a method which is wholly anterior to and more fundamental than the further business taken care of in task (b). And given this, a natural name will indeed be *de jure* rigid, since there can be no question of *inspecting* some possible world W to see what (if anything) a given natural name stands for with respect to it. On the contrary: supplying the name and stipulating that its bearer (at @) is part of W's domain is an essential prerequisite of saying which possible world W is, so that the question whether the name's bearer at W is the same as its bearer in @ always has the straight, legislated answer 'yes'; *there just is no other alternative*.

By way of contrast, however, consider how it would be decided which object (if any) a description 'the G' stands for at some possible world W. Generally, 'the G' stands for x *(at a possible world) if x* uniquely satisfies the functor 'G . . .' (at that possible world). And (essential properties apart) this is something which has to be 'read off' W's blueprint, and is only settled once task (b) in the specification of this has been completed (indeed, where 'G . . .' is complex, one needs further to apply the rules for generating the analogues of (ii) and (iii), the complex 'facts' of the possible world in question: see § 36). Given this, it could indeed just 'turn out' that some description stands for the same object at each possible world, and so is *de facto* rigid. But the point is that the relevant outcome is (at least) derivative on the task (b) part of the specification of the worlds in a way that has no parallel in the case of natural names. According to Kripke anyway, the specification of a name's bearer is always prior to this, and is settled once task (a) is completed.

This, then, is what seems to be the tacit background to Kripke's argument (1*)–(3). The task now is to assess this background.

40 A NON-MODAL BACKGROUND?

One crucial point, we have seen, is the idea that possible worlds are not 'discovered' but *stipulated*. Somehow, this feature of Kripke's modal semantics is to deliver the result that in stipulating a possible world one assumes (or perhaps ought to assume) that natural names provide one with a sort of 'direct access' to their bearers, which then serve partially to define the possible worlds one is interested in. Now, as I have already remarked, Kripke's modal semantics is not the only one in the market, and in particular there are other ('telescope') treatments which explicitly reject the stipulative approach. To this extent a full assessment of the background to (1*)–(3) would need to go into all of that. However, it would be inappropriate in the present sort of work to attempt a full-scale foray into the metaphysics of modality: so I shall let this issue pass. But even if Kripke's stipulative approach is granted there is no easy route from this concession to the crucial premiss

(2*) natural names are *de jure* rigid designators,

so that the anti-Russellian argument is by no means secured by that concession. For, as I shall now try to make clear, Kripke here is confusing at least two distinct notions, neither of which is especially much to do with modality, and neither of which, without further support, delivers any particular conclusion about natural names.

On the one hand, there is the purely abstract or formal idea that a possible world consists of a domain of objects whose comings and goings render true, with respect to that world, certain propositions. In this sense, the objects are primitive, or unstructured, with respect both to the worlds and the complexes ('facts') that render true the aforementioned propositions. Objects, we might say, are among the 'atoms' of which worlds are made, and are thus 'ontologically basic'. But of course, on the other hand, we do not in the normal run of things operate with this abstract conception of what a possible world is: for example, we are also interested in imagining, or stipulating, various concrete possibilities, as when we speculate about how things might have been had Thatcher resigned over the Westland affair. Nevertheless, there is a sense in which, when we do this, we actually determine, by direct means, the (partial) constitution of the possible world in question. We lay down, as it were, which particular 'atoms' help go to constitute the world. Hence one wants to say that we have, in *precisely this sense*, 'direct access' to the objects which are stipulated to be part of the world: they are just 'given' to us, to use Kripke's phrase. Even if we do not make the worlds what they are, we can at least definitely get hold of the ones we want to talk about.

Now all of this seems unexceptionable, so that it is harmless to allow that we are, in this sense, 'just given' the objects which we stipulate to be in the domain of some possible world. Moreover, we can also bring about these stipulations, sometimes, by using natural names: thus we say things like 'Suppose Thatcher had resigned over the Westland affair; would Heseltine have lived to tell the tale?', and so on. However—and this is an important point—there are other means of doing exactly the same thing which do not involve the use of natural names at all. For *any* way of indicating a set of objects whose possibilities are to be discussed—even corralling them into a circus ring—would serve just as well. Then we could say: suppose that *these objects* were painted orange; would they be visible at 100 paces? Furthermore, there seems to be absolutely nothing to stop us even from using *definite descriptions* for the same, stipulative purposes. For example: Let *W* be a world in which the first woman (actually) born in Leicester in 1951 exists. Now we have it: she, *that very woman herself*, is stipulated to be in *W*! Moreover, let *W* be a world in which she, that very woman, is born in Kayseri. There you are then: *she, that very woman*, might have been born in Kayseri!

Modality is, indeed, something of a red herring as far as the present point is concerned. For there is a sense in which *no* talk or speculation can go ahead unless it is first stipulated, or at least secured in some way, what the intended domain of the talk or speculation is to be. If I want to make a generalization about all the one-eyed women born in Thailand before the end of the Korean War, I need to indicate—usually just by saying so—that this is the intended domain of my remark 'Not one of them enjoys binocular vision'. As in the above modal cases, it is just *given* that *those women* are in the domain of my remark. But this is neither a point about modality, nor a point about natural names.

So far, then, there seems to be nothing at all to worry Russell in the modal arguments, apart of course from the points about scope: and even these, we have seen, can be accommodated by him (§35). Is there anything else? We need at this point to look back at the more abstract, formal conception of a possible world. For possible worlds are not just to be considered as the more or less arbitrarily specified items considered in the last few paragraphs. They are also used by logicians such as Kripke in order to provide rigorous semantics for formal languages containing operators such as '□' and '◇'. And, as was remarked in §36, the basic idea here involves a certain generalization of the procedure introduced by Frege for extensional languages. Moreover, as in the extensional case, formal treatments will start off with, or at least assume they are treating, a calculus similar to those beloved of elementary logic students, containing the usual predicate letters and variables, etc., and extensional operators such as truth-functors and quantifiers, as well as the new operators '□' and '◇'. Thus, the modal logician's procedure, in laying down modal semantics, *overlaps* to quite a considerable extent with the procedures adopted by those who merely treat extensional languages in the standard, Fregean way. Hence, such points as the one considered in §§ 9–10, to the effect that Fregean logics of generality require the specification of a domain of objects to be generalized over, will simply carry over to the modal case. But in these formal contexts the idea of 'specifying' a domain is a technical one, and is not to be confused with the homely enterprises concerning Thatcher and so forth described above. Rather, the idea that language somehow 'confronts' a domain of objects, over which generalizations can then be made, is in the formal case antecedent to the question of the interpretation of the language in question, since it is intended to be part of what the interpretation is. In the case of modal semantics this includes the interpretation of the operators '□' and '◇' also. Hence, we need to appeal to the idea of a possible world before we can even make formal sense of the operators '□' and '◇'. Hence—at least—we need to make a primitive appeal to the idea of a 'given' domain of objects which can be permuted in various ways.

Now we saw in chapter 1 that this sort of appeal, at least in a Fregean context, appears to commit one who makes it to the idea that Proper Names could at least be *introduced*, in principle anyway. Thus the same goes for the modal logicians who use Fregean ideas in the ways explained: they too are committed to making the appropriate kind of sense of the idea that an object, the thing itself, should be, for example, presented to a function, or stipulated to be in this or that domain or possible world. In short, Kripke is committed, to use Russellian terminology, to the idea of the *logically* Proper Name.

However, we saw that *this* commitment does not by itself show that *natural names* operate as Proper Names, nor even that a proposed translation of some natural name into a symbolism as a Proper Name is adequate for reasoning purposes (see §§ 10, 11, 18, 23). So, even if we grant, as we must, that Kripke's enterprise consists of an extension of basic Fregean semantic ideas to cover languages enriched by the modal operators '□' and '◇'; and even if we grant further, as I have suggested we do for the sake of argument, that Kripke's is the best approach to modality: even then, *nothing at all* follows about the status of natural names which is not already secured by the implementation of the original Fregean semantics.

Since nothing in particular does follow about natural names in this original case, we can conclude that not only is Kripke's point about 'direct access' to objects not especially to do with modality—since it comes up even for extensional Fregean approaches—but also that it is not much to do with natural names either: or not without further argument, anyway.[9]

It thus seems that no more real progress can be made in this issue between Kripke and Russell until we have more material at our disposal. In particular, there is the other main line of argument used by Kripke against Russell, mentioned at the beginning of the present chapter, which does not employ even explicit mention of modal matters. But, for reasons that will emerge slowly over the next three chapters, these arguments cannot be assessed properly on the basis of what is before us now. All that we can safely conclude at this point is that Kripke's modal considerations as presented above do not succeed in dislodging Russell's claim (ND).

Two pressing matters have so far been left dangling by our overall discussion. One, which has just re-emerged, is the thought that Fregean theorists are committed to the idea of the Proper Name: to the idea that we have a certain kind of direct access to objects we think and speak about. The other, which emerged from the discussion of Strawson and Russell in chapter 3, is that this issue is somehow rooted in the kind of meaning had by declarative sentences which are, as we would casually say, 'about objects': for we saw that one main plank of Russell's argument to the conclusion that Proper-Name treatments are afflicted by the Basic Problem is the complaint that such treatments could not give an adequate account of the statements allegedly made by uses of declarative sentences containing, for example, failed descriptions or vacuous natural names (§§ 16, 18). So at this point we turn to these dangling matters, starting with the second.

Further Reading

'Naming and Necessity' originally appeared in *Semantics of Natural Languages*, ed. D. Davidson and G. Harman (Dordrecht, 1972), and was later issued as S. Kripke, *Naming and Necessity* (Oxford, 1980) (page refs. are to this version). Other relevant works by Kripke are 'Identity and Necessity', in *Identity and Individuation*, ed. M. Munitz (New York, 1971), repr. in *Naming, Necessity and Natural Kinds*, ed. S. Schwartz (Ithaca, 1977); and 'A Puzzle About Belief', in *Meaning and Use*, ed. A. Margalit (Jerusalem, 1979).

For an early statement of the view that names are not synonymous with descriptions, see P. T. Geach, *Reference and Generality* (Ithaca, 1962), pp. 42–6, 122–4.

Excellent discussions of Kripke, and a partial defence ·of description-theories of names, are to be found in M. Dummett, *Frege: Philosophy of Language* (London, 1973), chap. 5 (App.), and M. Dummett, *The Interpretation of Frege's Philosophy* (London, 1981), chaps. 9, 10, and App. 3. For the sort of defence of Russell mentioned in § 35 see H. Noonan, 'Names and Belief', *PAS* 81 (1980/1). For more on the issue between Kripke and Russell see the Further Reading for chapter 8.

A useful collection of papers on possible worlds is M. Loux (ed.), *The Possible and the Actual* (Ithaca, 1979); for an introductory text see G. Forbes, *The Metaphysics of Modality* (Oxford, 1985); but, above all, for a sophisticated yet hugely clear and readable defence of 'telescope' approaches (§§ 36, 40), see D. Lewis, *On the Plurality of Worlds* (Oxford, 1986).

NOTES

1. 'Structural' ambiguities are to be distinguished from 'lexical' ambiguities, which occur when one or more words in a declarative sentence have more than one meaning: thus:

   There is a bat in the cupboard

   can either be used to say something which is of principal interest to a cricketer or baseball player, or instead to report the presence of a certain kind of flying mammal. In a 'logically perspicuous notation', one would of course use two different words for the two different meanings. In ordinary life, context and common sense usually save us from confusion.

2. Note that there are several other places where a negation sign could be inserted in Russell's formula—for instance, before 'Gy', before or after '$\forall y$', before '$x = y$'. . . . Of these, only the first would correspond to an operation on the English sentence of the 'The G is H' variety (it would yield a treatment of 'The non-G is H'). By no stretch, though, could any of these formulae—even the one just mentioned—be called (a symbolization of) 'a negation' of 'The G is H'.

3. By 'simple predication' we shall mean throughout a proposition comprising (a) an unstructured name with a bearer and (b) a primitive functor such as '. . . is fat' or '. . . moves': and we shall say that such a functor stands for a 'primitive function', which corresponds to a 'simple property' that an object can have. For simplicity, I ignore 2-place, etc. functors throughout this exposition of possible-world semantics.

4. Thus one is by no means committed, *without further argument*, to the

further (and perhaps ridiculous) conclusion that possible worlds (other than @) really exist somehow in all-embracing 'logical space'. (This issue, like many others to do with modality which are not directly relevant to the matter of Proper Names, will not be discussed—see LEWIS (1986).)

5. It is important to avoid confusion over how to assess the semantic value of an expression relative to a possible world. For example, the proposition 'Grass is green' is T *at* a possible world W if and only if W's grass is green: here we understand W's grass, greenness, etc. to be the same sorts of thing as @'s. But, of course, it may be that the proposition 'Grass is green', *as used in* W, is F: this will be so, for example, if the denizens of that world speak a language in which 'Grass is green' means that $2 + 2 = 5$. Similarly, 'Aristotle' will name (at W) whoever is Aristotle *at* W: but he may not be *called* 'Aristotle' *in* W. In general, then, distinguish the claim 'E has v at W' from the claim 'E has v in W' (where E is an expression and v is a semantic value). Note too the relativizations in 'T (at @)'—I shall sometimes also say '*actually* T (or F)': this is discussed further below.

6. There are complications here. Suppose we say that a is essentially G (see § 36). Then it would seem that 'Ga' ought to be a sort of necessary truth (since it cannot be F). But if, like most of us, a does not exist necessarily (i.e. exists only contingently), then there will be possible worlds which do not contain a and whose blueprints therefore do not appear to determine, in any obvious way, that 'Ga' is T. If, in response, we say that a property is essential if it is had by an object in every world at which the object exists, then existence, trivially, becomes an essential property of everything! For a discussion of these and related matters see FORBES (1985), chap. 2.

7. It is true that philosophers are not encouraged to see things in quite this way, mostly by Kripke's repeated claim to be attacking the 'Frege–Russell' theory of natural names. But this claim is just confused, as will be explained in chap. 5. Although Frege mentioned in a footnote that one might express the *Sinn* of 'Aristotle' with a description like 'the teacher of Alexander', he nowhere stated the view that names generally are thus associated with descriptions, and anyway he cannot be construed as adopting Russell's quantificational approach to names *or* descriptions. For Frege, both types of expressions are to be treated as Proper Names.

8. This gives the second way of meeting the point about structural ambiguities which was mentioned in § 35. Recall that the point there was that, according to Kripke, natural names differ from descriptions in that declarative sentences containing the former, such as 'Aristotle was necessarily fond of dogs', do not admit of more than one reading corresponding to the different scopes that may be allotted to '□' and the

allegedly abbreviated description. The point now is that if the description is a rigid designator, say, 'the last great philosopher of antiquity *at @*', then although there will still be a *syntactic* difference to note (between '□ (the *G* (at @) is *H*)' and 'the *G* (at @) is □ *H*'), this will have no *semantic* upshot of a relevant sort. That is, the two notionally different procedures:

(1) At each possible world *W* see if the *G* (at @) is *H* at *W*,

and

(2) Take the *G* (at @), and see if it is *H* at each possible world *W*,

are identical in fact. The defender of Russell could then claim that natural names abbreviate such *rigid* descriptions, and that this is responsible for the effective lack of two readings for the appropriate declarative sentences.

9. There is, perhaps, some acknowledgement of this in the preface to the book edition of *NN*, where Kripke rejects the idea that his point about names can be accommodated by the 'scope convention' suggestion discussed in § 35. He claims that his point is not merely that names and descriptions behave differently when mixed with modal operators, but rather that the unmodalized propositions:

(1) *N* is *H*

and

(2) The *G* is *H*

are understood differently by ordinary speakers. The claim here is that whereas (1) is so understood that it can only be true in situations where the (actual) bearer of '*N*' is *H*, the ordinary understanding of (2) allows that it might turn out false in such a situation—for example, because *N*'s bearer is not *G* (see *NN*, pp. 4–15). The appeal here seems to be to the sort of *meaning* that names are understood to have, and it is thus capable of being made quite independently of any particular possible world or modal framework: in effect, it amounts to the claim that whereas a name's bearer is essential to its meaning, the object which a description happens to fit is not essential to *its* meaning. This is the complexity in the notion of the 'modalization' of a proposition mentioned in § 35: one either considers the truth-value of the proposition which would result from adding a modal operator to the likes of (1) or (2), or one simply imagines what kinds of circumstances would make true or false the likes of (1) and (2). Cf. DUMMETT (1981), pp. 577–82, and n. 3 to chap. 8 below.

5
Meaning: The Essential Context

41 *SINN* AND *BEDEUTUNG*

So far the discussion has proceeded almost exclusively in terms of ideas deriving from Frege's theory of *Bedeutung*. But we noted in §6 that Frege later came to distinguish *Bedeutung* from *Sinn*, which he took to be a logically relevant type of meaning which somehow attached to expressions, but which is 'over and above' *Bedeutung*, although intimately related to it. In chapter 3, moreover, we saw that a proper assessment of Russell's main argument against Proper-Name treatments of the Candidates requires one to take account of the general notion of meaning, and of what role it plays in the overall application of Fregean semantics. So we now turn to this. I proceed by first describing as simply as possible the different jobs that Frege seemed to want *Sinn* to do. As in the case of the initial sections on the theory of *Bedeutung* (§§1–6), the exposition here will be relatively plain and uncritical: although, because Frege said comparatively little about *Sinn*, and because the issues raised are so complex, what I say will be somewhat more controversial.[1] Indeed, controversy will never be very far away from now on. The main cause of this is that it is very difficult to focus on what sort of animal meaning is, and on what sort of job it is supposed to do, so that all sorts of metaphysical and other preconceptions are brought to the topic, often with no very clear explanation, or even perhaps understanding, of how and why they are meant to bear on it. The impression sometimes given is that it is vitally important for philosophers to discuss meaning, but that they have not yet managed properly to identify either the target or the proper framework of the discussion. I hope to make the issues moderately intelligible in this chapter and the next.

42 INFORMATION CONTENT

In an intuitive sense, propositions convey *information about* the subject-matter they concern.[2] For Frege, the subject-matter itself is dealt with by the theory of *Bedeutung*, in which relations are set up between linguistic expressions and extralinguistic entities such as objects and functions. But he came to see that in specifying the *Bedeutung* of an expression one does not exhaust its information-content. This is very clear in the case of propositions: although, say:

$$2 + 2 = 4$$

and

The earth moves

have the same *Bedeutung* (T), they clearly say very different things, that is convey very different pieces of information. Of course, these two propositions are built out of components which themselves have different *Bedeutungen*, and it might be thought that this explains the crucial difference. But consider now:

(1) Hesperus is Hesperus

and

(2) Phosphorus is Hesperus.

From the point of view of the theory of *Bedeutung*, (1) and (2) are indistinguishable, not only in that they have the same *Bedeutung* (T), but *also* in that this value is determined in exactly the same way (namely by the presentation of Hesperus (that is, Phosphorus) to the function . . . *is Hesperus*). Yet the information conveyed is quite different: (1) is and always was a platitude to anyone familiar with the name 'Hesperus', whereas (2) had to be discovered by empirical means, and can still be news to those unversed in the ways of philosophers and the heavens. So, here there is a manifest difference between two propositions which is evidently not reflected at all at the level of *Bedeutung*: and Frege consequently said that while our two names have the *same Bedeutung*, they have *different Sinne*. Declarative sentences too have a *Sinn* ('express Thoughts'), said Frege, and the idea here is that the *Sinn* of a sentence is determined by the *Sinne* of its components (just as the *Bedeutung* of a sentence is determined by the *Bedeutungen* of its component). Hence the manifest difference in information-content between (1) and (2) is put down to the fact that they have different *Sinne* (express different Thoughts), and *this* is put down to the fact that 'Hesperus' and 'Phosphorus' have different *Sinne* (make different contributions to the Thoughts expressed). And the point seems to generalize. For instance, both

$$\ldots \rightarrow \ldots \quad \text{and} \quad -\ldots \vee \ldots$$

give the same values for the same pairs of arguments, so have the same truth-function as *Bedeutung*, and both

> . . . is a rational animal

and

> . . . is a featherless biped

take the same objects on to T, so stand for the same first-level function. Yet propositions made from these constructions with otherwise identical components could surely differ in terms of what information is conveyed, so in these cases too Frege said that *Sinn* as well as *Bedeutung* must be assigned. In what follows, however, we shall normally restrict attention to Proper Names and propositions containing them.

It should be noted that Frege's idea of *Sinn* as *information-content* has a certain technical edge to it (although it is not to be confused with the technical notion at the heart of 'information theory'). In ordinary talk, it sometimes seems correct to say that the information conveyed by a proposition varies from person to person or occasion to occasion. Thus, if you believe that all women are mortal, then the proposition 'Socrates is a woman' might convey to you, in the ordinary sense just mentioned, the information that Socrates is mortal. Arguably, the same can be said of all the concepts—meaning, sense, Thought, etc.—which philosophers use to allude to the Fregean notion. Thus, in a similar ordinary sense, in the context described above, 'Socrates is a woman' might be said to mean (to you), or to give you the message, or convey (to you) the Thought that Socrates is mortal. In his talk of *Sinn* or content, however, Frege is after the idea of an invariant core of literal or conventional meaning which attaches to expressions just in virtue of the fact that they play the role they do in the serious reasoning and information-stating uses which interest the logician (compare § 1): he is also, as we shall see in more detail below, after a notion that would be useful in the theory of communication.

This technical aspect of Frege's usage has, indeed, already explicitly surfaced. For we said that whereas:

> (1) Hesperus is Hesperus

is and always was a platitude to anyone familiar with the name 'Hesperus', the same could not be said of:

(2) Phosphorus is Hesperus

which, we said, can still be news to those unversed in the ways of philosophers and the heavens. The important word here is 'can': some knowledgeable people, in the ordinary sort of way mentioned above, might consider (2) to be just as platitudinous as (1). But Frege's idea is that there is a sort of *potential* for being informative in the case of (2) which is lacking in the case of (1), and the having of a different *Sinn*, according to Frege, is to account for this difference of potential. Whether or not Frege's notion can be made out in the way envisaged, however, is one of the controversial matters of which the sections to come are intended to give us a better understanding. So it would be unprofitable to try to discuss the idea further here, and I beg the reader to take it for granted for the time being (for more on this specific point, see chapters 6 and 7).[3]

43 MANNER OF PRESENTATION

For reasons which we must now start to make clear, Frege connected his notions of the *Sinn* and the *Bedeutung* of a linguistic expression by saying that the *Sinn* contains the *manner of presentation* of the *Bedeutung*; that is, it presents it *in* a certain way, *as* a certain kind of thing. The point is easiest to grasp initially in the case of descriptions (which for Frege, recall, are Proper Names). For instance both:

the Queen of Australia

and

the Queen of Scotland

have Queen Elizabeth II of England for *Bedeutung*, according to Frege. Yet they differ in *Sinn*, in Frege's view, precisely because otherwise identical propositions containing them could convey different information: compare, for example, the boring:

The Queen of Scotland rules Scotland

with the potentially enlightening:

The Queen of Scotland rules Australia.

This difference in *Sinn* Frege puts down to the different manners in which the descriptions present Queen Elizabeth: the first presents her as Australian Queen, the second as Scottish Queen.

One can try to fill out this idea somewhat by appeal to Frege's object/function distinction. Phrases like 'the Queen of . . .' can be regarded as functors which represent functions from objects to objects (compare '. . .²', §2), and then we can say that the function in question here yields Queen Elizabeth for either Australia or Scotland as arguments. We can then say this: the first description presents Queen Elizabeth as the value of our function for the argument *Scotland*, whereas the second description introduces the argument *Australia* in presenting her. Analogously, one might say that the difference in *Sinn* between:

Australia has a Queen

and

Scotland has a Queen

is to be traced to the fact that the two propositions present the same *Bedeutung* (T) in different ways, the first as value for the object Australia to the function . . . has a Queen, the second for the object Scotland to the same function.

However, it is doubtful that this method of trying to explicate manner of presentation will work even for descriptions, let alone for all Proper Names, or in the case of expressions generally: and one of the jobs that will exercise us is that of seeking for a different view of the matter (see especially chapters 6 and 7). Consider, for instance, the pair:

The Empress of Hesperus

and

The Empress of Phosphorus.

These could well both fit an individual—the same one, of course, because Hesperus is Phosphorus. Moreover, the two descriptions surely have different *Sinne* if any pair of co-referential Candidates do. However, one cannot explain this difference of *Sinn* in the way described above, namely, as due to the fact that the common value of the two descriptions results from taking distinct individuals as argument to the one function The Empress of. . . . One cannot do this, of course, because the common value is the result, in each case, of taking the *same* argument (Hesperus, that is, Phosphorus) to the common function. More generally, the proposal seems structurally unsound. The proposal is that we should explain the manner in

which the *Bedeutungen* of Proper Names '*a*', '*b*', etc. are presented
by appeal to the idea that these values are the result of taking objects
x, *y*, etc. as arguments to certain functions. But how are the objects
x, *y*, etc. presented? If Frege were to reply that these objects are not
presented in any particular manner, i.e. are such that Names for
them would not have a *Sinn*, then we should need to know a good
deal about these special objects: what could they be? (Russellian
particulars?—see §§ 24–5). As we shall see in § 60, they certainly
could not be ordinary material objects. If, on the other hand, Frege
were to reply that *x*, *y*, etc. are themselves presented as values of
certain arguments to certain functions, then the very same problem
arises again: which are these other arguments; how, if at all, are they
presented; and if not, why not?

Questions like these perhaps indicate that a wrong turn was made
at the beginning of this attempt to explicate manner of presentation:
and it is not, in fact, difficult to see where. For the fact is that the
obvious source of any difference in *Sinn* between the two descriptions displayed above is that they contain names which have different *Sinne* (namely, 'Hesperus' and 'Phosphorus'): identities or
otherwise which hold at the level of *Bedeutung* are just not relevant.
Indeed, the point here is exactly analogous to the examples

(1) Hesperus is Hesperus

and

(2) Phosphorus is Hesperus .

Here Frege posited (different) *Sinne* for the whole propositions, and
then *had to* explain this difference in terms of the difference of *Sinn*
of the two components 'Hesperus' and 'Phosphorus'. And the case of
our descriptions does not appear to be any different: here too we
have complex wholes with different *Sinne*, and the natural extension
of the Fregean model would be to put down this difference, too, to
the fact that the wholes contain parts with distinct *Sinne*. Thus we
cannot avoid, it seems, having to address the question of manner of
presentation for semantically primitive or unstructured expressions
(see chaps. 6 and 8).

It is worth noting here that we have passed close to yet another of
the many reasons why philosophers have yearned to say that natural
names abbreviate descriptions. For, of course, if we *could* say that
names like 'Hesperus' and 'Phosphorus' abbreviate different
descriptions, which are themselves made out of functors and Proper

Names, then we should have a clearish answer to the question, What *is* this difference in *Sinn* that is held to obtain between them, this difference of manner of presentation of the planet concerned? But since this avenue appears to be blocked, the suggestion seems worthless: although there may be other ways of explaining the *Sinn* of a name in terms of definite descriptions. This is a suggestion which we cannot fully evaluate until we have said more about the notion of *Sinn*, and even then not until we return to the topic of natural names (chapter 8). However, there is one important matter which we can straighten out here.

The attempt to explain manner of presentation for natural names just described would commit Frege to something that echoes Russell's:

(ND)   Treat natural names as descriptions.

That is, Frege would at least have to say that each natural name is 'associated with' a description which gives its *Sinn*. But be very clear that this would *in no way* commit Frege to Russell's quantificational account either of natural names or of descriptions. For it just is one thing to say that a name comes associated with a description which gives the *Sinn* of the name, and something else altogether to say, as Russell did, that the name in question is to be treated quantificationally. As it happens, Frege nowhere makes even the first claim, although it is true that his examples usually indicate that he has some such idea in mind. But he very definitely did not subscribe to anything like Russell's quantificational theories of descriptions and names: as has been repeated many times, Frege treated both types of expression as Proper Names.

Just to underline this fundamental difference between Russell and Frege, note too that while Frege certainly might well have tried to use (ND) or something like it to introduce the notion of *Sinn* for natural names, and while Russell definitely *did* use (ND), there is *no sense whatsoever* in which Russell thereby committed himself to the view that names have *Sinn*. On the contrary, he maintained that the quantificational approach made the notion of *Sinn* for *names* (and descriptions) redundant; although whether or not he could avoid positing *Sinn* for other expressions, for example, functors, is of course a different matter. For *Sinn* is to be or contain the manner of presentation of the object which a Proper Name stands for: and, according to Russell, natural names and descriptions just do not stand for objects because they are not Proper Names! As Russell repeatedly claimed in OD, and as we saw in chapter 2, one major advantage of his theories of names and descriptions is that he can account for them without having to 'assign them a meaning [= object] in isolation'. For Russell, these theories—pitched at Frege's level of *Bedeutung*—were *themselves* supposed to show how co-referential Candidates could differ in the ways to account for which Frege introduced the notion of *Sinn* (see §§16–20 and §46).

It is of course possible to define a 'designation' even for a Russellian description 'the *G*'. For Russell, such a description would translate into the second-level functor:

$$\exists x(\forall y(Gy \leftrightarrow x = y) \& \ldots x)'.$$

And the 'designation' of this functor will then be the object (if any) which uniquely satisfies the functor '*G* . . .' (Russell himself points this out at OD, p. 51). This seems to have led many to think that one could provide an abbreviated natural name *both* with a *Bedeutung* (= the 'designation') *and* a *Sinn* (spelled out by the Russellian second-level functor), and thereby produce an account practically equivalent to Frege's own. Thus it is very common to see mention of 'the Frege–Russell theory' of names, in *Naming and Necessity* and elsewhere. But this line of thought is seriously confused. Unlike a genuine Fregean *Bedeutung*, the 'designation' so defined plays no role whatsoever in the semantic account of how the name works. For the whole point of Russell's theory of descriptions, to repeat, is to give a way of treating these expressions *without* having to invoke a described object, by using second-level functors like the one above. In the context of this sort of approach, a defined 'designation' is a useless ornament. Given Russell's view, there is no more semantic point in calling the 'designation' of a description its *Bedeutung* than there would be in calling Lake Van the *Schmedeutung* of San Lorenzo de El Escorial. In neither case is any useful theoretical purpose being served. All of this can be summarized by noting the following claims:

(a) Descriptions have objects as semantic values

(b) Natural names have objects as semantic values

(c) Descriptions are quantificational

(d) Natural names are quantificational

(e) Vacuous names have no semantic value (unless one is arbitrarily stipulated)

(f) Failed descriptions have no semantic value (unless one is arbitrarily stipulated)

(g) Natural names have *Sinn*

(h) Descriptions have *Sinn*

(i) Natural names abbreviate descriptions.

Russell and Frege explicitly clashed over all but one of these central claims: Russell accepted (c), (d), and (i), and rejected all the rest; Frege did not pronounce on (i), although he might have been sympathetic, and accepted everything else *but* (c) and (d).

Thus the point, I hope, is by now abundantly clear: the *only* sense in which there is such a thing as 'the Frege–Russell theory' of names is that Russell did subscribe to, and Frege might have tried to subscribe to something like, the injunction (ND). And there is, also, just this much justification for the claim, which in some works has the standing of an unnoticed platitude, that in attacking this injunction one is attacking the idea that names have *Sinn*: (ND) could figure in a possible explanation of what it is for a name to have *Sinn*. But, as we shall see, there are other ways of explaining the idea of *Sinn* for names, which do not appeal to (ND): so this justification is not very significant.

44 PRESENTATION TO WHAT?

In some way—which we have yet to explain—the *Sinn* of a Proper Name is to be, or to 'contain', the manner of presentation of its *Bedeutung*. But manner of presentation to what? The answer is: Minds.

Strictly speaking, it was not *as a logician* that Frege introduced his notion of *Sinn*. If the aims of a logician are (i) to discriminate valid forms of argument, and (ii) to explain with a semantic theory what is being discriminated, then the theory of *Bedeutung* (along with its associated calculus, perhaps) suffices, at least for the uses of extensional language (§ 21) that interested Frege.[4] But as we noted in the Introduction, a semantic theory must be capable of interacting with a broader-based account of mind and language, since logic is supposed somehow to help govern correct thinking, and thinking is standardly conducted in a linguistic medium, or is at least capable of being so conducted. Now Frege was more than tacitly aware of this requirement for logical ideas to mesh with the broader framework. As was also noted in the Introduction, he believed that the logic of his time was hopelessly wrong largely because it was embedded in a quite wrong-headed conception of these wider matters, and he therefore took pains to indicate how he thought they should be conceived. His stress was on a version of what is called *realism*: crudely, his view was that the subject-matter of logic (and hence of the appropriate uses of language, and of the appropriate episodes of thinking) belongs to a reality that is external to and independent of the minds of thinking and reasoning beings. This may not sound a very exciting thesis—whoever thought things were otherwise?—but in fact philosophers have often, for various reasons, opposed this evidently commonsensical view with one or other versions of *idealism*, which holds (very roughly) that reality is *not* independent of minds and their activities or modifications (Russell may have been partly tempted by this view: see § 24). As it happens, the philosophy of Frege's time was shot through with idealistic themes, and this, as Frege often complained, had its due effect on contemporary approaches to logic, which were thereby encouraged to focus on the 'subjective' mind rather than the 'objective' world. (Another pressure which tended to result in the same effect was the idea, also vigorously opposed by Frege, that logic, being somehow concerned with thought, was a branch of empirical psychology: on this see the following section.) Frege roundly condemned these trends for robbing logic of its objectivity, which he thought was essential to it (here he was right), and only to be secured by his own theory of *Bedeutung* (although this last claim, unfortunately, is controversial, since it is perhaps possible to do 'objective' semantics in an 'idealistic' framework—see DUMMETT (1981), chap. 19). Here is a typical passage offered by Frege in defence of his theory of *Bedeutung*:

... if we could not grasp anything but what was in our own selves, then a conflict of opinion [based on] mutual understanding would be impossible, because common ground would be lacking ... There would be no logic to be appointed arbiter in the conflict of opinions (*The Basic Laws of Arithmetic*, p. 17).

Here Frege is defending his realistic semantic theory on the (controversial) grounds that nothing else would make logic objective enough to arbitrate in disputes between individuals. However, he speaks too of what we 'grasp' in expressing and arguing about our opinions, and mentions that 'mutual understanding' is essential if logic is to get the appropriate grip. In so doing he is going beyond the more technical aspects of logic and discussing how these matters mesh with a conception of what minds themselves 'grasp' or 'understand'. This takes us into the realm of *Sinn*: after all, it is the information expressed by language, its content, that we are properly said to grasp or understand. But notice how intimate the link is between the realms of *Sinn* and *Bedeutung*. In the very act of defending his view of the latter Frege slips into using language and notions appropriate to the former. And this much is surely right: the more technical aspects of logic cannot be left to 'wheel free' of whatever is involved when we grasp and communicate the opinions among which logic is intended to arbitrate. For a very large part of what counts as having a proper or adequate understanding of a proposition or of a propositional component is the ability to use it correctly in reasoning and inferring. Thus semantic theory itself is answerable to what we understand our language to mean, and must therefore 'harmonize' with a credible account of the cognitive capacities which are employed when the relevant stretches of language are used. And Frege's doctrine of *Sinn* is supposed to fill this gap by displaying somehow this 'harmony', thereby helping to answer the question, How does an understanding or grasp of the content of a stretch of reasoning commit one to respecting the logical principles, etc. derivable from the underlying semantics? For Frege, important work was to be done here by the metaphor of manner of presentation. We are to think of an expression's *Sinn* as something that is objective, in the sense that it can be grasped and communicated by more than one mind, and which serves to 'present' extra-linguistic reality to understanding minds in such a way that the expression's objective logical properties, described by Frege with the help of the presented extralinguistic items, will be manifest to those minds. Alternatively, it is sometimes said that *Sinn* (or a specification thereof) *determines* Bedeutung, in the sense that once *Sinn* has been specified, it has also been laid down what the presented *Bedeutung* will be.

45 *SINN* AND OBJECTIVITY

We now have the following programmatic model for explaining how a Fregean semantic theory is to mesh with mind and understanding. Because an expression conveys information it has a kind of content which is additional to the *Bedeutung* assigned by the semantics. This is the expression's *Sinn*, which does its job partly by presenting the

Bedeutung to the minds of those who grasp or understand the expression. Thus we have

$$Sinn = \text{information content} = \text{manner of presentation of } Bedeutung \text{ to mind}$$

Furthermore, Frege stressed that *Sinn*, just like *Bedeutung*, is to be *objective*, or mind-independent, so that, for instance, the same *Sinn* can be grasped by distinct minds, and thus communicated between them. So we can continue

$$Sinn = \text{what is grasped or understood (by different minds)} = \text{what is communicated between speakers}$$

The notion of objectivity, however, is difficult in any context, and it is necessary to be clearer about what exactly Frege is getting at here. So, suppose that X and Y are both of the opinion that the moon is made of green cheese, and are, say, disputing about whether it follows from a given premiss. In one sense, we have *two* opinions, namely X's opinion that the moon is made of green cheese, and Y's. This is analogous to the case where each has toothache, and we have two distinct aches. But even in this latter case there is a sense in which there is just one thing, a *sort of mental state* (namely, *having-a-toothache*), which is common to both X and Y: just as they could have the same height or weight or colour of hair. It is customary to mark this distinction in the following way. Where both X and Y have the same sort of toothache, there are two *token* aches (or mental states): namely X's ache and Y's ache. But in this situation there is only one *type* (of) state: namely, having-a-toothache. The tokens are, as it were, individual occurrences within individual minds: whereas alluding to the type is a way of approaching what these tokens have in common, relative to mental classifications.

Somewhat similarly, Frege was interested, in his theory of *Sinn*, not with *token* opinions, but with types: in our example he would be interested in the opinion-type *that-the-moon-is-made-of-green-cheese*. For Frege, a hyphenated phrase like this represents a type of opinion (or similar state of mind) whose properties, including the way it relates to the relevant parts of the theory of *Bedeutung*, are to be articulated by the theory of *Sinn*. And this gives one sense in which *Sinn* is the objective, since the focus is not on the nature of individual (token) opinions, but on their types relative to logical classification. That is, Frege's concern was not with individual token opinions, such as, say, X's opinion that the moon is made of green cheese, but rather with the logical and semantic classification of the type of opinion of which X's happens to be a token: for it is in virtue of being a token of the general type that X's opinion has the logical, etc. powers which it does. Frege here can be thought of as adopting an 'objective' or generalized stance towards his subject-matter, as opposed, say, to someone who 'subjectively' focuses intently and exclusively on the individual case (compare X's dentist's interest in X's ache with what X's own is likely to be!).

However, Frege intends more than this first sort of objectivity, although he tends to run together different sorts of consideration when explaining what he wants. For instance, he stresses that *Sinne* must be sharply distinguished from ideas, mental images, feelings, or any other *items to be found in people's minds*:

A painter, a horseman, and a zoologist will probably connect different ideas with the name 'Bucephalus'. This constitutes an essential difference between the idea and the sign's sense, which may be the common property of many and therefore is not a part or mode of the individual mind ('On Sense and Reference', pp. 59–60).

Frege seems here to have a number of points in mind. First, there is the one already made that *Sinn* is to do with types and not tokens (= 'part or mode of the individual mind'). But there is implied the extra point that a name like 'Bucephalus' is to be associated with a (type of) *Sinn* which is shared between different speakers (= 'common property of many'). This is extra because it is one thing to say that the *Sinn* I associate with the name is of a certain type, and quite another to say that the *Sinn* which someone else associates with it is of *the same type*: why should not each person have his or her own (type of) *Sinn*, just as some magazines encourage us to think that each has his or her own (type of) life-style? Obviously what Frege has in mind here is the idea of communication, which seems to require types of opinion to be shared (or at least shareable), and the related idea that for this to be possible there must be a core of literal or conventional meaning attached to words (compare § 42). But it is at least prima facie possible for individuals to have opinions, etc. which they cannot or just do not share, so the fact remains that there is a further point here. Thus the second way in which *Sinn* is to be objective is that there is to be one (type of) *Sinn* had by an expression, which is grasped by those familiar with the expression's use. In other words, *Sinn* is objective not merely because the focus is to be on the type of *Sinn* our words have, but also because different uses of the same expression, even by different speakers, are supposed to have the *same Sinn*.

There is, however, an important third point in the offing, which concerns the sort of investigations Frege considered logic and semantics to be. To make this clear we need first to go back to the toothaches mentioned above. We saw that it is possible to distinguish tokens from types (*X* and *Y* suffer their own tokens of the one type), so in this sense, having-a-toothache is no different from opining-that-the-moon-is-made-of-green-cheese. Similarly, as Frege indeed implies in the above passage, a zoologist and a horseman *could* both have (token) ideas of the same type: two exactly similar mental images, say, which are conjured up by 'Bucephalus'. But Frege makes it absolutely clear that the theory of *Sinn* has a different subject-matter altogether: he repeatedly says that ideas, etc. belong to the domain of *psychology*, and are therefore irrelevant to logic. However, if there is to be a further distinction between mental images, or feelings like toothache, or emotions, and *Sinne*, it will not be one to be made merely in terms of types and tokens, nor in terms of the shareability of types: since these distinctions apply right through.

It is impossible now to reflect on this issue without having in mind Wittgenstein's comprehensive demolition of the view that grasping a meaning is to be likened to occurrent episodes such as contemplating an image, having a feeling, and so on. And, as we shall see in §§ 49–50, one cannot make much sense of meaning unless one adopts a different approach altogether from the one attacked so effectively by Wittgenstein. But it is not clear that Frege ever confronted this issue, and anyway his present point is somewhat different. It involves the idea that certain types of state of mind (for example, having an opinion that so and so) stand in *logical relations* to one another which mimic those which obtain between propositions. Just as the proposition 'the moon is made of green cheese' entails the proposition 'something is made of green cheese', so an analogous relation holds between the *opinions* which sincere utterances of these propositions would indicate. So although, directly, the focus of logic is language, and (more specifically) certain relations that obtain between propositions, yet indirectly the target is thought, those aspects of mentality concerned with encapsulating and reasoning about information and putative matters of fact. Standardly, these mental aspects are or can be manifested in language, in the use of the same propositions directly studied by logic: hence the possibility that the latter enterprise will bear indirectly on the former matters. So, in this sense, logic is concerned with *thought*, and the laws of logic are thus, in a sense, *laws of thought*.

But this immediately makes it sound as though logic is in the same business as empirical psychology: for it too sets itself to look for such laws as there might be in the sphere of the mental. However, there is a crucial distinction to be made here, as Frege was very much aware. If, for example, you are of the opinion that the moon is made of green cheese, then you *should*, if the occasion arises, be of the opinion that something is. And this 'should' relates to logic, not to psychology. It is not being said that some psychological law sees to it that anyone with the first opinion has or is likely to have the second (although one always hopes that this will be the case). The point is that logic, rationality, *demands* this: people are just not thinking correctly unless their opinions are organized in this way. In connection with this, Frege alludes to a similar ambiguity in the idea of a 'rule of conduct'. On the one hand, this is a purely descriptive, anthropological notion, analogous to the psychological conception of a law of thought. One just looks to see how people carry on. But there is, of course, quite another interpretation of 'rule of conduct' in which it is not concerned with how people actually *do* behave, but rather with how they *should* behave. Hence, Frege says, logic is akin to ethics (*Posthumous Writings*, p. 4). Both, that is, are *normative* disciplines, concerned with aspects of how things should be.

Thus logic, on Frege's conception, turns out to be a discipline in its own right, distinct from merely descriptive empirical psychology. Its aim is to help characterize certain canons of right thinking by concentrating on the formal properties of its normal linguistic expression. So the third point buried in Frege's insistence that the study of *Sinn* must sharply distinguish it from ideas and other items of the mind is this: *Sinn* is to concern that aspect of (types of) opinions which is relevant to the determination, via the theory of *Bedeutung*, of the logical relations, etc. that obtain between them; and the study of this is just a *different discipline* from those psychological studies which may concern the relations that obtain between (types or tokens of) mental images, ideas, feelings, or whatever.[5] In short, Frege was absolutely opposed to what is sometimes known as *psychologism*—the importation of notions from empirical psychology into logic, or the doctrine that logic is a branch of psychology.

However, saying that *Sinn* does not belong to psychology is one thing. Saying something more helpful about where it does belong is something else—a very difficult something else: and it will take the second half of this chapter even to start to do this. Moreover, as we shall see, there is a way in which *Sinn is* psychological after all. For one can approach psychology in at least three different ways. One can think of it in relatively 'pure' terms, as aiming for a very general scientific analysis and understanding of types of mental phenomena—intelligence, memory, perception, and so on. Or one can think of it in a more 'applied' manner, as aiming for scientific generalizations and/or explanatory models which can be fitted on to specific pieces of behaviour in order to explain and/or predict them. Or, finally, one can think of it as being concerned with the given, phenomenological mode of being that we enjoy. This is Intentional or 'folk' psychology, and it is the realm that *Sinn* inhabits. As we shall see in more detail in the second part of this chapter, Intentional psychology gives expression to our ordinary, pre-scientific conception of what we, and other things with minds, are like *qua* conscious beings. According to this Intentional conception, we exist as rational agents who, among other things, have opinions or beliefs about the world, want certain things to happen or come about, and tailor our actions to suit, usually more or less rationally. From the point of view of Intentional psychology, the beliefs and wantings have *content*, in virtue of which they are about ('represent') the world: and *Sinn* is the content. So, in this way, *Sinn* does belong to psychology—Intentional psychology—from the point of view of which it is a sort of theoretical notion. That is, we think of ourselves as having beliefs and other states of mind, and these somehow relate to the world, and each other, and our normal rational behaviour. Content, or *Sinn*, is what we ascribe to these states when viewing them from the Intentional point of view.

This link—between *Sinn* and Intentional psychology—brings to light one more aspect of Frege's notion which will be increasingly important as we go along, and before turning to a more detailed description of the kind of thing *Sinn* is supposed to be, it will help to have this matter before us.

46 INDIRECT *BEDEUTUNG*

In § 20 we saw that propositions containing psychological words like 'believes' give problems for certain Proper-Name accounts. For instance, while:

(1) These astronomers believed that Vulcan orbits the sun

could well seem to be T, given the right sort of behaviour on the part of the astronomers, the proposal to treat the natural name as a Proper Name seems unable to account for this fact. For, since there is no planet Vulcan, there is no object to present to the function these astronomers believe that . . . orbits the sun. Again, one would expect that the propositions:

(2) Before there was any evidence that Hesperus is Phosphorus, most astronomers believed that Hesperus is Hesperus,

and

(3) Before there was any evidence that Hesperus is Phosphorus, most astronomers believed that Hesperus is Phosphorus,

to have *different* truth-values (the first T, the second F). But on the sort of account just mentioned this cannot be, since both propositions are guaranteed to have the same value (whatever the planet gives at the function before there was any evidence that Hesperus is Phosphorus, most astronomers believed that Hesperus is . . .).

Now these problematic propositions belong to Intentional psychology, and given what was said about this in the last section it should hardly come as a surprise that Frege appealed to his doctrine of *Sinn*, when suggesting solutions, albeit rather briefly, for both the above problems. Essentially, he just denied that propositions like (1)–(3) should be analysed in the extensional fashion just indicated: that is denied that one should logically divide a proposition of the form

X believes that C is so and so,

where 'C' is any Candidate, into the first-level functor:

X believes that . . . is so and so

and the Proper Name of an object 'C'. Rather, he claimed that words in psychological contexts do not have their usual (i.e. extensional) role, but instead take on another. In so doing he was, of course, taking the alternative course, which apparently did not occur to Russell, that we noted at the beginning of chapter 3. Moreover, as we also noted here, this line has an independent warrant: although, in extensional contexts, a proposition like:

(4) Hesperus is Phosphorus

may be regarded as having a truth-value as its *Bedeutung*, it can no longer be so regarded when it occurs as a component of an intensional proposition. For it is clear that, say,

(5) Shakespeare believed that Hesperus is Phosphorus

is neither guaranteed to be T, nor guaranteed to be F, by the truth of the embedded proposition (4). Now it follows that *if* (4) is considered to be a component of (5), and *if* we wish to account for the truth or falsity of the likes of (5) in terms of the semantic values of its components—and neither assumption seems avoidable—then we shall have to look for a different semantic value to assign to (4) when it appears in the likes of (5). Similarly, if this special intensional semantic value for (4) is itself to be determined by the semantic values of (4)'s components—and how else could one proceed?—then these components too will have to have a different semantic value from the normal one when they appear in intensional contexts. Otherwise, there would simply be no explanation of the fact that whereas (5) might have been F,

(6) Shakespeare believed that Hesperus is Hesperus

might, in the same circumstances, have been T. For the only difference between (5) and (6) is that an occurrence of 'Hesperus' has replaced one of 'Phosphorus'. Hence the envisaged difference in truth-value between them is due to the fact that the names have different semantic values in those propositions. But, extensionally speaking, according to Frege, these names have the *same* semantic value (the planet). So, in the likes of (5) and (6), names, like propositions, have a different *Bedeutung* from the normal one: they have what Frege called an *indirect Bedeutung*.

Frege identified *indirect Bedeutung* with *customary Sinn*. That is, he said that whilst a Proper Name is to be assigned a certain object (its bearer) as *Bedeutung* in extensional contexts, this will not be so for contexts governed by the psychological words. These are to be marked off as special contexts requiring special treatments, and this is to consist in the assignment of *Sinn* as *Bedeutung* to expressions when they occur in them. The solutions to the initial problem are then straightforward. If we can assume that 'Vulcan' has a *Sinn* (even though it has no bearer), then it matters not, with a proposition like (1), that the name has no bearer. For the *Sinn*, whose existence, we have assumed, is assured, will be assigned to it in that proposition, so there will be no overall failure of reference. Similarly, if we can assume that 'Hesperus' and 'Phosphorus' have *different Sinne*, then the argument that (2) and (3) are guaranteed to have the same truth-value just fails. For this argument assumes that it is the bearer, the (standard) *Bedeutung*, which is relevant to their truth-value: and Frege just denies this. It is the *Sinne*, he says, which are relevant to the truth-values of (2) and (3), and since these (we assume) are different, there is no reason to say that the pair of propositions are guaranteed to have the same value.

The general outline of this approach is certainly compelling. Is it not obvious that in using propositions of the form '*X* believe(s) that *P*', it is the *Sinn* or content of the proposition '*P*' which is relevant to the truth-value of the whole? Does one not, in using such a proposition, attribute to the subject(s) (*X*) a belief whose nature is to be specified by the content of the proposition '*P*'? However, the treatment is hardly complete as stated. In particular, if *Sinne* are to serve as *Bedeutungen* in the relevant contexts, we need to be told what sort of thing a *Sinn* is: and Frege himself is not very obliging here. We also need to know how (and why) the *Sinn* of, for example, 'Hesperus' *does* differ from that of 'Phosphorus'. Frege says little about this too, and we shall investigate the matter at some length.

Perhaps the most questionable aspect of Frege's treatment is that he links it with a particular conception of what it is for *Sinne* to be *objective*. For Frege, a *Sinn* is literally a sort of entity, abstract to be sure, and not to be found lurking inside anyone's skull, but still an entity for all that (and, what is more, an entity that exists for eternity). This is evidently one way of conceiving *Sinn* while making sure that the right sort of objectivity is secured. But as we shall see in §§ 49–50, this doctrine obscures more than it explains, and if anything is to be salvaged from Frege's view on the subject it will have to avoid this claim.

Despite these difficulties, however, the overall position to be defended in the remainder of this book is one in which a markedly Fregean notion of *Sinn* has ineliminable work to do.

47 MIND AND MEANING

We need to say rather more about understanding and the mind than we have so far. The theory of *Sinn* is intended to deal with the fact that thinkers interact with language in such a way that their thinking, if it is to be fully rational, must by and large respect the logical principles derivable from semantic theories of the language. One

therefore cannot theorize about *Sinn* without having some conception, implicit or otherwise, of what it is to think, at least when using
language; and this in turn means that one must also make commitments over what the mind is like. So this is what we must now do.
Matters such as these, however, have an enormous philosophy all of
their own, and it would be quite inappropriate in a work of the
present sort to try to deal with the topic in full. So I shall restrict the
scope of the enquiry in a number of ways.

In the first place, I shall not initially be explicitly concerned with
questions about the ontological status of minds—i.e. whether they
are immaterial substances that can perhaps exist independently of
the body (dualism), or just complex patterns of response to stimuli
(behaviourism), or brains (materialism), and so on. These are
important issues, and they are not entirely independent of the
matters that concern us, but we can usefully proceed without having
to trace out these connections to any great extent. Relatedly, I shall
not be concerned with questions about the essential nature of mind
as such—what possible guises it could appear in. My concern will be
with minds as we actually know them in the ordinary course of
things. In the second place, I shall be concerned only with certain
functions of the mind: namely those directly involved when thinking
and reasoning occur in a linguistic medium. These are what bear
most directly upon logic, and we shall have no dealings with emotion
or feelings or any other aspect of mentality. In the third place, we can
restrict attention even more by focusing exclusively on *understanding*. One cannot reason and think with the help of linguistic
expressions without understanding them, so in this sense understanding is the key notion. This, recall, is how Frege saw it, in that
Sinn is what is understood, or 'grasped', by the mind. So our focus
will be on this question: What general sort of thing is it for a thinker
to understand a linguistic expression?

Now minds typically manifest themselves in two rather different
ways. Each mind seems to have a direct appreciation of at least some
of its own doings which is not available to others. Thus, for instance, I
can feel my pains and enjoy my visual experiences in a way that
others cannot (although they may, of course, feel their own pains and
enjoy their own visual experiences). The idea here is that each of us
has a *first-person perspective* on just the one mind, namely, his or her
own, and is thereby able to know about certain goings on in the
aforementioned direct way. This is not necessarily to say that others
cannot know that I feel pain or enjoy a particular type of visual

experience.[6] It is merely to say that their 'access' to these facts is rather different from my own. They gain access from the *third-person perspective*: for instance, they may not feel my pain or enjoy my experience, but they can observe my behaviour and see how I am situated, and thereby get to know about my state of mind.

The exact status of this first-/third-person distinction is controversial: but we shall not need to go very far into this. For my limited purpose is to show that as far as our present interests are concerned, the third-person perspective is the correct one to employ. That is, it is reflection on behaviour and the situations of thinkers in their environments which provides the material for getting the best initial grip on questions about understanding and meaning. This leaves it open whether there are other aspects of mind best approached from the first-person perspective. I proceed by first discussing first-person approaches to understanding, which dominated philosophy after Descartes and until well into the present century, and which still sometimes have more influence than they should have (see §§63–5). A clear view of the defects of such approaches provides a good basis on which to build a third-person approach.

48 IDEAS AND UNDERSTANDING

Meaning can be thought of as a sort of 'life' possessed by inscriptions and other things. Words and so on are themselves inert, 'dead' things, marks on paper or sounds, just bits of the natural world. Somehow, they 'come alive' for an understanding mind and convey information, stand for things, express concepts, and so on. It is very natural to suppose that this life is itself *bestowed* by the mind (or minds in general). On the one hand, we have a material object, an inscription of 'London', say, and on the other, that great city on the Thames. What is it for the one dead thing to *mean* the other? Well, this certainly does not seem to be any ordinary relation between the two things, which just happens to obtain in the natural course of events. No ordinary survey merely of the space and causal mechanisms that lie between them, however detailed it may be, seems likely to hit upon an answer to the question. This suggests, what is anyway plausible in its own right, that a third thing needs to come into the picture: 'London' means London *for* something else—a mind, or some minds, for instance. But this in turn is very close to saying that minds themselves, when they understand 'London' to mean London, are somehow active in the process, even if they do not actually bestow the meaning relation. So the question about meaning drifts back, quite naturally, to a question about mind and understanding: what do minds *do* when they understand, say, 'London' to mean London?

If, as after Descartes philosophers were prone to do, one adopts an exclusively first-person approach to the mind, that is thinks of it as essentially a realm of experiences and feelings which are directly manifest to attention, one quickly passes on, from the conclusion of the last paragraph, to thinking of understanding as involving the occurrence of some suitable object of attention. 'Idea' is the more or less technical term used by philosophers around the time of Descartes and thereafter to refer to the posited items. Words were said to 'signify' ideas, things before the understanding mind's eye, which themselves then somehow give life to the words and enable them, indirectly, to mean things external to the mind. That is, we start off with the picture of Fig. 1, in which a word like 'London' is deemed to mean something else, the city. But then we are immediately at a loss to say anything more about the relation (represented by the dotted line) without introducing a third term, as in Fig. 2. And then this only helps if more can be said about how the third term of Fig. 2 mediates the mysterious relation of Fig. 1. Given the exclusively first-person perspective, we look for appropriate items present to attention, allegedly find ideas, and end up with the picture of Fig. 3 in which two relations now do the job of the original one.

means

'London'...................... [the city]

Fig. 1

MIND(S)

'London'   [the city]

Fig. 2.

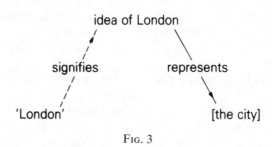

Fig. 3

This is the basic form of the traditional 'ideational' theory of how words mean things: they signify ideas in the mind and the ideas themselves represent the things. To understand a word is to associate with it an appropriate idea. But now the questions immediately spring up. What are ideas? Whatever they are, can they do the job in question: is it going to be easier to say how ideas can *represent* things than it is to say how words *mean* things? Does this theory yield a satisfactory conception of understanding, and if so how exactly?

It is a curious fact that the original users of 'idea' claimed to find the notion completely unproblematic: an idea, they would say, is just the sort of thing that one is aware of when contemplating the immediate contents of one's consciousness—just introspect and you'll find some examples, unless your mind is a complete blank! The fact is curious because it is now virtually impossible to see how anyone could have said this and believed it to be so straightforward. Of course, when people introspect, they usually become aware of (or make explicit to themselves) certain things that are going on—the fact that, say, they are warm or otherwise, that they can feel where their legs are in contact with things at various points, that they have been thinking about Vienna, and so on. But these are very different kinds of thing, and it needs further explanation why they are all being lumped together under 'becoming aware of ideas'. Neither were the traditional theorists particularly clear about what they really meant, despite their assurances that their notion is unproblematic. But they would tend, particularly when speaking of ideas in connection with the meanings of words, to slip into speaking of ideas as if they were mental images or similar replicas which could literally be summoned 'before the mind's eye'. Then, for instance, the idea of a cat would be thought of as a mental image or picture of a cat, derived perhaps from experiences of seeing cats, and it would be this image which would become annexed to the word 'cat', for instance, as a result of one's training in the language, and which would bestow upon the word the capacity to mean *cats*.

This view has an initial ring of plausibility. It certainly seems to locate meaning in the right sort of place, namely, in the conscious or reflective part of the mind. For, as we shall see in more detail below (§§ 51–3, 58–60), meaning is indeed a 'phenomenological' notion— it is something of which we normally have a kind of direct or immediate knowledge, and is in this sense one of the most familiar aspects of our existence, so that any account of it must also be an account of how we know it. And what could be more immediate or familiar than a contemplated mental image? Furthermore, we do usually learn words like 'cat' by being confronted with the animals, in the presence of someone who helpfully points and goes 'cat'. Perhaps also when we are thinking or speaking about cats we tend to summon up images of them (although not everyone, apparently, can form mental images). And perhaps, finally, it seems intuitively obvious how a *picture* of a cat can represent *cats*: there seems to be a clear resemblance or isomorphism between the two things, some- thing that is entirely lacking where the word is concerned ('cat' doesn't resemble cats at all). So if ideas are thought of as images and images are thought of as pictures, it can seem that a satisfactory explanation of the *means* relation of Fig. 1 above is provided by the *represents* relation of Fig. 3. For this is none other than the relation that holds between a picture and what it is a picture of—and this is just an allegedly primitive and unproblematic relation of *resemb- lance* (at least when the picture is a 'good likeness', one would have to add).

Is this ideational theory acceptable?

49 TROUBLES WITH IDEAS

No: despite the initial show of plausibility, the traditional theory is a total failure. In the first place, lots of words have meaning even though the notion of a *picture* of what they mean hardly makes sense: think, for instance, of 'if', 'so', or 'surely'. It may be replied that this is nothing very serious, since such words do not exactly mean things in the world either (there are no such things as ifs and sos), so that the original problem presented by the relation in Fig. 1 would not arise anyway, and some different account of such words would be needed (and this is true whatever one's theoretical stance). But think now of words like 'justice', 'honesty', or 'friend'. On the face of it these words *do* stand for things in the world (there are, for instance, such things as friends): but what would a picture or image of a friend be like? It is no good thinking here that one could get by with an image of a certain person, one's best friend for instance, as the meaning of 'friend'. For one thing, this would entail that most people mean different things by the word—since most people have different best friends—so it would be mysterious how we manage to communicate with it. For another, suppose your best friend is Ms X and that your idea of *friend* is the idea of Ms X. What now serves as the meaning of the phrase 'Ms X'?—certainly not the idea of her, unless 'Ms X' is to be synonymous with 'friend': but this is absurd, since these expressions do not even belong in the same grammatical category.

In any case, there is a deeper problem about taking a particular image as representing a range of different things (different friends or cats). The trouble is that the idea (if it is like a picture) will presumably have its own determinate properties. A picture of a cat is a picture of a certain sort of cat—a big black male one, say, with a chewed ear. This picture certainly resembles, we might allow, cats of that particular sort. But what of all the others—the dainty white females and all the rest? One reply is to say that, obviously, we can just choose to make a picture *serve* as a representative of a range of things, that is understand it in this way, as when a road sign depicts Everycar with a certain black outline. And this is true: we can understand *all sorts of things* to represent others (including words, remember). But this point is quite out of place here. For the whole idea of introducing images was to say what sort of thing it is for a mind to give life to inert things like words. The elucidation offered rests on the allegedly primitive and unproblematic sense in which a picture depicts something: 'cat' means cats thanks to the alleged fact that images of cats depict them. But this last idea, we are seeing, is problematic: how does a picture of a specific sort of cat depict cats in general? And to reply that we can make it *serve* in this role adds precisely nothing to the alleged explanation: we could have said as much, for instance, about the word 'cat' itself! This point is especially clear if one thinks of ideas, not as images in the mind, but as real physical pictures of such things as cats. Given the previous point that pictures have their own determinate representational properties which do not necessarily match those of all the things they are supposed to represent, we might say that such physical pictures are surely just as 'dead' and 'inert' as any word, and need the magic touch of the mind to bring them alive. But how does one add the magic simply by *placing the pictures inside the mind*? This suggests that our capacity to understand *pictures and images* is no clearer than our capacity to understand *words*, so that trying to elucidate the latter in terms of the former is pointless.

Another reply to the above difficulty about the determinate cat-picture would be to say that the images in question would be a bit sketchy, containing only enough detail to indicate that they are images of cats rather than, say, pine martens. Now it is not obvious that this suggestion would work even in the present sort of case: is there in fact, even for each kind of animal, a picture that contains *just* enough detail to rule out all other sorts of animal, yet remain sketchy enough not to exclude any of the appropriate sort? One is tempted here to think of caricatures and cartoons. But note now that the more stylized a picture becomes, the less plausible it is to say that it 'obviously' or unproblematically or intrinsically depicts the things it does, and the more plausible it is to think of it as being *made to serve* as a depiction—and this thought, we have just seen, is illegitimate in the present context. Furthermore, this resort to sketchiness seems to make little sense in some other cases. What would a sketchy picture of a *triangle* look like? If it had three straight sides which enclosed a space it would be a determinate triangle-picture after all. If it lacked any of these features why call it a picture of a triangle rather than a picture of the arrangement of lines it would actually be? Again, one could *treat* such an irregular shape as a representative of triangles: but the point at issue just now is how we manage to treat *anything* as a representative of something else, and in particular how we manage to make one thing represent a whole lot of things which differ in certain respects.

Things get even worse. Do even sketchy, cartoon-like pictures really have *any* unproblematic or intrinsic resemblance to things they depict? Wittgenstein's example (Fig. 4) suggests, perhaps, not. Is it a picture of a man walking up a hill, or a man sliding back down, or what? The answer is surely: it depends—for instance on the intentions and purposes of those who might produce and use the picture. Given these, the picture could *serve* as either of these things: without them, the matter remains indeterminate, and this suggests that the picture itself has no, or anyway not enough, intrinsic representational power of its own. It is true that *we* should find it

F<small>IG</small>. 4

most natural to take the picture in the first way, as of a man climbing up a hill. But is this a fact (wholly) about the picture or a fact (at least partly) about us? Well, consider a tribe who spend most of the day landing by parachute on hilltops and then sliding down backwards on a slurry of tinned lager and dead flies. These folk would find it quite natural to take the picture in the opposite way, and I sympathize. Their customs, even if they seem rather strange to some of us, are in fact no stranger than those of many visitors to the Alps, and it is anyway wrong to accuse the members of this tribe of wantonly misreading or misusing the picture in question. If so, this is surely because the picture does not itself fully determine what it represents, but has to be *interpreted* or 'taken' one way or another. Neither will it help to imagine that more details could be added in order to make it plainer which way the above picture should be 'taken'. If we add words, for example 'Man climbing a hill', then we should have gone in a circle, since the original idea was to explain the meanings of words in terms of the powers of pictures! And if we add, say, an arrow pointing upwards, then this only relocates the original problem. Can we not imagine a tribe of 'macho archers' who from time immemorial have fired arrows backwards (as we would say) in order to make their sport more difficult? In such a culture, it would be perfectly natural to take the picture of an arrow in the opposite way from the way we do. And again, although there may be a sense in which 'macho archery' is a perverse misuse of a wonderful instrument, the same cannot be said, *given this practice*, of the consequent use of the arrow symbol. On the contrary: *anything else* would be perverse (see W<small>ITTGENSTEIN</small> (1953) §139).

It is a contentious point, which I shall not pursue, whether it makes sense to say that pictures have *any* intrinsic representational powers of their own. All we need for the present argument is the milder claim that pictures, at least those sketchy enough to have a hope of surviving the arguments of the last paragraph but two, can legitimately be understood in more than one way. Given that this is indeed the case, this shows that the core to the original problem about understanding and meaning remains unanswered.

If all of this is on the right lines, then the proposal enshrined in Fig. 3 is broken-backed. The original idea, recall, was to elucidate how we understand words to mean things. If we are referred to the fact that we understand pictures to mean things, this hardly looks like progress unless the way that pictures mean things is itself unproblematic. Thus, the claim that pictures have primitive or intrinsic powers of representation is absolutely indispensable to the theory under discussion, and once it is undermined, the theory collapses.

So far our attention has been on general words like 'cat', rather than on Candidates, which are more central to our concerns. This is reasonable enough: if, as seems obvious, the notion that the meanings of general words are ideas or mental pictures is just hopeless, then it is highly doubtful that the same type of proposal will work for Candidates. But it is illuminating to look more closely at the matter. In the case of descriptions, indeed, the matter is straightforward. Whether or not a quantificational treatment is proposed, the fact remains that a description 'the G' itself contains general words, and its meaning is in some sense to be explained as deriving in part from their meanings. So the hopelessness carries over straightaway. If the ideational theory cannot cope with 'G ...', it cannot cope with 'the G'. Natural names and demonstratives may be slightly different. Of course, in so far as these too are to be treated as descriptions in line with Russell's Official View (§ 24), the original point holds. But what if, as seems obligatory (§ 25), this Russellian line is rejected? The suggestion which springs to mind is simply that the meaning of, say, 'London' will just be an image or mental picture of London, which enables the word to mean the city by being a true or accurate likeness thereof, presumably built up by the mind in virtue of its contacts with the city. But then the objections spring up. What if one has no such image, whilst happily using the word nevertheless? Why should the picture unambiguously resemble London, especially in that majority of cases where there has been no direct contact at all? Pictures in books and magazines of one large modern city tend to look like those of any other. These objections, indeed, mirror some of Kripke's objections to description treatments which will be discussed in chapter 8: for instance, the claim that an individual's description may not 'fit' the actual bearer, and the claim that an individual may anyway associate *no* (non-trivial) description with a name (see § 74). And this is not at all surprising: once one thinks of the meaning of a name as a picture it is a relatively small step to the idea that a description of what is depicted could serve to give expression to this meaning; and this is rather like embracing a description theory of names. Thus one may suspect that one further motivation for description theories of names has been provided by the ideational theory of meaning which we have been discussing. And by the same token, the inadequacy of this theory hardly enhances the prospects for description theories.

To return to the main theme. In view of the objections pressed in the present section, our traditional theorists may well back off from the claim that ideas are picture-like images. For the problems illustrated above all make play with this identification. But an idea, our traditional theorists may now say, is really a completely different kind of mental item, more like what we should call a *concept*. And isn't it indeed true that we talk almost indifferently of the ideas or concepts which people associate with words, and take this to be the sort of thing that underwrites their understanding? No doubt this is so. For example, we say such things as '*X* has now acquired the concept horse: she at last has some idea of what they are, so at least knows what you mean when you tell her to fetch one.' But what, after all, *are* concepts, and how do they see to it that words can mean things? They are certainly not images, as we have been seeing. But then this question becomes acutely embarrassing for the philosopher who concentrates exclusively on the first-person perspective. If our understanding of words is constituted by the presence in our minds of these items, and if the first-person perspective is employed, we ought to be able to turn them up on introspection. Try it. Speaking for myself, I am aware of nothing of the sort (I'm not even sure what it would be like to introspect a concept, although of course I *have* plenty of them). Experience has taught me that I am not alone in failing to turn up the requisite thing, so it seems that the latest suggestion is in trouble.

Is the problem here due to concentrating on the first-person perspective, or to the obscurity of 'concept'? I think the answer is 'both'. We saw that Frege sharply distinguished *Sinne* from ideas and other similar objects of consciousness, and instead thought of them as abstract entities of some sort (§ 46). In this way he thought the objectivity of logic and the possibility of communication were secured. But however objective a *Sinn* may be on this kind of approach, the *Sinne* need to be 'grasped' by minds if they are to characterize the understanding. And what sort of thing is this 'grasping'? On the first-person approach, it will have to be something that goes on before the mind's eye: some mental act or aspect of experience or whatever. But, again, see if you can catch yourself attending to abstract entities that you 'grasp' and which thereby somehow invest your words with meaning . . . As I suspect you will now appreciate, this just is not a very promising line of approach.

However, the problem here is more than a mere extra problem for the first-person theorist. Talk of what it is to grasp meanings must chime, so to speak, with the psychological facts as they present themselves to us: as we remarked in §48, meaning is a phenomeno-logical notion, so that any account of it must at the same time be an account of our experience and knowledge of it. But the idea that we are literally interacting with abstract eternal *Sinne*, which inform our minds with understanding and our words with meaning, is clearly a total fantasy: understanding, we know, is nothing like that! Thus we shall see that, although it is useful and legitimate to speak of Thoughts, and *Sinne* generally, as if they were objective entities (i.e. to 'reify' them), this is a manner of speaking with little or no elucidatory value, and must it be backed up by a more concrete conception of what it is for us to understand language as meaningful. In short, talk of *having* ideas or *grasping* concepts is systematically misinterpreted, not only by the first-person approach—although the point is especially easy to isolate here—but also by *any* approach which tries literally to treat understanding as a sort of intercourse with certain kinds of entities. Such reifying talk is in need of elucidation. However, appealing to introspection is just no help: casting about in the consciousness to see what *really* goes on when a concept is grasped turns up a blank, and no progress whatsoever has been made on the question of what sort of thing understanding is, of what goes on when the understanding mind invests words with meaning.

Only one course seems open: switch perspectives.

50 BEHAVIOUR AND UNDERSTANDING

It immediately comes as something of a release to look at these matters from a third-person perspective. Wittgenstein said that 'if we had to name anything which is the life of the sign, we should have to say that it was its *use*' (*The Blue Book*, p. 4). This can be made to mean all sorts of things, but, interpreting it as innocently as possible, we end up with something of a platitude. To be able to understand a language is standardly to be in possession of a complex web of practical skills and abilities. This includes much more than having the ability to blurt out complex strings of sound which appear as words. In the first place, utterances are supposed to be appropriate to the context in which speakers find themselves. What counts as 'appropriate' varies according to the context and the purposes at hand, but in standard simple cases of making reports about the local arrangements of observable material objects, 'fit' is all-important. If a word means cats then its presence in such a report is only fully appropriate if there is, indeed a cat in the offing. An inappropriate use in the presence of a good dummy is excusable enough: the absence of this sort of thing brings problems. At the limit, persistent lack of fit between the use of the word and the comings and goings of cats just undermines the idea that a speaker understands the word to mean cats. This is only a small part of the story, of course. For instance, a normal understander of language is also required to be sensitive to the promptings of others. Other things being equal, the order 'Get me a cat' ought to be followed by a suitable dispatch, and ideally a cat or an excuse should be produced. Again, at the limit, persistent failure to deliver the goods undermines the claim that the recipient understand the word to mean cats.

Naturally, these quick remarks require a formidable array of qualifications. Perhaps we can make sense of the notions of behaviourally inert classifiers of the passing show, of dumb and passive understanders of all that goes on, of perverse total liars and utter disobeyers. What is more, not all words mean, or pick out, *things* (recall the ifs and sos of the previous section), and many of those which do do not mean observable things ('electron') or things observed by all apparently competent understanders ('Julius Caesar': see §§79, 83). But the basic point remains. Standard and central exercises of understanding minds are found in the complex pattern of events involving uses of linguistic tokens by agents, and the agents' responses to and actions upon their environment. Roughly, the meaning of a word is to be gleaned from its role in the pattern of life followed by its user(s). This is where the phenomenon of understanding is to be found. To underline the contrast with the ideational view, we may say that although the mind is indeed active in bestowing meaning on words, the nature of the activity is more like riding a bicycle, or operating a chainsaw, than entertaining an image or paying attention to any other sort of mental item. Words are instruments, not inert labels: understanding involves *using* the instrument, not associating it with a piece of mental furniture.

Given this third-person view of the matter, to come upon the phenomenon of understanding is part and parcel of coming upon things whose behaviour, etc. is complex enough for them to be considered as possessors of a psychology, whatever that in fact amounts to. We distinguish, perhaps not very sharply, or even completely consistently, between things like sticks and stones, which do not think or reason or appreciate their surroundings, and others, like human beings and (perhaps) dogs, which do. The last example, though controversial, indicates that the capacity to use and understand language is not obviously an essential part of having a mind. But the very fact of the controversy is to a large extent due to the lack of linguistic ability on the part of dogs and similar animals. So while it is indeed controversial whether the capacity to understand language is *essential* to mind, it is not to be denied that it is a central component of obvious standard cases. We ourselves are the best examples we know of things with minds, and it cannot be denied that a crucial core of our psychological mode of being is constituted by our linguistic ability. Given this, one would *expect* to encounter the phenomenon of understanding at the same level at which other mental phenomena are encountered: and from the third-person perspective, this is in behaviour seen as such.

51 THE INTENTIONAL STANCE

The 'seen as such' in the last sentence is meant to pick up the following idea. In the normal course of things, to consider the career of something as an example of mindful activity is to classify the relevant goings-on partly in terms of a specific and distinctive net of concepts and classifications. Thus we speak of the thing's noticings, choices, intentions, decisions, beliefs, desires, and so forth. In short, we classify it with the notions of Intentional psychology (§§ 45–6). This is in marked contrast to the way in which the careers of mindless things such as stones are described. A stone may move and be the agent of all sorts of modifications in its surroundings, but when we speak soberly and literally of these things we do not employ the sorts of Intentional classification just mentioned, and we speak instead of forces and other physical mechanisms, within and without the stone itself, wreaking their blind and mindless effects.

This distinction between two radically different ways of describing and classifying phenomena is the distinction, to use some jargon, between the *Intentional stance*, which is what we characteristically employ when describing and classifying something with the help of the psychological vocabulary mentioned above, and the *physical stance*, which is the one taken towards such things as stones. Adopting the Intentional stance towards one another is the heart of our normal interpersonal manner of interacting, and it provides the framework within which our life together takes place and makes sense. We just do see ourselves and each other as choosers, believers, desirers, and all the rest. To say that we 'see' each other in this way is, partly, to say that these are the terms in which we make sense of, that is see pattern and intelligibility in, one another's doings. To take a simple example: if a woman suddenly springs up and leaves the room, this occurrence may be rendered understandable, and in some manner explained, by a description of the affair according to which she noticed a noise in another room and decided to go and investigate. Given such an account of the matter, we see why things happened the way they did: the woman's movements make sense to us. This sort of Intentional explanation, or way of rendering intelligible or understandable, is in evident contrast to what would be appropriate in the case of a stone which suddenly rolls away across the floor and out of the door. To understand what happens here, we should seek a physical explanation, couched explicitly in terms of sufficient antecedent forces and so on, and would not take ourselves to know why things happened as they did unless we found one. Talk of the stone deciding to take a roll outside would not be acceptable.[7]

We have said that the understanding of language is typically to be found in competent linguistic behaviour, in correct uses of linguistic expressions and appropriate responses to those of others. Because this involves linguistic *behaviour*, the phenomenon of understanding falls under the general purview of the Intentional stance. That is, seeing a woman as an understander of her words is itself part of the larger enterprise of understanding her and her doings in the Intentional way. 'She understands "cat" to mean cats' is itself an Intentional description, something that, in appropriate circumstances, could render some of her doings intelligible (for example, her production of certain noises; her responses to shouts of 'cat!'; her general interactions with cats). Thus, if we had to say where the phenomena of meaning and understanding are known in their most familiar form, we should reply that they are to be found all around us, at the same level at which we appear to each other as Intentional beings, beings to be understood and made sense of as believers, reasoners, etc. In this sense there is nothing hidden or mysterious about understanding and meaning—we confront them all the time in our normal activities. (This is not to deny, of course, that it may be mysterious how beings could be the way we simply are.)

Notice that adopting the Intentional stance towards our woman seems to involve understanding her in (apparently) two different senses. Thus, as we have just seen, we could understand her production of certain noises by viewing her as one who uses 'cat' to mean cats: but at the same time, *we* thereby understand those noises themselves as meaning cats (in her mouth at least). The distinction to be observed then is between understanding *her* (as an Intentional agent), and understanding *her words* (as meaning, for example, cats). But the things distinguished are intimately related. As already noted, central cases of things with minds, that is things towards which it is appropriate to take the Intentional stance, will be things with language. And the plain fact is that language normally plays such a dominant role in the behaviour of a subject which has it that there will be little headway to be made in rendering this behaviour intelligible (from the Intentional point of view) unless the language which the subject uses can be interpreted. For instance, attributions of beliefs, desires, intentions, etc. will often only be possible when our subject's linguistic expressions of these states of mind can be interpreted. So, understanding *her* will involve understanding her *words* (in her way). Thus, if an Intentional subject has language at all, *one will understand her fully only if one understands her words*. To this extent, as I said, the two senses of 'understand' are intimately related.

Indeed, one can say more. If she has language at all, understanding her (as an Intentional subject) involves seeing her as an understander (of her own words) and it involves understanding her words (in her way) oneself. But *this* is to say that the goal of an Intentional understanding of a subject with a language is to make communication, linguistic interaction, possible. For if both she and ourselves understand her words to have the same meanings, then only physical disabilities or taciturnity can stand in the way of at least elementary communication. Mutual understanding (of words and doings) is the supreme end of Intentionality. Or, in other words, in coming to a full

Intentional understanding of a subject with language one comes to replicate or reproduce, *in one's own mind*, the thoughts expressed by the subject in her utterances. To understand Intentionally is to 'think in sympathy'. This point, to which we shall return in §58, is of crucial importance to a proper appreciation of the notion of meaning.

52 MEANING-FACTS

Let us call the facts about individuals which make their production of and responses to noises correctly interpretable as meaningful uses of language, and thus as exercises of understanding, *meaning-facts*. Then one crucially important point here is that meaning-facts, as normally encountered, are 'open to view': meaning-facts, that is, are directly available to be apprehended by appropriately situated and equipped Intentional observers. To say this is to say more than that understanding is exercised in such observable things as interactions with the environment at large. Such interactions are available to be observed by anyone, even someone incapable of interpreting the words used. The further point is that those capable of interpreting the words used will themselves understand the words, take them as loaded with meaning as they are produced. This is evident from the observation above that the Intentional understanding (of a thing with language) will itself require one to understand the language used, so that mutual communication should at least be possible. In communication, the experience of meaning is standardly direct: one does not normally consciously apprehend another's words and go on to decipher them (nor are there usually any problems about finding words for what one wants to say). On the contrary, it is the meaning in the words which is apprehended directly. This is a special case of a more general phenomenon at the Intentional level. Standardly, one does not as it were observe the brute movements of a subject and go on consciously to decipher them as a certain kind of action (although this can happen, of course). What one does in standard cases is to apprehend movements straight off as actions, and often one is quite at a loss to produce a less 'loaded' account of what went on. So, for instance, one could see a woman as, say, *signing a cheque*, and whilst this no doubt would involve her in all sorts of arm, hand, eye, and other movements, one would not normally be able to describe these in any more informative a way than as, collectively, constituting the signing of a cheque (compare §§63–4). In this sense, Intentional facts generally and meaning-facts in particular are utterly familiar: they suffuse our normal waking experience, and our conscious lives are largely constituted by a fabric of them. This is exactly as things should come out, given, as we have said, that meaning is a phenomenological notion.

This point in turn has important repercussions for our enterprise of making specific proposals about the meaning of this or that sort of expression. In one way, because meaning-facts are utterly familiar in the way just described, specific meaning-theoretic proposals should themselves be quite unmysterious, and should make reference to facts about the use of words which, at least once made explicit, seem almost trivial. Or, to put the point less contentiously, such a level of description should at least be possible (it is then, as we shall see, a matter for argument whether anything more analytical or explanatory is possible, desirable, or obligatory: see §§ 61–5). The immediate reality of our lives as self-conscious, reflective beings is largely constituted by the meaning-facts we generate and encounter as users of language and understanders of such users, and just because this is conscious mental activity, reflection on it ought to be capable of unearthing features of it which are familiar, or at least recognizable as features of the conscious life we live.

These observations about the openness to view of meaning-facts may serve to dispel a residual unease that some may have felt at the shift from the first- to the third-person perspective. As we remarked in § 48, part of the initial plausibility of first-person accounts resides precisely in their concentration of the conscious aspects of understanding, since this is clearly one way of trying to capture the fact that meaning, as a phenomenological notion, must in some sense be an object of consciousness, at least in the sense that it is part of the 'life of the mind' as we encounter it. Correlatively, it may have been felt that this point was lost sight of in the switch to a third-person perspective: does this not direct attention away from the life of the mind and towards blank, merely physical, movement? However, the implied criticism is mistaken. We must distinguish a narrow sense of 'consciousness', in which the (perhaps mythical) immediate arena of an individual point of view is intended, and a somewhat broader sense where the focus is on phenomena as they present themselves to minds in general. As we said above, it is behaviour, *seen as such*, that constitutes the true phenomenon of understanding. Here 'seen as such' means: as apprehended by the Intentional understander. Behaviour so apprehended is, as it were, illuminated by Intentional understanding, absorbed into the conscious realm of familiar things as seen from the Intentional vantage-point. Thus, one must also distinguish two senses of 'behaviour': the narrow or physical sense in which it applies merely to bodily movements seen as such, and the wide or Intentional sense in which it is seen as 'loaded' with significance and purpose, as in the cheque-signing case. This, second way is how we practically always see our *own* behaviour—including, of course, linguistic behaviour—and it is also how we all normally see one another's.

53 LOCATING MEANING

We wanted to say something about mind and meaning. This brought us to the question: What sort of thing is it for a thinker to understand a linguistic expression? (§47). We went on to discuss the traditional ideational view, which attempts to answer this question in the context of an exclusively first-person perspective on minds (§48). According to this approach, understanding involves associating an idea (an item present to attention) with the expression in question. Despite its initial promise, not least in respect of the fact that it treats meaning as a phenomenological notion, this view was found to be severely flawed, and the first-person perspective unhelpful (§49). So we switched to the third-person perspective (§50). That section produced this short answer to our question: typical understanding involves being able to use the linguistic expression in the course of engaging in appropriate interactions with others and the environment. In more detail: to be an understander of a word is to be a species of Intentional agent, one whose behaviour (involving the word and otherwise) can potentially be (and, standardly, actually is) correctly described and made sense of in terms of attributions of mental states like beliefs, desires, intentions, and so on (§51). Normally (if not always) this will involve being a member of a community of similar Intentional agents who share and act upon the environment (and each other), and communicate in open mutual Intentional understanding. Typically, if not essentially, to understand is to share an Intentional form of life with other understanders (§52).

Now this can hardly be *wrong*: aren't these precisely the settings in which we know at first hand the phenomenon of words being understood? Certainly the description rings much more truly of our common general experience of what understanding words is like than does the first-person account of § 48. So I suggest that the only sensible criticism can be that our answer does not go deep enough; that we want a more informative account of the notions of understanding and meaning than this phenomenological approach gives.

Some such critical thought as this dominates modern approaches to meaning. In turning their backs (not always for the best reasons) on the ideational conception of meaning, philosophers soon came to realize that the correct focus for an account of meaning was linguistic behaviour (again, not always for the best reasons). Hence it has become customary to employ the metaphor of the Radical Translator or Interpreter, that is someone who, innocent of anterior understanding, sets out to recover the essential meaning-facts of a Tribe by observing the characteristic comings and goings of its members. The thought is that by reflecting on the procedures and problems of such a Translator, we should come to see the kind of thing that meaning is: for precisely what happens as the Radical Translator moves from the situation of uncomprehending outsider to that of an understander of the natives' words, is that their meaning becomes manifest. But it is then a smallish step to the realization that this procedure means seeing the behaviour in a more or less Intentional way, as produced by the beliefs, etc. that drive behaviour generally, and in particular the linguistic behaviour at the focus of the enquiry. But then the trouble starts. For various reasons, philosophers have been and continue to be suspicious of Intentionality: either because the Intentional locutions make trouble for the well-understood basic Fregean logic (compare chapter 2); or because the philosophers are behaviourists (in the 'narrow' sense mentioned in the previous section); or because the methods or classifications of Intentional psychology are 'unscientific'; or because its notions are said to need a 'materialistically acceptable' analysis. What often results is a search for some suitably respectable substitute for meaning—some notion that will either explain meaning in terms acceptable to the philosopher concerned, or perhaps do the explanatory psychological job (near enough) that meaning seems to do, but in what is alleged to be a philosophically more respectable framework. At the limit, the idea that meaning has to be explicated or defined exercises such a grip that it is undertaken for its own sake, with Intentional locutions being fetched back in for the purpose. Such is the stuff of much modern philosophy of meaning—and most of it, I should say, is completely wrong-headed. Unfortunately, however, it will not be possible to demonstrate this here, and I shall

have to content myself, in chapter 6, with a fairly detailed consideration of just one—extremely influential—'scientific' approach to
meaning.

Thinking about meaning is desperately difficult—all the more so, it
seems to me, because insufficient attention is paid to the question:
How does meaning enter the picture in the first place? This is the
question that the present chapter has tried to answer, and it has done
so by ultimately locating meaning in the Intentional point of view.
The background sketched out in the foregoing sections may well
seem vague, or obscure, or mysterious: and it is certainly very
incomplete. But my hope is that there is enough both to ring fairly
true and to show what sort of thing philosophers set themselves to
theorize about—and eliminate or replace—when they turn to the
matter of meaning.

It will be helpful at this point to see how these Intentional
ruminations fit in with the general sketch of Fregean *Sinn* given at
the beginning of this chapter.

54 *SINN* AGAIN

Sinn, for Frege, is to be co-ordinate with understanding and
communication, and an account of the *Sinn* of a specific word is to
be an account of how the *Bedeutung* of the word is presented to
minds and of how this makes it appropriate for thinking involving
the word to respect the semantics determined by the *Bedeutung*.
Bedeutungen, for Frege, are extralinguistic entities, so *Sinn* is to
mediate the relationship between minds and their extralinguistic
world. This ties in with the third-person elucidation of understanding in the following obvious way. According to this elucidation, to
understand a word is to be able to use it in the course of one's general
dealings with the environment (including those features of it which
are fellow speakers), and specifically with those bits of the environment which the word means (i.e. cats where the word is 'cat'). But this
embraces communication (in so far as other speakers are involved)
and the Fregean *Bedeutungen* of the words concerned. So it seems
fruitful and permissible, to say the least, to embed specific doctrines
about *Sinn* in one's more general Intentional account of those who
'grasp' it. That is, to say in more detail what sort of thing it is for
speakers to have certain *Bedeutungen* 'presented' to them will be to
focus on certain interactions between these speakers and the extralinguistic entities in question. More specifically, it will be to focus on

those interactions which inform the Intentional view we can gain of these speakers as subjects (a) who have beliefs, desires, intentions, and so on with respect to the 'presented' entities; (b) who communicate with us about those and other things; and (c) whose reasoning with the word in question (if it is to be rational) must be sensitive to what is laid down by the theory of *Bedeutung* (among other things), which theory itself invokes the presented things themselves. On this approach, we treat *Sinn* as an (Intentional) psychological phenomenon: to see uses of words as having *Sinn* is to see those uses from the point of view of an Intentional understanding of the behaviour and functioning of which they form a part.

We have a clutch of semantic issues left over from the earlier chapters, and have already seen that their resolution turns on what is said about meaning. And we have now put meaning in context, and outlined some of the roles it is supposed to play. In so doing we have also put the semantics in context. The context is Intentional psychology, and it is with reference to this that the outstanding issues will be tackled.

Further Reading

Frege's chief works on *Sinn* are 'On Sense and Reference', which can be found in *Translations From the Philosophical Writings of Gottlob Frege*, ed. P. T. Geach and M. Black (Oxford, 1960), and 'The Thought: A Logical Enquiry', trans. A. and M. Quinton; *Mind*, 65 (1956), repr. in P. F. Strawson (ed.), *Philosophical Logic* (Oxford, 1967). See also Frege's *The Basic Laws of Arithmetic*, trs. M. Furth (Berkeley and Los Angeles, 1964), pp. 12–25, and his *Posthumous Writings*, tr. P. Long and R. White with the assistance of R. Hargreaves (Oxford, 1979), pp. 2–8, 126–51, 191–6.

For discussion of Frege's notion see M. Dummett, *Frege: Philosophy of Language* (London, 1973), chaps. 5, 6, 11, 17, and M. Dummett, *The Interpretation of Frege's Philosophy* (London, 1981), chaps. 3, 5. See also G. Evans, *The Varieties of Reference*, ed. J. McDowell (Oxford, 1982), chap. 1.

For the 'ideational' theory of meaning see J. Locke, *An Essay Concerning Human Understanding*, ed. J. Yolton, vol. ii (New York, 1961), Bk. iii, chaps. 1–4. The view is discussed in I. Hacking, *Why Does Language Matter to Philosophy?* (Cambridge, 1975), Pt. A. Wittgenstein attacks the view trenchantly in *The Blue and Brown Books* (Oxford, 1958), pp. 1–45. See also S. Blackburn, *Spreading the Word* (Oxford, 1984), chap. 2.

For the notion of Intentional stance see D. C. Dennett, *The Intentional Stance* (Cambridge, Mass. 1987). The approach to meaning defended in §§ 50–4 is generally influenced by L. Wittgenstein, *Philosophical Investigations*, tr. G. E. M. Anscombe (Oxford, 1953), esp. Pt. ii, and D. Davidson,

Essays on Actions and Events (Oxford, 1980), Essay 12, and D. Davidson, *Inquiries into Truth and Interpretation* (Oxford, 1984), Essay 10. For the idea of 'thinking in sympathy' see W. V. Quine, *Word and Object* (Cambridge, Mass., 1960), pp. 218–19, and also G. McCulloch, 'Scientism, Mind, and Meaning', Pt. II, in *Subject, Thought, and Context*, ed. P. Pettit and J. McDowell (Oxford, 1986), and J. Heal, 'Replication and Functionalism', in *Language, Mind and Logic*, ed. J. Butterfield (Cambridge, 1986).

Philosophical work on meaning has been very heavily influenced, and distorted, by Quine's destructive attacks, most of which are based on the (correct) claim that meaning cannot be given a scientifically respectable explication. See especially: 'Two Dogmas of Empiricism', in W. V. Quine *From a Logical Point of View* (Cambridge, Mass., 1953), and chaps. 2 and 6 of W. V. Quine, *Word and Object* (Cambridge, Mass., 1960), where the idea of the Radical Translator (§ 53) is introduced. For a careful treatment of the question whether meaning is somehow unacceptable because it cannot be given a respectable scientific explication, see G. Macdonald and P. Pettit *Semantics and Social Science* (London, 1981), esp. chaps. 1, 2. For the idea of defining meaning in terms of intensional locutions (§ 53) see M. Davies, *Meaning, Quantification and Modality* (London, 1980), chap. 1.

The criticism of Frege's account of the existential quantifier mentioned in § 42 n. 3 is to be found in C. Chastain, 'Reference and Context', in *Language, Mind and Knowledge*, ed. K. Gundeison (Minnesota, 1975).

NOTES

1. Even terminology is an irritating problem. Frege used '*Bedeutung*', the ordinary German for 'meaning', in a somewhat technical sense when presenting his mature views. Consequently, it has been usual to translate it as 'reference' (sometimes '*nominatum*', sometimes 'designation'). '*Sinn*' is usually then translated as 'sense'. However, there is now a tendency to translate '*Bedeutung*' as 'meaning' (perhaps with a capital 'M'), for example, so as not to prejudice questions about *how* technical Frege's usage was. However, this is singularly unfortunate, since 'meaning' has come to be used by philosophers writing in English as more or less interchangeable with 'sense' (although sometimes the latter term is reserved for its specifically Fregean connotations). So there is now a growing source of potential confusion, 'meaning' being used to allude to *both* terms of Frege's crucial distinction! Given that the distinction is anyway so controversial as to have spawned any number of different technical locutions (see § 6, n. 7), more chaos is likely to ensue than even this most difficult of areas should produce. I shall try to avoid trouble by using the German words when speaking of Frege's doctrines, and I shall always use 'meaning' in the traditional way, that is to cover matters which for Frege belong to the realm of *Sinn*. Elsewhere, I am as guilty as anyone

of allowing locutions to proliferate. My excuse is that no other course seems possible: my hope is that context will ease the burden.

2. In what follows I always use 'information' in a broad sense, to cover 'misinformation' too. On this usage, both 'Mick Jagger is a man' and 'Mick Jagger is not a man' are pieces of information: although, of course, only the first is *correct*.

3. It is helpful to bear in mind here that Frege's idea that a Proper Name *stands for* an object has a similar technical edge. For, of course, in ordinary talk, we should say that definite descriptions stand for objects, or even that 'a dog' sometimes stands for a dog (namely the one which prompts an utterance of 'there's a dog coming towards us: its name is "Entwhistle"'). But the first fact cannot, by itself, refute Russell's claim that descriptions are not Proper Names (i.e. do not have objects as semantic values): and the second fact, similarly, cannot by itself undermine the Fregean idea that quantifiers do not stand for objects, but instead stand for second-level functions. In the first place, our ordinary talk of meaning, reference, etc. is loose and largely untheoretical. And in the second place, to the extent that it is theoretical, it might be wrong—like any other theory. For good examples of bad arguments against Frege on quantifiers like the one above, see CHASTAIN (1975). See also, for the related phenomenon where descriptions are concerned, §§ 68–70 below.

4. He was principally concerned to account for the reasoning used in mathematics: although his examples clearly indicate an interest in scientific reasoning in general, and others, notably QUINE (1960) have stressed the adequacy of Fregean extensional ideas for such purposes.

5. The reader may wonder why this third point is made in terms of 'objectivity': does not psychology at least intend to be an objective study of the mind? Part of the problem here is a certain confusion on Frege's part: when he speaks of ideas and *Sinne* he tends to speak of them as objects, and then, since images are thus 'subjective' (belong to the consciousness of the individual subject), whereas *Sinne* are supposed to be 'objective' (communicable), he tends to relegate ideas to the 'merely subjective or psychological'. However, this could be cleared up by a more careful use of the type/token distinction, as deployed in the present section. Could there not then be an objective psychological study of the different *types* of ideas, even if it is to be distinguished from logic? A further problem here is that many people, including many psychologists, subscribe to an extremely unsatisfactory conception of ideas, etc., even construed as types, according to which they are 'inside the mind (or head)', therefore not available for public observation, and therefore not the business of objective science. Frege definitely held this view (see, for example, 'The Thought'): and he was not atypical of his time. Such a view of the mind is almost bound to lead scientists to some form of behaviourism: as indeed it did at the beginning of the present century.

6. Although there are arguments, of course, which try to show that because I cannot know another's mind from the first-person perspective, I cannot know another's mind at all (concerns in this area go under the heading 'The Other Minds Problem'). Such matters will not delay us in the present book: for an exposition see CARRUTHERS (1986), Pt. I.

7. Note that it is not being denied that one could similarly take the physical stance towards the woman, and explain her movements in terms appropriate to a stone. The point is only that this would be a very different type of explanatory enterprise to embark upon. See chap. 6, §65 for more on this sort of point.

6

Demonstratives: The Elements of Externalism

55 DEMONSTRATIVES

Now that we have the Intentional background in place we are in a position to consider properly proposals to treat the Candidates—natural names, descriptions, demonstratives—as Proper Names. I shall proceed as follows. Starting with the demonstratives themselves— expressions like 'this', 'that', 'he', 'she', etc., as used to speak of observable objects in the immediate environment—I shall set out to explain and defend what seems to me the most natural way to develop a Proper-Name account of these expressions which harmonizes, as we have seen it should, with the Intentional point of view. And the main critical responses against which this attempt will be tested are complaints based on the observation that Proper-Name treatments generally fall foul of the Basic Problem. In the present chapter the sharpest claws of these complaints will be drawn: although others will remain to be confronted in the following two chapters, which concern descriptions and natural names respectively.

The discussion of demonstratives, along with the corresponding consideration of the Basic Problem, falls naturally into two parts. In the first (§§56–60), I describe what will be called the FS ('Frege– Strawson') treatment of demonstratives which, as a Proper-Name treatment, confronts the Basic Problem. And we shall see how the FS theorist might try to argue that the Basic Problem is no problem at all (§58). But after further amplification of the FS treatment, we proceed to the second part of the discussion, where the Basic Problem rears its head once more, this time in a form which most contemporary philosophers seem to find irresistible (§61). The remainder of the chapter is then devoted to showing how and why it should be resisted.

56 SIGNIFICANCE

In chapter 3 we noted Strawson's claim that in giving a Proper-Name account one should distinguish different kinds of meaning possessed by expressions and sentences containing them. For example, one might distinguish between the *significance* of the English sentence:

(1) That is a horse,

and the *statements*, assessible for truth or falsity, which may or may not be made by different uses of that sentence. Thus someone might use (1) when speaking of Red Rum, and thereby make a true statement about the Grand National hero, whilst someone else might use the same sentence and make a false statement, say about a seaside donkey. Our first task in the defence of Proper-Name treatments is to show how well this sort of claim fits in with our common-sense ideas about the use of demonstratives.[1]

One picks up the significance of linguistic expressions in the course of general training in the use of language. Part of what is learned here is the fact that 'that' (as it stands alone in sentences like (1)) is a sort of reusable device of a non-specific kind, which can be used to pick out salient objects of any type (although it is not polite to use it of persons). This acquired knowledge meshes with general competence in predication (the use of phrases like '... is a horse') and yields the further knowledge that a sentence like (1) is itself a non-specific reusable device, capable of being used to say indefinitely many different things. Of course, the learning of a language (especially a first language) is a cloudy and complex affair. Somehow, out of a total immersion in a form of life, driven by unlearned tendencies and bolstered by explicit training and correction, the normal learner eventually emerges as a competent speaker. Such things as can be said about the processes involved here are the business of, for instance, developmental psychology. But our interest is with the final product of the learning process: namely, the Intentional state of being of the competent language-user as described in the last chapter. As Strawson puts it, those in this state act as if they have imbibed, when learning the meaning of the demonstrative 'that', '*general directions* for the use of the expression to *refer to* or *mention* particular things' (see OR, p. 9; compare § 30). The suggestion here is not that speakers could generally state explicitly what these directions are, nor is it even that all speakers are aware that they have in fact picked up 'general directions': although it is a moot point how ignorant of such things an otherwise competent speaker could remain after careful reflection. The suggestion, rather, is that we, as somewhat detached observers of native speakers, can classify the activities of using the expression as activities which conform to these general directions.

The key notion involved in the Strawsonian 'general directions' is that of *referring to* an object, or picking it out as a subject of possible discourse. Now, as we have already mentioned (§42 n. 3), one must be careful with notions like 'referring to an object': although we do have a natural or pre-theoretical idea of this, and although this natural idea has some correspondence with the key notion of Proper-Name treatments, it is a mistake to read too much into this correspondence without more ado (§11). So it will be instructive at this point to consider the natural idea at more length, to see to what extent it corresponds with what a Proper-Name treatment of demonstratives would have to say.

Where demonstratives are concerned, reference to material objects is obviously bound up with psychological notions like perceiving, noticing, paying attention to, and so on. These are 'face-to-face' relations which can hold between speakers and objects in their vicinity, and it is clear that one or more of them will usually hold (or have held) between a speaker and an object when the former refers to the latter with a demonstrative. More than this, it is difficult to imagine creatures with language who could stand in the face-to-face relations with objects but who lacked all capacity for making, or at least learning to make, demonstrative reference to them. Moreover, it is equally hard to imagine creatures capable of using demonstratives to pick out material objects but who could not stand in 'face-to-face' perceptual relations, of one sort or another, with those very objects. However, one must not overstate the extent to which demonstrative reference and face-to-face relations are linked together. In the first place, it is possible to bring off deferential or 'assisted' reference, as when someone at the other end of the telephone mentions a troublesome cat, and you say 'that animal ought to be castrated'. Here reference is surely accomplished, thanks to the assistance of the other speaker, even though you may never have stood to the cat in any of the psychological relations mentioned. As we shall see (§§79, 83), assisted reference is a rather difficult notion, but to the extent that it occurs, it transcends direct links between demonstrative reference and our 'face-to-face' psychological notions. Again, one's very position in space can perhaps assist a reference, as when, blindfolded, one points to where there happens to be a man and says 'I'll go with that one'. Still, in dealing with demonstratives we are concerned in the first instance with the most direct psychological relations imaginable between speakers and the material world, and the use of these expressions is part of our most intimate cognitive contact with our material surroundings. We just are (or are associated with or whatever) physical objects of a certain size, and we move and live among, and take immediate notice of, other objects of a comparable order of magnitude. In a sense, this sort of thing is basic with respect to all our other doings and knowings about the world at large. Arguably, we cannot bring anything at all to pass unless we act on something within reach: similarly, we get to know about remote parts on the basis of our concrete interactions with what is relatively local—books, other people, clouds on the horizon. To this extent we exist in a vicinity of consciousness and awareness, a 'cognitive field' populated by given objects, and demonstrative reference is a basic feature of this fundamental aspect of our Intentional existence (compare Russell on acquaintance, § 24; and also § 58 below).

Consequently, it is plausible to suggest that assisted reference and similar phenomena are parasitic on basic face-to-face encounters, which initiate 'chains' of co-referential uses of demonstratives and other expressions. Either one's assistor stands in such a relation to the object concerned, or further assistance is provided by someone who . . . stands in an appropriate face-to-face relation to the object (for further discussion of this see §§ 78–9). The case involving the blindfold is an evident exception: but then this sort of case is subsidiary or parasitic in a different way. Making demonstrative reference is a prelude to or component of one's general round of interactions, including the gathering and spreading of knowledge and information, with items in the more-or-less immediate environment. And such a round of activity cannot even get off the ground unless the item(s) concerned can be perceived or otherwise kept track of. So unless, in a case like that involving the blindfold, one is in a position either to remove it or be assisted by someone not similarly fettered, the act of reference will necessarily remain isolated and without further upshot. It is clear that nothing very useful is to be learned about mind or language from staring, howsoever hard, at such cases.

I have said that face-to-face encounters and associated acts of demonstrative reference concern objects in one's 'vicinity'. This is a nice vague word (its technical synonym is 'context'). As far as *space* is concerned, your vicinity is an area allotted to you for some given purpose, usually with you located somewhere near the centre. Limits will depend (at least up to a point) on purpose. From the point of view of a police enquiry into a burglary, the vicinity within which suspicious persons may relevantly have been seen lurking is a few streets. In international politics, a vicinity can be a chunk of continent, an ocean, or even more if you have airbases abroad. Relative to the use of demonstratives, however, vicinity is initially circumscribed precisely by the range of the cognitive abilities which are involved with the face-to-face uses, and it is then extended in various ways. That is, perceiving, noticing, and paying attention to objects requires them to be 'in range'. What this involves will vary according to the object's size, the condition and type of the perceptual apparatus and medium, the nature of the terrain, and so on for quite a bit. But some grip on what is involved can be achieved by thinking about how you normally interact with and think about the things around you. The range of physical interactions is initially limited by motor abilities. Perception tends to extend further than such abilities, although they can then be supplemented by the use of transport or rifles (for example). The range of perception too may be extended by things like telescopes and information networks involving telephone, radio, and television—although it is contentious to what extent one can perceive through such networks. Assisted reference, and background knowledge about the environment, based on earlier perceptions and other sources, can also supplement one's powers of interchange with it, and (in some cases) enable one to refer. But here we shade off into issues involving the use of natural names and other devices, which will concern us in chapters 7 and 8.

Normally one refers demonstratively to things with the express purpose of communicating something to someone else who will also usually be present in the vicinity. When the intention succeeds this is usually because the hearer also notices or whatever the thing referred to (we come back to whether this is either a necessary or sufficient condition in §§61–4). Implicated too here is the Intentional recognition by the hearer of the speaker as one with an intention to direct attention, get across a message, and so on. In making such an intention clear, various devices may be pressed into service: for instance, speakers can point at referred-to objects, or indicate them in some related physical way—sometimes just by looking at them. They can also use semantic devices, and supplement a demonstrative with other words to narrow down the possibilities. Thus someone may say 'That *animal over there* is a horse', relying on such things as the fact that only one animal is over there, or anyway salient enough in that region to be the natural focus of attention. There are also more subtle clues, such as relevance to the previous topics of conversation, and the expectation that one's hearers will be charitable. If we have been discussing the comings and goings of frogs, and I say 'That one arrived yesterday', then (other things being equal), you should take me to be making a relevant remark in the situation, and thus referring to a salient frog rather than a nearby letter. Again, if we are confronted in ideal viewing conditions by a cat and a bulldozer, I might say 'That is a tom', meaning, of course, the cat. But perhaps nothing in my gestures and orientation or in the previous discourse gives a clue as to which of the two I refer to. Still, charity dictates that I be seen as trying to say something sensible, and it is not sensible to call a bulldozer a tom in the conditions mentioned: so an intended reference to the cat would normally be communicated.

Notice that there is room here for divergence between what the speaker intends to say, and what the hearer picks up. At least where demonstrative utterances are concerned, the speaker's intention is normally paramount, in a fairly strong sense, because of the reusable nature of the expressions. For their semantic contribution is not fixed once and for all, but is left open from use to use: and it is the initiator of a reference chain who in this way sets up the rules of the game. But intentions to refer can be misconstrued, and the hearer(s) may fasten on to the wrong object. Perhaps in the example mentioned above the relevance clues were particularly weak, and you (understandably but wrongly) took me to be speaking of the letter rather than the frog. In such a case it is certainly misleading to say either that I referred to the letter whilst intending to refer to the frog, or that something about the letter was (erroneously) communicated (see § 69 below). However, from that point on, the letter may be in the game, and stay there. You repeat your version of what was said, you try to act on what you thought I meant and throw the letter into a stagnant pond, and so on. In this sort of way, the authority of the original speaker can be subverted. As we shall see in chapters 7 and 8, such facts as these are of some importance to theories of descriptions and natural names. Indeed, many of the matters touched on briefly in the present section will be taken up again as we investigate in more detail the idea of referring with Proper Names.

What we have been describing are the sorts of things that we learn to engage in when we learn how to use, that is learn the significance of, demonstratives. The foregoing platitudes are the result of reflection on what is involved, from the Intentional standpoint, in having learned to use and understand those expressions. These are some of the relevant meaning-facts: to be able to do such things, and to be capable of appreciating (to some extent, after reflection) that this is what one can do, are what learning the significance of demonstratives is all about. And nothing we have said so far is in any way incompatible with a Proper-Name treatment of demonstratives: on the contrary, if anything.

57 STATEMENT AND THOUGHT

Continuing the Strawsonian theme, we should say that learning the significance of a demonstrative equips one with the ability to make statements with it (assuming, of course, that other linguistic abilities are already in place). Statements, recall, are what concern logic, because it is these which are assessed for truth or falsity (§§ 27, 29). Now, according to Strawson, under either of the two interpretations carried forward from § 29, one needs an object to make a logically relevant statement with a sentence containing a demonstrative, and the semantic or logical nature of the resulting statement depends upon the identity of the object referred to. Thus a use of our sentence

(1) That is a horse,

where 'that' refers to Red Rum, will make a (true) statement about that very animal. Had another object been referred to—say the seaside donkey again—a different (false) statement would have been made; and had no object been referred to, then there would be no statement at all: or at least, no statement of any logical relevance would have been made, and the utterance would be 'written off' from the point of view of logic. Call any account of demonstratives which makes these claims *Strawsonian*. A Strawsonian account has it that when a demonstrative is used one *must* refer to an object if a statement with a truth-value is to be produced. In effect, Strawsonian accounts add a doctrine about statements to the ordinary Proper-Name view, perhaps in accordance with the idea, discussed in chapter 5, that a bearer of logical properties, a statement or meaning, or whatever, is to be involved in the relationship between the Fregean semantics and the use of the language. So let us suppose that anyone who wishes to defend a Proper-Name account of demonstratives will incorporate the *Strawsonian ingredients*: (i) the object (if any) referred to by a use of a demonstrative is essential to the logical or semantic nature of the resulting statement (if any), in the sense that (ii) uses of sentences containing failed demonstratives do not issue in statements that determine a semantic value.

This Strawsonian proposal is obviously somewhat similar to that of Frege, to the extent (a) that uses of sentences containing failed Candidates are assigned no semantic value (except for purely formal purposes—see § 30), and (b) that some further aspect of meaning is said to be involved in the production of semantic value. One difference is that Strawson speaks of *statements made*, whereas Frege speaks in terms of *Thought expressed*. But given a little straining, the two ways of speaking can be identified. As we shall see in the second part of this chapter, the strain involved is quite significant: Frege held that a sentence containing a failed Candidate might still express a Thought even though it would be assigned no semantic value, whereas one interpretation of the Strawsonian ingredient involves the claim that *no* statement would be made in such circumstances.[2] But the issues raised here, which are linked to the Basic Problem, are extremely vexed and controversial, and it will actually help if we try for the time being to force the main Strawsonian and Fregean proposals into the same mould. This will squeeze out, in an illuminating way, some of the more crucial issues that the embedding of semantics in Intentional psychology raises: issues that are at the centre of a hot contemporary debate.

Initially, indeed, it is not at all difficult to identify Fregean Thoughts and Strawsonian statements, at least where the use of demonstratives is concerned: on the contrary, there are at least four apparently good reasons for doing just that. First, although Frege himself actually said rather little about demonstratives, one of the things he did say was that understanding uses of sentences containing them requires 'knowledge of certain accompanying conditions of utterance, which are used as means of expressing the [Thought]', since this knowledge is needed for the Thought's 'correct apprehension' ('The Thought', p. 24). This is certainly *compatible* with saying that one needs to invoke the object referred to in order to character-ize, or 'apprehend correctly', the Thought expressed: after all, the object itself is one of the 'accompanying conditions'. And this in turn is at least compatible with saying that any Thought expressed where there is a lack of an appropriate object to invoke will be logically improper (for much more on this see §§ 58–9).

Second, Thoughts and statements are similar in that they are the things assessible for truth or falsity, i.e. both function as that which determines truth-value. Third, Frege identified Thought expressed with the *information carried* by the use of the appropriate sentence: and it seems right to say that pieces of information (and misinformation: see §42, n. 2) belong to the realm of statement, rather than, say, to that of significance. For, considered merely as a reusable linguistic token, sentence (1) conveys no information in itself. It is about no aspect of the world: for example, it is not assessible for truth or falsity, so the question whether it conveys *mis*information evidently cannot arise. On the other hand, one could certainly convey *two* pieces of information with two successive uses of the one sentence, speaking truly of Red Rum then falsely of that seaside donkey. Here we should have two applications of *one* unit of significance—that of (1)—but *two* pieces of information: and it so happens that we have two statements also. Fourth, there is perhaps room within the Strawsonian approach for an interpretation of the Fregean idea that the Thought should contain the 'manner of presentation' of the object (§43). For, in using (1) to make the statement about Red Rum, one is evidently referring to the horse in a certain way, *as* (for instance) a salient feature of the immediate vicinity, and so in this sense the statement presents the horse in a certain manner—which is to be contrasted, for example, with the manner in which it would be presented by the phrase 'that murky shape behind the bushes'. Reflection on the significance of 'that' might then furnish insight into the sort(s) of manners in which an object can be presented when picked out with 'that' (for more on this see §60).

On the strength of these four reasons, then, let us try to effect the identification of Fregean Thought and Strawsonian statement, and speak of the statement made/Thought expressed by a use of a declarative sentence. What we arrive at is a Proper-Name treatment of demonstratives ('the FS treatment') that seeks, as it should, to harmonize with the Intentional notion of meaning. The FS treatment captures the flavour of the Fregean semantics, forges a link with the relevant notion of information, and attempts to locate the treatment within an Intentional framework by suggesting a way in which the metaphor of manner of presentation might be cashed out by appeal to the notion of significance. The next three sections will be devoted to spelling out some of the implications of the FS treatment.[3]

58 DEMONSTRATIVES:
THE BASIC PROBLEM BANISHED

Many readers will no doubt already have noticed one glaring feature of the FS treatment: it encounters the Basic Problem. For the treatment implies that there will be no logically relevant statement made/Thought expressed by a use of a sentence which contains a failed demonstrative. In other words, uses of such sentences will be viewed by the FS theorist as involving some serious linguistic malfunction (see §§ 29–30). Imagine this sort of case. Someone is in unknown, difficult terrain. Like Richard III, she is anxious to find a horse to save her kingdom. Her anxiety makes her hypersensitive— so much so that she imagines a clip-clopping behind her and swings round, exclaiming as she does so

(1) That is a horse

—and refers to nothing. Would she have given expression to a logically relevant statement or Thought, that is said anything true or false? Our FS theorists says 'no' on both counts. Can this be acceptable?

The issue here, of course, is essentially that which divided Russell and Strawson in the disagreement discussed in chapter 3. That disagreement was specifically about descriptions, but we noted that it could be applied to the case of natural names and demonstratives (which Strawson, indeed, explicitly considered), and it is this last application that concerns us here. Initially, the Russellian point in the present case would be that the utterance of (1) should be given the semantic value F, rather than neither T nor F, as Strawson recommended. However, we saw that little progress is to be made if the debate is conducted on this ground: we need to see why it matters whether F is assigned or withheld. This, we saw at length, in turn involves enquiring into whether the utterance would make a semantically relevant statement: and we shelved the discussion at that point precisely because we had no clear idea about statements or what they might *be* or *do*. Chapter 5 was intended to fill this gap, first by outlining Frege's theory of *Sinn*, and then by locating the notion in Intentional psychology. So we ought to be able to press the results of that chapter into service now, and use them to answer the question, Would the utterance of (1) in the imaginary circumstances above make a statement/express a Thought with logical relevance?

As we saw in chapter 5, we give expression to our Intentional understanding of individuals by the ascription to them of sayings, beliefs, desires, and similar psychological states or actions, using reports of the form, say, 'X believes/said that P', where 'P' is to convey the content or substance of the ascribed Intentional state or act. If the FS treatment is to be accepted, then, its proponents must say that their notion of statement made/Thought expressed is the appropriate kind of content to be ascribed in such reports. So to see how the FS treatment might cope with the above example, and hence the Basic Problem, let us first consider what is involved in reporting the saying of someone who has *successfully* picked out an object with a use of sentence (1), and see how the FS treatment can accommodate *this*.

Of this subject we could say:

(2) She said that that is a horse.

Sentence (2) as a whole begins with a demonstrative ('she'), and so (according to the FS treatment) a use of it (the whole of (2)) could only itself make a statement/express a Thought of logical relevance if an appropriate person were around to be referred to by 'she'. Similarly, one could only normally manage to get this report across to a hearer capable of picking out the appropriate woman. But what are we to say of the second occurrence of 'that'? To get a grip on this, imagine that the situation is as follows: the subject (S) of the report has used (1) twice: once to speak of Red Rum, and once to speak of you-know-what. Which of these sayings would be ascribed by a use of (2) in which 'she' refers to S?

It seems clear that there is *no answer* to this question given just the present information: a use of (2) could surely serve to ascribe *either* saying, depending on other matters. What other matters, exactly? Well, suppose that Red Rum is present before the Reporter (R), and R picks out Red Rum with the second occurrence of 'that'. Assuming that all other expressions are used with the same meaning as they had in S's mouth, R would surely here have ascribed to S her original saying about Red Rum, and not the other one about our seaside donkey. To see this, imagine R using (2) whilst trying to obey the order 'Tell us one of the true things S said', rather than the order 'Tell us one of the false things S said'. So we can say as a first shot that to succeed in reporting a given saying originally made with the help of a demonstrative use of 'that', it at least *suffices* (other things being equal) to use a report in which 'that' occurs and picks out the object referred to in the original saying (this claim will be modified somewhat in §60).

So far so good: these evident facts about how we should report demonstrative sayings are clearly in line with the FS treatment. But given the FS conception of statements made/Thoughts expressed with the use of demonstratives, according to which the object referred to is essential to a statement/Thought's logical or semantic identity, we shall plainly have to go further, and claim that ascriptions of the sayings considered above *necessarily* involve a reference to or invocation of the relevant object. For how otherwise could the report be a report in which we ascribe *that very statement/Thought*, which itself concerns the object, rather than some other? We can, of course, make 'oblique' or non-committal reports of sayings originally brought off by uses of (1) without referring to the relevant objects: for example, we might say 'She said something', or 'She said something apparently about a horse', etc. But normally when we are concerned to provide Intentional descriptions of someone we are interested in ascriptions which are much more specific than this. Indeed, this is a general point about the enterprise of describing states of affairs, and is not something that is confined to Intentional psychology alone. Thus someone might survey the passing scene, itself devoid of Intentional subjects, and say, 'Something is taking place', or 'An object is interacting with another one', and succeed in speaking truly. But for most purposes such idle descriptions are useless, and our need is for much more specific information: *what* is taking place; *which* objects are interacting; and *how*? Something similar holds for Intentional descriptions: to the (very large) extent that we are interested in acquiring a detailed Intentional understanding of others, we need to know the precise nature of their sayings and doings. If we are told that someone *said something*, our characteristic response is: said *what*? At the limit, such questions are requests for the import, or substance, of the speaker's words—that is, according to the FS theory, they are requests for the very statements made/Thoughts expressed. But since, according to this theory, the logical or semantic identity of a statement made/Thought expressed by a use of (1) will turn on the identity of the object referred to in the making of that statement/expression of that Thought, it follows that it will be *necessary* to invoke this object if a precise specification of the original saying is to be given in a report like (2).

With these points in mind, then, let us return to the case of our hypersensitive speaker who used (1) but failed to refer to an object.

Because of the reference failure, the FS theorist will say that there was no logically relevant statement made/Thought expressed by this utterance, and that, therefore, in this sense, there will be no saying to report with a use of (2). However, this theorist can still agree that the original subject did, in a sense, *say something*: in the sense, that is, of uttering a perfectly grammatical and significant English sentence. Indeed, one could go further, and say that the following report would be true of her:

(3) She said, 'that is a horse'.

One could also, of course, given the appropriate circumstances, say many other things about her: for example, that she thought she heard a horse behind her, that she at least *tried* to make a statement/express a Thought about a horse, and so on (see § 61). Need anything more be said about the situation?

For at least two reasons, the FS answer 'no' is perfectly acceptable. In the first place, there is the link between information and statements/Thoughts. Frege intended the *Sinn* of a sentence to be the information content it carried: furthermore, as we saw in § 57, the idea of information expressed seems to belong at the level of statements (because, for example, the notion of *mis*information seems to require that of falsity, which itself is assigned to statements made). Would the imagined use of 'That is a horse' convey any information? It would seem not: since the utterance is not about anything, there is nothing for it to be information about. Furthermore, what possible use could the alleged piece of information be? Normally one wants information to do such things as help with manipulations of and other interactions with the environment. Now certainly, as already remarked, all sorts of information could be gleaned *from the fact that an utterance occurred* (i.e. from the fact that (3) is true). Knowing the facts of the situation, or failing this, just given that the speaker is generally honest, one would gather that she thought a horse was in the offing. Given, furthermore, her general reliability as a gatherer of information, those ignorant of the full facts of the situation might claim to have evidence that a horse indeed was in the offing. But *this* is all information to be gleaned from the fact that (3) is true, and so it is no embarrassment to the FS theorist, who of course admits as much. The further question then at issue is whether there is any *extra* information, expressed by the original utterance of 'that is a horse', which the FS theory cannot accommodate. And it seems that there is no such information.

In the second place, imagine trying to report accurately the alleged substance of the saying. The most straightforward way would be to try:

(2) She said that that is a horse.

But there are evident difficulties here. Certainly the ordinary sort of procedure described above, in which one would tie down the original saying by referring with the second occurrence of 'that' in (2) to the object referred to in the original utterance, would not be possible. *Ex hypothesi*, there is no such object, since our hypersensitive subject was imagining things. Yet standing alone, and without a context in which the second 'that' picks out an object, (2) is just mysterious: an appropriate response would be 'Said *what* is a horse?'—and there would be no point whatsoever in scanning the surrounding countryside to try to come up with an answer. So (2) itself would be no use, and the FS theorist—who maintains as much—is still avoiding difficulty.

One immediately thinks of looking for some *other* way of reporting accurately the alleged substance of the saying: for example, a report of the form:

She said that . . . is a horse,

where the replacements for the dots would not induce the puzzlement that would attend a use of (2). And this is very close indeed to asking for a paraphrase or restatement of the original utterance 'That is a horse', which does not depend for its semantic nature on the existence of an appropriate object: precisely the sort of thing that we saw Russell trying to provide in § 17 with his theory of descriptions. Given a Fregean semantics, only Proper Names and quantifiers can occupy the gap in '. . . is a horse'. In the present sort of case, where there is no appropriate object, the FS Proper-Name treatment of 'that' delivers no proper statement, no semantically active unit. So a quantifier treatment is proposed instead: as Russell might say, we need a description 'the so and so' to replace 'that', and need to offer a quantificational account of this description.

Now, in a sense, nothing could be easier to provide. Certainly in the vast majority of cases, the speaker will be so situated, and her hearers will be sufficiently aware of these relevant facts that it would be a simple matter to come up with a suitable description. For example, one can imagine such tricky things as 'the thing she thought she heard behind her', or 'the source of the (apparent) noise that caused her to turn', etc. Such descriptions could then easily be slotted into the context '... is a horse', and the resulting sentence given a quantificational paraphrase in one of the ways described in §17. Given this, one could then also produce some such report as:

(4) She said that the thing she (thought she) heard behind her is a horse,

with the description construed quantificationally.

However, it is implausible to claim that this sort of Russellian move accords with normal Intentional practice. In the first place, although one certainly *might*, in recounting the story of our hallucinating subject, use something like (4): '... and then she said that the thing she thought she heard behind her was a horse, and then she swung round'—it would be odd to do so. Such a report naturally invites the question 'What was it—the thing she thought she heard behind her?', and so is, to that extent, misleading: the recounter of the episode would at this point have to backtrack, and (if able to) explain the situation more fully. Furthermore, consider the reactions of such observers there may have been of the original episode. As we shall see in §60, the direct observers of demonstrative sayings are in the best possible position to gain a full and accurate Intentional understanding of what is going on. But it is hard to see why such observers would *need* to provide a Russellian paraphrase of the unhappy saying. Certainly they would have enough grasp of the situation to pinpoint the speaker and her surroundings accurately enough to implement the Russellian proposal in practice: they would, for example, be able to view her as one object situated among others to which they can straightforwardly refer. In the absence of this, it is doubtful whether they could even begin to proceed as reporters of a saying in that context—how could they, if they could neither locate the speaker nor form an opinion of what sort of interaction with her environment prompted her utterance? But if they can do all of this, they certainly know all the relevant facts of the situation, and will know how unfortunate the saying was. So what use would they have for a Russellian paraphrase? As we have already seen, there is no interesting sense in which a piece of information would be lost to them. The knowledge that our speaker believed a horse to be in the offing, and the fact that this may furnish evidence that there is indeed a horse nearby, would in no way be enhanced by the ingenious production of a quantificational saying.

So why bother? Given our present view of things, it seems that there is *just nothing to be gained* by going in for the obsessive *ad hoc* production of Russellian paraphrases of sentences involving failed demonstratives, and we seem none the poorer without them: there is as yet no evident theoretical need to posit a logically relevant statement or Thought when reference fails. Indeed, it seems that we can now go further. Given that such unhappy utterances neither give expression to a useful piece of information, nor reveal facts about the speaker which somehow cannot be accommodated by the FS theorist, there seems to be no obstacle to doing away with the caginess inherent in the phrase 'logically relevant statement or Thought'. For, apart from the sort of facts reportable by some such sentence as:

(3) She said, 'that is a horse',

there seems to be *nothing* relevant about the original unhappy utterance. So let us try to have done with the matter, and say straight out, from now on, that *no* statement/Thought is produced by an utterance of a sentence containing a failed demonstrative. For it is now very unclear what possible use there could be for the idea of the logically enervated sort of statement/Thought, lacking a truth-value, for which we have so far striven to leave room (for more on this see §§61–5).

In any case, the Basic Problem, at least where demonstratives are concerned, seems now to be no problem at all, and so cannot be considered an objection to the FS treatment. We shall therefore consider it banished for the time being: although it will return to torment us in §61.

59 GENUINE SINGULAR THOUGHTS: EXTERNALISM

So far, the Proper-Name approach to demonstratives, in the guise of the FS treatment, has held up pretty well: it can accommodate the facts evidently involved in the ability to use demonstratives (§56), and seems also to tally with normal practices of giving expression to our Intentional understanding of users of demonstratives (§58). If, however, the account is to be taken seriously, it needs to be spelled out in more detail: and the task of this section and the following one is to do just this. First, we shall see at greater length what sort of philosophy of mind it implies: the discussion here will refer back to the third-person conception outlined in chapter 5. And second, we need to see how, if at all, the account can accommodate the sorts of intensional facts described in §§ 20 and 46, which Russell at least took to be incompatible with Proper-Name treatments of Candidates.

In identifying the Fregean notion of Thought with the Strawsonian notion of statement in the above manner, proponents of the FS theory commit themselves to the doctrine of *genuine singular Thoughts*. There are different versions of the doctrine, but what they all have in common is the following: there are Thoughts, i.e. logically relevant contents of sayings and other psychological attitudes, which *essentially* concern or contain the object which would be referred to by the thinker of the Thought in giving an accurate expression of it. In other words, the doctrine is that such a Thought only exists, as something to be entertained or asserted or whatever, *if the object exists*, so that *thinking a genuine singular Thought about a* will be like, say, *sleeping with a*: neither is possible unless *a* exists.[4]

This doctrine about Thoughts is in turn a special case of a more general doctrine about the mind: *externalism*. According to the externalist, at least some states of mind—typically those like seeing, hearing, noticing, etc., which are bound up with the capacity for demonstrative thinking and uttering—are essentially relational or world-involving, in that as we know them to be, they require their subjects to stand in psychologically relevant relations to items contained in their environment. On the face of it, externalism is the appropriate doctrine to hold of a great deal of our Intentional, or mental, life. For example, actions are typically described in terms of more or less of their causal upshot. Not only do we speak of each other as doing such things as going to *London*, riding *a bicycle*, eating *a cake*, and so forth, but we also categorize actions according to whether or not they have a certain type of outcome: one can only be described as having *killed* someone if they (eventually) die as a result of one's intentional interactions, more or less direct, with their body. Again, one is only said to remember doing so and so (as opposed to *seeming to remember*) if one did, in fact, do so and so: and one is only said to see a cow if there is, indeed, a cow that one sees. And there are other well-known examples: for instance, it is often claimed that one can only have Thoughts about natural substances like water, or types of thing like cats, if one is appropriately related to examples of the substance or of the type of thing—so that inhabitants of worlds without water or cats typically just cannot have Thoughts about these things (see PUTNAM (1975), chap. 12;

PETTIT and McDOWELL (1986), Introd.) In what follows, however, we shall restrict attention to externalism in so far as it bears on the treatment of the Candidates, and thus incorporates the doctrine of genuine singular Thoughts.

Opposed to externalism about the mind is *internalism*: the doctrine that mental states, properly so-called (or 'purely mental' states) are not essentially relational or world-involving, but instead have an 'intrinsic' nature of their own which is not dependent on relations that may hold between the thinker and the 'external' world. The most famous and influential internalist is Descartes, who claimed that the 'contents of his mind'—his thoughts, beliefs, experiences, and so on, which apparently disclosed to him a world of physical objects—did not in fact require the existence of this world in order to be the thoughts, etc. that they were, but might instead, for all their essential nature required, be 'pure' thoughts, etc. induced in him by a malignant demon, the sole other inhabitant of the Universe. This sort of internalist stance is still extremely common, and we shall have to confront arguments based on it in §§61–5. As with externalism, however, we shall largely restrict attention to aspects of internalism which bear on the topic of the Candidates.[5]

The internalist view of the mind is, of course, closely related to the typically Cartesian adoption of the first-person stance discussed— and rejected in so far as it bore on the topic of understanding—in chapter 5. Not surprisingly, then, the externalist view is closely related to the third-person stance preferred in that chapter. Indeed, one may be tempted to suppose that the two oppositions—first-person v. third-person, and internalist v. externalist—amount practically to the same thing: for example, in so far as mental phenomena are best approached by way of the Intentional stance, which as we saw is a third-person view of thinkers and agents as interactors with their embedding environment, it might seem that externalism is obligatory. Ultimately, we shall see that this thought is correct; unfortunately, we shall also see that the matter is by no means simple or straightforward.

Nevertheless, some support for externalism may be obtained as follows. As seen from the normal Intentional perspective, a person's mental life is 'interlaced', as it were, with facts, items, and situations of the world at large. If we regard subject S as having killed victim V, then we see S's Intentional, mental career as involving, among other things, certain interactions with V and V's subsequent actual worldly death. Similarly, if we regard S as knowing that Red Rum is a horse, then we relate S to the state of affairs or whatever that consists in Red Rum's being a horse. But of course, things are not always so straightforward: S may falsely believe that Red Rum is a cow, and there is here no corresponding actual state of affairs consisting in Red Rum's being a cow to which S can be related. However, one can appeal here to the background semantics, and the associated notion of information discussed in §§ 42 and 57, which the FS theorist tries to accommodate with the theory of statement/Thoughts. For there is the genuine singular statement/Thought, the piece of (mis)information to the effect that Red Rum is a cow, whose semantic nature (articulated by the theory of *Bedeutung*) determines that it is to be assigned F: and ascribing the false belief to S involves relating S to this statement/Thought, and hence (according to the FS theorist) to Red Rum. More generally, we can consider attempts to do semantics in the manner of Frege as attempts, in part, to describe possible structures of Thought about the world at large. For as we saw in chapter 5, the nature of our mental life is to a large extent determined by the structure and nature of the language that we use: and Frege's semantic theory is an important component of a powerful account of what this structure is. In other words, the idea is that in describing one another's mental life we (among other things) 'tag' each other with pieces of information (or misinformation) about the world: and the FS theory is then part of an account of the logical structure or nature of the pieces of information involved when demonstratives are in play.[6]

Furthermore, in this context, the particular form of the FS treatment, we saw, seems entirely appropriate: in so far as our concern is with the notion of information about the world, and intentions to give expression to items of information about objects supposed to exist in a thinker's vicinity, it is correct to deny that there would be any information, and hence statement/Thought, expressed by a sentence containing a failed demonstrative. To this extent, then, externalism is vindicated: if there just is no information with which to 'tag' the appropriate subject, and that is how we normally characterize a subject's state of mind, why *should* there be a corresponding state of mind to be characterized? Hence the externalist can draw support from two sources: on the one hand, from the fact that, as conceived from the Intentional point of view, our mental lives certainly are world-involving, or interlaced with items, etc. of the world at large; and, on the other, from the fact that the best available approach—the Fregean one—to the characterization of the logical structure of language (and thus states of mind) would treat demonstratives as Proper Names, and hence assign objects to them. To this extent, the onus is very much on those internalists who would oppose the FS treatment to make out their case. As we shall see in §61, there is an allegedly powerful and generally accepted argument, related to the Basic Problem, which is intended to do just this. But we shall also see that it does not work.

60 DEMONSTRATIVE MANNERS OF PRESENTATION

So much, for the time being, for the philosophy of mind presupposed by the FS treatment. I turn now to the elaboration of the second aspect of it mentioned at the beginning of the previous section: its accommodation of the intensional aspects of propositional attitude ascription.

Consider again the case where S has used:

(1) That is a horse

to speak truly of Red Rum. In §58 we saw how plausible it is to join the FS theorist in claiming that it is *necessary* to pick out Red Rum when making an accurate or detailed report of this saying with:

(2) She said that that is a horse.

But before that, we also suggested that, other things being equal, it could be *sufficient* to do this. Putting these two ideas together, we get very close to saying that reporting or specifying a statement/ Thought originally made by way of demonstrative reference to object x amounts merely to restating this statement/Thought, partly by referring to the appropriate object x, in the course of producing a report with a sentence like (2). Or, in other words, we seem to arrive at the conclusion that sentences standing in the gap of true reports like 'S said/believes that ...' serve to express the statement/Thought which they would express if used alone by the subject (S) in a sincere assertive utterance (compare DAVIDSON (1969)).

This view is rather similar to Frege's view, described in §42, that sentences in contexts like 'S said/believes that ...' stand for their *Sinne* (Thought expressed) rather than their (customary) *Bedeutung* (truth-value). However, as we noted at the time, this idea is sorely in need of further development: in particular, we need to say what kinds of entity *Sinne* are if we are to make it work—what *are* statements/Thoughts?

Note that in asking such a question we are not falling into the error of construing thinking as an activity which involves a mysterious sort of interaction between thinkers and abstract entities. For one does not have to take such 'reifying' language literally, but can regard it instead as a useful manner of speaking which helps one make explicit certain complexities of the relevant subject-matter (compare § 49). In this case we reify Thoughts in order to make explicit some of the complexities involved in the activity of thinking about demonstratively available objects. And two things here are straightforward enough. The first is that we must, as Frege himself did, think of statements/Thoughts as *complex* entities, that is, as entities whose nature is determined by their constituent parts, which themselves correspond to the constituents of the sentences which give expression to them. Otherwise it is just mysterious why we can only accurately express and identify statements/Thoughts by using the appropriate sentences. The second is that FS theorists might as well agree that the object referred to by 'that' in an utterance of, say, 'That is a horse' is itself one of the constituents of the resulting statement/Thought. Otherwise it becomes exceedingly obscure how such theorists could continue to maintain that the relevant object is essential to the statement/Thought's nature, in the very strong sense that the statement/Thought could not exist at all if the object did not exist. So let us say that, according to the FS theory, the statement/Thought expressed by a successful use of a sentence containing a demonstrative, such as 'That is a horse', is a complex entity consisting *at least* of (i) the object x referred to by the demonstrative (for example, 'that') and (ii) the *Sinn* of the corresponding first-level functor (for example, '... is a horse').

It will be convenient to list the components of statements/Thoughts in the following way: where U is some utterance of a sentence containing a demonstrative, which is or could appropriately be made by some actual subject in giving expression to a statement/Thought genuinely entertained, we shall write:

$$ST \backslash U = \{\ldots\}$$

('the statement/Thought expressed by $U = \{\ldots\}$'), where the dots in the brace brackets are to be replaced by expressions standing for the components of the statement/Thought in question. Thus, for example, we so far have it that $ST \backslash W$—the statement/Thought which results from S's successful use of 'That is a horse' in speaking of Red Rum in utterance W, is

{Red Rum, the *Sinn* of '. . . is a horse'}.

A different utterance (W^*) of the same sentence, in which, say, Ferdinand the seaside donkey would be referred to, would result in ST\ W^*, the statement/Thought:

{Ferdinand, the *Sinn* of '. . . is a horse'},

which is, as we should want it to be, of course, a different statement/ Thought from ST\ W because it has a different component (Ferdinand instead of Red Rum).

Now, as we saw in chapter 5, Frege argued that merely assigning an object as *Bedeutung* to a Proper Name will not suffice to characterize the Name's *Sinn*, that is, will not serve to specify the expression's contribution to the *Sinne* of complex expressions in which it occurs. Thus, for example, the propositions:

Hesperus is visible now

and

Phosphorus is visible now

differ in the respects discussed in §§ 41–3, even though, if the natural names are treated as Proper Names, these propositions will be identical from the point of view of the theory of *Bedeutung*. Thus, Frege concluded that one must acknowledge that the names have *Sinne*, which would contain the 'manners of presentation' of the relevant planet.

To say this is, of course, compatible with saying that in order to provide a *Sinn* for a Proper Name, one must *also* provide a *Bedeutung*: for the suggestion is merely that in characterizing *Sinn* one must *do more* than merely specify an object; and this leaves room for the idea that one cannot characterize a *Sinn* by *doing less* than specify the object. Thus, it is so far possible for the believer in genuine singular Thoughts, for whom an object referred to by a Proper Name is itself a component of the statement/Thought expressed, to accept Frege's point as stated. What we might suspect, however, is that the *Sinn* of, say, 'that' as used by S to refer to Red Rum in utterance W will not be Red Rum alone, so that the above list of the components of ST\ W, namely:

{Red Rum, the *Sinn* of '. . . is a horse'}

is so far incomplete, and will have to contain an *extra component*, corresponding to the 'something more' which will be added in the characterization of the *Sinn* of the demonstrative.

This suspicion is, furthermore, fairly easy to substantiate by way of examples. For instance: Mercedes arrives at the railway station and sees the two ends of what happens to be one exceptionally long train (The Passengergobbler), whose middle portions are hidden from her by a building. But she does not realize that she sees the two ends of the same train: on the contrary, she has excellent reasons for supposing that what she in fact sees are the protruding ends of *two* trains. For, contrary to the usual practice of the operator, both ends are attached to a locomotive, since—again contrary to usual practice—The Passengergobbler is exceptionally long. What is more, Mercedes knows nothing of the possibility of providing a train with two locomotives, one to pull and the other to push: and it is anyway common for the operator to allow trains going in opposite directions to stand back to back at the same platform. So she justifiably and sincerely expresses herself thus:

> *this train* [pointing at the end nearest her]
> *is not the same train as*
> *that train* [pointing at the other end].

This case is strikingly similar to one in which someone might intelligibly deny that Hesperus is Phosphorus—and, for the same reason: one and the same object is presented in two different manners, in such a way that someone like Mercedes can labour on under the illusion that there are in fact two objects. Hence it is plain that our attributions of statements/Thoughts to Mercedes will have to reflect the fact that, as used by her in the described situation, 'this train' and 'that train', despite in fact referring to the same object, have different *Sinne*. For example, Mercedes would vigorously resist the idea that the utterance displayed above expressed the same statement/Thought as would be expressed in the same circumstances by:

> *This train* [pointing at the end nearest her]
> *is not the same train as*
> *this train* [pointing once more at the end nearest her].

These posited differences in *Sinne* would certainly be borne out by our attempts to understand Mercedes and her doings from the Intentional point of view. For example, she might refuse to walk to the far end of the platform to enter the train, exclaiming as she does so

> No, I don't want to get into that train, I want to get into this train: I want to go to Valladolid, and *this train is going to Valladolid*. According to the (as usual) inaccurate station information-board, *that train is going to Valladolid*. But I know better; it isn't!

In the circumstances, all of this would make perfect sense, and would need to be reflected in the statements/Thoughts which we ascribed to Mercedes in characterizing her state of mind. In particular, we should have to regard Mercedes's two utterances:

> (*U1*) This train is going to Valladolid

and

> (*U2*) That train is going to Valladolid

as expressing different statement/Thoughts. For, as we have just seen, she accepts the claim made in (*U1*), and refuses to accept that made in (*U2*). But given the facts of the situation this is a perfectly sensible thing for her to do, and cannot be assimilated to cases of extreme irrationality in which a person both accepts and refuses to accept one and the same claim. So we have to say that Mercedes here gives expression to two *different* statement/Thoughts, so that

> ST*U1* = {The Passengergobbler, M, the *Sinn* of '. . . is going to Valladolid'}

and

> ST*U2* = {The Passengergobbler, N, the *Sinn* of '. . . is going to Valladolid'},

where M and N are the *two different manners* in which The Passengergobbler is presented to Mercedes.[7]

What might M and N be? Here it is clear that Mercedes thinks of the Passengergobbler as a train—witness the explicit qualification to her demonstratives—and it is almost as clear than whenever *anyone* thinks of a demonstratively available object they will think of it as a particular kind of thing, whether or not any used demonstratives are qualified: although, of course, they may think of the object as being the *wrong* kind of thing. It is thus plausible to suppose that M and N will have some kind of 'conceptual' component, supplied, in this case, by the *Sinn* of '. . . is a train'. However, this cannot in general be all there is to demonstrative manner of presentation, simply because *M* and *N* need to be *different*. Neither is it plausible to suppose that the ways in which Mercedes thinks of The Passengergobbler could be specified by some uniquely identifying description—although, no doubt, she could construct such a description if she wished. Rather, the train just strikes her—twice!—as 'that/this train'. What more is involved here?

One answer available to the FS theorist, which we noted briefly in §57, is that *M* is the significance of 'this train', and *N* is the significance of 'that train', where significance is the sort of meaning had by demonstratives which is picked up in the course of general training in the use of them to pick out objects (see §56). This answer is certainly adequate to the extent that it yields the obligatory result that *M* and *N* be distinct: for whether or not it is possible to say very much in detail about the significance of a particular demonstrative, it is clear enough that 'this' and 'that' as used as demonstratives have different 'shades' of meaning. For example, we learn to use 'this' normally of things which are fairly near to hand, and 'that' of things rather further away. And analogous things can perhaps be said of the correct employment of other demonstratives: 'she' is normally used of females, 'he' of males; 'I' refers to the speaker, 'you' to the person addressed, 'we' (except in the mouths of the imperious) to the speaker together with his or her associates; and so on. Furthermore, as we also noted in §57, this suggestion indeed appears to make some sense of Frege's metaphor of 'manner of presentation': thus we could say that 'you' presents the person who is actually addressed *as the person addressed*, as opposed, say, to 'she', which might on the same occasion present that same person as the relevant, indicated female.

As in cases already considered, it will perhaps be thought that there is some oddity in thinking of the significance of an expression as an entity, which we seem to need to do if we are to say that it is a component of any statement/Thought expressed with a sentence in which it occurs. For although we do speak of people as *learning the significance* of this or that expression, it is unhelpful, as we have seen, to represent such things literally as a kind of interaction between the person concerned and some entity. But again, 'reifying' talk need not be taken literally: we can regard it instead as a useful manner of speaking. In this case, we reify significance in order to make clearer the theory of manner of presentation under consideration. (Subject to this qualification, we can anyway regard significance as a sort of function, which takes a speaker's occasion or context of utterance (for example) as argument, and yields (where reference succeeds) an appropriate object—the one referred to—as value.

This, then—the identification of manner of presentation with significance—is one option which the FS theorists might try, and which is sometimes suggested by philosophers working in this area (see, for example, PERRY (1977), MCGINN (1983)). However, the alert reader may well already have anticipated an apparently devastating objection. What is to stop us changing the Mercedes example slightly, so that instead of $(U1)$, she comes out with

(*U1**)   *That train* [pointing to the end nearest her]
          is going to Valladolid—

i.e. uses 'that train' *twice* to refer to The Passengergobbler? Nothing else about the example need change, so that Mercedes remains, as before, sanely and justifiably convinced that she confronts two trains. But since, in the new example, the significance of 'that' will occur in the Thoughts expressed by both utterances, we shall only have the *one* manner of presentation to work with, and will consequently have to say that the two utterances express the same statement/Thought—i.e. we shall have to say that $ST\backslash U1^* = ST\backslash U2$— and thus be left powerless to distinguish this case from those cases of extreme irrationality in which someone both accepts and refuses to accept one and the same statement!

It will not do to reply that Mercedes would here be guilty of some subtle misuse of one of the demonstrative phrases. It is true that in setting up the original example we conveniently supposed that it would be natural for Mercedes to use 'this train' of what she considered to be the nearest train: but this is a very dispensable feature. First, provided that both ends of The Passengergobbler are sufficiently far away from her, there would be no misuse in using 'that train' twice over. Second, we could anyway imagine that she is equidistant from the two ends, and replace 'the end nearest her' and 'the other end' in the description of the relevant utterances with 'the end to her left' and 'the end to her right', without changing any other essential feature of the situation.

This latest twist in the tale suggests that units of significance are just the wrong sort of thing to serve as manners of presentation, if only because there are not enough of them to go round. And the suggestion is borne out by the following, different sort of case. Pilar also arrives at the station, and in many respects her situation is parallel to that of Mercedes: Pilar also considers herself to be confronted by two trains on account of The Passengergobbler's unusual length, her ignorance of the fact that one train can have two locomotives, and so on. And she expresses herself with the same sentences as used by Mercedes (in the episode as originally described): in particular, she gives sincere expression to one of her beliefs with

(U3)   *This train* [pointing to the end nearest her]
        is going to Valladolid.

Now suppose we ignore the recent objection, and reinstate the idea that manner of presentation is to be explained in terms of significance. This would mean that

$ST \backslash U3 = \{$The Passengergobbler, M, the *Sinn* of '. . . is going to Valladolid'$\}$.

But of course, given the reinstated idea, we also have it that

$ST \backslash U1 = \{$The Passengergobbler, M, the *Sinn* of '. . . is going to Valladolid'$\}-$

and putting together these two equations, we arrive, of course, at the conclusion that:

$ST \backslash U1 = ST \backslash U3$:

that is, we get the result that Mercedes and Pilar, in the described circumstances, express the same statement/Thought with their utterances (U1) and (U3), and so to this extent have the same beliefs about The Passengergobbler.

So far, not so bad, it may seem: why shouldn't they be equivalent in this respect? But I have suppressed a detail. Pilar is blind, and, unlike Mercedes, she does not base her judgements on what she can *see*, but bases them rather on what she can *hear*: for example, she hears the two locomotives ticking over at the two ends of the platform. Now, in one harmless sense of the term, there is no doubt that The Passengergobbler is presented to Pilar in a quite different (type of) manner from that in which it is presented to Mercedes. In the first case we have an aural manner of presentation and in the second we have a visual manner. Just to make this vivid, imagine yourself presented with an item, say a telephone, which you can see, and can also hear ringing. You have here two modes of access to the same thing: two ways, as it were, of apprehending it. Moreover, it is very plausible to go further, and to suppose that these two modes will be involved in different ways in which you will be able to think about the telephone: for example, you may believe, for excellent reasons, that you can hear one telephone, but see another, so that you intelligibly think to yourself 'That phone [ringing] is not the same phone as that phone [visually present]'. Here we have no irrational denial of a truism: we have an intelligible Thought which, in the circumstances, concerns one and the same object, which, therefore, must be presented in two different manners. However, we have the same unit of significance used twice (that of 'that phone'), so *it* cannot serve as the appropriate kind of manner of presentation (compare the case of Mercedes in the modified example). On the other hand, though, we have perfectly good candidates for the job: namely, the particular aural and visual manners in which, in a perfectly ordinary sense, the telephone is presented to you. So why not let *them* be the relevant components of the Thought?

If we take this sort of idea seriously we shall also have to say that The Passengergobbler is presented to Mercedes and Pilar in different manners, and thus deny that $ST\backslash U1 = ST\backslash U3$, i.e. affirm that with their utterances ($U1$) and ($U3$) they respectively express different statements/Thoughts. And, for at least two reasons, this seems the right conclusion to draw. First, our Intentional efforts to understand the two women will be drastically different: knowing that Pilar is blind we should expect very different sorts of responses from her than we should expect in Mercedes's case. For example, if we asked them both to double-check their beliefs that they confronted two trains, we should expect Mercedes, say, to go and look more carefully, and Pilar, say, to run her hands along the carriages: analogous remarks apply if we try to persuade them of their error and they refused to accept anyone's word for it. One natural way of explaining this Intentional difference is to say that they need to falsify *different* statement/Thoughts, that their *different* reactions flow from *different* states of mind: and this is exactly the sort of option made available by the proposal to identify manners of presentation in the way mentioned in the last paragraph. Second, it is arguable that Pilar cannot so much as *understand* what Mercedes thinks about the train: certainly, if she has been blind from birth she just will not know what it is like to have things presented to her in a visual manner, so that there will be some aspect of Mercedes's state of mind—its visual 'quality'—which is inaccessible to Pilar. This is, indeed, just an application of the undeniable and common idea that congenitally blind people just cannot fully understand essentially visual concepts or ways of classifying things, such as those expressed by colour-words. Thus it is eminently sensible to say that Pilar's own thoughts about the train—which she obviously can understand—are different from Mercedes's, which she cannot. (Of course, unless she is congenitally deaf, Mercedes would be able to understand Pilar's thoughts: but this is neither here nor there. If it were, however, I should indeed insist that poor Mercedes is congenitally deaf.)

What we are suggesting, then, is that Frege's somewhat meta-phorical notion of 'manner of presentation' can in fact be interpreted quite literally when demonstrative Thoughts are being considered: for at least in central cases, where as we have seen the use of demonstratives is part and parcel of enjoying face-to-face en-counters with objects, the appropriate objects just are presented to us in certain ways. Note too the contact with Russell's idea that in order to Name objects one must be 'acquainted' with them. This too, as we briefly remarked in § 56, can be taken almost literally when demonstratives are in play. We perceive 'given' things under certain aspects—from this or that visual perspective; as coloured; as noisy; as feeling rough; and so on. Furthermore, as those who concentrate on the first-person perspective are quick to point out, there is no doubt that such perceptual aspects—the ways given things appear to us—'flavour' or condition our thinking, and help to make it the sort of thinking that it is. If there are or could be any creatures which perceived the world in ways very different from the ways in which we do, or which perhaps did not perceive at all, but somehow managed to think 'blindly' about their environment, then one cannot sensibly deny that their minds, their characteristic mode of mental existence, would be drastically different from our own, and we should find them, from the Intentional point of view, strange and alien (see NAGEL (1974) and McCULLOCH (1988c)).

However, although what we are appealing to here is a character-istically first-person phenomenon, this does not imply that we have by now given up the third-person stance outlined in chapter 5, or have in any way compromised the externalism of the FS theorist. For the conception of statement/Thought which results is as externalist as ever: in particular, nothing we have said counts against the FS claim that there can be no statement/Thought expressed by a sentence containing a demonstrative unless the demonstrative refers to an object. All we have said is that such statement/Thoughts have a 'subjective' or first-person component, which consists in the precise way in which the relevant object is presented to the thinker of the statement/Thought as a perceived item. But these 'subjective' aspects need not be thought of as somehow beyond the pale of, that is as inaccessible from the point of view of, the externalist, third-person stance. For there is nothing to stop appropriately situated reporters from taking up the point of view of, say, Mercedes, and having The Passengergobbler presented to them in the same manners as those in which the train is presented to her: such reporters can, for example, stand where Mercedes stood and view the scene as she saw it. (Recall the point made in § 51: unless you can 'think in sympathy' with your Intentional subjects you will not have gained the best possible Intentional understanding of them.)

Now, as we mentioned briefly in § 47, there are sceptical arguments, usually based on exclusively first-person, Cartesian preoccupations, to the effect that one person just cannot know what the 'subjective' aspect of another's state of mind is like—and if these claims could be established that would show that our communal grip on the sort of statement/Thoughts we have been describing would be put at risk. For, although we could stand where Mercedes stands and see the scene which Mercedes saw there would be no guarantee that our 'subjective appreciation' of the scene would be the same as hers: and this would mean in turn that we could not know that we were thinking the same Thoughts about the scene as she herself had thought—for we would not know that we had hold of the right subjective component of Mercedes's original Thought. However, it is not clear who might use this argument as an objection to the form of externalism we have defended. It could hardly be used by a champion of internalism, since according to internalists the entire essential nature of Thought is 'subjective', and so vulnerable to the very same objection. Could it, then, be used by even more thorough-going externalists than our FS theorist, who wanted no truck whatsoever with 'subjective' aspects in their theory of Thought? This is very doubtful. As I have already said, the objection is nourished by Cartesian, and hence internalist, preconceptions: the 'subjective' is thought of as something radically inaccessible, 'inside the mind (or head)' and therefore simply unknowable from a third-person point of view. But how could an argument based on externalism start off from here? On the other hand, the notion of 'subjectivity' which I have offered to the externalist is quite innocent: we do know that scenes strike us, in perception, in certain ways which are flavoured by the perceptual apparatus used and our particular perspective. We also know that many of us share the same type of perceptual apparatus, and can adopt one another's perspectives if we are able and willing to move around. Furthermore, and for this reason, we have little practical difficulty in understanding one another as thinkers of demonstrative Thoughts: we just can, with the right sort of effort and imagination, take up one another's point of view on the perceptually available world, and come to gain the appropriate kind of Intentional understanding of one another. Why should any externalist committed to theorizing about the nature of Thought want to make trouble for these manifestly sensible contentions?

It is true that the sorts of Thoughts envisaged by the above account would be relatively 'inaccessible' to many other thinkers. In the first place, it is a general consequence of genuine singular Thought-doctrines that only those in a position to refer to the target object of the Thought will be able to 'apprehend' that Thought, and so be in a position to gain a full Intentional understanding of the subject. Others will have to make do with less accurate specifications ('she was confronted by a train, which she thought was two trains back to back: so she said "this train is not the same train as that train", referring as she did so to its two ends'). But there is nothing very strange about this: is it not, rather, a fact of Intentional life? However, in the second place, there will be further sources of inaccessibility on the view canvassed above. For even if I can refer to the object to which you refer when giving expression to one of your genuine singular Thoughts, that will not suffice for me also to apprehend that very Thought, and so will not suffice for me to gain the most accurate possible Intentional understanding of you. To do that I should also have to simulate or reproduce for myself the exact manner in which the relevant object was presented to you. But, again, this is no more than one should expect. Unless we are prepared to use our imaginations, and move around, we really shall not be able in general to appreciate the way in which the environment strikes our subject, and so—obviously—will not know to the highest possible degree of accuracy what is going on in the subject's mind. For many ordinary purposes this just does not matter: given that we know which objects are concerned, and that we have a rough idea of how the subject relates to the context, most Intentional purposes will not be subverted. But if we want the full facts, and the best possible Intentional understanding of what is going on: then, of course, we shall have to work for them!

I conclude, then, that there is no reasonable objection, based on suspicion of the 'subjective', to the kinds of manners of presentation which have been described above: and given the other arguments in their favour, I offer them to the reader as the right sort of thing to play the role of demonstrative manners of presentation in a Proper-Name account of the demonstratives. Obviously there is much more to be said about them: but I shall pursue that matter no further here. Rather, I shall at this point turn back to the Basic Problem: for we now have before us the materials necessary to consider the afore-mentioned objection, based on the Problem and considered by many to be irresistible, to the doctrine of genuine singular Thoughts.

61 *DOPPELGÄNGER*:
THE BASIC PROBLEM RETURNS

Helen and Ellen are very much alike. They can be as similar as you please in purely physical terms—atom-for-atom replicas, say—but for some small details. Their environments are very similar too: again, let them be atom-for-atom replicas, except for an important feature. The important feature is a horse (Cowdell). Helen's immediate environment contains Cowdell, Ellen's lacks him (and every other horse or similar object). The situations are much as described in §58. Each needs a horse to save her kingdom; each is hyper-sensitive; each seems to hear a clip-clopping behind; each consequently swings round exclaiming 'That is a horse'. But remember the difference. In Helen's case she really does hear Cowdell, despite her hypersensitivity, and so really does refer to him as she swings round. However, Ellen is not so lucky. The small physical quirk that distinguishes her from Helen happens to make her imagine a sound just like that which Cowdell produced behind Helen. But there is no horse or any other source of the imagined sound behind Ellen. As she swings round she refers to nothing.

According to the FS account of demonstratives Helen expresses a statement/Thought (about Cowdell), but Ellen expresses none. Given the links we have made out between meaning and Intentional psychology this means that while we can ascribe a certain Thought to Helen, for example in the course of explaining her reaction in swinging round and exclaiming, we shall not be able to proceed in this way with Ellen: for instance, there will be no appropriate belief or similar state of mind attributable to Ellen whose content is expressed by her use of the sentence 'That is a horse'. And, from a consideration of '*Doppelgänger*', examples such as these, opponents of the genuine singular Thought-doctrine claim to derive the afore-mentioned allegedly insuperable objection to it. In outline the objection is easy enough to state: it is simply that *Doppelgänger* such as Helen and Ellen are 'obviously' or 'intuitively' *psychologically equivalent*, and that the FS theorists are *committed to denying this*, and so must have gone wrong somewhere. In particular, the objection continues, it must be wrong to say that whereas Helen thinks a Thought, Ellen thinks none: since to say this is precisely to deny the 'obvious' or 'intuitive' psychological equivalence. In other words, the FS approach simply gets the psychology wrong.

However, although that is the general outline of the objection, the fact is that its exact force, and the exact nature of its premises' authority, are exceedingly difficult to pin down. But obviously enough the argument is a close relation of the Russellian complaint about the Basic Problem. As originally presented, that complaint focused on the alleged semantic inadequacies of Proper-Name treatments. But we saw in chapter 3 that it soon resolved itself into a problem about meaning: now, we see, it manifests itself as a problem about psychological explanation. This should come as no surprise though, for as we saw in chapter 5 meaning is itself an Intentional-psychological notion: it is precisely the thing to which accounts of how semantics fits in with mind and language must appeal.

·I shall proceed here as follows. First, I shall describe three possible problems which one may find with the FS treatment of Helen and Ellen: *The Hole-in-the-Mind Problem*, *The First-person Symmetry Problem*, and *The Third-person Symmetry Problem*. And I shall go on to indicate ways in which the FS theorist might deal with these problems, by appealing to the externalist philosophy of mind described in the foregoing sections. This will serve to bring to the surface the internalist presuppositions which underlie the *Doppel-gänger* argument: and I shall then, finally, go on to suggest why these internalist presuppositions need not trouble the clear-headed ex-ternalist. But first, the three problems:

(1) The Hole-in-the-Mind Problem

Imagine how things would seem to Ellen from the first-person perspective: would not some such thought 'Ah, that is a horse!' flash before her mind as she imagined the sound? Yet the FS theorist seems to imply that her mind was a blank! But, clearly, it would at least *seem* to Ellen that she thought something about a horse: and can it be possible to seem to think something yet fail to do so, as the FS theorist is committed to saying? In short, the FS theorist seems to posit a gap or 'hole' in Ellen's mind where a Thought (even if logically enervated) should be. But now consider our view of Ellen as an Intentional agent. It was no inexplicable accident or mere reflex that made her swing around and exclaim as she did. The episode was a direct result of her functioning as a psychological agent, and one therefore justifiably expects it to be explicable in psychological terms by the ascription to her of a suitable state of mind, such as a horse-related belief. But how can this be if one denies that any Thought (even a logically enervated one) was expressed? Thoughts, we said, are precisely the things that one needs to ascribe in order to explain, in Intentional-psychological terms, others' behaviour. So how can there by a psychological explanation without them?

(2) The First-person Symmetry Problem

Now consider Helen. As we said, Helen and Ellen can be as similar as you please but for their relations to a nearby horse and the precise physical accompaniments and causes of their auditory experience. In particular, then, Helen would surely be very similar indeed to Ellen from the psychological point of view. Subjectively, for example, things seem the same to both of them: they both at least seem to hear a horse, and both at least seem to think something appropriate (thus if Ellen had been confronted by a horse, then it would have been presented to her in precisely the same way as Cowdell is presented to Helen: compare § 60). Indeed, from the first-person point of view, Helen and Ellen are indistinguishable: if one could somehow 'freeze' the scene, leaving them momentarily unconscious, and *interchange* them before starting everything up again, neither would notice any difference. Yet despite these parallels FS theorists are committed to saying that Helen and Ellen are asymmetrical from the point of view of Intentional psychology, since these theorists are committed to saying that whereas Helen thinks a Thought about Cowdell, Ellen thinks nothing of the corresponding type. But can there really be psychological asymmetry in the face of so much subjective similarity?

(3) The Third-person Symmetry Problem

Indeed, the parallels between our two subjects are not merely confined to how things seem to them. For they both react in the same way (each swings round exclaiming 'that is a horse!'). The rub now is that while Helen's performance can be explained in Intentional terms by the attribution to her of the genuine singular Thought posited by the FS theorist, Ellen's, we have seen, cannot be explained in this way. And this means that their reactions—swinging round and exclaiming—even though they are exactly the same, will be explained in very different Intentional terms (if, indeed, Ellen's reaction can be explained at all). But surely here we have similar effects which—especially given the other, subjective parallels—cry out for explanation in terms of similar clauses: contrary to what the FS theorist would offer.

These, then, are the three problems. How might the FS theorist respond?

62 INITIAL EXTERNALIST RESPONSES

Taken by itself, the *Hole-in-the-Mind Problem* carries little weight. For although it is true that the FS theorist has to deny that Ellen thinks a Thought which she tried to express with 'That is a horse', this does not yield either the implausible conclusion that her mind was just blank, or the unsatisfactory conclusion that her reaction is psychologically inexplicable. In the circumstances the FS theorist can agree that each of the following is true:

List 1

    Ellen thought she heard a horse behind her
    —She thought there was a horse behind her
    —She seemed (to herself) to refer to a horse
    —She seemed (to herself) to think about a horse—

and there is clearly plenty of scope here for explaining why she reacted as she did. Naturally, wanting a horse as badly as she did, Ellen swung round because she thought she heard a horse behind her. Indeed, from the *first-person point of view*, there is no 'hole' in Ellen's mind at all: by definition, and as emphasized in the formulation of the *First-person Symmetry Problem*, Ellen is no different from Helen from this point of view—and there is no 'hole' in Helen's mind *at all*. And to emphasize this, the FS theorist could even agree that Helen could be described thus:

List 2

> Helen thought she heard a horse behind her
> —She thought there was a horse behind her
> —She seemed (to herself) to refer to a horse
> —She seemed (to herself) to think about a horse—

although to say such things about Helen would clearly be misleading because, as we shall see in more detail below, there are more accurate descriptions of her available. But if one wanted to display the considerable first-person parallels between Helen and Ellen, one could certainly do so in the above way with *List 1* and *List 2*. And there is nothing here so far to bother the FS theorist.

Then what sort of 'hole' in the mind does the FS theorist posit? Clearly, the answer is that Ellen is lacking the kind of relational or world-involving mental state explained in §§ 59–60: in this case it is the belief that that [Cowdell] is a horse. But it is not really very contentious to suppose, as the FS theorist does, that this 'hole' will not, as it were, show up from Ellen's own point of view. For something similar goes for very many uncontentiously relational mental states: as sceptics have a habit of pointing out, one can seem to see a cow without (really, actually) seeing a cow; one can seem to remember being at Buckingham Palace for tea yesterday without really doing so (since the occasion never took place); one can seem to know that so-and-so without really knowing (for example, because so-and-so is false); and so on. In cases like this it is absolutely standard to point out that the fact that a subject seems to be in a certain mental state does not guarantee that the subject really is in that state: so there is nothing particularly mysterious about the FS theorist's use of this notion. Perhaps it is less common to be told that one could actually seem to *think* something without really thinking it: but there are other examples of this. For example, you think you have at last got a clear understanding of Descartes' ontological argument for the existence of God; a friendly passing tutor asks you to explain; and you produce a garbled, incoherent 'explanation' which makes no sense, even to you. One minute you seemed to have the thoughts there, the next minute you realize there was nothing at all! And consider also the 'profound' thoughts which can occur with seeming lucidity in dreams, but which dissolve as soon as you wake up: or how easy it is, I am told, to seem to yourself to make perfect sense when drunk, even though your sober companions realize you are babbling incoherent nonsense.

For these reasons the *Hole-in-the-Mind Problem* is no problem at all for the FS theorist: so let us move on to the *First-person Symmetry Problem*. At first glance, however, this 'problem' is just as spurious. For, as we noted above, the FS theorist can certainly acknowledge the considerable degree of first-person symmetry between Helen and Ellen, for example by allowing the misleading characterization in *List 2* of Helen's state of mind. However, it has to be admitted that the FS theorist is committed to a divergence in the Intentional characterizations of Helen and Ellen from this point on. For example, the two stories might continue thus:

List 3

> Ellen hallucinated that there was a horse behind her
> —She tried (but failed) to refer to a horse
> —She tried (but failed) to express a Thought with her utterance

and

List 4

> Helen heard that there was a horse behind her
> —She referred to this horse
> —She expressed the Thought that that [Cowdell] is a horse.

That is, the description of Helen, unlike that of Ellen, will continue in a relational or world-involving vein. And perhaps the *First-person Symmetry Problem* can now be seen as a challenge. For, as we saw above, the FS theorist had better acknowledge that *Ellen's* reaction can be given an Intentional explanation in terms of the seemings, etc. described in *List 1*. But then, if *List 1* can furnish the materials for an explanation of Ellen's reaction, surely *List 2* can furnish an explanation of Helen's precisely similar reaction. So—the challenge goes— what *use* is the excess baggage posited in *List 4*?

The FS theorist can reply as follows. When we provide Intentional descriptions of a subject's states of mind we normally do so with a view to maintaining an 'ongoing' account of their behaviour. Thus, for example, we should normally be interested in what Helen does after the initial episode of hearing Cowdell: she might stalk the beast, corner him, grab him by the nose, mount him, and so forth. We see this subsequent activity of Helen's as integrated, or 'held together', by the beliefs, desires, and other states of mind which it is reasonable to ascribe to her, given—for instance—her immediate situation and background project of getting a horse at all costs. In particular, we focus not merely on the more-or-less fleeting experiences as described in *List 2*, but on the more stable states of mind—memories, the continuing belief that that [Cowdell] is a horse, and so on—which, along with her continuously updated perceptions, guide her subsequent doings. But, as we saw in § 59, the standard way to characterize thoughts and beliefs is by 'tagging' subjects with pieces of information about their environment: in this case, we 'tag' Helen with information about the object (Cowdell) towards which her efforts are directed. In short, then, the 'excess baggage' in *List 4* reflects the fact that our normal Intentional interest in subjects is an interest in the subjects as interactors with and modifiers of the things that surround them in their environment: we are interested in explaining, for example, why Helen *stalked Cowdell, grabbed him by the nose*, and so on. These, note, are externalistically described actions: and the usual Intentional explanations would themselves be couched in externalistic terms. Thus, we know that Helen wants a horse at all costs; hence, in the circumstances, she wants *Cowdell* because she can see *him* before her, and believes that *he* is a horse. So she grabs *him* by the nose: and so on.

Contrast Ellen. Although she starts off like Helen, both in terms of how things seem from the first-person point of view, and in terms of how she swings round and exclaims, the similarities soon run out. Even if we suppose that she is so hypersensitive that she hallucinates visually in such a way that the scene visually strikes her as Helen's strikes her; and even if we suppose further that Ellen makes stalking movements like Helen's, subsequently grabs out into thin air, and so on: even so, the things to be explained would be quite different from those to be explained in Helen's case. In the one case we have an intelligible pattern of activity directed at the catching of Cowdell: in the other, we have an apparently deranged war dance, complete with triumphant shrieks of 'I'll get the brute!' So there can be no easy complaint about the fact that the FS theorist would offer drastically different explanations of the two women's reactions, simply because the *things to be explained* are so different: sensible tracking of a horse as against deranged war-dance.

And at this point it becomes clear how the FS theorist might reply to the third problem, the *Third-person Symmetry Problem*. For although it can be written into the example that, in some sense of 'behave', Ellen and Helen might behave in *precisely the same way*—for instance, they might have started out in exactly similar postures, and in reacting and uttering their bodies might have moved, etc. in exactly the same ways—the fact remains that our normal Intentional aim is not to explain 'behaviour' thus characterized. We normally do not even notice with any particular accuracy how persons move their bodies (compare the example of signing a cheque in § 52): rather, our normal focus, as stated before, is on agents and their interactions with items in their environment. And at this level of description and explanation, as we saw in the last two paragraphs, there is third-person *asymmetry* between Helen and Ellen, so it can hardly be offered as an objection that at this level of description and explanation the FS theory implies that different explanations of the two actions would be given. As we noted at the beginning of the previous section it is only reasonable to expect parallel explanations when one has two examples of the *same* kind of phenomenon: and in the case of Helen and Ellen, as we have seen, we have two very *different* kinds of behavioural phenomenon to explain. Thus, the third 'problem', like the two before it, is no trouble to the FS theorist (see McCulloch (1988a)).

But at this point the proponent of the *Doppelgänger* argument might try to bite back. For although there are third-person asymmetries in the example I have considered we can surely just imagine a different continuation of the initial Helen–Ellen story, according to which their careers develop in a parallel manner, *even as viewed from the normal, externalist point of view*. For example: both women, upon seeming to hear a horse, immediately rush off to find their lieutenants; tell a story about a horse to be found in a nearby field; dispatch foot-soldiers to collect it; start to issue new orders to those around them to marshall the troops for a new assault—and so on. With a little ingenuity we could surely here describe parallel stories in externalist terms, and then point out that—contrary to what is 'obviously' or 'intuitively' required—the FS theorist would still be committed to giving asymmetrical explanations of these symmetrical careers: for example, in Helen's case in terms of the Thought/memory that Cowdell is nearby, and in Ellen's case in terms of the delusory memory that there is a horse nearby. Is not this the real basis of the entire *Doppelgänger* objection? (see Carruthers (1988)).

It had better not be. The mere fact that the careers of Helen and Ellen *can* be described in the same externalist terms is not enough to show that these careers must succumb to the same Intentional explanation. For example, both Harold Wilson and Margaret Thatcher *went to see the Queen upon winning a General Election*, and *went off to form a Government after being asked to do so*. But this clearly does not mean that there have to be parallel Intentional explanations of these two courses of action. There may be such a thing; more likely, there is not: either way, the existence of symmetrical descriptions of the careers does not, by itself, show that symmetrical explanations are required. Neither is this a special feature of Intentional explanation. From the fact that two episodes can be described as examples of *one object interacting with another*, it clearly does not follow that it is reasonable, much less obligatory, to look for parallel explanations of the two cases. Before any two cases which *can* be described in the same way present an example of a pair of cases which need to be explained in a parallel fashion, it needs also to be shown that the level of description is of the 'appropriate' kind—whatever, exactly, that is (see McCULLOCH (1988b)).

Obviously, then, we need to examine more carefully what the proponent of the *Doppelgänger* argument has in mind when speaking of third-person symmetries. And, more generally, we have by now surely seen enough to be suspicious of the bare assertion that *Doppelgänger* 'intuitively' or 'obviously' are psychologically equivalent and therefore should succumb to symmetrical psychological explanations. For the discussion of the three 'problems' above shows that, from an externalist perspective, it is quite intelligible to discern Intentional psychological differences even in the face of considerable first-person and third-person similarities. Thus, those who nourish their capacity for having intuitions—and derive their sense of what is 'obvious'—from careful attention to actual externalist Intentional explanatory practice are very likely simply to disagree over what the *Doppelgänger* examples show. So if we are to get any further on this matter—and most discussions seem simply to stop at this point—we need to examine more carefully the presuppositions which underlie the *Doppelgänger* attack.

63 INTERNALISM:
THE SUBJECT-CENTRED UNIVERSE

Doppelgänger considerations are very special thought-experiments. We have to imagine someone like Helen who is attributed a genuine singular Thought about something like Cowdell. Then we are invited to imagine someone else like Ellen, exactly the same in all respects except those facts about the presence of objects which affect the presence of a genuine singular Thought. And there is nothing to stop the example being tailored in such a way that these facts just seem to have no essential bearing on how the subjects register the situation and move their bodies in response. Indeed, as we have seen, the cases can simply be defined as ones in which two subjects are both subjectively and—at one level of description—'behaviourally' equivalent. The root idea here is that one simply imagines that the objective worldly target of the Thought—Cowdell—is 'spirited away', and *everything else remains exactly as it was*: including, we are invited to agree, all the psychological facts.

In all essentials this procedure repeats Descartes's famous strategy, mentioned in §59, which he used to try to establish *internalism*—the view that thoughts, etc. are not essentially world involving, but can exist just the way they are even if the world they appear to depict does not. Descartes too, with his device of the malignant demon, imagined the worldly targets of thought to be spirited away, and maintained that all the essential psychological facts would remain. Of course, there are important differences between Descartes and at least some modern employers of his strategy. One crucial difference is that Descartes imagined that even his *body* might not exist though his thoughts, etc.—even thoughts, etc. 'about' his body—would remain just as they were: and he went on from this to try to establish that *he*, the subject of these thoughts, was therefore identical with no material thing, but was an immaterial substance. But modern internalists do not normally follow Descartes even as far as the first step, and instead—and we saw in the description of the *Doppelgänger* example—treat their subjects as physically embodied agents. Furthermore, as noted in §59, most modern internalists believe that thinking subjects are not immaterial, but physical. This second point will not be considered further here, but will be touched on briefly in §65. As for the first—the fact that modern internalists consider their subjects to be physically embodied agents—the main point involved here is a shift of perspective. In chapter 5 we noted that Descartes approached psychological phenomena from an exclusively first-person point of view. But we also saw there that such an approach is fruitless for many psychological phenomena, including the central ones of meaning and understanding, which are better approached from the third-person point of view. And this point is generally acknowledged, to some degree or other, even by modern internalists, and is reflected in their aforementioned treatment of their subjects as physically embodied agents.

Another crucial difference between Descartes and the modern employers of his strategy concerns the extent, as it were, of their internalism. Descartes, rooted as he was in the first-person standpoint, formulated an extremely severe form of internalism. But once subjects are seen as physically embodied agents one can hardly ignore the fact—explicitly imagined away by Descartes—that they are situated in a physical environment. And this at least seems to open up the possibility of different varieties of internalism, some of which incorporate externalist components. Thus, for example, one may try to be an externalist about perception, in the sense of agreeing that seeings, etc. are essentially seeings *of* items and situations in the world, but an internalist about thoughts concerning natural substances such as water, and hold that, say, *the thought that water is wet* could exist even if there were no such thing as water. Or one might try to be an externalist about such thoughts as this, but an internalist about singular Thoughts, and hold that, say, Helen's Thought *that that [Cowdell] is a horse* could exist even if Cowdell did not: for example, one might claim that Ellen could think this very same Thought. Now there are evident difficulties here: 'selective' internalists will have to explain pretty carefully what their principle of selection is, and will have to motivate their internalism in such a way that the arguments do not simply carry over and undermine the externalist parts of their doctrine. As it happens, most of the claims made by internalists seem applicable to *any* psychological phenomenon which purports to represent the environment. But we shall not consider these matters in any depth, and instead merely concentrate on internalism with respect to singular Thoughts.

Despite the important differences between Descartes and his modern followers which we have noted in the last two paragraphs, the fact remains that the essential strategy for establishing internalist claims is the same. In both cases we are invited to 'spirit away' the worldly targets of the relevant psychological phenomena, and to see or 'intuit' that these phenomena remain as they were. In both cases we are encouraged to adopt a certain view of the matter, to see the facts in a certain way: namely, as *subject-centred*. That is, we are encouraged to think, as it were, in terms of a *subject-centred Universe*: here is the subject, thinking about the world; there, set over against the subject, is the rest of the Universe, such as it be. This is obviously the view taken by Descartes himself, and is implicit in his exclusively first-person stance. But it is equally present in the modern approaches, even if slightly less obviously. For consider again the case of Helen and Ellen. It is *defined* into the situation that they are indistinguishable from the first-person point of view: otherwise, clearly enough, it could not be claimed that they are psychologically equivalent. But it is also, equally, defined into the example that they 'react' or 'behave' in the same way: otherwise, equally plainly, it could not be claimed that they ought to be explained in parallel ways. However, we saw that it will not do here merely to point out that they both fall under some one behavioural description, even if this is couched in externalist terms: as we saw in the case of Harold Wilson and Margaret Thatcher, this is not enough, by itself, to motivate the call for parallel explanations. So what exactly are we supposed to imagine? Clearly this: that *their bodies move, and perhaps continue for some time afterwards to move, in the same ways*. Thus, although it is true that modern internalists do not 'home in' on the subject to anything like the extent that Descartes did, it is undeniable that they do not widen their perspective to anything like that of the ordinary, Intentional view of subjects either: in focusing on the subjective and 'behavioural' similarities between *Doppelgänger* they remain a long way short of the Intentional point of view, which, as we have seen at some length, is strongly externalist. In short, whereas the Intentional conception of behaviour is externalistic, the conception appealed to by proponents of the *Doppelgänger* argument is behaviour as 'mere physical movement' (compare § 52), even if they do not always *describe* it as such.

But it is undeniable that our normal Intentional practices do not involve us in focusing narrowly on how subjects move their bodies in response to the promptings of the environment. Even in cases where demonstrative Thoughts are concerned, we tend, as the story of Helen exemplifies, to see subjects in terms of their Intentional actions on the items around them, and often do not even notice the particular details of their bodily movements. And most Intentional explanatory projects are even further removed from the sort of subject-centred project envisaged by the internalist. When we write biographies or case-histories, or *curricula vitae*, or work hard to penetrate the reasons for the movements of this or that author's mind, or give people advice, or phone up to say why we shan't be coming to the party after all—when we are engaged in these typically Intentional projects, we are undoubtedly formulating a complex mixture of descriptions and redescriptions of actions, on the one hand, and Intentional explanations of these on the other. But the actions—the things to be explained—are rarely conceived of in the narrow behavioural terms recommended by the internalist: similarly, the posited mental states—the things which are supposed to do the explaining—are conceived of in a correspondingly externalist way, and are 'tagged' by appropriate pieces of information about the world. To this large extent, Intentional psychology is not subject-centred at all: on the contrary, the subjects of Intentional psychology are thoroughly 'mixed' or interlaced with the external world, both as a result of how their actions are typically conceived, and as a result of how their mental states are individuated. Since none of this can be denied, it is therefore clear that the *Doppelgänger* boot is on the other foot: it is not the externalist at all who distorts or misrepresents the psychological facts; it is the *internalist* who does this. Far from the *Doppelgänger* example showing that the FS theory and similar offshoots of externalism must be wrong, it serves instead to show how far off the psychological track modern followers of Descartes have remained, even after they have acknowledged the futility of approaching Intentional phenomena, as Descartes himself did, from the first-person point of view. It is a sheer, unthinking mistake to switch to the third-person perspective whilst uncritically carrying over the subject-centred orientation.

64 DEMONSTRATIVES:
THE BASIC PROBLEM GOES AWAY AGAIN

In §58 we saw how stress upon the fact that our usual means of identifying Thoughts involves 'tagging' subjects with pieces of information suggests that the Basic Problem, at least where demonstratives are concerned, is no problem at all. This suggestion was further borne out in that section by a consideration of how we might go about reporting the Thought allegedly expressed by a sentence containing a failed demonstrative. What we concluded was that whilst it might indeed be possible to produce a report of some quantificational Thought in such circumstances it could not be claimed with any justice that such a report would deliver an accurate Intentional characterization of the relevant subject. So we considered the Problem banished, and went on to develop in more detail the FS treatment of demonstratives, both by articulating the externalist philosophy of mind which it presupposes and by considering how it might best accommodate the Fregean notion of manner of presentation. What these two lines of development brought out was how well the general FS approach fits in with the actual Intentional facts; and given that this is exactly what any semantic theory has to do, as we saw in chapter 5, it follows that §§58–60 yield a powerful argument in favour of the FS treatment.

We next turned, in §61, to consider the *Doppelgänger* objection to externalism, which is itself related, in the ways described, to the claim that Proper-Name theories fall foul of the Basic Problem. We described three problems for externalism that the objection might seem to uncover, and then went on to show how these problems are, given an externalist perspective, quite spurious. So we then turned to a consideration of the internalist presuppositions of the *Doppelgänger* objection, which go back, as we saw, to Descartes's famous thought-experiment involving a malignant demon. But we saw that this Cartesian strategy, even when improved by being employed from the third-person perspective, simply distorts the Intentional facts by recommending a sort of subject-centred point of view which is quite alien to the normal Intentional stance: and that it therefore can hardly be employed to show that the FS treatment, and other externalist treatments generally, are not in accordance with the Intentional-psychological facts.

We should now conclude that the objection fails, and that internalism as a philosophy of mind is irremediably flawed: and we should also conclude, given the previous arguments put forward in its favour, that the FS treatment of demonstratives is very likely correct, at least if a broadly Fregean approach to semantics is adopted, and perhaps anyway. At this point, at least as far as demonstratives are concerned, the Basic Problem has gone away for good.

There may remain a little resistance to this conclusion among internalists. I shall therefore conclude this chapter by presenting some fairly respectable thoughts behind the modern impulse to internalism. We shall in this way see that there may be something to be said for internalism: but nothing that need trouble the externalist.

65 THE ROOTS OF INTERNALISM

Descartes's own treatment of internalism is tangled up with a number of other broad concerns, including the reconciliation of science with religion on the grounds that any self-respecting body of knowledge, including science, must rest upon theological foundations. There is in his work, furthermore, a kind of bewitchment brought about by concentration on the first-person point of view to which anyone can become prey. In a sense, modern philosophy has barely recovered from this. At least at the point of entry of many undergraduates, most of the characteristic philosophical problems— 'sense-data' and the 'external world', other minds, general scepticism, the self—are set up in terms that go back, more or less directly, to Descartes and the schools of philosophy, including British empiricism, on which he had a profound influence. It is not too surprising, therefore, that philosophers such as the internalists described in the preceding sections should find certain Cartesian appeals to 'intuition' overwhelmingly conclusive. I say this, not because I think it is in general a good thing to dismiss opponents with explanations of why they cannot help believing what is manifestly false—on the contrary, it is plainly a pernicious practice—but because, in this particular case, it is hard to think of any other reason why externalism should be greeted with the incredulous stares that it usually encounters. For, as I trust the preceding sections have made clear, it is a very plausible and, indeed, somewhat unexciting doctrine, in harmony with the commonest experience of the Intentional facts of life.

However, the present situation is complicated by the fact that philosophical prejudice has become mixed up with, and apparently supported by, some apparently perfectly reasonable views about the explanation of behaviour. In the first place, if a broadly naturalistic point of view is taken towards humans—if they are seen, that is, as a fundamentally natural phenomenon at the end of the usual kind of evolutionary chain—then there is a sense in which the human individual is a sort of *physical system*, complex and puzzling and rather unlike any other known physical systems, to be sure, but physical for all that. But once this kind of stance towards individuals is adopted, certain things seem inexorably to follow, the chief one being that everything which the individual 'does'—all its actions and interactions on and with the environment—should be explicable in terms (a) of the forces, etc. acting upon it, and (b) its own 'internal' nature—its inner states, etc. In this sense a human individual is no different from a stone, except of course that its receptivity to incoming forces will be much greater, and its inner states will be much more complex and flexible, and will also exhibit a kind of internal development or maturation hardly to be found at all in the case of the stone.

Now, suppose we imagine a pair of *Doppelgänger* who are *complete* atom-for-atom replicas embedded in distinct but replicated environments. Two such perfect *Doppelgänger* are Kate and Kath. Both hate to be touched by spiders and both feel atom-for-atom replica spiders, Rupert and Nigel respectively, crawling up a leg. Both lash out. On an externalist account of psychological states, these reactions are not explained symmetrically: they lash out, Kate because she felt Rupert, Kath because she felt Nigel. And because Rupert is not Nigel, feeling the one is not the same as feeling the other. However, any demand for explanatory symmetry would only obviously be reasonable if they are thereby behaviourally equivalent. But are they? Naturally, since they are atom-for-atom replicas, their limbs describe the same arc. But in externalist terms, they behave differently: Kate *crushes Rupert*, Kath *crushes Nigel*—and these are different types of behaviour (for instance you might be rewarded for performing the one, punished for performing the other).

However, given the aforementioned naturalism, there will surely have to be explanatory symmetry at some level. The mess of particles that is Kate and the mess of particles that is Kath start in the same initial conditions and comprise elements which obey the same laws. So a fully informed and suitably situated physicist would be able, in principle anyway, to give us symmetrical explanations of ensuing motions of the matter that comprises limbs (I ignore the possibility of indeterminacies here). By the same token, moreover, our pair will be *physiologically* equivalent, so that any structural or functional physiological explanation that applies to one will apply to the other. Note too that, with respect to these levels of explanations, Rupert and Nigel are quite likely to be entirely irrelevant, since their physical or physiological effects on the women could presumably easily be replicated (what matter here are the inputs to the women's nerve endings, after all). So we can say both that explanatory symmetry is indeed guaranteed at these levels, and also that the explanations will be *radically internalist*: only matters within the subjects' skin need be mentioned.

Now even if this does not echo Cartesian obsession with the first-person stance, things are otherwise, it seems, as regards the idea of the subject-centred point of view: quite the reverse. Thus modern internalists are naturally profoundly impressed by such points, not least because they can seem to chime in with the aforementioned internalist prejudices already present in the tradition. But it must also be conceded that the naturalism is plausible in its own right. It is pointed out too, in this connection, that one standard role for the attribution of psychological states (especially when a third-person perspective is adopted) is the explanation of behaviour. And since, given the naturalism, it is the case that behaviour (as Intentionally understood) just is, at bottom, bodily movement comprising the motions of limbs (i.e. behaviour-as-bodily-movement), which can itself be explained in a radically internalist way at the physical and physiological levels, it seems reasonable to hope that there will also be a level of *psychological* explanation which is also radically internalist. That is, given the thought deriving from naturalism that mental states, as the producers of behaviour, have to be, in a sense, *internal* causal states of the mechanism that drives the limbs and other mobile parts of the body, internalism about the mind seems obligatory. And there are various ways of trying to make the idea more concrete. For instance, one thought is that the mind, material or otherwise, is unintelligible unless conceived on a computational model, for instance as a 'syntactic engine', that is a manipulator of internal structures which can properly or by analogy be considered as *symbols*. Thus there is a literature concerned with the so-called 'language of thought' (see FODOR (1976)). Such symbol-manipulation will obviously start from a certain position ('memory', etc.), be in response to incoming signals of the appropriate type ('perception'), and issue in outgoing signals (that produce 'behaviour' at the surface). Clearly, since Kate and Kath are perfect physical *Doppelgänger*, any possible internalist description of this type will apply to both if to either, so given *this* 'scientific' conception of psychology, they will be psychologically equivalent, and explanatory symmetry will hence be guaranteed.

I have no general disagreement with the naturalism mentioned above: on the contrary, it seems clear to me that any general metaphysical stance with a hope of being correct must accommodate it. Neither do I need to try to dampen the aspirations of those who hope for an internalist, 'scientific', psychology: although I suspect that more circumspection is required here than is customary. But however this may be the flaw in the claim that the above currents of thought undermine externalism should be obvious. From the fact that mental states, *considered as internal mechanisms of the human individual*, should be susceptible to internalist classification, it of course does not follow that mental states, *considered as Intentional states of the human agent*, are either classif*ied*, or even classif*iable* internalistically. For the possibility remains—of course, it is *actual* if the conclusions of this chapter are broadly correct—that Intentional classifications and explanations *just are* externalistic, so that even if they might have been, or might conceivably become, internalistic (and these are both highly debatable suppositions), still the fact would be that they *are* not, so that doctrines such as the FS treatment, which try to reflect this, could scarcely be criticized for being externalistic.

So the naturalism, even if correct, *cannot* undermine externalism: and neither should one expect it to, if the arguments for §§ 58–63 are right. Since there is such a huge gap between naturalistic premisses and anti-externalistic conclusion, it seems reasonable in this case to appeal, as I did above, to the presence of unthinking philosophical prejudice. But either way, despite the respectable roots described above, there is nothing in modern internalism to trouble the clear-headed externalist.[8]

Further Reading

The literature on the main topic of the present chapter is burgeoning at a rate which is alarming even by modern standards. A useful route into the matter is provided by J. Perry, 'Frege on Demonstratives', *PR* 96 (1977), S. Blackburn, 'Thought and Things', *PAS, supp. vol.* 53 (1979), and chap. 5 of C. McGinn, *The Subjective View* (Oxford, 1983).

For the seminal discussion of externalism in the theory of meaning see chap. 12 of H. Putnam, *Mind, Language and Reality* (Cambridge, 1975). For the doctrine of genuine singular Thoughts see J. McDowell, 'On the Sense and Reference of a Proper Name', *Mind* 86 (1977). For an application of the idea to demonstratives see G. Evans, 'Understanding Demonstratives', in *Meaning and Understanding*, ed. H. Parret and J. Bouveresse (Berlin, 1979) and, for the very best work on the topic, the marvellous G. Evans, *The Varieties of Reference*, ed. J. McDowell (Oxford, 1982), esp. chaps. 4–8.

Internalist reaction to Putnam's original claims takes off from J. Fodor, 'Methodological Solipsism Considered as a Research Strategy in Cognitive Psychology', *BBS* 3 (1980); repr. in *Representations* (Brighton, 1981). See also chap. 9 of S. Blackburn, *Spreading the Word* (Oxford, 1984). An excellent discussion of internalism and Fregean *Sinn* is H. Noonan, 'Fregean Thoughts', in *Frege: Tradition and Influence*, ed. C. Wright (Oxford, 1984). See also the companion article H. Noonan, 'Russellian Thoughts and Methodological Solipsism', in *Language, Mind and Logic*, ed. J. Butterfield (Cambridge, 1986), esp. pp. 69–71, where the *Doppelgänger* argument is explicitly deployed. For a similar approach see P. Carruthers 'Russellian Thoughts', *Mind* 96 (1987); and compare J. Fodor, 'Individualism and Supervenience', *PAS, supp. vol.* 60 (1986). For a useful collection of predominantly internalist papers on meaning see A. Woodfield (ed.), *Thought and Object* (Oxford, 1982); and for the externalists see P. Pettit and J. McDowell (eds.), *Subject, Thought, and Context* (Oxford, 1986).

The argument from Descartes mentioned in §63 is to be found in the first two *Meditations*. See R. Descartes, *Meditations*, in *The Philosophical Writings of Descartes*, vol. 2, tr. J. Cottingham, *et al*. (Cambridge, 1985). For the seminal discussion of the treatment of propositional attitudes in terms of possible worlds (§59) see J. Hintikka, *Knowledge and Belief* (Ithaca, 1962).

For the issues concerning the computational model of the mind, and the 'language of thought' (§65), see J. Fodor, *The Language of Thought* (Hassocks, 1976); and for scientific realism see S. Stitch, *From Folk Psychology to Cognitive Science* (Cambridge, Mass., 1983), chaps. 10, 11 and P. Churchland, *Scientific Realism and the Plasticity of Mind* (Cambridge, 1979), Introd. and chap. 4. See also G. McCulloch, 'Scientism, Mind, and Meaning', in Pettit and McDowell (1986).

For the notion of subjectivity briefly discussed in §60 see T. Nagel 'What is it like to be a bat?', *PR* 83 (1974); repr. in *Mortal Questions* (Cambridge, 1979).

NOTES

1. The general type of distinction between significance and statement has become a commonplace of the theory of demonstratives although, as ever in this sort of area, there are various different terminologies which may or may not correspond to genuine theoretical differences. The most common terms used to refer to significance are: 'input-sense', 'character', 'role', and 'linguistic meaning'.

2. However, it is also possible to query the enthusiasm with which Frege held the view that there could be *Sinn* without *Bedeutung*. See EVANS (1982), pp. 27–30.

3. Because of the overlaps just mentioned, and also because of those to be developed in the following sections, it is entirely appropriate to yoke together the names of Frege and Strawson in the manner just described. However, it should not be thought that the views of the historical figures exactly coincide in all details: the idea being developed is, rather, that they might well have as regards all points of substance. The most conspicuous differences are that Frege, as remarked above, sometimes said that there could be a Thought even when reference with a Proper Name failed, whereas Strawson was rather more cagey on this matter: and that Strawson did not explicitly address the idea of manner of presentation (or, indeed, any other Intentional aspects of the use of demonstratives).

4. A note on terminology: what I have here called genuine singular Thoughts are sometimes called Russellian (singular) Thoughts because Russell, with his doctrine of 'singular propositions', was perhaps the first writer in the modern discussion to draw attention to the possibility; see EVANS (1982), pp. 42–6. However, 'singular' contrasts with 'general', and Russell, of course, is even more famous for the idea that propositions involving many Candidates are not singular, but general (quantificational), so there is a real danger of fostering misunderstanding if Evans's terminology is adopted: seeing 'Russellian' in a discussion of treatments of Candidates is likely to put the reader in mind of quantificational approaches. So I use 'genuine'. But in the context of Fregean semantics it might seem that this epithet serves no purpose: why not just speak merely of *singular* Thoughts? But in fact, there is an important possible distinction here, since some think that there are distinctively singular Thoughts (i.e. Thoughts about objects which cannot be expressed in quantificational or 'purely general' terms), which nevertheless are *not object-invoking* (see NOONAN (1986), CARRUTHERS (1987)). The motivation for such views is discussed and criticized in §§ 61–5. Of course, when such alleged Thoughts are given expression to in the *absence* of an appropriate object, they are logically enervated (see §§ 57–8).

5. More accurately, Descartes believed (and tried to argue) that at least two of the contents of his mind required the existence of something which corresponded to them in an appropriate way—namely, his idea of himself as a thinking thing, and his idea of God. (He perhaps also held a similar view of thoughts about abstract things like numbers and geometrical shapes.) Of course, Descartes believed that since his idea of God corresponded to God (i.e., since God exists), he could also be confident that his normal experiences, etc. really did disclose a world of physical objects to him. But this did not make him into an externalist after all: it merely indicated that he considered himself to have God-given reason for supposing his experiences, etc., which he continued to believe to have an internalist nature, in fact and in general are reliable indications of the 'external' world. Note too that, although Descartes himself was a sort of dualist (he believed that the mind is an immaterial substance distinct from the body, with which it merely interacts), this aspect of his view of mind is strictly independent of internalism. In the first place, it seems consistent to be a dualist, but to insist that the mental states of the immaterial substance have an externalist nature (so that, for example, such a substance would not be able to have thoughts about cats unless it were appropriately related to them). And in the second place, as we shall see in §§ 63 and 65, most modern internalists are not dualists, but believe that the mind is fundamentally material.

6. Thus it is sometimes proposed to treat propositional attitudes as involving relations to (sets of) *possible worlds*. A possible world, we saw (§ 36), can be (at least partially) specified by way of a (permissible)

blueprint: and such a blueprint itself comprises (a) a domain of objects, and (b) a (permissible) assignment of these objects to the members of a set of first-level functors. Once such stipulations are made we saw that one can then apply the normal Fregean rules for, for example, truth-functions and quantifiers in order to build a description of a course of history which at least might have transpired. But now consider: each person's total stock of beliefs, for example, when fully articulated at any one time, comprises just such a story, actually false (and perhaps not even permissible) in nearly all cases, of how the world has gone (and will go). Thus, 'the world according to S'—that is, S's beliefs at any one time about how things are overall—can be represented by means of a blueprint for a (perhaps impossible) world. And note here the extent to which S's mind, so characterized, is 'interlaced' with worldly items: for example, the (actual) objects of the blueprint's domain. See HINTIKKA (1962).

7. In characterizing Thoughts thus I ignore certain irrelevant complications. For example, the time at which an utterance is made can contribute to the Thought thereby expressed. If I knowingly speak twice of the very same object x, at time t', saying, 'This is red', and at the later time t'', saying, 'This is green', still I do not necessarily either contradict myself or change my mind about what I originally said, since I might succeed in speaking truly on both occasions: for example, if the original red object is painted green between t' and t''. It is customary to mark this sort of phenomenon by including a time specification in the description of the Thoughts concerned: thus we might represent the two Thoughts just mentioned as:

$$\{x, M, \text{the } Sinn \text{ of '} \dots \text{ is red'}, t'\}$$

and

$$\{x, N, \text{the } Sinn \text{ of '} \dots \text{ is green'}, t''\}$$

respectively. As the following discussion will bring out, M and N here may or may not be identical: but the presence of the two time specifications ensures that these two Thoughts are compatible. See LEWIS (1980) for discussion of such indexicality.

8. To be fair, this may not be quite the end of the matter. For there is in modern philosophy a strong current of *scientific realism*, one of whose principal themes is that proponents of each account of how things are and why things happen faces a stark choice: either this account must be somehow reducible to, or capable of being displayed as a special case of, the best scientific theory of the phenomena in question; or failing this, it is to be *eliminated*, in the sense that although it may be retained as a handy approximation for practical purposes, its proponents must accept that it is not really true, howsoever useful and familiar it may be (see CHURCHLAND (1979)). Now, given that Intentional psychology is externalistic, it may be under pressure here, given the internalist drive derivable from naturalism: if everything the human individual 'does' can

be explained internalistically, why not just *eliminate* Intentional psychology? Here is not the place to confront this argument (see McCulloch (1986)): but no matter. Even if the conclusion is derivable, the most that it shows is that talk of externalistic Thoughts should be eliminated too: but this, of course, leaves untouched the claim, defended in the present chapter, that the Thoughts expressed by sentences containing demonstratives, eliminable or not, are genuine singular Thoughts, rather than the quantificational sort preferred by Russell (which would also be eliminated along with the rest of Intentional psychology).

The issues in this area are often discussed in terms of a distinction between *wide* and *narrow* contents. Wide contents are the kind of world-involving Thoughts favoured by externalists, whereas narrow contents are best construed as the kind of logically enervated Thoughts favoured by most internalists. The principal thesis of the present chapter is *not* that narrow contents have *no* work to do—that matter has been left open—but rather that they do not have any useful work to do in Intentional psychology. See Putnam, and Fodor (1980).

7
Descriptions: Thought and Talk

66 DESCRIPTIONS: PROPER NAME OR QUANTIFIER?

At the end of chapter 3 we left Russell and Strawson nose to nose over the treatment of descriptions, with Russell proposing a quantificational treatment, and Strawson favouring a Proper-Name approach. Russell was worried in particular by the Basic Problem, and one principal merit of his treatment is that this Problem does not arise for sentences containing descriptions. But Strawson too supposed himself have avoided the Problem. Although, as he conceded, a present-day use of a sentence like

(1) The present king of France is bald

would be assigned no semantic value on a Proper-Name treatment, he claimed that this is not a fault in the treatment but rather a fault in those who use failed descriptions. The treatment works smoothly given the assumption or presupposition that its Proper Names have objects to refer to. If this presupposition fails then sentences containing them do not receive a semantic value: but one should not blame the treatment for that. In any case, if one so wishes, it is possible to secure assignments of arbitrary semantic values to otherwise failed descriptions, for formal purposes, for example in the manner discussed in § 30.

Now we also saw that in the background of this narrowly semantic dispute was a meaning-theoretic disagreement about statements, with Russell (in effect) affirming and Strawson (in effect: see §§ 29, 58) denying that a present-day use of (1) would issue in a statement, that is serve to express an intelligible item fit for logical or semantic assessment. But we had to shelve that matter pending the investigation into meaning mounted in chapter 6. Now we have to reopen the argument. Of course, we have already confronted the parallel issue with respect to demonstratives in chapter 5. And we decided that a Proper-Name treatment, and the corresponding genuine singular-Thought doctrine enshrined in the FS account, should be upheld as an accurate and illuminating account of demonstrative reference and thought. In other words, at least where demonstratives are concerned, the meaning-theoretic aspect of the Basic Problem is no problem at all. However, it would be hasty to conclude from this that we can swiftly close the debate over descriptions in favour of Strawson. As was described in some detail in §§ 56–7, the use of demonstratives is tightly bound up with face-to-face encounters with objects, and thus with perceptual and related capacities: and the communication and reporting of demonstrative Thoughts requires, as we saw in §§ 58 and 60, that the original referred-to object be kept track of by those who receive or report the Thoughts expressed. But the phenomenology of the use of descriptions is quite different from this, in the main. Characteristically, descriptions are used precisely when we are *not* face to face with the object we intend to speak about. One might then say this: when we cannot gain 'access' to an object by demonstrative means, we often introduce what we take to be a uniquely identifying description, and thereby pick out the object in that way. Thus our ordinary talk is peppered with phrases like 'my house', 'your car', 'her husband', 'this bike's previous owner', 'Barbara's cat's tail', which we use to 'pin down', usually with the help of auxilliary demonstratives and natural names, objects to which we have no 'direct' access. And this characteristic difference between demonstratives and descriptions opens up the possibility of a mixed strategy (§ 31), on which the former expressions are treated as Proper Names, and the latter in a Russellian, quantificational manner.

What could motivate such an approach? Well, we saw in § 24 that Russell distinguished between knowledge by acquaintance and knowledge by description, and held that one could only Name objects of which one had the first kind of knowledge. It is true that Russell intended these claims in a stiflingly Cartesian manner, with the consequences discussed and rejected in §§ 24–5. However, as we have already seen, one can accept the Principle of Acquaintance as expressing a rather bland truth about thinking. The doctrine gives expression to an important and familiar fact about the conscious thinking mind: that it is, in some sense, 'in contact' with, able to 'survey', or is transparently 'aware of', much or most of its own central activity. Furthermore, with the account of demonstrative Thought put forward in § 60, we began to see how these somewhat metaphorical characterizations, as well as Frege's own 'manner of presentation' metaphor, might be cashed out in terms of subjects' perceptual grasp of the scenes before them which contain the referred-to objects.

So let us introduce a mildly technical notion, and say that, *by definition*, one who Names an object must be 'Acquainted' with it: and let us see, on the basis of a consideration of descriptions, whether anything epistemologically interesting can ultimately be squeezed out of this. For the hard fact, as already remarked, is that the noted ways of glossing the plausible Russellian and Fregean claims about Naming in the case of demonstratives are typically not available in the case of descriptions. Thus we can say, at the very least, that anyone who proposes a Proper-Name treatment of descriptions has to address and give satisfactory answers to the following two questions:

(a) Is 'knowledge by description', despite Russell's claim to the contrary, a suitable type of epistemic relation to underwrite the use of Proper Names?

and

(b) Does the introduction of descriptions provide us with suitable manners of presentation of the described objects?

In considering these questions we already have something to go on: perceiving, noticing, and the thinking of associated demonstrative Thoughts, etc. provide *examples* of Acquaintance. So our consideration of descriptions can take the form of an enquiry into the nature and possible range of epistemic relations which may underlie the use of Proper Names, using the demonstrative case as a benchmark. That is, we can approach the matters raised by question (a) and (b) by seeing whether, and if so how, one might extend or imitate the FS treatment to provide a Proper-Name treatment of descriptions.

However, we shall see that it is a delicate and complicated business, even given the discussion of demonstratives, to get a proper grip on what really divides Russell and Strawson at the meaning-theoretic level. It will be useful to start by looking at some of the things we actually do with descriptions.

67 UNDERSPECIFICATION

One of the battery of objections brought by Strawson against Russell in OR concerns the fact that the descriptions we use often do not fit just one object. Speaking of one's kitchen, for instance, one might say

(1) The table is covered with cabbages.

But if we do a straight Russellian expansion on this, absurd results seem to flow: for instance, is not

(2) $\exists x(\forall y(y$ is a table $\leftrightarrow y = x)$ & x is covered with cabbages)

obviously *false* since there is more than one table? Yet (1) as normally understood could surely be true in an appropriate context despite this. Furthermore, how many users of (1) would be ignorant or foolish enough to intend to say what is conveyed by the massively false (2)? Here, as Strawson himself implies, the use of the description is rather like the use of a demonstrative, and he has been followed in this by others, notably Donnellan who distinguishes a demonstrative-type use of descriptions (see §68), and by some who have claimed that 'the', at least sometimes, is tantamount to the demonstrative 'that' (see HORNSBY (1977), and §70 below).

Such underspecification is so common that the Russellian had better have a good response. One is that we just do, very often, trade in the ludicrous and massive falsehoods which a Russellian treatment would apparently deliver. Luckily, however, contextual matters such as, in the above case, the presence of only one salient table, help us to 'see through' the massive falsehoods to the utterance's prompting facts. We can see, as it were, what truth the speaker was trying to express with the massive falsehood. What this response appeals to is a distinction between (a) what is literally said, and (b) what the speaker *intends* to say (and perhaps manages to get across). In the described use of (1), for example, the Russellian can claim that what is literally said is given by the Russellian paraphrase, and is false if there is no unique table. However (the response continues), the speaker did not intend to say this, but intended rather to say something about the table concerned: and this could well be obvious to the speaker's audience, so that the message is delivered. And what Russell appeals to here is a general distinction, which will be considered in more detail below (§§78, 70): one often uses the wrong words but still succeeds in getting across what one wanted to say nevertheless. For instance, I may say 'Put more jelly on my plate', and, even at the highest tables, receive another helping of *bombe* for my dish.

Such a response, however, clearly needs more defence. For the defender of Strawson can simply ask, in reply, why we should bother with the silly falsehoods when we have before us the manifest intentions of the speaker to say something about a particular table. Why not just treat 'the' as a sort of demonstrative: one that can even, perhaps, transcend the direct epistemic links associated with uses of 'that'? And this is the large question about descriptions that we are trying to focus on.

There is another Russellian response to the charge based on underspecification. In cases like that involving (1) it would usually be easy to fill out the description as required in order to specify uniquely. One might say: 'the table in my kitchen', or something like that. As we saw in the discussion of demonstrative thoughts (§ 58), resourceful Russellians can usually think of something like this to offer. However, it is obvious enough that one who offered such detailed descriptions could not in general avoid Candidates altogether—notice the 'my kitchen' in the above example—and the ubiquitous demonstratives that would usually be incorporated in these tricky descriptions are themselves to be treated as Proper Names (compare §§ 24–5). So if some Candidates are to be treated as Proper Names, why not all of them? This encompasses the large question about descriptions we are hoping to focus on.

Just to underline how elusive the issues can be here, consider finally another Russellian reply. We said above that (2) is massively false. And with respect to the domain that includes the world at large this is right, since there are many tables in the world. But we often more or less tacitly *restrict* our intended domain. If I drop my tea-set and exclaim 'Every cup is broken', I am not insanely intending to project my plight on to the entire Universe, and am therefore somewhat misrepresented by a construal which has me uttering a massive falsehood. If, visiting a farm, I say 'All the cows are in the shed', I do not absurdly imply either that the shed is gigantic, or that there are no cows beyond the farm's limits. What such examples illustrate is the fact that we can and do restrict the domain we intend to be generalizing over. And why should not the Russellian exploit this fact in order to accommodate cases of underspecification? Thus, back on the farm, if I say 'The cock is late getting up today', I cannot normally sensibly be taken as implying (or presupposing, for that matter) that there is only one cock in the entire Universe. And, similarly, (2) above could be true relative to the intended domain of the remark since there is only one table in it.

Quite how we restrict domains, and what contextual and conventional matters are deployed when we do it, are difficult enough questions to raise. But it is plain that some work would be done in these accounts by the ideas of an accepted or 'given' range of objects known, etc. to the relevant participants, and we have seen at enough length that such ideas bring with them Proper Names. So again: if some, why not more? Russell or Strawson?[1]

68 REFERENTIAL AND ATTRIBUTIVE?

In his very influential article 'Reference and Definite Descriptions' (RDD), Donnellan suggested that, in a sense, both Russell and Strawson were right. For Donnellan claimed that there are two distinctively different ways of using descriptions, namely the *referential* and the *attributive*. And he suggested that Strawson's approach gets the flavour of the former type of use, whereas Russell's is more appropriate to the latter. This has suggested to some a mixed approach, somewhat different from that mentioned in §66, on which descriptions will somehow be divided up into those which (along with demonstratives) should, and those which should not, be treated as Proper Names. Furthermore, as we shall shortly see, the referential/attributive distinction is held to turn on epistemological matters; and this further enhances its apparent relevance to the question before us, given the Russellian idea that demarcation within a mixed strategy turns in part on Acquaintance and related epistemological notions.

Donnellan's distinction can be illustrated as follows. Consider two very different circumstances in which you might use, say:

(1) The woman who libelled me is unbalanced.

In circumstance A, you have just been reading a scurrilous rag in which you are seriously libelled in an unsigned article by what is evidently a disturbed woman. You have no other information about the writer, and have no idea who she may be beyond the trivial one that she wrote the libellous article, sometimes contributes to the scurrilous rag, and so on. You register your opinion of this unknown woman by coming out with (1). According to Donnellan such an utterance involves using the description in the *attributive* way: you have no one definite or otherwise identifiable in mind, but merely intend to speak of the woman, whoever she may be, who libelled you. Somewhat similarly, we might idly speculate about the heaviest fish in the sea—whatever and wherever it may be—and again have no better grip on what we are talking about than the description provides.

Time goes by, however, and you eventually find yourself in circumstance B, in a courtroom faced by Ms X whom you are suing for the aforementioned libel. The first time you catch sight of her you notice her long grey beard and glittering eye and, shocked, come out with (1) once again. This time, says Donnellan, you use the description *referentially*: you have a certain, independently identifiable woman in mind, and you pick her out with the description. But you need not have used it: according to Donnellan, the description functions here as an 'inessential tool', and you might well have said what you wanted to say by referring to Ms X in some other way, or by pointing or whatever. And, just to underline this point, Donnellan says further that in such a referential use the intention to refer to Ms X could succeed *even if the description does not fit her*: even if, say, you go on to lose the case, or even if it turns out that Ms X did not even write the offending article (or any other that libelled you). Somewhat similarly, you might say of a woman at a party that she is drunk, by pointing and saying, 'The woman in the corner drinking Guinness is drunk', even though, as it happens, the woman concerned is actually drinking carbonated dandelion and burdock.

A Russellian quantificational approach seems, at first blush, to be required in the case of an attributive use. For in sorting out, as it were, who (if anyone) you pick out with the description, the descriptive material used does essential work. What you try to do is to narrow down the field by providing a uniquely identifying description, and the object described (if any) has no relevent part to play in your efforts. And in a sense (which we shall have to look into), you do not know who (if anyone) you are talking about, so to the extent that this implies that you are not Acquainted with the relevant object, your description here does not serve as a Proper Name.

Equally, a Strawsonian Proper-Name approach seems, at first blush, to be required for the referential use. Indeed, it seems obligatory if, as Donnellan maintains, the description need not fit the object referred to. For in such cases the Russellian treatment could capture the wrong object. For instance, if you utter (1) referentially in circumstance B where Ms X is innocent of any libel against you, but where, as it happens, your description is uniquely satisfied by Ms Y, then (on a Russellian treatment) what you say will be true if Ms Y is unbalanced, whereas (according to Donnellan) what you actually say with this referential use is true if *Ms* X is unbalanced. In any case, given that (in circumstance B) you are face to face with Ms X, and are thereby Acquainted with her, there is no obvious objection (based on epistemological grounds) to a Proper-Name treatment.[2]

Can we agree, then, that Donnellan's distinction provides the basis for a mixed strategy approach to descriptions, with epistemological matters involved in the demarcation criterion? Not without more effort, since these views as stated limp on most legs. In the first place, in RDD at least, Donnellan speaks coyly of referential and attributive 'uses', and the links between such talk and semantics are not straightforward. For instance, a Russellian might try to accommodate the facts surrounding referential uses in one of the ways described in § 67. Suppose I use 'the G' referentially to predicate 'H' of object x with an utterance of 'the G is H'. On a Russellian treatment what I say would be rendered thus:

$$\exists x (\forall y (Gy \leftrightarrow x = y) \mathbin{\&} Hx).$$

The Donnellan complaint then is that this could well misrepresent what was said, most strikingly if x fails uniquely to satisfy 'G' (for example, as in cases of underspecification, or—if we have to accommodate such examples—as when the intended referent simply fails to be a G). In such a circumstance the complaint is that the Russellian paraphrase would be false (or would capture the wrong object): yet for all that x may be H, and I may well fully intend to be saying this, and may well get my message across to my listeners (if any), and thereby (apparently) speak truly with my utterance of 'the G is H'. However, we have already seen in § 67 that the Russellian can try to accommodate cases of underspecification either by insisting that the description used should be filled out so that it *does* specify uniquely, or by making the 'domain restricting' move. What is more, in dealing with cases where the intended object is a non-G, the Russellian can invoke the distinction between (a) what I literally say and (b) what I intended to say (and perhaps manage to get across). In this sort of case, the Russellian will claim that what I literally say is given by the Russellian paraphrase, and is false if there is no unique G (in the intended domain). But (the reply continues) I do not intend to say this: I intend to say something about x, and this could well be obvious to my listeners, so that my message is delivered (see KRIPKE (1977)). And since what the Russellian appeals to here is a general distinction, as we saw in § 67, there is nothing obviously *ad hoc* or otherwise suspicious about this manœuvre: although, as we are well aware, we still await convincing reasons why one should go to lengths to defend a Russellian (or a Strawsonian) treatment.

So the Russellian can apparently accommodate the referential uses. Conversely, can the Strawsonian accommodate the attributive? Again, on the face of it, yes. We can allow that the Strawsonian treatment copes adequately with referential uses precisely because they so resemble the use of demonstratives (but see § 70). But, as we noted in § 66, the phenomenology of the use of descriptions is quite different from that of demonstratives, in the main, since descriptions are used precisely when we are *not* face to face with the object we intend to speak about. When we cannot gain 'access' to an object by demonstrative means, we often introduce what we take to be a uniquely identifying description, and thereby pick out the object in that way. But might not one's treatment of these descriptions just as well be Strawsonian, i.e. involve treating the descriptions as Proper Names? The main problem, as we said when describing attributive uses, is that the speaker, 'in a sense', need not know who, if anyone, is being described. Thus, given that Naming must be underwritten by Acquaintance, it may look as though not all such uses can involve Proper Names. But what is this 'sense' in which attributive users of descriptions do not know who (if anyone) they are describing? Well, as we saw above, one can certainly tailor the examples so that the *only* access to the described object enjoyed by the speaker is given by the description itself, and perhaps a few other trivial means of identification. But why should not these be enough? Do you know who 'the G' refers to (if anyone)?—why, the G of course! Perhaps this reply is beside the point: perhaps there is a more interesting sense of 'knowing who' someone is, more closely related to the notion of Acquaintance which we have already introduced, to which Donnellan is trying to draw attention with talk of referential and attributive uses. But nothing so far said gives any clue as to what this may be (see § 71).

By themselves, then, Donnellan's examples neither motivate a mixed strategy to the treatment of descriptions nor even, as far as we have been able to tell, help in the dispute between Russell and Strawson. However, they do encourage us to focus on the underlying issue over the matter of Acquaintance, since they emphasize two very different ways in which uses of descriptions can provide us with access to objects, only one of which—the referential—at all resembles the way in which demonstratives serve to do this. So I propose to consider these examples in more detail: but first we have to assimilate a crucial complexity in the doctrine of Acquaintance which they help to bring out.

69 EXPRESSING AND ENTERTAINING

We have said that in order to Name something one must be Acquainted with it (§66). But the idea of Naming straddles two intimately related but none the less distinct notions: that of *referring* by linguistic means, and that of *thinking* an appropriately related genuine singular Thought. This in turn is a special case of a general distinction between (i) using an expression to *express or convey* a Thought, and (ii) *grasping or entertaining* the Thought thus conveyed or expressed. Usually, of course, one entertains the Thoughts which one expresses: this is a simple consequence of the fact that we usually know what our words actually mean. But people *can* obviously use words intelligibly, with many of the usual consequences of so doing, *without* understanding what they are saying (and therefore without entertaining the relevant Thought). Clear cases are those where one acts as a mouthpiece for someone else, and successfully delivers a message which one does not understand. Here, the *linguistic* aspects of the performance can be described in the normal way, as in:

This messenger just reported that the sky is blue.

But suppose the messenger is and always has been blind. In this case she just will not understand what it is for the sky to be blue, for the plain reason that she will not understand the word 'blue'. So it would be at best misleading to describe her thus:

This messenger believes that the sky is blue—

for if the messenger does not understand the message she is delivering she cannot entertain it even as a supposition, and so cannot believe it—even though she may believe that her report is true (say, because she implicitly trusts those who dispatched her). Again, a secretary can be left to pass on a telephone message which he himself simply does not understand—'Professor Jones said that she has unearthed a fallacy of equivocation in the argument to the conclusion that the model of canonical grounds or commitments cannot be developed for past tense contents: she'll be in touch next Wednesday.'

Thus we can say that 'mere mouthpieces' with respect to a particular Thought T are those who *express* T with some utterance, but who do not, for one reason or another, *entertain* T. Now it is unlikely that this is a very sharp distinction, if only because a propensity to use a sentence in appropriate circumstances itself counts as a large part of what it is to be able to understand that very sentence (see §§ 50–2). Furthermore, for this and other reasons, the notion of understanding is not 'hit or miss', but is something which can be present in degrees. Thus one can have a fairly secure grasp of a Thought; or a partial and incomplete grasp; or a very tenuous grasp; and so on. Those who have corrected the work of others or marked examinations will be very familiar with this. It is usually fairly clear what examinees are trying to *say*: the difficulty comes when one tries to decide how many of these sentences are grasped or understood, and if so *to what extent*. Some aspects of this kind of vagueness or looseness will concern us later: however, the fact remains that we can make sense of the idea of 'mere mouthpieces'— those who express a Thought but do not entertain it—so that the distinction between expressing and entertaining has at least some applications.

Where Proper Names are concerned we have arguably already encountered something very similar to the mouthpiece phenomenon, when we considered the case of the blindfolded person who, pointing at a man, says, 'I'll go with that one' (§ 56). Here reference may well succeed, in the sense that those to whom the remark is addressed could know which object is relevant to any possible repercussions of the utterance: for example, perhaps the group as a whole is employing this rather bizarre method for deciding who gives whom a lift home. Furthermore, we can make tolerable sense of the idea that there is a genuine singular Thought T^* expressed here, at least to the extent that *if* the blindfold were removed *then* the man referred to would be presented to the utterer in a certain visual manner (see § 60). Yet T^* is clearly—by definition—not entertained by the utterer when it is first expressed. Of course, our subject may well be able to think about the man in question in some other way—for example, as 'the person I pointed to': but this would not be to think about him in the manner involved in T^*. For upon removing the blindfold our subject may exclaim 'That one is the person I pointed to!': and this is clearly a different Thought from that which would be expressed in the same situation by 'That one is that one'. So we can say that the mouthpiece phenomenon occurs specifically where Proper Names are concerned.

More relevantly to our own immediate interests, there is a phenomenon closely related to the mouthpiece phenomenon which occurs when a subject expresses a Thought about one object but, at the same time, is really entertaining Thoughts about another one. Defenders of Russell on descriptions will claim that we have already seen an example of this in the discussion of Donnellan. Confronting Ms X in the courtroom in circumstance B you say, 'The woman who libelled me is unbalanced', clearly intending the remark to be about Ms X. Unbeknownst to you, however, it was Ms Y who libelled you, not Ms X. According to the Russellian quantificational treatment of descriptions, at least, what you say here—the Thought to which you actually give expression—concerns Ms Y, in the sense that you will not speak truly unless Ms Y is unbalanced. But even the proponents of this view can concede, as we saw, that what you *intend* to say concerns Ms X, and that you may well succeed in the circumstances in getting across to others the message that Ms X is unbalanced. But if—as we should—we concede this much, then we can surely hardly balk at admitting that what you *entertained* at the time of utterance was a Thought about Ms X, which was not, therefore, the Thought which you *expressed*. So that here—if Russell is right—we have a case of someone who expresses one Thought—about Ms Y—whilst at the same time entertaining another—about Ms X.

And whether or not we accept a Russellian treatment Donnellan is right to draw attention to the fact that in so far as our aim is to gain or develop an accurate Intentional understanding of the utterer in the circumstance, the correct procedure would be to ascribe Thoughts about Ms X to the subject, and not Thoughts about Ms Y whom— we have supposed—is completely beyond the subject's ken. And this, as we shall see in the following section, is something that should be acknowledged even by a Proper-Name treatment of the description which would assign *Ms* Y to it.

For another example, consider the sort of botched exchange briefly mentioned in the discussion of demonstratives (§56). A group of us are discussing a certain frog, and there is no mistake among us about what we mean with our repeated uses of 'it', 'that brute', and so on. Then an outsider joins in, and gets the wrong end of the stick: she thinks we mean a salient alligator. She says things like, 'I bet it would rather be in the water', 'I don't like those greenish warts on its skin', and so on. Given the antecedent understanding generated among ourselves, and lacking any indication of her mistake, we are fully entitled to construe her remarks as being about the frog, and in this sense her demonstratives refer to it. There is, admittedly, some strain in saying this, since upon discovering the true state of affairs we should say, quite naturally, that she had all along *really* been referring to the alligator. But, notwithstanding this, until the misunderstanding is discovered, her remarks will have all the expected repercussions (in the context) of remarks about the frog, as our responses would make very evident. And consider again the request for more jelly (§ 67): I may well intend to ask for *bombe*, but I could hardly complain at being the occasion for the despatch of servants in search of something red and trembling.

Now we can draw two important morals from the foregoing discussion. In the case involving the frog and alligator, and in the sense just explained, our outsider is referring to the frog. Nevertheless, she most certainly need not be *thinking* about it—she might not even have noticed it sitting there on the alligator's head—and to the same extent she does not stand to it in any interesting cognitive or epistemological relation whatsoever. Unless and until she discovers it, and/or unearths the misunderstanding, the frog is, psychologically speaking, nothing to her. Yet she is certainly entertaining (demonstrative) Thoughts about, and is thus Acquainted with, something; namely, the alligator. This will be clear to her, and clear to us if her subsequent doings expose her misunderstanding. So the first moral to draw is this: such examples, silly as they may look, show that the Acquaintance principle can only plausibly be maintained as a principle about Naming 'in thought', that is as a constraint on the *entertaining of singular Thoughts*. For, to all the wider *linguistic* intents and purposes, our unfortunately mistaken woman is Naming the frog and expressing Thoughts about *it* with her remarks about warts and water, and yet she certainly need not know or even believe anything about it at all, even that it exists, to do this. So Naming, in the merely linguistic sense, itself need make no specific epistemological demands of those who bring it off, and one thus need not be Acquainted with something in order merely to. *express* Thoughts about it.

Now Naming, 'in thought', for us, means having genuine singular Thoughts, since we have adopted that doctrine as giving the best way of incorporating Proper-Name treatments into the Intentional background. So the second moral to draw is this: if we are to get to the bottom of the issue between Russell and Strawson over the treatment of descriptions, the correct strategy is to focus on the *kind of Thought* that are *standardly* entertained and expressed by users of descriptions. That is: we set out to see whether the FS treatment of demonstratives could be expanded or imitated to yield a tenable Proper-Name treatment of descriptions; and what we have now arrived at is the more specific question whether at least some uses of descriptions are best seen, as uses of demonstratives are, as *standard* ways of giving expression to genuine singular Thoughts entertained by their users. So let us now consider the question: Are descriptive Thoughts—the sort of Thoughts we normally express and entertain when using definite descriptions with their accepted, normal meaning—genuine singular Thoughts?[3]

70 DESCRIPTIVE THOUGHTS

The question needs to be approached in stages. In the first place there is certainly nothing wrong with saying that paradigmatically referential uses of descriptions arise from the fact that the relevant utterer is at least *entertaining* a genuine singular Thought. As you confront Ms X in the courtroom scene described above she is perceptually presented to you in the sort of manner discussed in §60, and the structure of the Thought entertained is exactly the same as those demonstrative singular Thoughts discussed in chapter 6. You say

(1) The woman who libelled me is unbalanced;

but the entertained Thought which gives rise to this utterance clearly has this structure:

{Ms X, M, the *Sinn* of '... is unbalanced'},

where M is the appropriate demonstrative manner of presentation of Ms X. And in the circumstances, of course, you may well have used, say:

She is unbalanced,

or even

That woman (who libelled me) is unbalanced.

So to this extent—i.e. while the focus is on the Thought *entertained* by the speaker in the particular context of a referential use—there is some truth in the claim that the description in (1) functions as an 'inessential tool' or that 'the' in its referential appearances is very like the demonstrative 'that' (compare §67).

However, none of this shows that the Thought *expressed* is the same Thought as the one here *entertained*. For, as we have already seen, a defender of Russell on descriptions could simply insist that in this case the use of (1) serves to express the Thought that

$$\exists x (\forall y (y \text{ libelled me} \leftrightarrow y = x) \ \& \ x \text{ is unbalanced}),$$

even though, as we have said, this was not the Thought which the user of (1) entertained or intended to express. Furthermore—and this is very important—not even *Strawson* need agree that the Thought expressed in referential uses is the same as the Thought entertained. Suppose as we did before, for example, that Ms *X* in fact did not libel you, but that it was Ms *Y*. Then it is open for Strawson to say that the description 'the woman who libelled me' is a Proper Name of *Ms* Y, and that consequently the Thought *expressed* by (1) is the Thought

{Ms *Y*, *N*, the *Sinn* of '. . . is unbalanced'}:

and this is a different Thought from that entertained, which as we have seen is

{Ms *X*, *M*, the *Sinn* of '. . . is unbalanced'},

since it contains a different object and a different manner of presentation (for more on which see below). So not only are the facts attending referential uses of descriptions compatible with a quantificational treatment: they do not even unequivocally suggest the sort of Proper-Name treatment which, by claiming that 'the' as so used is tantamount to the demonstrative 'that', would here identify the Thought expressed with the Thought entertained.

This leads us to the second type of case to be considered. For, as we said in §66, users of descriptions characteristically are *not* perceptually presented with the object described (if any), so that a Proper-Name treatment of descriptions will not in general be able to appeal to demonstrative manners of presentation when characterizing the types of Thought which, on such a theory, sentences containing descriptions will be used to express. And this is plain enough in the case just considered: if the description in the appropriate use of (1) is treated as a Proper Name of Ms *Y* then *N*— the manner of presentation contained in the Thought expressed— will not have a demonstrative or perceptual character.

The line to take here is evidently to appeal to the idea of descriptive or *conceptual* manners of presentation, and correspondingly to distinguish *descriptive* from *demonstrative* genuine singular Thoughts. For example, one could say that just as we have the general capacity for thinking about objects under this or that perceptual aspect, as in demonstrative cases, so we can also, perhaps by analogy, acquire the capacity to exploit conceptual means of thinking about objects, for instance by framing what we take to be uniquely satisfied descriptions of the form 'the G'. Where we succeed in this, the proposal continues, we succeed in thinking about the described object as being uniquely G. A Proper-Name treatment of this type would thus have it that the Thoughts *standardly* expressed by sentences containing descriptions, and thus the Thoughts entertained by users who are faithful to this standard usage, are of the form $\{x, N, ***\}$, with x the described object, N the appropriate *descriptive* manner of presentation, and *** the *Sinn* of the rest of the sentence. On such an account, what we learn when we learn to use descriptions is that an expression of the form 'the G' refers to the object (if any) which is uniquely G, and is fit for giving expression to *descriptive genuine singular Thoughts* about that object under the appropriate descriptive or conceptual manner of presentation.

If this sort of line is taken then referential uses such as that described above could be dealt with as follows. Confronted by Ms X, and entertaining the relevant demonstrative Thought about her, you expressed yourself with an utterance of (1). But, unfortunately, this use of the description was an inappropriate vehicle for the expression of that Thought, since—given the treatment of descriptions just proposed—the correct use of (1) is for the expression of a distinct descriptive singular Thought about the unique satisfier of the description. Not that your mistake is in any way inexplicable. For it derives straightforwardly from the fact that you entertain a false belief to the effect that

She = the woman who libelled me.

Given this false belief, you naturally assumed that you could use the description and the demonstrative interchangeably for many purposes, and so you came out with (1). This diagnosis assimilates the sort of referential case just considered to others where the presence of a false belief leads to an inappropriate attempt to express a Thought entertained. Believing that Mitterrand is the king of France, and that he is bald, you say 'The king of France is bald'. Believing that bats are birds, and that there is a bat in the next room, you say 'There is a bird in the next room'. And there is this much to be said for the diagnosis: if you had not been under the impression that Ms X had libelled you, you would certainly not have used (1) to say what you were thinking about her.[4]

Such an approach can also, of course, accommodate cases where your referentially used description *does* fit the demonstratively presented object (for example, if Ms *X* really did libel you; or if you had said 'the woman who allegedly libelled me is unbalanced'). For here the claim will simply be that your *true* identity belief of the form '*d* = the *G*', with '*d*' a demonstrative referring to the appropriate object, led you to use a co-referential expression in saying what you wanted to say. Such a case is like one in which you think 'this is a featherless biped', but say 'this is a rational animal'.

It is, naturally, open for the determined lover of referential uses to resist this diagnosis, and insist instead that 'the' sometimes really does function as a demonstrative. However, since such an account could not adequately cope with all or even typical uses of descriptions, which as we have seen occur when the described object is not perceptually present, the claim would amount to the proposal that 'the' is actually ambiguous. And it is difficult to see what could justify this claim. As we have just seen, it will certainly not do merely to appeal to Donnellan-type examples of referential uses. All the facts in such cases can evidently be accommodated easily either by Russellian quantificational accounts or by the sort of Strawsonian Proper-Name account recently described. Furthermore, these accounts have the virtue of simplicity, since they posit no ambiguity for 'the'—a posit which is, moreover, surely rather surprising to say the least. So the prospects for a demonstrative sense of 'the' do not look at all promising—unless someone just wants to *stipulate* one, of course—and I shall consider the proposal no further.

The reader will note with a sinking feeling that this leads us straight back to the question with which we started this chapter: should we accept Russell's quantificational account of descriptions, or should we accept the sort of Strawsonian Proper-Name approach recently outlined—or should we, perhaps, adopt a mixed strategy and treat some (uses of) descriptions one way, and some the other? However, the intervening sections have not been in vain, for they have put us in a position to discern that there are in fact *two different questions* here. One is a straight question about descriptions as we standardly understand them:

> *Qu. 1*: Do descriptions in, say, English standardly contribute to the expression of (i) *general* Thoughts of the kind delivered

by a Russellian treatment, or (ii) (descriptive) *singular* Thoughts of the type delivered by the Strawsonian account: or sometimes the first, sometimes the second?

The other is a question about the nature of Thoughts:

> *Qu. 2*: *Are there such things as* descriptive singular Thoughts of the Strawsonian type, i.e. genuine singular Thoughts which present objects under descriptive or conceptual manners, *whether or not sentences in English containing descriptions standardly express them*? For example, could we just introduce a new style of description, say 'der *G*', and *stipulate* that such expressions will be Proper Names as characterized in the Strawsonian account given above? (compare KAPLAN (1978)).

And the second question is both philosophically more interesting than the first, and also in a certain sense prior to it. For if there could not be such things as descriptive singular Thoughts, then the first question would answer itself in favour of Russell's or some similar quantificational treatment. Furthermore, the proper concern of the philosopher of language is not with detailed anthropological questions about this or that tribe, but with more general questions concerning possible structures of Thought. So from now on our focus will be on the second question: Are there such things as descriptive singular Thoughts?—although it will eventually be possible to attempt some sort of answer to the first. I shall argue forthwith that although we can make some sense of the claim that there are such Thoughts, there are definite epistemological limits to which of them we are capable of entertaining. Not any old Proper Name of the form 'der *G*' will make available descriptive singular Thoughts for us to think, *even if we understand the functor* 'G . . .'. I shall then go on to draw from this conclusion an important moral for semantics.

71 BACKWARD-LOOKING AND OUTWARD-LOOKING DESCRIPTIONS

In our discussions of externalism we noted that one of the principal reasons for adopting genuine singular Thought doctrines is the fact that the gaining of Intentional understanding involves a view of the agent as one item among many in the environment, and that from this point of view the agent is seen as standing in psychologically relevant relation to some of these environmental items. If, then, the doctrine of descriptive singular Thoughts is to be made out, it has to be shown that we do or could make Intentional sense of others by the ascription to them of such Thoughts. For Thoughts are nothing—to us at least—if they cannot figure in the gaining of this type of understanding.

Where the ascription of *demonstrative* singular Thoughts is concerned our focus is on agents and their more-or-less immediate possibilities for action. We see Helen acted upon by Cowdell when he makes a noise behind her, and her subsequent reactions to him are partly made sense of by the ascription to her of demonstrative singular Thoughts about him (§§ 58, 62). Given such a focus, more distant objects such as those she can only speak of by introducing descriptions or using names are simply not in the picture. Given this immediate focus these distant objects are beyond her ken. But widen the view and the picture changes: start to wonder about how she might act in the future, what she could do on the basis of a conversation, or upon receipt of a letter, and the distant objects come swimming in. If the kingdom is indeed saved she'll set to tomorrow and see that the blessed blacksmith who contributed to her woes gets his just deserts! Thus one may try to make out a case for descriptive singular Thoughts.

Typically, as we have already remarked, we formulate descriptions in the absence of the described object (if any) when we have pretty good evidence or reason to believe that there is a unique satisfier of a certain first-level functor. We know that people have parents, and so are happy enough to speak of *Barbara's mother*, *Maureen's maternal grandfather*, and so on, even though there may be a sense, highlighted by Donnellan and mentioned in § 68, in which we do not know who these people are. Similarly, we speak of the place where Barbara was born, or Maureen's home, even though, in the same sense, we perhaps do not know what or where these places are. What the defender of our descriptive singular Thoughts would say here is that, whether or not the descriptions used are quantifier phrases or Proper Names in their common English acceptance, we can anyway make sense of the idea that those who formulate the descriptions can or could be ascribed descriptive singular Thoughts about the objects concerned.

Let us call such uses of descriptions, if there are any, *object-indicating*, where by this we mean that the description, whether or not it is a Proper Name, is used because the relevant speaker is

entertaining a descriptive singular Thought about the object concerned. Are there such uses?

From a certain viewpoint, the ascription of descriptive singular
Thoughts seems to have real Intentional work to do: and this
suggests that there are indeed object-indicating uses of descriptions.
The viewpoint is the 'retrospective' one taken, for example, not only
by writers of memoirs and biographies, but also by each of us in so
far as we understand agents in the light of their histories. For in doing
this we typically see agents as acting in part on the basis of their
memories or recollections of past demonstrative encounters: thus
we ascribe Thoughts with the help of descriptions such as 'the man
she spoke of yesterday', 'the place she started out from this morning',
and so on. Because of these links with demonstrative encounters,
which as we saw in chapter 6 typically involve those concerned in
entertaining genuine singular Thoughts, there is a good deal of
plausibility in claiming that *these* uses of descriptions, arising as they
do from straightforward encounters with the described objects, are
object-indicating. Furthermore, given that much of our normal
Intentional practice is 'ongoing', in the sense that it involves understanding agents in the light of their previous careers (compare § 62),
it follows that our Intentional accounts of agents are typically
suffused with such 'backward-looking' descriptions, so that object-
indicating uses are hardly an exceptional case. It does not follow
from this, as we have already said, that backward-looking uses of
descriptions are uses of Proper Names. Neither does it follow that
the Thoughts which give rise to such uses are always the 'pure' type
of descriptive singular Thought with which we are concerned. For it
may be that some of the Thoughts in question, based as they are on
memories of perceptual and demonstrative encounters, are a certain
kind of demonstrative Thought (compare § 60), in the sense that the
recollection of the encounter (and not merely the recollection that it
took place) partly flavours the manner in which the remembered
item is presented in the Thought (see EVANS (1982), chap. 9). But I
shall ignore this complication here: and in any case, we can always
restrict attention to cases where no such quasi-demonstrative
element is present, but where a description is still introduced on the
basis of a past encounter with an object.

Even if, however, we adduce backward-looking uses as pointing
to cases where descriptive singular Thoughts are entertained, there
are other cases involving the introduction of descriptions—'outward-
looking' uses—which have a very different structure, and where, I

shall now suggest, it is mistaken to claim that the uses of the descriptions are object-indicating. The most striking examples to consider are cases where a process of speculation will actually determine which of a number of descriptions (if any) will eventually succeed in picking out an object. Imagine, for example, that a group of people—perhaps an entire population—finds itself facing a choice whose outcome will have far-reaching implications, perhaps for a century or more. In this kind of case it is necessary to speculate about the likely consequences of this or that decision, and consequently the members of our group find themselves talking about 'the outcome under option A', 'the proposed power station at location X', 'the best site given option B', and so on. The crucial point here is that many or most of the descriptions used will never apply to any object, simply because at most one of the envisaged projects will be completed. Yet, for all that, these droves of failed descriptions are clearly introduced on the basis of entertained Thoughts about how the future may be—but Thoughts which are not, by definition, descriptive singular Thoughts. For on the one hand, we can make clear sense of the lives and day-to-day activities of the speculators on the basis of their utterances which contain the failed descriptions: 'This woman thinks that the proposed power station at location X will ruin the dairy industry there'; 'This man is afraid of the political repercussions of building the motorway in that Tory heartland'; 'This group has been trying for years to drum up support for the landing strip at location Y'. And on the other hand, the alternatives formulated with the help of failed descriptions really do, as it were, engage with the world; that is, they are serious and successful attempts to characterize how things will be given certain other assumptions, and so need to be treated as full-blooded, logically relevant uses of language. Otherwise, they would not be able to function, as they certainly can, as plans on the basis of which relevant long-term projects in the world could proceed.

Thus, not only would it be absurd to dismiss the speculation as involving, at least where failed descriptions were used, a serious linguistic malfunction (compare § 29): it would also be wrong to see it as involving a sort of make-believe, not really of central concern to the logician/semanticist. The speculation could occupy the serious working thoughts of large numbers of people for many years; hundreds of thousands of (ideally) closely reasoned words might issue, shot through with the descriptions concerned: 'If option B is taken up, then the power station at L − − − M − − − − − will have to be completed by 1995. But then we can expect the local people to mount a peaceful protest, so the police will need riot control equipment . . .'. The plain truth, of course, is that speculations like these involve the formulation of serious enough, logically relevant Thoughts: but they are not Thoughts about objects in the sense intended by the singular-Thought approach, but are indeed 'merely descriptive' or general in character and, therefore, cry out for characterization in something like a quantificational manner.

The point here is not simply that, since most of the speculative descriptions fail, we cannot treat *all* of the uses as object-indicating (compare §22). The point, rather, is that *none* of them—even the successful ones, if any—should be so treated. For it makes *no difference at all* to our Intentional practices of ascribing Thoughts to the users of the descriptions whether or not their descriptions eventually succeed. As has already been remarked, we can make perfect sense of the activities of the users of the descriptions quite independently of whether any of the descriptions actually pick out objects in future states of affairs. And the fact is that much of our day-to-day Intentional understanding of one another is conducted, not in the cool repose enjoyed by the writer of memoirs, but in the heat of the moment; for example, the careers of those engaged in the speculative projects would unfold as they actually happened before the eyes of most of those interested in giving an Intentional account of them—their superiors, their assistants, their husbands and wives, and so on. To the large extent that these people do not—cannot, as they go along—adopt the retrospective point of view to which the notion of descriptive singular Thought most naturally belongs, it is clear that they could make no use of that notion when ascribing Thoughts to their subjects on the basis of their uses of descriptions such as 'the power station at L – – – M– – – – –'. That is, it would just fly in the face of the Intentional facts to allege that the standard type of thought ascribed on the basis of uses of such descriptions is singular. In so far as typical observers operate in the midst of their subjects' activities, and try, as we put it in chapter 5, to *think in sympathy* with their subjects, these observers literally cannot and so do not see their subjects as related to the satisfiers (if any) of their speculative descriptions, and to this extent the described objects (if any) are irrelevant to their Intentional purposes. And the users of the descriptions themselves, of course, do not occupy a more advanced position in this respect. If there is no Intentional work to be done by the Thoughts in question, one cannot possibly change this just by deciding that it shall be different. So, overall, we might say that the introduction of such outward-looking descriptions serves as a prelude to future activities and projects, of which the described object (if any) is a more-or-less remote 'target', rather than as a means of drawing attention to objects which we encounter and respond to. Correspondingly, the Thoughts from which uses of such descriptions arise are not descriptive singular Thoughts.

These considerations also suggest that the phenomenon of outward-looking descriptions is not merely restricted to cases involving objects which may or may not exist in the future. For we can certainly speculate, more-or-less idly, about objects which are so remote from us that the ascription of descriptive singular Thoughts to us can have no Intentional application. For example, we might fill in a few dreary hours speculating about the possible species and whereabouts of the heaviest fish in the world, even though we have had no more direct dealings with the animal than are provided by very general knowledge about the existence of fishes, variations in sizes among animals, and so on. Observers of our efforts would be able to make perfect sense of our activity as we speculate—we keep sending out for reference books and atlases, make telephone calls to the local zoo, and so on—and it would make no difference whatsoever whether or not they had any better idea than ourselves on the whereabouts and identity of the appropriate fish, if there is one. And this means that uses of descriptions of this nature—roughly, when our Thoughts are not focused on the past encounters we have had with objects, but rather 'face outwards' to the world beyond our experience—are also not object-indicating.

All of this is to be contrasted with cases involving demonstratives. In such cases, as we saw in chapter 6, objects thought about under demonstrative manners of presentation stand in more-or-less direct psychologically relevant relations to the thinkers concerned, and it is an essential part of our normal Intentional view of such thinkers that their actions are seen as actions on and interactions with such objects. By the same token, uses of failed demonstratives both can and should be seen as involving both a serious linguistic malfunction and a consequent failure to think a singular Thought of the type intended. For although we can imagine 'local' cases where a failed attempt to think a demonstrative Thought gives rise to a certain course of action—witness Ellen's comical attempts to 'catch a horse' in §62—the actions themselves cannot be seen as serious activity, and should instead be explained away as having resulted from the sort of malfunction taken seriously by the FS theorist. But one just cannot sensibly take the same line with the serious and prolonged careers of our serious users of outward-looking descriptions.

Note that we seem at last to have unearthed the sort of demarcation criterion between different types of Thought 'about objects' to which Russell gestured with his distinction between knowledge by acquaintance and knowledge by description (§ 24). For on the one hand, uses of backward-looking descriptions, grounded as they are in previous demonstrative encounters with objects, provide plausible examples of cases where singular Thoughts are entertained, and so offer one way in which our technical notion of Acquaintance can be stretched to cover cases other than Thoughts involving face-to-face demonstrative encounters. And on the other hand, uses of outward-looking descriptions provide clear examples of the formulation of Thoughts about objects which are not singular, but are instead essentially general or descriptive, and which therefore are not underwritten by Acquaintance with the described objects (if any). Could this in turn help with the dispute between Russell and Strawson?

72 THE 'GOD'S-EYE' VIEW:
SEMANTIC ALIENATION

What we have been saying suggests the following position. On the one hand, there are clear cases, involving the use of 'backward-looking' descriptions, where the appropriate ascription of descriptive singular Thoughts, whether or not these descriptions actually are, as normally understood, Proper Names, seems perfectly defensible. On the other hand, however, there are other cases, involving the use of outward-looking descriptions, where the ascription of descriptive singular Thoughts cannot be carried through in general, even though the uses of these descriptions arise from the fact that appropriate Thoughts are being entertained by the users of the descriptions. Now it might seem that reflection on these matters could furnish an argument to the conclusion that one or other of Russell and Strawson is right over the restricted question whether descriptions in, say, English standardly contribute to quantificational or singular Thoughts. For example, if descriptions are typically or usually used in an outward-looking manner, then one might argue that it would have become commonly accepted that quantificational Thoughts are what normally get paired with uses of descriptions. Such a practice would, as it were, harden into a convention concerning the use of descriptions. On the other hand, if backward-looking descriptions are the norm, then the opposite conclusion would be suggested. Then again, perhaps a mixed approach would be more appropriate: or perhaps the matter is indeterminate.

Now, either way, there is a sense in which we are clearly not equipped to pursue this empirical anthropological matter here: and it is, anyway, hardly a philosophical question *in itself*. Nevertheless, there is one more important thing to be said about the debate. For the nature of the distinction between backward- and outward-looking descriptions *is* a philosophical question, since whether or not it marks a possible demarcation line between Proper-Name and quantificational senses of these expressions, it certainly seems to represent a limit to the singular Thoughts which we entertain on the basis of our introduction of descriptions. And this is clearly no mere anthropological claim about English-speaking tribes, which might well have been different, but is, rather, a philosophically important conclusion about the nature of the Thoughts which creatures like us can entertain. However, it would be a mistake to suppose that everything here is clear and untroubled. On the contrary, the issues involved soon become very murky indeed, to the extent that it is rather doubtful whether our distinction can be drawn at all sharply. To see this, consider the following sort of example, which is rather different from those described above.

A detective surveys the footprints outside the forced window and the fingerprints on the blown safe at what is evidently the scene of a crime. She satisfies herself that only one person gained entry, and starts to say things like 'the person who broke in here must have come over that wall: I imagine he or she must have had a car, with perhaps an accomplice keeping watch', and so on. Now, such an example certainly resembles the sort of backward-looking case considered above, since although the detective does not introduce the description on the basis of a demonstrative encounter, she does so on the basis of encounters with clear traces of the described object. We might say that she has clear evidence, although evidence that falls short of direct testimony of her senses and memory, that her introduced description fits an object. Furthermore, given a sufficiently wide view of the detective's subsequent activities, she could perhaps be seen as 'tracking' the culprit(s), and as guided in this by the Thoughts that her enquiries enabled her to formulate: she follows the scent, picks up more and more evidence, gets closer and closer, and finally, some weeks later, makes an arrest. Asked 'Why did she arrest this man?' we might say: She was soon on to him; he left lots of clues, she knew what big feet he must have because he left a footprint, she managed to trace the stolen car which he used, and so on. Nor need this view of her be exclusively retrospective: for example, we might ourselves have witnessed the crime, and so be capable from the outset of seeing the detective as related in psychologically appropriate ways to the person she eventually arrests.

But now consider again the description 'the heaviest fish in the world'. Our introduction of this is based on no previous demonstrative encounter: nevertheless, there is a sense in which we have 'evidence that falls short of direct testimony of our senses and memory, that our introduced description fits an object'. Furthermore, given a sufficiently well-informed observer, and a sufficiently wide view of the matter, our activities clustered around the introduction of the description might well be seen as relating us to the appropriate animal. For example, we might decide to throw in our jobs and put all our efforts into tracking down the beast, and eventually, somehow, succeed. How exactly, if at all, does this example differ from the one involving the detective? One thought is that whereas the evidence which prompts the detective's formulation of a description is relatively concrete, the evidence that leads us to introduce 'the heaviest fish in the world' is abstract, and put together out of general knowledge—that there are fishes, that fishes have some weight or other, that some are heavier than others, that it is extremely unlikely that at any one time two fishes should have exactly the same weight and also be heavier than all other fishes, and so on. But why should the type of evidence matter? It might be different if the evidence in one of the cases were exceptionally weak—although this would then simply introduce questions concerning how strong evidence must be to ground the use of an object-indicating description—but this does not apply here. In so far as we have a sense of the strength of evidence, the evidence that there is a heaviest fish in the world is surely quite overwhelming.

A better reply is to point out that whereas the detective's evidence actually derives from the activities of the described object, that is consists of traces left behind by the thief, our evidence about the fish does not. In the first case, one may say, the detective is literally responding to the described object from the start, and thus stands in genuine psychologically relevant relations to the criminal: to use

Kaplan's vivid phrase (see KAPLAN (1969)), the criminal has 'made a mark' on the detective. In the case of the fish, and the other sorts of outward-looking cases considered above, such literal contact with the described objects is signally lacking.

This suggestion forms the basis of many attempts to draw the kind of distinction we have been discussing. However, it is unclear whether anything very sharp can be wrung from it. For example, I may start to speculate one day about the first woman born in Leicester in 1951: and as far as I am concerned she is as remote from my life as the heaviest fish in the world. Nevertheless, it is possible, for all I know, that she has 'made a mark on' me: we might have attended the same schools, for example, or I might have brushed against her in a pub one day last April. Furthermore, it could be, in the imaginary case where I start to speculate about her, that my odd decision is somehow partly caused—unbeknownst to me, of course—by some such unnoticed encounter with her. Would I be Acquainted with her?—I suspect not, but cannot see any clear reason in support of this, except for the somewhat circular one that she has no 'psychological reality' for me. Moreover, it is clear that no great philosophical ingenuity is required in order to serve up any number of intermediate cases like this, where 'marks' of different strength and nature are made on the hapless formulators of descriptions. It does not seem very plausible to suppose that anything clear-cut is to be salvaged from this.

This is not to say, however, that the distinction argued for in the previous section is bogus: it is merely to say that it does not have very sharp boundaries; and this is compatible with there being clear exemplifications of the two extremes. Nor is it to say that descriptions could not be ambiguous as normally understood, sometimes contributing to the expression of singular Thoughts, and sometimes to the expression of general ones: but it seems rather far-fetched to suggest that an appreciation of the sort of arcane matters just mentioned has come to be built into the ordinary practice of ordinary users of descriptions, so that they operate, as it were, with some means for filtering out the intended meanings.

Such possible ambiguity aside, therefore, I suggest that we should side with Russell overall. For there is a measure of asymmetry between the two ends of our spectrum of situations involving descriptions. We have a firm grip on the matters involved at the demonstrative end (chapter 6), and an explanation of how quantificational descriptions might come to be used as a result of demonstrative encounters (§70). On the other hand, we have no use for descriptive singular Thoughts at the other end of the spectrum: it is no part of the Intentional point of view to attribute singular Thoughts on the basis of outward-looking uses. Short of positing a rather unlikely-looking ambiguity, therefore, we should adopt a broadly quantificational approach to descriptions.

Someone might object that this conclusion is unwarranted; all that has been shown, it may be said, is that we do not, where outward-looking cases are concerned, *entertain*, either as users or ascribers, descriptive singular Thoughts. But this, the objection continues, leaves untouched the Strawsonian claim that descriptive singular Thoughts are what get *expressed* in such uses (compare §69). Why should it not be like this: we learn in general, in association with ordinary demonstrative cases, what it means to say that:

(D) 'the *G*' stands for the *G*,

and in this sense descriptions serve in English as Proper Names. But then the language, so to speak, runs away with itself, and allows outward-looking instantiations such as:

(*D**) 'the heaviest fish in the world' stands for the heaviest fish in the world

which, in our ignorance, we fail to understand in their 'intended' meaning. Nevertheless, the objection concludes, (*D**) gives expression to a true Thought about the relevant description, even if we have no Intentional use for this Thought, or for certain consequences of the semantic account of descriptions based on (*D*).

Anyone who objects thus has simply forgotten why one should bother with the details of natural-language semantics. It is certainly true that we can regard formal systems as giving an ideal model to which natural languages are intended to approximate. It is also true that, in so far as such models are to help in the assessment of particular pieces of reasoning, we can assess a piece of reasoning that involves 'local' failures of reference, as in uses of failed descriptions on a Proper Name approach, even whilst 'writing off' these uses from a logical point of view. For example, Strawson might say that the inference 'Everything moves, so the present king of France moves' is valid *in the sense that if* the necessary presuppositions of the reasoning had held, then it would have been a move to a conclusion which has to be true if the premiss is (compare §30). Furthermore, we can certainly make sense of the general idea that serious attempts to say something of logical relevance can fail due to reference failure: demonstratives provide a dramatic example (chapter 6). But these failures too are 'local'—set against a background of generally successful attempts. The present proposal for descriptions, on the other hand, is relatively 'global' in its extent: in so far as uses of outward-looking descriptions are a set and institutionalized feature of the use of descriptions generally (compare §71), the proposal amounts to the claim that we regularly and systematically misuse and misconstrue our own language, both in that we neither entertain the Thoughts we are expressing, nor, in practical terms, 'write off' all those droves of uses of failed descriptions which, as strict semanticists, we should certainly write off.

But this is ridiculous: what point and purpose is there in the claim that we are, in this systematic sort of way, *semantically alienated* from our own language? This is not a contribution to Intentional psychology, nor to the general anthropological enterprise that seeks generalized self-understanding (compare §12), nor to logic. Once it is granted that outward-looking descriptions do not serve as Proper Names *for us*, what possible use could there be for the 'qualification' that, nevertheless, they are *really* Proper Names? Who for?

What tends to happen here is that enthusiasm for the semantic aspects of externalism (§59) leads, via an excess of zeal, to a misconception over what natural-language semantics is supposed to achieve. One imagines subjects interacting with their wider environments, and imagines pinning down their sayings with the help of the objects on which the utterances are targeted. Given the third-person perspective on mind and meaning, and given the evident facts about, for example, the use of demonstratives and associated devices, such an approach, we have seen, is justifiable. When descriptions come into play it then seems entirely natural to view them as devices for expanding our means of referring to objects: we cannot pin down 'distant' objects perceptually, but we certainly seem able to do so descriptively, and as we have been seeing, if a sufficiently wide view is taken of subjects' relations to their environments, then a straight extension of a Proper-Name treatment looks harmless in many cases. And even when such an account cannot accommodate the Intentional facts, as in outward-looking cases where only 'purely descriptive' Thoughts are ascribed and entertained, this still seems to leave the semantic component of the Proper Name account intact. 'Given a sufficiently wide point of view, of course we can *at least refer to* the otherwise unknown objects', one tries to say. But whose wider view are we here adopting? In the case of demonstrative thinking, anchored as it is by perceptual relations between speakers and/or hearers and the demonstrated objects, we just imagine ourselves in the position of actual participants in the exchanges. Perhaps someone who is blindfolded cannot perceive or whatever the object picked out, but other participants can, and can also know enough about the situation to see the utterer, given a sufficiently wide view of the matter, as engaging with the object. But things are not really like this in the outward-looking cases: in such situations, characteristically, none of the speakers or likely hearers knows of the true situation—whether or not the description succeeds, if so why. So, at this point, those over-impressed by externalism just imagine themselves as sufficiently clued-up, god-like spectators on the proceedings. From *this* perspective it is known whether or not, and if so what, the description picks out: and so from this perspective it seems plain that we are confronted by uses of Proper Names. But such 'god's-eye' semantic theses are mere ornament, as we have seen, and add nothing to any useful enterprise for which semantic theses might be required.

A rather similar point will surface in chapter 8, when we come to consider certain uses of natural names. But as far as descriptions are concerned it seems to me to be decisive. On the assumption, then, that uses of outward-looking descriptions are neither rare nor untypical, and leaving aside the rather unlikely possibility of an ambiguity in 'the', I conclude that the dispute over descriptions is to be resolved in favour of quantificational rather than Proper-Name approaches.[5]

Further Reading

In addition to the works cited in the Further Reading for chaps. 2 and 3 see also K. Donnellan, 'Reference and Definite Descriptions', *PR* 75 (1966), S. Kripke, 'Speaker's Reference and Semantic Reference', in P. A. French, *et al.* (eds.), *Midwest Studies in Philosophy*, vol. ii (University of Minnesota, 1977), D. Kaplan, 'Dthat', in *Syntax and Semantics*, ed. P. Cole, vol. ix, *Pragmatics* (New York, 1978), J. Hornsby, 'Singular Terms in Contexts of Propositional Attitude', *Mind*, 86 (1977) and M. Davies, *Meaning, Quantification and Modality* (London, 1980), chap. 7.

For the demarcation problem mentioned in § 72 see D. Kaplan, 'Quantifying in', in: *Words and Objections: Essays on the Work of W. V. Quine*, ed. D. Davidson and J. Hintikka (Dordrecht, 1969); repr. in Linsky (1971), Pt. ix; and esp. G. Evans, *The Varieties of Reference*, ed. J. McDowell (Oxford, 1982), Pt. ii.

NOTES

1. Note too that the Russellian and Strawsonian accounts could even sometimes be, to all material intents and purposes, equivalent. It is presumably a more-or-less arbitrary matter, often, quite what counts as being in the intended domain of this or that remark. So why not, when the kitchen table is available, just treat *it* as the intended domain of (2)? But then Russell's account would no more be insulated against the Basic Problem than is Strawson's! How can one successfully stipulate that a non-existent object shall be the domain of one's variables?

2. Note that one can accept much of the anti-Russellian spirit of Donnellan's claims about referential uses without going to the length of saying that 'the *G*' can sometimes have the legitimate linguistic function of meaning, or referring to, a non-*G*. Although writers often proceed as though taking seriously the idea of referential uses is all of a piece with going to this length, this is in fact a mistake. As we shall see in § 70, it is perfectly consistent to say that (*a*) at least some uses of descriptions are to be given a Proper-Name treatment, even though (*b*) such a use is only linguistically correct, and therefore fit for semantic assessment, if the invoked object is indeed a *G*. Think of a similar thesis concerning uses of 'that (this) *G*'.

3. In making the distinction to which we have been drawing attention, namely that between (i) the Thought (if any) which one's words express, and (ii) the Thought (if any) which one is actually entertaining and trying to express with those very words, we leave room for various possible combinations. One can entertain one thing, express another (as in the frog and alligator example, and the *bombe* example); entertain nothing, express something (as in the blind messenger example, and the blindfold example); or entertain something, express nothing (I think that my beer is too warm, and, rather overestimating my linguistic abilities, I tell the Italian waiter that '*mon cervesa eta deux calor*'). In the discussion that follows we shall tend to restrict attention to the first type of case. It exhibits what I shall call *semantic alienation*: as a speaker one uses the sentence in order to give expression to a certain Thought one is entertaining, but in the context of an account of the sentence concerned which associates a different Thought with it.

4. Donnellan actually considers other types of case which could not be dealt with in exactly these ways. For example, I may manage to convey that *x* is in his counting-house by saying 'The king is in his counting-house' even though I know full well that *x* is not really the king. This could be so, for example, if my intended audience all believe *x* to be the king. But even this is not strictly necessary, as Donnellan also points out. We may all know full well that *x* is not the king, yet archly or just cynically so speak of him, and manage to communicate. However, these cases do not

seem to me to tell us anything interesting about descriptions in particular. As far as the first case is concerned, it just can be necessary or expedient to use an incorrect word given the sort of audience who would not readily understand anything else: 'OK', one assures the very superstitious, 'all the demons have left this woman now' (i.e. her fever has subsided). Similarly, the second case is also an example of something much more general, namely, 'in-house' humour or irony: thus one junior lecturer may advert to the recent promotion of a colleague by saying 'I see that x has become one of the Chosen Few'. Would Donnellan really want to argue that, say, there is a distinctive use of 'Chosen Few', worthy of the attention of semanticists and logicians, according to which it means 'promoted lecturer'?

5. The matters underlying the distinction between backward- and outward-looking descriptions, and the related ones suggested by Donnellan's referential/attributive distinction, are highly relevant to the cluster of issues usually discussed under the heading 'the *de re / de dicto* distinction'. However, the relevant literature is so confused and confusing that I have not attempted to explain the matter here. But very roughly, the issues divide as follows:

De re notions	*De dicto* notions
referential uses	attributive uses
object-invoking treatments	quantificational treatments
object-indicating uses	narrow scope occurrences
wide scope occurrences	outward-lookingness
backward-lookingness	

8
Natural Names: Practices and Problems

In chapter 4 we considered Kripke's modal arguments against Russell's doctrine that natural names abbreviate descriptions, and reached a negative conclusion: those arguments do not themselves, despite the many appearances to the contrary, amount to any general refutation of Russell's view. If they are interpreted blandly as points about the scope behaviour of names and descriptions, they seem not to result in conclusions which Russell could not accept (§§ 33–5). If they are set within Kripke's modal semantics then they look weightier; but, at bottom, the key anti-Russell move involves a claim—as yet undefended—about the semantics of natural names, and our access to their bearers, to which talk of modality seems largely irrelevant (§ 40). However, the suspicion lingered that there is *something* in this idea that certain expressions (even if they are not natural names) give us 'direct access' to objects, and are therefore to be treated as Proper Names, especially given the point from § 10 that the *introduction* of Proper Names ought to be possible in principle if Fregean semantic approaches are to apply. And this idea has since been developed in the chapters on demonstratives and descriptions, and enshrined in the doctrine of genuine singular Thoughts. Our final task now is to re-examine the case of natural names in the light of these developments, and in particular to attempt a proper evaluation of Kripke's influential arguments against Russell.

Notice that the intervening discussion has shown that the original question about the relationship between names and descriptions actually embraces several issues. One involves the question whether names, in their standard use, contribute to the same type of Thoughts as do descriptions. And this itself is a complex question, since we have seen that the question of the correct treatment of descriptions is itself a rather elusive matter. So it is best, overall, to refocus the original question about names: do they standardly contribute to singular Thoughts, or to general ones: and, if the first, are these always or at least sometimes descriptive singular Thoughts, or are they of a different type? In addition to this there is the further question, analogous to the one discussed in § 72, whether a Proper-Name treatment of natural names would entail that what pass for competent users of the names are sometimes not in a position to *entertain* the Thoughts to which the names contribute in their standard usage. For example: would such an account of names imply that at least some users of them are *alienated* from the Thoughts to which these names standardly contribute, and if so is this acceptable? We obviously shall have to tread very carefully.

As was remarked in chapter 4, Kripke's attack on Russell actually has two main strands: one comprises the modal arguments, and the other, intertwined with these, comprises a somewhat independent examination of a number of different description theories of natural names. Kripke claims to find all of these theories wanting, not merely in detail but in principle, and for reasons quite different from those discussed in chapter 4. His main thesis here is that any description account of natural names is based on a radically mistaken idea of how they operate in natural language: and in support of this thesis Kripke sketches a 'picture' of how names operate which, he claims, is much more faithful to the actual linguistic facts than anything delivered by description accounts. However, matters are a good deal less clear than one might initially suppose. Although, it is true, Kripke has produced a number of powerful considerations which seem to tell strongly against certain types of description theories of names, we shall see that analogues, or close cousins, of those considerations seem also to apply to Proper-Name accounts. Consequently, I shall suggest that the position over names is not: bad old description theory v. plausible new Kripkean approach. Rather, it is more like this: neither approach seems to deliver a wholly satisfactory theory of names, although each has plausible elements in it. Indeed, we shall see that there is a sense in which they have parallel virtues and vices. But, first, let us review Russell's suggestion about names, and the difficulties that can be raised against it.

74 THE 'INDIVIDUALISTIC' DESCRIPTION THEORY: FOUR OBJECTIONS

Which descriptions are natural names supposed to abbreviate? The obvious suggestion here is that *individual users* of a natural name will 'associate' with it some description which they take to apply to that name's bearer, and which they would supply on demand. How else could one accommodate the idea that a use of a natural name is in fact a use of an abbreviated description? Moreover, if speakers are asked 'Who/What is *N*?', with '*N*' some natural name with which they are familiar, they will often reply by giving a description. Much the same goes if they are asked 'Who/What do you mean by "N"?' Thus one would expect a speaker to offer, say, 'The great leader of the British people during the Second World War' if asked 'Who is Winston Churchill?', or 'Who do you mean by "Winston Churchill?" '; and so on. We might therefore try:

(IND) A natural name '*N*' as used by speaker *S* abbreviates the description which *S* would offer in reply to 'Who/What is N?'

This suggestion, however, is open to a number of apparently devastating objections, of which I shall describe four in the present section. Then in the following three sections I shall consider how a supporter of Russell might respond.

The first objection, which I shall call the Availability Objection, is that not all speakers will always meet the requirement. In Kripke's words:

Usually the properties in question [out of which the descriptions will be made] are supposed to be some famous deeds of the person in question. For example, Cicero is the man who denounced Catiline. The average person, according to this, when he refers to Cicero, is saying something like 'the man who denounced Catiline', and thus has picked out a certain man uniquely.... [But in] fact, must people, when they think of Cicero, just think of *a famous Roman orator*, without any pretension to think either that there was only one famous Roman orator or that one must know something else about Cicero to have a referent for the name (*NN*, pp. 81–2).

Now this seems right—I think inspection will reveal that most of us are happy to use at least *some* natural names with which we associate no uniquely identifying description of the appropriate sort. An obvious Russellian reply to the difficulty would be to say that we need to find or invent such a description before we can subject our propositions containing the natural names in question to the proposed treatment. But what if we do not know enough to do this? And, surely, we are often quite happy to use natural names in all sorts of conditions of ignorance where the demand to supply a nice description cannot be met. For instance, I blush to admit that the only information I associate with 'Marco Polo' is that it is supposed to name a Venetian who travelled to China in the olden days and lived there for a time, and either did or did not return. I doubt if this picks out a unique individual. Yet this is a name with which I am, so to speak, familiar, and I could well find myself using it in an argument or when showing off my knowledge of the Orient. But it seems that I cannot rephrase what I would be saying in the way required by Russell, and so cannot apply his semantics.

The second objection, which I shall call the Reference Objection, is that even if an individual *can* offer a description in answer to the 'Who is N?' question, our understanding of natural names allows us to make perfect sense of the idea that the description offered may not 'fit' the name's actual bearer. For example, suppose that someone offers 'the Roman military leader who invaded Britain and once decisively crossed the Rubicon' for 'Julius Caesar'. The thought is that even in offering the description the speaker, if pressed, would and should admit the (howsoever remote) possibility that this may be a *misdescription of Caesar*. But if this thought is generally correct—i.e. holds of any description which an individual might offer—then the present individualistic Russellian proposal enshrined in (IND) is certainly mistaken, since the thought implies that individual speakers enjoy 'access' to the bearers of natural names which is independent of the fit which may obtain between that bearer and the descriptions which the speakers believe to be satisfied by it. And if this is so, natural names are semantically independent of the usual descriptions offered by individuals, and so cannot abbreviate them.[1]

Again, I think there will be wide agreement here with Kripke's general point. Certainly, we might very often be prepared to acknowledge that we had given the *wrong answer* to a 'Who/What is N?' question, in the sense of acknowledging that N—the bearer of the name—does not actually answer to the description offered in our reply. And we can easily imagine more radical examples. For example, one can imagine someone even more ignorant than myself of Marco Polo, who thinks that this is a name of a Catalan who spent many years in Sri Lanka, and who did all kinds of things which Polo never actually did. It seems that no description offered by this speaker will fit Marco Polo: but, for all that, the whole point of the story is that this speaker is still *referring to Polo*—is regrettably ignorant of the career of the bearer of 'Marco Polo'—despite this lack of fit, so that the access to the name's bearer simply cannot be underwritten by the descriptions which this speaker might offer.

Just to underline this sort of point, Kripke further considers what should be said if the 'wayward' sort of description offered by the ignorant speaker just mentioned happened to be satisfied by an object. For example, suppose that there really was a Catalan, born in Barcelona, who did all the things associated with 'Marco Polo' by our ignorant speaker. Then the proposition:

The Catalan who went to Sri Lanka (etc.) was born in Barcelona

as used by our speaker would be true. But since, according to the description theory based on (IND), 'Marco Polo' is the ignorant speaker's abbreviation of the above description, this would entail that, at least as used by this speaker:

Marco Polo was born in Barcelona

would state a truth about this unknown Catalan. But this seems absurd. The problem with such speakers is not that they mysteriously utter bizarre truths about unknown individuals, but rather that they are ignorant on the subject of the real bearer of the relevant name: this, after all, was simply made part of the story, with no apparent strain.

The third objection, which I shall call the Proliferation Objection, is that no *one* description would turn out, on the approach based on (IND), to be *the* description that a natural name abbreviated. For example, one speaker might offer 'The teacher of Alexander' when asked 'Who is Aristotle?', another might offer 'The last great philosopher of antiquity', another might offer 'The pupil of Plato born in Stagyra', and so on. This would ensure that different speakers would attach different meanings to the one name, and one unwelcome consequence of this is that communication starts to look like a problem: would not users of names very often simply be talking at cross purposes? But in fact the Proliferation Objection, if correct, is rather more damaging than this. For the awkward truth appears to be that not only would different speakers tend to offer different descriptions for some given name: also, the same speaker might well offer different descriptions on different occasions, and not because this speaker keeps altering the meaning that the name is supposed to carry, but because *any one of a number of descriptions would do as answer to the 'Who is N?' question*. And again, this seems right: I do not myself, for example, associate one particular description with 'Aristotle', which description I take to be abbreviated by the name. Rather, if asked 'Who is Aristotle?' I should be inclined to reply 'a famous Greek philosopher', and then to add more detail as the situation seemed to demand. It is true that in adding this extra detail I should be giving a number of descriptions, or at least an account out of which such descriptions could be manufactured: but the fact remains that I should not regard any one of these as having any special connection with 'Aristotle'.

All of this looks rather bad for the proposal enshrined in (IND), but before considering how a Russellian might reply we should note one final objection, which I shall call the Inextricability Objection. Consider the nature of the descriptions which could plausibly be offered as abbreviations of names on the approach under consideration; for example, the 'Julius Caesar' description canvassed above: 'the Roman military leader who invaded Britain and once decisively crossed the Rubicon'. This contains at least two natural names ('Britain', 'the Rubicon') and a word made out of one ('Roman'). What are they doing there? Well, consider a quantificational translation of the description: say,

$\exists x (\forall y ((y$ was a Roman military leader & (y invaded Britain & y once decisively crossed the Rubicon)) $\leftrightarrow x = y$) & ... x).

Any proposition containing 'Caesar' would go into a proposition containing the above quantified clause, and it would be the semantics of this new proposition which a Russellian account of the original proposition would invoke. But the whole idea was to *eliminate* natural names, and to replace them by Russellian descriptions, in order to avoid the problems which allegedly arise when these natural names are treated as Proper Names. And this will plainly be a waste of effort if the translations involve expressions which will give rise to the same problems. Yet if the problems arise for 'Julius Caesar', then surely they *will* also arise for 'Rome', 'Britain', 'the Rubicon', and so on. Or if not, we certainly need to be told why: is not one name much like another? For instance, suppose the Russellian is motivated by the thought that Julius Caesar, for all we know, may not have existed even though it is certain that the name can be used to make logically relevant statements (compare § 22). Then why should it be supposed that matters are less problematic for the names in the proposed description?

One inescapable point here is that we take a great deal on trust about how the world is and has been, and imbibing all this is at the same time our basic training in the use of many of the natural names and other words we are familiar with. For example, we do not first learn, say, a whole lot of geography or history in purely general terms, and then find out that this or that country or person has this or that name. Neither do we first learn a lot of names—'France', 'Kurdistan', 'Kemal Atatürk', 'Ho Chi Minh'—and then go on to find out about their places in the overall scheme of things. Rather, things are like this: in picking up what passes for much of our knowledge we acquire what passes for mastery of many of the names that we use. And the way that we acquire the relevant information seems to ensure that, in general, natural names will inextricably 'hang together' in bunches, so that any attempt to eliminate all names is doomed to failure. Just try, for each natural name with which you are familiar, to make up a description which (a) you take to be true of the name's bearer, and (b) contains no other natural name. I am confident that most of you will find this an extraordinarily difficult thing to do.

To summarize, there are four serious objections to the Russellian suggestion (IND):

> *Availability*—not all speakers can oblige with a description;
>
> *Reference*—an individual's description could actually be false of the relevant name's bearer;
>
> *Proliferation*—no *one* description seems to have any special connection with a given name, either among speakers in general, or even when attention is fixed on one particular speaker;
>
> *Inextricability*—names cannot in general be eliminated in favour of descriptions since the offered descriptions themselves will usually contain names.

Can Russell possibly survive in the face of these objections?

75 AVAILABILITY AND THE MOUTHPIECE PHENOMENON

The Availability Objection certainly shows that one can at least *use* a natural name without being able to provide a description which one takes to apply to its bearer, and hence, according to the Russellian, without knowing what the word means. However, a determined Russellian could try to hang on to (IND) by appealing here to the 'mouthpiece' phenomenon discussed in §69, and claim that although such benighted speakers can indeed *express* Thoughts by using the name in question, they simply cannot *entertain* these Thoughts, and so do not understand the name in question. And this is not completely arbitrary or *ad hoc*: although it is not, admittedly, a reply that one could imagine being made by Russell himself, given his somewhat Cartesian predilections (see below). Despite Kripke's claims about what 'most people' associate with the name 'Cicero', the fact remains that resourceful speakers can usually think of some description to go with a name: and what kind of understanding of such a word does one have, we might ask, if one can think of little or nothing to say about its supposed bearer? As we saw in chapters 5 and 6, a large part of understanding a word normally consists in being able to use it correctly in appropriate circumstances: what distinguishes mere mouthpieces is their inability to do more than parrot what they have been told. And surely this is all one would be doing if one knew little more about a name than that it was supposed to be the name of a Roman orator.

There is what appears to be another possible Russellian response, in any case. Recall my lamentable state of ignorance regarding Marco Polo. Even given this, there is certainly one thing which may help to provide me with a description with which to replace, say, 'Marco Polo': namely, that this was the name by which he was known. Thus, if I were to add 'and was called "Marco Polo"' to my woefully inadequate description, this would be very likely to turn it into one which specified uniquely. Now one actually has to be rather careful here, since we sometimes refer to objects using names by which they were *not* known. For example, the founder of modern Turkey, whom people now refer to as Kemal Atatürk, in fact was known as Mustapha Kemal for most of his life. Thus, if this Russellian trick is to be successful, some indication of when or by whom the bearer of some name '*N*' was known *as N* must be built into the appropriate description: Atatürk is the man *generally called* 'Atatürk'—and so on. Or, as a limiting case, one might offer something very tricky like 'the person/thing I am now calling "*N*"'.

Kripke roundly objects that such 'tricky' descriptions involve a circularity:

... as a theory of reference it would give a clear violation of the non-circularity condition. Someone uses the name 'Socrates'. How are we supposed to know to whom he refers? By using the description which [it abbreviates]. According to [the tricky theorist], the description is 'the man called "Socrates"'. And here ... it tells us nothing at all. Taking it this way it seems to be no theory of reference at all. We ask, 'To whom does he refer by

"Socrates"?' And then the answer is given, 'Well, he refers to the man to whom he refers.' If this were all there was to the meaning of a proper name, then no reference would get off the ground at all (*NN*, p. 70).

Part of what Kripke means here is the following. Some people have been attracted to description theories of natural names because they thought this could help them say something substantive about, or even define, the reference relation that holds between a name and its bearer. Some say it is particularly odd that natural names, with no evident descriptive content, can manage somehow to pick out or latch on to extralinguistic objects. These people might think that the idea of a description 'fitting' an object is somehow clearer, and so they may be attracted to description theories on this account. Now one may query this motivation: why should it be thought *particularly* odd that names refer to objects, and is it really any less odd that descriptions manage this incredible feat? But this is not to the present point. What is relevant is that someone motivated in this way could not sensibly make unbridled use of the tricky Russellian approach because descriptions like 'the thing I *call* "*N*"' make flagrant use of the idea of *calling* someone by a name: and this just is the reference relation that our theorist is trying to eliminate (compare *NN*, p. 73). In other words, the account simply presupposes what it is supposed to be defining.

This may seem straightforward enough. However, the objection does not obviously apply to the sort of Russellian account we are considering. For our Russellian is not explicitly motivated by the desire to eliminate or explicate the naming relation, but merely by the desire, say, to solve or avoid the Basic Problem. And this is something that can come up quite independently of (and antecedent to) worries about how linguistic expressions manage to refer, since until one has a proposed semantic account of a language one cannot raise questions about the intelligibility or otherwise of its semantic relations. Certainly, there is perhaps a residual problem here about how reference could 'get off the ground' (as Kripke puts it). Perhaps the notion of 'calling' contained in tricky descriptions would not even be *available* unless some primitive word-object correlations had been set up and known to obtain. Perhaps there is here some further support for the idea that there should be *some* Proper Names. But it does not follow from this that any *natural names* are Proper Names. The most that this could show is that we could not employ tricky descriptions—because we would not understand what it is to call someone such-and-such—unless we first became familiar with the general idea of using expressions—for example, demonstratives—as Proper Names.

Nevertheless, there is something unsatisfactory about the tricky descriptions, which is linked to the circularity objection: they are clearly *derivative*. If all a speaker S can offer when asked 'Who is N?' is the reply 'The person called "N"', then it is clear that this speaker is little more than a mouthpiece, on a par with someone who, asked to explain what is meant by 'tadpole', replies 'a tadpole is a thing called a "tadpole"'. Obviously, such a reply is true: equally obviously, if this is all the speaker could offer on the matter—i.e. if the speaker could neither say nor do anything more to indicate an understanding of 'tadpole'—then that speaker is a mere mouthpiece. And exactly the same applies to those speakers who can only offer tricky descriptions. The tricky proposal is thus, at bottom, no different from the first Russellian reply to the Availability Objection, which appeals straight off to the mouthpiece phenomenon.

Now it is important and true that Kripke could rightly claim here that this sort of appeal to the mouthpiece phenomenon involves a significant shift of ground by the Russellian. As we shall see in more detail below, one of Kripke's main positive proposals is that naming is an essentially *social* phenomenon. Normally, he says, individuals pick up names in their dealings with other speakers and the world, in all sorts of ways, and usually just assume that these are names of people, things, places etc. which thereby come to be known about. In a typical case:

Someone, let's say, a baby, is born; his parents call him by a certain name. They talk about him to their friends. Other people meet him. Through various sorts of talk the name is spread from link to link as if by a chain (*NN*, p. 91).

On the other hand, the original Russellian picture enshrined in (IND) is more like this:

One is isolated in a room; the entire community of other speakers, everything else, could disappear; and one determines the reference for himself by saying—[for example] 'By "Godel" I shall mean the man, whoever he is, who proved the incompleteness of arithmetic' (ibid.).

The point here is that by appealing, tacitly or otherwise, to the mouthpiece phenomenon, the Russellian at the same time acknowledges that there must be some important ways in which an individual's use of a name can be dependent on what other speakers do or have already done: there must be more substantial facts about the meaning of a name with respect to which the mouthpiece's use is derivative. But it is clear that making this acknowledgement cannot amount, by itself, to the renunciation of some kind of description approach to names. All that need be acknowledged is that there must be some users of a name—the 'authoritative' ones—who can offer a non-derivative description of which the name can then be said to be an abbreviation. Moreover, the general move away from the sort of 'individualism' enshrined in (IND) is surely to be applauded. The very existence of the mouthpiece phenomenon, with respect to any type of word, indicates that some speakers are likely to be more authoritative than others: and common sense, stripped of the invasive Cartesian notion that each individual is a kind of nugget of pure Thought whose essential psychic nature can be specified quite independently of all other things, surely demands the sort of 'socializing' of meaning recommended by Kripke. So while Kripke certainly does score a significant point against description theories with the Availability Objection, the chief outcome of this is to make those theories more defensible.

We can say, then, that a plausible response to the Availability Objection would involve the Russellian in appealing to a social model of naming in which (a) some speakers are mere mouthpieces, and (b) there are authoritative speakers in addition. What of the further objections?

76 AUTHORITY: REFERENCE AND PROLIFERATION

According to the Reference Objection we can in general make perfect sense of the supposition that the description (if any) offered by a speaker may not actually fit the bearer of the name which is supposed to be the description's abbreviation. And according to the Proliferation Objection there will anyway not in general be just one description of which it is plausible to say that the name abbreviates it.

The socialization of the description account may well offer some escape route from these objections. For, as we remarked in §69, understanding is not a hit-or-miss phenomenon, but is something that can come in degrees. Thus, the Russellian might say that as well as being used by the very benighted sorts of mouthpiece considered in the previous section, a name is also commonly used by a spectrum of 'intermediate' speakers, who are rather more informed, even though they still fall short of full mastery precisely because they are not authoritative users. And by this the Russellian might mean: they do not know the authorized description which the name really abbreviates. So of course, the Russellian might go on, one frequently encounters the wrong answer to 'Who is *N*?' questions: and of course different speakers offer different answers anyway. But all of this happens because lots of speakers are not authoritative.

Such a reply appeals to the idea that there will be at least one description—the one offered by authoritative speakers—which does have a special relationship with the name, and is such that it is in some sense *guaranteed* to be true of the name's bearer (if of anything). And one can certainly imagine cases where the acknowledgement that a proffered description may not actually fit the bearer of a name would be difficult, or even impossible, to elicit. For example, I do not seriously entertain the possibility that Rosalind McCulloch is not the woman with whom I spend most of my time; neither do I doubt in any serious way whatsoever that Nottingham is the city just north of the river Trent between Derby and Grantham, or that Ronald Reagan was the President of the United States during 1987, or that Barcelona is the principal Catalan city, and is on the east coast of Iberia. And it may well be that Russell could try to exploit such points in producing an account of authoritative speakers.

However, even if such an account could be made out, it does not appear to meet the Proliferation Objection. For if there *are* any authoritative speakers in the above sense, then I am certainly authoritative with respect to the name 'Rosalind McCulloch'. Yet I do not consider any one of the very large number of uniquely identifying descriptions which I associate with my wife's name as having a special role to play in giving its meaning. And the same seems to go for all the other names with respect to which I would be authoritative on any reasonable account: 'Leicester', 'The River Trent', 'Robert Black', and so on. Rather, I associate a whole range or cluster of descriptions with each name, no one of which I take to be the one that the name abbreviates.

Neither, however, do I consider all such descriptions to be on a par: for example, I consider 'the river that flows through Nottingham and Newark' to be far more closely associated with 'the river Trent', in the sense of being something that one would expect an authoritative speaker to know, than I do, say, 'the river that G. W. McC crosses every morning on his way to work'. Similarly, if there is to be a viable notion of authoritativeness at all, it will be more important to know that London is the capital of England than to know, say, that it is the only large city within twenty miles of Bushey, or the place where a certain pair of silk stockings was mislaid. So at this point Russellians might appeal to the idea that a name can serve indifferently as an abbreviation of one or more of a range or cluster of descriptions which are known by authoritative speakers to apply to the name's bearer if to anything, so that it has, in this sense, either several legitimate meanings or one rather 'loose-jointed' meaning given by the relevant cluster of descriptions. Such suggestions have been made:

> Suppose we ask the users of the name 'Aristotle' to state what they regard as certain essential and established facts about him. Their answers would be a set of uniquely referring descriptive statements. Now what I am arguing is that the descriptive force of 'This is Aristotle' is to assert that a sufficient but so far unspecified number of these statements are true of this object. Therefore, referring uses of 'Aristotle' presuppose the existence of an object of whom a sufficient but so far unspecified number of the statements are true. To use a proper name referringly is to presuppose the truth of certain uniquely referring descriptive statements . . . (SEARLE (1958), p. 94).

Now it is not clear what the details of such a view would look like, nor whether they would be all that easy to work out: but it is not obvious that this could not be done.

Where are we? We saw in § 76 that Russellians might try to answer the Availability Objection by appealing to a social model of naming in which (*a*) some speakers are mere mouthpieces, and (*b*) there are authoritative speakers in addition. To this, Russellians hoping to meet the Reference and Proliferation Objections would need to add (*c*) that even moderately informed users of a name may well still count as intermediate users only, (*d*) that authoritative speakers do abbreviate descriptions with names, even though (*e*) there is no one description that is thus abbreviated, but rather a whole cluster of them. But even if this could be successfully carried out, of course, there still remains the Inextricability Objection. Could Russellians cope with this?

77 INEXTRICABILITY AND MIXED STRATEGIES

In discussing the Inextricability Objection we saw that the way in which we normally acquire our overall knowledge of things seems to ensure that, in general, natural names will inextricably 'hang together' in bunches, so that any attempt to eliminate all names is doomed to failure. A moment's thought should convince anyone that it just is not possible to produce, for each name, a name-free description for it to abbreviate. This goes even for authoritative speakers, if such there be: one needs to know that London is the capital of *England*; that the Trent flows through *Nottingham* and *Newark*; that Caesar invaded *Britain* and once decisively crossed *the Rubicon*. Of course, we may be told that these analyses need to be taken further: 'Britain', 'the Rubicon', and so on must themselves be eliminated from these descriptions. However, we saw that this could not go on forever: some names will be left at the end of such a process.[2]

This does, however, leave the Russellian with a possible reply. This would involve the suggestion that there are *different kinds of name*: that we can certainly incorporate *some* natural names within the Russellian rewritings of propositions containing, say, 'Julius Caesar', which names, for reasons we need to be told, can legitimately be treated as Proper Names. This is a mixed strategy approach to the treatment of natural names (compare § 31): a proposal that some names are more 'problematic' than others when it comes to Proper-Name treatments, and that these must be treated quantificationally, although it is permissible to use the less problematic sort of names in forming the relevant descriptions (compare Russell's Official View, § 24). But then, of course, we can ask some awkward questions here. Which are the favoured expressions? Why do they not give rise to the problems which prompt the Russellian alternative? (Or if they do, why does this not matter?) If 'we' can Name some things—such as each other—with demonstratives and natural names, for example when offering paraphrases of problematic natural names, etc., what is it about the allegedly problematic names that marks them out as special? In short, the Russellian who made the above suggestion would need to address the difficult matter of *demarcation* (compare §§ 29 and 71–2).

Still, one can imagine the sort of things that might be intended. Names of friends and acquaintances, places visited, demonstratively available objects, and so on, are unproblematic: and names of distant things such as spatially or historically remote individuals are problematic, precisely because we do not enjoy an intimate mode of access to these objects. Neither is it obvious that this sort of programme could not be carried out. However, it has to be admitted that the description theory is being forced, under the pressure of the four objections introduced in § 74, into an ever more complex form. We saw in § 76 that the Availability Objection necessitates appeal to a social model of naming in which (*a*) some speakers are mere mouthpieces, and (*b*) there are authoritative speakers in addition. To this Russellians hoping to meet the Reference and Proliferation Objections would need to add (*c*) that even moderately informed users of a name may well still count as intermediate users only, (*d*) that authoritative speakers do abbreviate descriptions with names, even though (*e*) there is no one description that is thus abbreviated, but rather a whole cluster of them. To this, on account of the Inextricability Objection, we now have to add (*f*) that a mixed strategy is to be adopted towards natural names. Furthermore, there are awkward questions in the wings: Who are the authoritative speakers? How much does one need to know in order to qualify? Which are the authorized descriptions for, say 'Aristotle' (always assuming, of course, that this is 'problematic')? How can names be used to communicate Thoughts if they have a 'loose-jointed' meaning? What is the demarcation criterion? On top of this, further-more, it seems that at least some names—the 'unproblematic' ones— *can* be treated as Proper Names. How?

As I have already remarked, it is not clear that these matters could not be successfully dealt with. However, the sheer size of the task might make it appear that perhaps description theorists are on the wrong track: should one need to become involved in such com-plexities in accounting for the semantics of natural names? This suggests the following idea: since some natural names, it appears, would be treated as Proper Names even by Russellians, let us investigate the possibilities for providing such treatments. Perhaps it will then appear that no such complexities as those described above will need to be considered. With such a thought we certainly arrive at the start of a well-beaten path.

78 AN ALTERNATIVE APPROACH: BAPTISMS AND PRACTICES

Kripke provides the basis for modern Proper-Name treatments of natural names:

Someone, let's say, a baby, is born; his parents call him by a certain name. They talk about him to their friends. Other people meet him. Through various sorts of talk the name is spread from link to link as if by a chain (*NN*, p. 91).

And for the vast majority of cases, Kripke's description is undeniably correct. Names of people, pets, ships, cities, stars, rivers, mountains, and buildings—to take a few central examples—normally get into the language as a result of more or less formal ceremonies or baptisms where (normally) a group of speakers, confronted by some newly created or discovered object in which they have a certain interest, decide to call it by a certain name. And an important feature here is signalled by the word 'confronted', for in nearly all cases the named object is perceptually present to those who name it. This in turn suggests that, at least in these cases, those who introduce a name do so on the basis of genuine singular Thoughts which they entertain about the object concerned: 'Let's call this dog "Felicity"'. This means that, again in these sorts of cases at least, the introducers of names are Acquainted with the named object, so that the basic requirement for treating the name as a Proper Name of the object will be met (§§ 60, 66). Furthermore, the principal Russellian objection to such a treatment, which invokes the Basic Problem, immediately loses most of its force. For as we saw in detail in chapter 6, the Basic Problem is really no problem at all where demonstratives are concerned: and where names are introduced on the basis of demonstrative encounters with the named object, it is consequently difficult to see how the name could be more problematic than the associated demonstratives. So is it not plain that natural names are *explicitly introduced* as Proper Names?

However, it would be implausible to suggest that names introduced on the basis of such demonstrative introductions are synonymous with the appropriate demonstrative, in the sense of serving to express the demonstrative manner of presentation of the object carried by the appropriate use of, say, 'this dog'. For as was mentioned in § 60, such manners of presentation, and the Thoughts of which they are components, are 'transitory', in the sense that they are only available to those appropriately situated in the contexts in which they are expressed. And this means that if the introduced names were synonymous with the demonstratives in the above sense, they would soon start to lose their meaning, which could anyway not be passed on to others not present in the original ceremony: and both outcomes are manifestly at odds with what actually happens. So a better proposal for a Proper-Name treatment of names would be that although names can be introduced via the use of demonstrative manners of presentation of the objects concerned they serve to convey distinct manners of presentation of those very same objects. The basic idea would be, perhaps, that a name could be treated as a Proper Name which presents its bearer in what we might call a *demonstrative-based* manner, where this means something like: those who introduce such a name do so on the basis of having demonstrative Thoughts about the relevant objects, and by introducing the name they enable themselves to present the object to one another in speech even when it is not demonstratively present. Given the facts about the introduction of names just adduced this claim looks quite promising.

Kripke himself says surprisingly little about the details of how names operate once introduced, beyond the claim that later uses of the name standardly refer to the objects named in the introduction ceremony in virtue of the existence of a *reference-preserving causal link*. X introduces a name as a name of Y, and passes it on to Z who resolves to use it in the same way as X, and thereby picks up the ability to name Y (which can then be passed on to W). Neither does Kripke discuss the sort of Thoughts to which names contribute, although this is partly due to his tendency, discussed in §44, to dismiss the idea of *Sinn* for names on the basis of his rejection of description theories. There are, however, further possible reasons here which will be outlined in §80.

Gareth Evans has given a much more careful account of how names operate once introduced, and it will be instructive to consider now the shape of his account, which stresses the extent to which names figure in ongoing naming *practices* involving many speakers (see *The Varieties of Reference* (*VR*), chap. 11). I shall call the resulting theory the 'Kripke-Evans' (KE) theory of natural names: although, as was the case with the FS theory of demonstratives, I do not mean to imply that the theory so named captures faithfully the considered views of the philosophers whose names have been annexed.

The use of a natural name 'spreads outwards' from the introduction ceremony in at least three characteristic ways. The first way concerns the future uses of those present at the ceremony. Typically, they will continue to use the name as a name of the object originally named. Neither is this continued use normally supported merely by memories of the original ceremony. Rather, it will be continually updated and reinforced by further demonstrative encounters with the object. One or other of the parents of newly born children are almost constantly by their side, often for years. The discoverer of a mountain may remain in minute-to-minute contact with it for weeks, and, with or without others, may constantly return. Some of the inhabitants of a new town or village will never again fail to be in demonstrative contact with it. Hamsters, irritatingly, have to be administered to daily. In such cases it is very plausible to think of a natural name as a vehicle for an ongoing and distinctive type of Acquaintance, which fills the gaps, so to speak, between demonstrative encounters, and thus enables one to 'keep track' of the object concerned, perhaps throughout one's life. Of particular importance here is the idea that those who are Acquainted with a name's bearer in this way will typically (a) have a well-developed capacity for *locating* the object as needs require, and (b) the ability normally to *recognize* the object, with little or no difficulty, when it is encountered. This is particularly obvious for permanent fixtures like buildings and villages, and—in very many cases, at least—only marginally less so for moveables like people and animals, which usually thread rather predictable paths between well-established haunts, and are in this and other ways locatable in the framework of immoveables.

The second way in which the use of a name spreads involves the induction into the practice of new users, not present at the original ceremony, who nevertheless may be introduced, in demonstrative encounters, to the named object: 'Meet my wife, Betty'; 'This is Jim, our hamster'; 'See that hill? It's called "Old John"'. If, as they usually do, such new users allow themselves thus to be drafted into the pre-existing naming-practice, they undertake to use the name in accordance with established usage, and so are in this mild sense 'deferential' to those who already participate in the practice. What this means, among other things, is that even if something goes wrong when the new user is introduced—say the wrong object is demonstrated, or the new user picks up on the wrong object—even so, the name henceforth names, on the lips of the new user, the object which is actually named by the members of the practice. Thus, suppose you mistakenly or mischievously point out to me Rupert Murdoch and say 'That is Robert Maxwell': or suppose you really do point out Maxwell, but I take you to be pointing out Murdoch, who is reclining nearby. In both cases my subsequent utterances of 'Robert Maxwell sounds Australian' will be taken by others as (false) remarks about Maxwell, and although there is a sense in which I intend to be making remarks *about Murdoch* (since I am, after all, entertaining Thoughts about him—see §§69–70), nevertheless, since I will also have the overriding intention to refer to *the actual bearer of the name*, I will consider myself to be responsible for the (howsoever excusable) falsehoods that I perpetrate. For example, I should recognize as just any call there might be for me publicly to retract my remarks about how Maxwell sounds.

This feature of the use of names—that they figure in established practices, and that those newly introduced to the practice are deferential in the foregoing sense—underlines the main point of the Availability Objection, which is that speakers need not be able to produce a description that they take to be true of the names they use. For I may forget how I came to acquire the use of 'Maxwell', and most of the other things I took myself to believe about him, without necessarily losing the ability to refer to him by name. Here my continued ability is *clearly* underwritten by the existence of the practice, rather than by any alleged ability to provide an identifying description. Moreover, even if I do remember certain things, and upon being asked 'Who is Maxwell?' reply, 'The pleasant Australian-sounding fellow who X pointed out to me last night', it is clear that my description will not be true of the man I refer to with 'Maxwell': further, I am very likely to acknowledge this possibility, simply because I acknowledge the possibility that my induction into the 'Maxwell' practice might have been infected by the kind of error which in fact, unknown to me, did infect it. And this, of course, underlines the main point of the Reference Objection. Furthermore, since there is just no apparent need for speakers to associate descriptions with a name in the sort of intimate way required by Russellian accounts, it is not surprising that the main point of the Proliferation Objection holds. And finally, given that names appear to be bound up so closely with our ability to keep track of ourselves within a more-or-less broad 'frame of reference', comprising objects with which we can enjoy demonstrative encounters from time to time, Inextricability should equally come as no surprise.

In short, not only does the KE theory of names look plausible in its own right, but it also makes it perfectly understandable why Russellian description theories should be prey to the four objections we have mentioned. Furthermore, we saw that even the Russellian seems obliged to treat some natural names as Proper Names (§77), so that something like the KE treatment would seem to be required *anyway*. These are good points in favour of any theory: and given the daunting complexity into which the Russellian was driven as a result of trying to meet these objections, it might seem overwhelmingly clear that the above Proper-Name theory should be adopted, and that the Kripkean orthodoxy has finally been vindicated.[3] However, as we shall now begin to see, things are not quite this simple.

79 PRODUCERS AND CONSUMERS: ACTIVE AND PASSIVE

At the beginning of §78 I mentioned that there are three character-istic ways in which a name 'spreads outwards' from its introduction: and we only considered two of them in that section. The third one is discussed explicitly by Evans in *VR* (pp. 376 ff.). Self-consciously invoking the social character of naming, Evans called those who come into demonstrative contact with the bearer of a name they use *producers*, since they are the introducers of the name into the language, and/or those whose interactions with the named object, and other activities, serve to keep the core of the practice going. Such users Evans then contrasts with *consumers* who will be, for example, those who have no demonstrative contact with the named object, but who merely join the practice on the basis of what they are told: 'the group which owns this newspaper is run by a man called "Robert Maxwell"'; 'I come from a village in Leicestershire called "Houghton-on-the-Hill"'; 'We used to have a hamster called "Jim"'. Let us say, apparently in accordance with Evans's intentions (*VR*, p. 376), that one is a consumer *by definition*, if one's use of a name is not backed up by demonstrative encounters with the named object. It follows from this that even moderately educated people are consumers with respect to a large proportion of the names they use. For a great deal of what we learn about the world and its history is taken on trust, and in learning all of this we are inducted, at the same time, into scores or perhaps hundreds of naming-practices which concern objects that we shall never encounter. The rich and famous, the great and good, the geographically and historically remote: most of us know most of these, if at all, 'by name' only, and our uses of their names—our abilities to refer to them—are underwritten by the pre-existing practices to which our education binds us. Because of this, it is clear that 'consumerism' is an extremely important phenomenon in the operation of natural names, and that any decent treatment of names must therefore give a reasonable account of it.

Now those who enjoy no demonstrative access to a name's bearer are clearly deferential to those who already belong to the relevant practice in the sense already mentioned in § 78: they take themselves to be bound to the established usage of the name in question. But they are likely also to be deferential in a somewhat different sense, at least to the extent that their activities have little or no bearing on whether or not the practice continues. For example, many such users of names play no part in the generation of information about, or in the development of the tradition concerning, the relevant object. Rather, they passively and literally consume the fruits of others' efforts, that is, defer to them on all matters of substance. In so far as these consumers continue to refer with the relevant names, they do so only by dint of the fact that the practice already exists, and is maintained in existence, by courtesy of others. If the efforts of these others ceased, in the sense that neither the gathering of first-hand information about the bearer, nor the refinement of the tradition concerning it, were to continue, then our 'passive' consumers would soon lose all contact with the bearer. This, for example, is how things can get 'lost in the mists of time'.

But there is a crucial distinction to be made here among con-sumers. For, as has already been tacitly acknowledged, it is not only *producers*—those who enjoy demonstrative access to the name's bearer—who keep a practice 'going'. Many thousands of archae-ologists, historians, philosophers, translators, and other scholars, for example, work incessantly to keep alive the traditions concerning those figures and other objects from the past, great and small, who and which are in various ways still of interest or relevance. In a somewhat similar manner, geography teachers, and students of current affairs, keep others in touch with the spatially remote without themselves, necessarily, enjoying demonstrative access to these things. Thus, although experts on Aquinas, for example, may be deferential in the *first sense* to the original producers who knew the great man personally, as well as to a vast army of consumers[4] who over the years kept the light burning, it is clear that they are not really deferential in the *second* sense. That is, such experts certainly only manage to refer at all because there is a pre-existing practice into which they were inducted: but the practice is not maintained for them by courtesy of others. On the contrary, it is these 'consumers' who now keep the light burning.

For some purposes, then, we might well wish to superimpose upon Evans's producer/consumer distinction a rather different 'active/

passive' distinction. Active users will then be (a) Evans's producers, and (b) those consumers who help to keep a practice going. Moreover, this active/passive distinction coincides almost exactly with the distinction to which we saw the Russellian appealing in § 75: namely, the distinction between mere mouthpieces and others. Passive consumers, by definition, are those who just parrot sentences containing the relevant names without really knowing what they are talking about: for example, inattentive history students, casual observers of billboards, people who talk loudly about the situations in Afghanistan and Nicaragua on top of the Clapham omnibus. So the first complexity forced on the Russellian treatment by the Availability Objection applies equally to the KE Proper-Name treatment: and this is, of course, not in the least bit surprising, since the mouthpiece phenomenon just does occur, even with respect to Proper Names (§ 69).

What is perhaps a little more surprising, however, is the fact that something resembling the *second* Russellian complexity (§ 76), forced by the Reference Objection, also seems to apply to the KE approach. For it is not exactly easy for the proponents of this view simply to *abandon* the producer/consumer distinction in favour of the active/passive one. For, as we have seen, those who understand a name do so, according to the KE approach, precisely because they are presented with the name's bearer in a *demonstrative-based* manner (§ 78): they have the ability to think of it and keep track of it even when it is not demonstratively available to them. But a crucial element in the gaining of this ability is the fact that these users enjoy regular and repeated demonstrative access to the name's bearer. One might thus say that whereas producers, who do enjoy such demonstrative access, are authoritative users of the names, the consumers—even the active ones—are not, precisely because they do not enjoy such access. But active consumers are clearly not mere mouthpieces either, because of their role in the continuation of the practices: so the KE theorist, like the Russellian did in response to the Reference Objection, has apparently to appeal to the idea of *intermediate* users of names. Moreover, such users qualify as more than mere mouthpieces in virtue of the fact that they associate a number of informative, although not authoritative, descriptions with the name: how else do they keep the tradition going? And this is just as the Russellian would say: so on this score, at least, the KE approach and the Russellian alternative are rather similar (but see § 83)—although, of course, we still have an important difference over what is involved in being authoritative. We shall return to these matters in §§ 83–4.

Thus facts to do with the Availability and Reference Objections force complexity on to both Russellian and KE treatments: not only this, but each theory responds to the difficulty in substantially the same way. And as we shall now begin to see, the KE treatment can similarly be pushed into the sorts of changes forced on the Russellian by the Proliferation and Inextricability Objections. For all that has been said so far, it seems that the KE treatment can retain the idea that a name has associated with it just one sense which it expresses in each of its uses: and this would be an apparent advantage over the Russellian approach which, we saw in § 76, seems to have to appeal to multiple or at least 'loose-jointed' meanings somehow provided by clusters of authorized descriptions. However, this apparent advantage has been undermined: ironically enough, by Kripke himself.

80 A PUZZLE ABOUT BELIEF

Kripke takes up the question of *Sinn* for names in a paper, 'A Puzzle About Belief' (PB), which is in many respects as significant as the celebrated *NN*. He starts from the thought that, in *NN*, he has given strong reasons for supposing that names are intersubstitutable in modal contexts: for if names are rigid designators then they refer to the same thing at every possible world at which they refer at all. So if 'N^*' and 'N'' are actually co-referential, they are necessarily co-referential, and there can thus be no possible world at which N^* is G and N' fails to be G (and vice versa). Thus if we have either '$\Box(N^*$ is $G)$' or '$\Diamond(N^*$ is G)', we can safely infer the corresponding proposition containing 'N''. However, as Kripke concedes, intersubstitutions of names in *psychological* contexts do not look remotely truth-preserving. Mary, firmly convinced on the basis of good evidence that George Orwell is not Eric Blair, behaves in all the usual ways in which one would expect her to behave if the reports:

(1) Mary believes that Orwell wrote *Animal Farm*,

and

(2) Mary believes that Blair did not write *Animal Farm*,

were true. For example, she repeatedly and sincerely asserts 'Orwell, not Blair, wrote *Animal Farm*'. If, however, substitutions of these co-referential names were allowed, then we could go from (2) to:

(3) Mary believes that Orwell did not write *Animal Farm*.

But whilst (3) may not itself contradict (1), it is clearly a very misleading, if not obviously false, report of Mary's state of mind: more than this, we sorely need an explanation of why Mary, rationally and even justifiably, believes both that Orwell wrote *Animal Farm* and that Orwell did not write *Animal Farm*. *Sinn*, as we have seen in previous chapters, is precisely the sort of thing to be appealed to by such an explanation.

Moreover, as Kripke also concedes, he himself seems to need at least to prohibit intersubstitutions in some contexts in order to back up his claim that names are rigid designators. For, even if '□ (Orwell is Blair)' *is* true, as Kripke maintains, 'Orwell is Blair' is not an obvious candidate for the status of a necessary truth. On the contrary, the great majority of philosophers, at least before *NN* was written, would insist that 'Orwell is Blair' might have been false. Kripke accuses such philosophers of suffering from a sort of illusion: when they seem to themselves to envisage a possible world at which Orwell is not Blair, what they are really doing is imagining a world at which, say, someone just like Orwell, but distinct from Blair (and thus Orwell), happened to write *Animal Farm* and do all the other things for which Orwell is in fact famous. Thus, says Kripke, it is not really possible, but merely imaginable, that Orwell might not have been Blair. However, it is not, of course, even imaginable that Orwell might not have been Orwell: hence we at least cannot intersubstitute co-referential names in contexts governed by 'It is imaginable that . . .'.[5]

Kripke thus contemplates a sort of 'impure' theory on which even rigid designators need to be assigned a *Sinn* for some purposes (PB, p. 244). But his discussion immediately takes a dramatic turn: first, he argues that the doctrine that names have *Sinn* cannot be upheld; next, he describes a case in which occur problems like those to which (1)–(3) give rise, *even though no principle of substitution is involved*; then, he concludes that he has unearthed what appears to be a paradox at the heart of the practice of ascribing reports like (1)–(3) (i.e. Intentional psychology). Now if this last conclusion were right, of course, this really would be an implicit and extremely destructive attack on *Sinn*, which as we have seen belongs squarely at the centre of Intentional psychology (chapters 5 and 6). But we shall see that the conclusion can be resisted, albeit at a certain cost. In any case, care must be taken to distinguish this implicit attack from Kripke's explicit attack on *Sinn* which was mentioned at the beginning of this paragraph. For the explicit attack, as usual, takes the form of an attack on the idea that names abbreviate descriptions (PB, pp. 244–8): and this, as we have seen (§43), is not at all the same thing as the idea that names have *Sinn*.[6]

However this may be, Kripke's main argument for his 'paradoxical' conclusion is beautifully simple. We have already seen that names normally function at the heart of practices involving perhaps many speakers (§78): and he essentially just exploits this fact. More precisely, what Kripke exploits is the idea that someone could *unwittingly* join the same practice *twice over*, and thereby gain, as it were, two competences with (what happens to be) the one name. But of course if it is not realized by the speaker that one name is involved twice over, then the speaker could end up in a state just like Mary's apparently inexplicable state of rationally and justifiably believing that Orwell wrote *Animal Farm*, and that Orwell did not write *Animal Farm*. And this time there would be no point in trying to disallow 'substitutions' of co-referential names, for none would have been employed.

For example, Mary by day maintains regular and diligent attendance at the office at which she works, and often sees there a certain John Smith, who is mousy, quiet, clean-shaven, and diffident. In her daily dealings with this man she counts as a normal producer in the naming practice, and thus counts, by the usual standards, as understanding the name 'John Smith'. For although they do not enjoy a very close relationship at the office, Mary has the same kind of day-to-day demonstrative encounter with John Smith as do many of the other producers in the practice. Anyway, over a period she comes to the conclusion, amply based on her dealings with him, that he is not exactly an extrovert. Indeed, we can say on the basis of her sincere assertions that:

(4) Mary believes that John Smith is not an extrovert.

Mary has another life. By night she regularly and assiduously visits the Frillyknicker Club where she encounters, from time to time, a number of her colleagues from the office. She also frequently comes across a certain John Smith who is raven-haired, noisy, bearded, and rumbustious. At the club she counts as a normal producer in the appropriate naming-practice, and thus counts, by the usual standards, as understanding the name 'John Smith'. For although they do not enjoy a very close relationship at the Club, Mary has the same kind of night-by-night demonstrative encounter with John Smith as do many of the other producers in the practice. And, at length, she comes to the conclusion, amply based on her dealings with him, that he is an extreme extrovert. Indeed, we can say, on the basis of her sincere assertions, that:

(5) Mary believes that John Smith is an extrovert.

Naturally she does not suspect for a moment that the diffident office John Smith is the rumbustious Club John Smith.

But, of course, he is.

81 PROLIFERATING BELIEFS

If there is enough overlap between office-workers and Clubbers, it is not possible to claim here that there are two practices involving two typographically identical names of the one man. If some, but not all, of the relevant producers know well enough of John Smith's way of keeping business and pleasure separate, then we can neither argue that a 'proper' grasp of the name involves a knowledge of this fact, nor that the practice is somehow riddled with confusion (one man regularly and universally being thought to be two). The situation as described could thus involve just one practice, just one name, and thus—given that a name has the same *Sinn* in each of its uses—just one Thought that John Smith is an extrovert. Does Mary have a belief whose content is this Thought, or does she not? Her behaviour at the office suggests not: witness (4). But her behaviour at the Frillyknicker Club suggests otherwise: witness (5). Further, to reply 'both' is a contradiction; to reply 'neither' flies in the face of her rational behaviour, linguistic and otherwise; and to favour one resolution rather than another is arbitrary. Neither are things like this: Mary's state of mind 'flickers', so that each evening she starts to believe that John Smith is an extrovert, only to set it aside for its opposite in the morning. On the contrary, she maintains ongoing beliefs which she regularly expresses with sentences containing 'John Smith'. The trouble is, the beliefs appear to be contradictory. Yet neither is Mary being irrational: she knows about the law of non-contradiction, and regularly reviews her beliefs to weed out possible inconsistency. When she does so she often, of course, notes that she would sincerely report herself with both 'John Smith is an extrovert', and 'John Smith is not an extrovert'. But she cannot regard these as contradictory any more than I can regard my sincere assertions 'Cambridge [England] is not in North America' and 'Cambridge

[Mass.] is in North America' as contradictory; and for the same reason: the names are believed to have different bearers. Unfortunately, though, I am right and Mary is wrong, so from the point of view of the theory of *Bedeutung*, Mary's assertions are contradictory, just like 'Orwell wrote *Animal Farm*' and 'Blair did not write *Animal Farm*'. Even more unfortunately, although one can try to deal with this Orwell/Blair case by appealing to the idea that the two names have different *Sinne*, so that the two sentences expresses different Thoughts, one cannot make this appeal in the John Smith case: for *there is only one name*. This apparently leaves us both impotent to explain the obvious fact that Mary's state of mind is not contradictory, and unable to answer satisfactorily the simple question 'Does Mary, or does she not, believe that John Smith is an extrovert?' This is Kripke's 'paradox'.

Broadly speaking, I should say that there are only two lines of solution to this ingenious problem. One is to proliferate *Sinne* for names, and to claim that there is in this sense no such thing as *the* Thought that John Smith is an extrovert (even when the same John Smith is intended), but rather a cluster of different Thoughts which the appropriate sentence can express. This might involve, for example, trying to generalize the notion of *demonstrative* manner of presentation discussed in §60: Mary is, after all, in a very similar situation to that of Mercedes and Pilar when they confront The Passengergobbler. Or it might involve going back to the socialized version of a Russellian description theory, which also, we saw, has to proliferate meanings for names (§76). The second line of solution is to conclude that the notion of *Sinn*, along with Intentional psychology generally, is just shown to be unstable, and ultimately untenable, by such examples. A third apparent option, that we should just give up on the idea that *names* have *Sinn*, does not appear to me to be a genuine alternative. In the first place, as I have just remarked, an exactly parallel problem occurs with demonstratives: recall that in one version of the story Mercedes uses 'That train' twice over. And in the second place there still remains the problem of explaining why Mary is not simply irrational. If the explanation here is done in Intentional terms, then it is hard to see how this differs from proliferating *Sinne* for names. And if it is done in some non-Intentional terms, say in terms of the kind of 'scientific psychology' mentioned in §65, then one would have given up on the Intentional stance after all.

I do not believe that the second option—that of giving up on

Intentional psychology—is worthy of serious consideration, and I do not believe that people who advocate it know properly what they are saying. But I cannot argue this here, and I shall merely record the comment that if one were to take that line the discussion about names could stop at this point. For we have been concerned to know whether a Proper-Name treatment of names is better than a description treatment: and by 'better' we mean 'more faithful to our given understanding of the meaning of natural names'. But this is, of course, an Intentional project (see §45), and therefore of no further interest to one who has dismissed the Intentional enterprise.

So we are back with Russellian approaches versus KE approaches once more: and note one important thing. Just as, on examination, the KE treatment seems to need to go in for distinctions parallel to those forced on to the Russellian by the Availability and Reference Objections (§§75–6, 79), so it now seems poised, in the face of Kripke's puzzle, to proliferate *Sinne* for names: which is precisely what the Russellian had to do in the face of the Proliferation Objection.[7] So the argument used against the Russellian approach in §77—that it seemed to involve rather a lot of complexity—is now trained almost squarely on to the KE approach, and so is becoming less and less of a reason for merely abandoning the Russellian approach as a completely lost cause. Both theories would be complex: the details of neither are altogether clear.[8]

I turn now to a further twist in the tale.

82 DESCRIPTIVE NAMES

Some names are not introduced in the demonstrative manner described in §79, but are rather introduced in a stipulative manner on the basis of a description presumed to fit an object. For example, scholars may discover an important series of documents, author unknown, and say 'Let's call the author of these documents "Chapman"'. Or astronomers, noticing significant perturbations in the movements of a planet, may decide that they are due to the presence of a hitherto undiscovered heavenly body, and even though this body remains unobserved, may say 'Let's call the cause of these perturbations "Persephone"'. Or idle speculators, intent on passing away a rainy afternoon, may say 'Let's call the heaviest fish in the world "Kim"'.

Let's call such names 'descriptive names'. Not any name introduced by way of a description will count, in what follows, as a descriptive name. For the mere fact that a description is employed at a name's introduction does not by itself rule out that those introducing the name may also have demonstrative access to the object concerned: and in such cases the practice involving the name will then approximate to the KE picture described in previous sections. But it is possible for there to be 'pure' cases, where the introducing description (and perhaps trivial variants of it) provides the only access to the bearer of the name: and these are what concern us here. Arguably, they are not very common in natural languages: but they are possible, and interesting, as we shall see. For after its introduction, a practice may grow around the use of the descriptive name: large tomes may come to be written about Chapman, wherein his thoughts are expounded and his possible identity speculated upon ('there is the following evidence that Chapman was in fact either Shakespeare or Bacon, or perhaps both . . .'); efforts may be made to observe Persephone, and its probable mass calculated; the likely whereabouts of Kim may be guessed at, more or less desultorily. However, again, these practices will not, in every case, involve those concerned in having demonstrative encounters with the named object—although they may, of course, culminate in such encounters, for example if Persephone is observed and subsequently visited. But what are we to say of the pure cases?

On the face of it, they provide the best possible examples of names which *do* abbreviate descriptions. Certainly the obvious sort of Kripkean objection have no force here. For example, at least around the time of a descriptive name's introduction, the relevant description provides a new user with the only possible access to what the practice concerns, and it is therefore obvious that speakers just will not count as understanding the name unless they know that it was introduced by way of the description actually used to stipulate its bearer: although they may well, of course, be able to use the name— as mere mouthpieces—to express whatever Thoughts it contributes to. Thus the fact that some users of the name may not be able to *supply* the appropriate description is neither here nor there, since such users literally do not know, therefore, what they are saying, but are mere mouthpieces. By the same token, neither will properly competent users acknowledge that the description may not fit the actual bearer; how could it fail to, if the bearer is *stipulated* to be the object, if any, which fits the description?

Thus it is plausible to claim that a knowledge of:

(1) 'N' is (stipulated to be) the G

is a necessary condition for understanding any descriptive name 'N', and therefore of understanding sentences containing 'N'. Can we say further that knowledge of (1) is sufficient for understanding 'N'? Again, this is very plausible: given normal linguistic competence, what more could one need to know, beyond (1) itself, in order to understand 'N'? But if a knowledge of (1) is both necessary and sufficient for understanding 'N', this in turn strongly suggests that (a) 'N' and 'the G' are synonymous, so that (b) the Thoughts expressed by sentences containing 'N' are the very same Thoughts as would be expressed by the corresponding sentences containing the description instead of the name. And this last conclusion is, moreover, independently plausible: how could one make available a whole new batch of Thoughts simply by introducing a new term by way of a stipulation like (1)? How could the progression:

The G is H;
Let's call the G 'N';
N is H,

by itself, make it the case that the final sentence came to express a completely new Thought (compare *VR*, p. 50).

Nevertheless, Kripke denies that names introduced in the above ways are synonymous with the relevant descriptions. For he distinguishes in general between *fixing the referent* and *giving the meaning* of an expression, and he holds that it was a crucial mistake of description theorists to conflate these two distinct things (see *NN*, pp. 53–60). Whereas, says Kripke, (1) may well serve to fix the referent of 'N'—i.e. lay down what it shall refer to—it does not follow that (1) thereby gives the meaning of 'N' as being the meaning of the description 'the G'; on the contrary, says Kripke: 'N', as a natural name, would thereby be a rigid designator, whereas the description need not.

However, even if a descriptive name is in this way *not* equivalent to the introducing description, it is implausible to deny that the description *somehow* contributes to the name's *Sinne* (Kripke, of course, is barely able to formulate this thought given the terms in which he usually sets up the discussion, where 'having *Sinn*' = 'abbreviating a description'). Furthermore, by definition, a descriptive name cannot present its bearer in the sort of demonstrative-based manner mentioned in §78: for in the 'pure' cases, there is no demonstrative contact between the users of the name and its bearer (if any, indeed). How can the KE theorist accommodate this? One obvious reply is to appeal to the idea of the descriptive singular Thought introduced in chapter 7. Since it appears to make sense to suppose that we can think singular Thoughts about objects under a descriptive or conceptual manner of presentation, and there is an obvious candidate, in the shape of introducing description, from which the appropriate conceptual manner of presentation may be culled, one might attempt to regard descriptive names as contributing to descriptive singular Thoughts. Of course, to say this would not necessarily be to say that the name is, after all, synonymous with its introducing description. For it may be that descriptions, as normally understood in natural language, do not themselves contribute to genuine singular Thoughts at all, but serve rather in the formulation of purely general Thoughts (see §72 and the end of the present section). And if this is indeed the case then one could claim that some name 'N' presents its bearer in genuine singular Thoughts as being uniquely G, without also having to claim that 'N' is thereby synonymous with 'the G'.

Unfortunately, this attempt to deal with descriptive names by the KE theorist cannot in general work, essentially for the reasons set out in §72. At least in those cases where the introducing description is of the outward-looking variety, there is no point at all—semantic, Intentional, or logical—in saying that the expression is a Proper Name. It cannot serve as a Proper Name *for us*, and since the way it serves us is the basis of the only real interest we can have in it—it does not matter at all to us what the thing looks like from a god's-eye perspective—it just is not a Proper Name. But, of course, there will be a more or less perfect overlap between (i) names introduced by way of outward-looking descriptions, and (ii) 'pure' cases of descriptive names. There may be a slight grey area, where, although there is no demonstrative contact between the introducers of the name and its bearer, the relevant object may still have 'made (enough of) a mark' on the introducers for the description to be backward-looking (compare §§71–2). This would be a 'pure' descriptive name which could, conceivably, count as a Proper Name (imagine the detective of §72 saying 'Let's call this thief "Diego"'). But for the rest this cannot be, and the result is that the KE treatment, like the Russellian, would need to adopt a mixed strategy (§77). Admittedly, there are differences: since descriptive names are rare, they only necessitate a small modification in the KE treatment, whereas, if the Russellian approach is to be a serious alternative, rather than a small modification to an otherwise nearly correct KE treatment, its supporters would presumably argue for a more significant use of a mixed strategy. Moreover, this argument could not be based on the observation that the 'problematic' names are those introduced by way of descriptions, for the same reason (see §84). Still, here is yet another way in which the hard lines of the KE approach need to be softened and smudged if an accurate theory is to be produced.[9]

Why is Kripke and those who follow him on descriptive names so confident that they do not abbreviate their introducing descriptions? One can trace the argument to the thought that whereas

(2) The G is necessarily G

can be interpreted in two different ways, depending on the relative scopes of the description and the modal word, there is only one way of taking

(3) N is necessarily G.

And this, if true, straight off seems to show that 'N' and 'the G' are not exactly synonymous. The doctrine of different types of designator is then employed as a semantic explanation of this alleged difference (see §§38–9).

Now in the general case, as we saw in chapter 4, Kripke is on strong ground over the modal point, although we also saw that there are other explanations of the modal facts which are compatible with a description treatment of names. But in any case the issue is rather less clear-cut in the case of descriptive names. For the fact is that 'pure' cases, as we remarked above, are not very common, so one cannot expect many speakers to have very strongly developed 'intuitions' over how many ways there are of taking a modal sentence containing a descriptive name. What is more, 'intuitions' can be influenced and refined by other relevant facts: and given the above argument to the conclusion that descriptive names *just are* synonymous with the relevant descriptions, and anyway cannot be Proper Names, we seem to have before us just the sort of fact which might persuade us that there are scope choices to be made in respect of a sentence of the form of (3), where 'N' is a (pure) descriptive name. Nor would resisting Kripke's claim about descriptive names amount to denying his general distinction between fixing the referent and giving the meaning. For, as we noted above, a name may be introduced by way of a description in circumstances where demonstrative access to the bearer is available, and where it is therefore plausible to see the name as a Proper Name of the object concerned.

In such a case the description would merely serve as an 'inessential tool' (Donnellan's phrase: see §68) for picking out the name's bearer: that is, it would fix the referent without giving the meaning. But such impure cases are a case apart, and allowing Kripke's distinction here does not force us to apply it everywhere.

This, then, is one way that Kripke's attack on a description theory of *descriptive* names might be resisted. However, there is another way, which involves *accepting* that there are no scope choices to be made where sentences of the form of (3) are concerned even when '*N*' is purely descriptive. For, as we saw in §35, there are other explanations, compatible with a description theory, of these scope phenomena. For example: if it is a general convention among us that natural names are to be given the widest scope available, then this itself would rule out scope choice with respect to the relevant sentences. Moreover, such a convention could be grounded, as we saw in §78, n. 3, in the fact that many names certainly start out as Proper Names among the producers of the relevant practice. And why should not such a convention apply even in the case of descriptive names: if names are usually given wide scope, and a name is introduced in a pure case by way of a description, is it not completely intelligible to suppose that this new expression will be governed by the conventions which govern other natural names, and that it too should therefore always be given wide scope?

To take this line would not necessarily be to commit oneself to the claim that it is possible to generate new Thoughts on the basis of a progression like:

> The *G* is *H*;
> Let's call the *G* '*N*';
> *N* is *H*.

For there is no doubt that 'synonymy' is itself a rather complex notion, so that one could say *both* (a) that a descriptive name makes the same contribution to a Thought as does its introducing description, and (b) that, nevertheless, the two expressions are not exactly synonymous (compare '✕' and '★' in §35). One might say, for example, that the ordinary notion of synonymy (and meaning) embraces both what we are here calling *Sinn*, and what in chapters 3 and 6, following Strawson, we called significance: after all, Strawson proposed, precisely, that we make this sort of distinction within the rather rough notion of meaning with which Russell was operating. Then we could say that just as a general grasp of the sort of expression a demonstrative is would involve knowing that these expressions are standardly used in perceptual encounters with objects presented in certain ways, so a general grasp of the sort of expression a natural name is would involve knowing that, in the standard types of case described in § 78, a natural name is used by a group of speakers to pick out, even when it is not demonstratively present, a certain object which serves, as it were, as the focus or target of the whole activity. And this itself, for the reasons given there, could underlie a general convention to the effect that names should always be given wide scope. Thus, although it is indeed, at the beginning, both necessary and sufficient to know that:

N is (stipulated to be) the G

if one is to count as understanding 'N', this is not enough to show that 'N' and 'the G' are exactly synonymous. For knowledge of the above stipulation can only be operative in the context of general linguistic competence: and such competence will include the knowledge, described above, that natural names have their own distinctive type of significance (see DUMMETT (1981), pp. 572–4).

83 CONSUMERS AGAIN

The position we have now reached is that a properly worked-out KE theory, like the Russellian alternative, would be quite complex: it would involve appeals to the mouthpiece phenomenon and (perhaps) to the idea of 'intermediate' speakers (§ 79), would proliferate *Sinne* for names (§ 81), and would need to employ a mixed strategy (§ 82). Moreover, there is a significant overlap between the two appoaches in respect of the detailed treatments which they would offer for specific names. As we saw in § 78, it is hardly to be denied that nearly all natural names are Proper Names at least among producers: moreover, the Russellian is committed anyway to a mixed strategy, according to which at least some names would be treated as Proper Names (§ 77). Putting these two points together, the result seems to be that Russellians and KE theorists should give exactly the same treatment to names as used by producers: they should treat them as Proper Names. What is more, since, as we have just seen, descriptive names cannot, at least in the majority of cases, be treated as Proper Names, the two approaches should presumably offer parallel, quantificational treatments of descriptive names.

However, despite these considerable overlaps, the position so far is that the KE treatment 'wears the trousers': except for the anyway atypical case of 'pure' outward-looking descriptive names, KE theorist and Russellian alike should offer Proper-Name treatments of names. Thus, if anything interesting is to be salvaged from the Russellian approach—if, that is, any serious qualification is to be forced on to the KE theorist—then it will have to emerge out of the treatment of names as used by speakers who are not producers. With this in mind it will help if we now look more closely at the 'intermediate' users. Intermediate users as so far characterized, recall, are those who are neither authoritative speakers nor mere mouthpieces: 'active consumers' on the KE picture (§ 79), speakers who offer non-authorized descriptions on the Russellian (§ 76).

The first thing we have to note is that the Russellian characterization of intermediate speakers is no longer applicable in every case. If, as we have acknowledged, we should regard natural names with respect to which we are producers as Proper Names, then there is a sense in which the Russellian notion of 'authorized description' becomes redundant: at least as regards the names to whose bearers we have demonstrative access, we should acknowledge that understanding such a name involves being Acquainted with its bearer, rather than associating with it an allegedly authorized description. Given this, the mark of an intermediate user of such a name can no longer in general be an inability to provide an authorized description: rather, the Russellian is now obliged to accept a KE-type characterization, according to which one large class of intermediate users consists of the active consumers (Russellians can, of course, retain their characterization of intermediate speakers for those names—for example, descriptive names—which should be treated as abbreviations of descriptions: see below). But do active consumers hold out any hope for the Russellian?

Now, the KE theorist might try to deal with active consumers either by (i) denying that they have any better grasp of a name's meaning than do mere mouthpieces, (ii) claiming that a name takes on a new and different meaning when used by active consumers, or (iii) by claiming that even consumers—or the active ones anyway— can understand a name in the same way as producers can, despite lacking demonstrative access to its bearer.

However, option (i) is not at all credible. It would involve, for example, having to claim that there is no difference, as far as understanding the name 'Aristotle' is concerned, between the most learned twentieth-century scholar, and the man on the Clapham omnibus who heard yesterday that a girl called 'Aristotle' invented syllogistibolic logic in 1950. It would mean that education does not in general teach us a great deal about distant parts and times, but instead merely puts us in a position to parrot a lot of sentences that we do not really understand. Such a suggestion is clearly absurd.[10]

On the other hand, option (iii) is mysterious: how can a manner of presentation which is demonstrative-based, that is available to certain speakers as a result of their day-to-day demonstrative encounters with a certain object, somehow become enshrined in a practice so that even those who are *not* in a position to encounter the object can nevertheless have the object presented to them in that way? Moreover, since, as we have seen, the KE theorist is committed to proliferating *Sinne* even among producers (§ 81), there can be no such thing as *the* demonstrative-based manner of presentation enshrined in a practice. Given, furthermore, that what makes producers' understanding of a name distinctive is clearly the fact that their uses of the name are entwined with their day-to-day inter-actions with its bearer—this is, after all, a key insight of the KE approach (§ 78)—it cannot sensibly be denied that an active con-sumer's understanding of a name is essentially different from that of a producer.

This leaves the KE theorist with option (ii): a name takes on a different meaning for active consumers; or, rather, takes on mean-ings of a different kind from those demonstrative-based ones grasped by the producers. How is this to be filled out? The only obvious line for the KE theorist to take here is to say that active consumers have the relevant object presented to them under *descriptive or conceptual* manners of presentation. In receiving education as a consumer one learns a lot of presumed information about the bearers of lots of different names, and the idea would be that one thereby comes to think descriptive singular Thoughts about them (§ 70). And it is indeed true, as we saw in § 79, that the mark of active consumers, as opposed to mere mouthpieces, is that they associate a certain amount of putatively identifying material with the name.

Now there are obvious affinities here with Searle's 'cluster' theory (§ 76), according to which one's grasp of a name is somehow underwritten by the idea that an unspecified but significant number of a cluster of descriptions fit an object. However, this nod in a Russellian direction on behalf of the KE theorist would not amount to a capitulation, of course. For the envisaged KE theory would still be a Proper-Name treatment—active consumers would be held to think singular Thoughts, involving descriptive manners of presentation, about the bearers of the names—whereas, of course, the Searle-type theory was presented above as an option for a quantificational approach (Searle's own intentions on this matter are difficult to divine: it is possible, even, that he would reject the sort of contrast I have made). Thus the two theories would still be divided by their responses to the possibility that a certain name may lack a bearer, as when, say, a practice grows around a hoax or legend. According to the KE approach, such a fact would rob the utterances of the participants in the practice—even those of the active consumers—of their intended type of content. There just would not be available for expression any appropriate descriptive singular Thoughts to which, on this KE approach, uses of the names are supposed to contribute. Whereas, on the other hand, a quantificational treatment could hold that Thoughts are expressed by active consumers' uses of the name whether or not it had a bearer (§§ 16–18).

There would be other differences too. For example, if a treatment of a name is to be a genuine description theory, then it must say that an object will count as the name's bearer if and only if that object satisfies (enough of) the descriptive material alleged to give the meaning of the name. Thus it is apparently ruled out that (for example) the active consumers of a practice should come to associate with a name a cluster of descriptions which all happen to be *false* of the name's actual bearer: as Searle puts it, 'any individual not having at least some of [the properties commonly attributed to him] could not be Aristotle' ('Proper Names', p. 95). At the same time, it is also implied that a name might take on a new bearer in the course of its history, as when, for example, a name starts out as a name for x, who is known to the practice's producers, but ends up among active consumers as a name for a distinct individual y on account of the fact that many or all of the relevant cluster of descriptions happen to fit y rather than x.

A proponent of the KE approach is likely to reject both ideas. In the first place, since the active consumers are alleged to think descriptive singular Thoughts about the object which actually started out at the focus of the practice—the object Named by the relevant producers, which has subsequently 'made (some kind of) a mark' on the consumers—room is left within the KE account for the idea that even the active consumers should come to hold only false beliefs about that very object: in which circumstances they would, of course, have come to think of it under inappropriate descriptive manners of presentation. Such a case might, for example, be considered to be analogous to a case in which someone, badly tricked by the light, say, thinks of a perceptually present sage-bush under a demonstrative manner 'that leopard'. Similarly, a KE theorist is not forced to conclude that if the descriptions associated with the name happen to fit some object distinct from the one at the focus of the original practice, then the name has become, among the later users, a name of this distinct individual. For an important insight of the KE treatment is that entrants to a naming-practice are 'deferential' to those who introduced the name at least to the extent that they take themselves to be naming the object known to the producers at the core of the practice (§78). Of course, a name *can* change its bearer—as when, for example, a practice comes, through widespread error, or imposture, to centre on a different individual than that which it originally concerned. In such a situation, as time goes by and assuming that the original object disappears from the scene, the practice's producers use the name in the course of expressing and entertaining demonstrative singular Thoughts about the new object, and after a time it becomes pointless to deny that this object has become the bearer of the name (see VR, pp. 388–91). But the fact remains that this kind of reference-change—which could also, of course, be recognized by the Russellian—is a different phenomenon from the one mentioned above, which involves a change of reference for a name not merely when another object 'contaminates' a practice, but also when, for whatever accidental reasons, the cluster of descriptions associated with the name by active consumers happens to be satisfied by a new object. We shall return to this point below.

We thus appear to have at least two options, which differ in the ways just described, for dealing with the uses of names made by active consumers. One involves a fairly straightforward extension of the KE treatment, whilst the other involves a rather dramatic employment of a mixed strategy, according to which names with respect to which all remaining speakers are consumers—and there are a very great many of them where educated speakers are concerned—would be treated, not as Proper Names, but in accordance with some version of the 'cluster' description theory. I shall now complete my examination of the Proper Name by suggesting that the latter alternative is, on the whole, preferable.

84 RUSSELL REINSTATED?

The first point to be noted is that it is somewhat inappropriate to continue to regard active consumers as 'intermediate' speakers, given the suggestion implicit in this label that these speakers have a somewhat deficient understanding of the name concerned (compare §76). For although an active consumer's grasp of a name is, as we have seen, certainly *different* from that of a producer, this in itself is no reason to hold that this grasp is also in some way inferior. After all, the meanings of words do evolve through time as they come to take on and shed different connotations and inferential links with other words. Furthermore, even in cases where a word comes to take on a cruder or less subtle meaning than it formerly had—as is the case with 'fabulous' in the 1960s, say—such a situation is not happily described as one in which later competent speakers have a deficient understanding of the word. Rather, such speakers understand their word perfectly well: it is just what they understand is a blunter instrument than that from which it has derived. For recall that the principal reason for crediting speakers with an understanding of the meanings carried by their words is in the course of making Intentional sense of these very speakers (chapter 5). From this perspective, once speakers have become inducted into the normal contemporary practices involving the use of a certain word, there is just no more to be said on the score of their competence: they are fully-paid up participants in the game.[11] And what is the point of taking a different view of a name like 'Aristotle'? Even if there is a sense in which the grasp of active consumers is somehow inferior to that of producers—and it is by no means clear, as we shall see, that this supposition is correct—the inferiority attaches, as it were, to what is grasped rather than to the manner of grasping, and active consumers are thus perfectly authoritative with respect to the contemporary meaning of the name in question.

If this is correct, then whichever of our two opposing treatments of names as used by active consumers we adopt, it should incorporate a dynamic, rather than a static, distinction between authoritative and intermediate speakers. And, on the face of it, either approach could incorporate such a feature. For we have seen that the essential difference between active and passive consumers turns on the richness of the descriptive material associated with the name (§79): and given this the authoritative speakers will be the ones who are sufficiently *au fait* with the cluster of authorized descriptions; the speakers to whom one should turn for proper instruction in the correct use of the name. But there is here no bar to the idea that the membership of this cluster should change through time as the body of information associated with the name itself changes, and, as it were, the conception of the name's bearer implicit in a practice itself thereby shifts. According to the KE approach, what would be shifting here would be the descriptive manners in which the bearer of the name is presented to the active consumers. According to the Russellian approach, it is not a matter of changing manners of presenting the bearer, but rather a matter of changes in the cluster of descriptions of which the name is somehow to be construed as an abbreviation.

At any one time this will make it possible to distinguish between authoritative consumers on the one hand, and a spectrum of increasingly passive intermediate speakers on the other, who will know less and less of what is important about the name until, at the limit, they count only as mere mouthpieces. Of course, one cannot expect matters here to be sharp or clear-cut: given someone who knows merely that, say, Aristotle is the man called 'Aristotle' by the scholar at the end of the street, what more does this speaker need to get to know to become an authoritative speaker? The matter obviously needs investigation (compare DUMMETT (1981), pp. 188ff.). However, such a labour, awkward as it may be to undertake, cannot be avoided merely by appealing to the KE picture. For, as we have seen, KE theorists too, if they are to give a satisfactory account of names as understood by active consumers, are required to give an account of the kinds of descriptive manners of presentation under which, on this KE approach, such users think of the names' bearers. These are problems which just seem to be inherent in the very idea of the natural name, and they can in no way be avoided simply on the strength of breezy incantations of KE sympathies.

This point is missed so often because of the influence of the sort of god's-eye perspective mentioned in § 72. From this sort of perspective a naming-practice is thought of as extended in space (and especially time), and the following view is then very tempting. An object comes to be known as 'N' by a group of speakers who both introduce the word into the language and maintain it in operation. Others join in somewhat at the fringes, deferring to those who know best, and come to be able to perform the useful but humble task of spreading the word to those even more benighted. One who adopts this sort of view is almost certain to favour the KE approach to active consumers, and almost as likely—vainly if I have been right so far— to try to avoid the question of characterizing properly the understanding of a name enjoyed by such speakers. By the same token, sympathy for the Russellian approach to active consumers is likely to be involved with a closer interest in their actual Intentional situation: for it is by paying attention to this, after all, that one gets to see that the grasp of the name enjoyed by such speakers, and the way in which this grasp is involved with the descriptive material associated with the name, cannot simply be discounted. In trying to decide between the two approaches, then, it will profit us to focus on this clash of perspectives.

Evans introduces this matter with the following passage:

Everyone who is introduced to the 'Homer'-practice nowadays learns 'Homer was the author of the *Iliad* and the *Odyssey*'; and everyone who is introduced to the 'Robin-Hood'-practice learns more or less of the legend: the bandit in Sherwood forest who used a longbow, who robbed the rich to give to the poor, and so on. These facts, which are of course known to speakers, make possible the general use of such a name with an intention other than the simple intention of using it to refer to whatever is the referent of a name in a given practice. . . . Thus, inside the long-lived practice of using the name 'Homer' and 'Robin Hood', there develops, so to speak, a secondary practice of using the name *as if* it were governed by the stipulation 'Let us use the name "Homer" to refer to the author of the *Iliad* and the *Odyssey*' . . . (VR, pp. 394–5)

Evans goes on that people in such a 'secondary practice' make

further uses . . . of the name—building on what they know to make new assertions ('Homer was a master of narrative'), to express desires and wishes ('I wish I had met Homer'), to give commands ('Write out a page of Homer's poetry'), to make jokes, and so on . . . (ibid.).

That is, at least some active consumers tend to behave with a name as if it served, for them, as an abbreviation of the description(s) commonly associated with it. So, for example, the scholar interested in the style in which the *Iliad* is written will certainly use the name 'Homer' as short for, say, 'the author of these poems', and as far as the relevant purposes would be concerned the thought that Homer might not have written the *Iliad* would be conceptually improper or irrelevant: on this usage Homer just is whoever (if anyone) wrote the poems in question. Such usage therefore conforms to what the Russellian treatment would offer, and is at odds with the KE approach: for according to such a theory, the thought that Homer might not have written the poems—for example if the man at the centre of the original 'Homer'-practice had stolen some manuscripts from an unknown wandering scribe—ought always to be open, at least in principle, and thus can never be conceptually improper.

Now what Evans says here is, of course, true enough: but it is also rather understated. For he might have gone on that such 'secondary' users of names also write books, engage in field trips, put on lecture courses, and generally engage in the practices and careers character-istic of non-technological sections of colleges and universities and, more broadly, of those who are engaged in the development of a proper cultural appreciation of themselves by studying the art and ideas of former or distant cultures. Moreover, it is only from the god's-eye perspective that such activities could possibly be seen as 'secondary' practices operating 'inside' some broader context. For, of course, from a *contemporary* perspective, such activities consti-tute the core of the practice *as it has become*: from this perspective, there is a sense in which there is *no* broader context within which the so-called 'secondary' uses of names by active consumers are to be seen as somehow derivative or make-believe. And this, of course, means that the Russellian treatment is here rather more plausible than Evans makes it sound. For, once we agree that active con-sumers are not 'intermediate' speakers in any interesting sense, but rather have a perfectly good grasp of the meaning that the names have come to have, we are bound to take their own understanding of the word as the crucial thing upon which to focus when giving an account, as meaning-theorists, of the meanings of the names in the relevant uses. So if the active consumers understand the names in a way that is captured by a Russellian account, then the Russellian account is to be preferred to any rival, such as the KE treatment, which fits the relevant understanding less well. To suppose other-wise is to fall into the error, mentioned in §72, of supposing that there is some point to the idea that speakers might be semantically alienated, in a systematic and institutionalized way, from their own language.

Evans, however, rejects a Russellian treatment of names as used by active consumers on the grounds that

Our use of at least personal proper names is governed by a picture of how they are endowed with a reference—[*the KE picture*]—and this means that we would simply not think of saying, if asked to defend our assertion 'Homer was the author of the *Iliad* and the *Odyssey*', that 'I was under the impression that "Homer" was just the name we give to the author . . .'. (VR, p. 396)

Rather, Evans goes on, we are kept 'in a position of permanent deference—sensitive to information which we ourselves do not possess about the person whose name we are using' (ibid.). In other words, names never really, despite the appearance given by 'secondary' practices, become attached definitionally to descriptions in the manner alleged by the Russellian.

Now it is far from clear that active consumers would 'not think of saying' what Evans puts into their mouths. Russellian treatments of names have struck many—experts and lay persons alike—as extremely plausible, if not platitudinous, and it is very common indeed to find newcomers to the topic saying exactly the kind of thing cited by Evans. Nevertheless, there is something right about his claim. In the first place, as we have already noted (§ 76), it is not plausible to hold that names *generally* come associated with just one description: 'Homer', indeed, is quite exceptional in just this respect. Rather, a credible description theory should maintain that names are normally associated with a more or less vaguely delineated cluster of descriptions which collectively, somehow, invest it with its meaning: so that, for example, one will not count as understanding such a name properly unless one associates with it enough of the appropriate cluster. Given this, it is indeed normally reckless to tie a name too tightly to just the one description, as the aforementioned newcomers to the topic can normally swiftly be persuaded. But such a result, of course, leaves the cluster theory intact.

In the second place, Evans is certainly correct to the extent that active consumers do not ordinarily suppose that the relevant names were explicitly introduced as descriptive names, or as the focus for a cluster of identifying descriptions. Rather, as he points out, it is part of normal active consumers' understanding of a name that it has come down to them by the appropriate kind of reliable mechanism, starting off with producers and then spreading in the sorts of ways described in §§ 78–9. But this, too, is compatible with a Russellian cluster theory. For it can hardly be maintained that one could be properly authoritative with regard to the contemporary meaning of a name such as 'Aristotle' or 'Aquinas' without having at one's fingertips a fair amount of the presumed history of the named individuals and their work. Moreover, given the acknowledged facts about how names are supposed to pass down to active consumers, a

Russellian might even suggest that some or all of these descriptions should be weighted quite strongly, so that if enough of them fail to apply to anything, the relevant name would be deemed to lack a bearer (for more on this, see below). And it is true that a proper induction into, say, the 'Aristotle' practice does not involve a blind acquaintance with the texts, divorced from all sense of time and place: this is true even of philosophical inductions, which are notorious for their ahistorical bent. Hence, any cluster theory worth its salt would of course include the stipulation that among the cluster of authorized descriptions there will normally be historical and biographical material. Indeed, exactly the same would be maintained by any KE treatment worthy of attention: for, as we have seen, the task of deciding what kinds of beliefs and abilities are required for a proper active consumer's understanding of a name is not one that the KE theorist can shirk. The difference between our two alternatives resides not in what counts as a proper active consumer's understanding of a name, but rather in the account of what is thereby understood: descriptive singular Thoughts according to the KE approach, quantificational ones according to the Russellian.

However, given all this, it may well be objected at this point that a great fuss is being made over not very much: if the accounts are so similar, then what does it matter whether we say one thing or the other? And Evans himself remarks at one point that it 'is quite striking how little it matters what we decide' (VR, p. 394): and one should be sympathetic here. Nevertheless, there are arguments on both sides: what is more, paradoxically, there is a sense in which the 'it doesn't matter' response plays into the hands of the Russellian.

The main tactic of the KE theorist is to press the question of what should be said in the event of the discovery that most or all of the descriptions associated with a name by active consumers turn out to be false of the object named by the producers of the practice. For example, what should we make of the putative discovery that there indeed was a Greek known to the producers of what is in fact our 'Aristotle'-practice, but that he was a philosophically innocent soldier of fortune: a soldier of fortune, the thought continues, who one day happened to stumble on the unpublished manuscripts of a recently deceased reclusive genius, ('Baristotle'), which manuscripts he thereafter passed off as his own (we may suppose that the ancient Greeks were very gullible)? If such a story were in fact true then most members of our cluster of 'Aristotle'-descriptions would thus be true of Baristotle. Should not the Russellian, faced with such a discovery, conclude that 'Aristotle' is in fact our name for Baristotle: and is it not equally obvious that so to conclude would be wrong; that we really would all along have been using 'Aristotle' to refer to the soldier of fortune, the focus of the original naming-practice?

However, all that is really obvious is that we should be in a mess over our uses of the name 'Aristotle'. Certainly, there is a sense in which the soldier of fortune comes into the story: after all, it was his name and later presumed exploits that were incorporated into the practice that we joined. But there is equally a sense in which Baristotle, also, comes into the story: after all, we should certainly decide that in our future disquisitions on *Nichomachean Ethics*, and all the other books written by Aristotle, their provenance should be made clear; moreover, we should ensure that our future attributions of greatness and so on would be laid at the right door. But given the 'Baristotle' supposition, should I have said just now that the *Nichomachean Ethics* was 'written by Aristotle'? This is the question at issue, and it is this question which has an air of unreality about it. On the one hand, the soldier of fortune was named by the producers of the relevant practice: furthermore, as noted above, the Russellian might weight this fact in such a way that 'Aristotle' remains, even on a Russellian treatment, as a name of the soldier of fortune. But, on the other hand, it is clearly in closer accord with our original intentions when using 'Aristotle' that the name, if used at all in future in connection with the works and the tradition surrounding them, should be used as a name of Baristotle. KE theorists can try to insist, if they like, that such a decision would amount to a deliberate change of reference for the name 'Aristotle', and go on to reiterate the claim that, before this decision, 'Aristotle' was 'really' a name of the soldier of fortune, and 'Aristotle did not really write the *Nichomachean Ethics*' expressed a true Thought. Russellians, even, might agree with this, depending on how they weight historical and biographical detail.

But what does *any* of this add to the story as originally told: that something went wrong in the transmission of the name; that most members of the cluster of descriptions associated, on any account, with a proper contemporary understanding of the name 'Aristotle', are not true of the man named by the producers of the 'Aristotle'-practice? What is added to this by the competing semantic claims? Now we have seen at length (chapters 5 and 6; §§ 71–2) that semantic claims like these stand or fall to the extent that they contribute to the Intentional illumination of speakers, characteristically by forming the basis of an account of the Thoughts expressed and entertained by these speakers. But it is clear, as we have indeed already suggested, that however natural the KE verdicts on active consumers may look from the god's-eye perspective, things are quite otherwise from the Intentional point of view. As far as our understanding of fellow speakers' uses of 'Aristotle' is concerned, it is clear that there is *nothing to be gained* by an insistence that such speakers are 'really' expressing descriptive singular Thoughts about someone who did not write *Nichomachean Ethics* and all the other books, despite the fact that the paramount, communicated intention of such speakers would normally be to speak of the author of the relevant works.

It thus emerges that the most striking feature of such cases—and the real basis of the 'it doesn't matter' response—is that the normal communicative, etc. purposes served by names as used by active consumers are rather indifferent to the sorts of questions which we have just seen to divide Russellians and KE treatments of these uses. But this actually favours the Russellian. For the most glaring of such questions to which active consumers' uses of names are in many ways indifferent is the question of whether or not the name used actually has a bearer at all. As in the case of outward-looking descriptions (§ 71), there is a clear sense in which the Intentional business of understanding the linguistic and other behaviour of active consumers can proceed with total indifference to the question whether the name concerned actually names anything. We do not hesitate to ascribe Thoughts to one another on the basis of our uses of, say, 'Aristotle' or 'Robin Hood', and the success of our Intentional efforts would by no means be undermined by the discovery that these names had no bearers. Naturally, many propositions which we had formerly believed to be true, such as 'Robin Hood lived near Nottingham', we should now have to mark down as false, or qualify with 'according to the legends . . .'. But this, of course, goes no way towards showing that a KE treatment must be right after all. On the contrary: a Russellian treatment would support the change in truth-value, whereas a KE treatment, in a sense, would do no such thing (compare §§ 26–30). For if, as the KE theorist claims, contemporary uses of, say, 'Robin Hood lived near Nottingham' are intended to function as a means of expressing genuine singular Thoughts about the name's bearer, which is presented to contemporary users under descriptive manners of presentation, then we ought to decide, upon discovering that the name has no bearer, that no Thoughts were ever expressed by any uses of this name, and that our so-called Intentional understanding of people who said things like 'I'm going to visit the forest where Robin Hood lived' were, in fact, illusory. But this is plainly absurd: not, indeed, because it can never be right to take such a drastic line with sincere attempts to use Candidates in order to formulate Thoughts (compare chapter 6), but because the Intentional facts point the other way in this case (compare § 72). Insisting on the KE line with regard to active consumers is thus, at bottom, analogous to insisting that outward-looking descriptions are Proper Names. Both claims fly in the face of Intentional reality due to overemphasis of the god's-eye point of view. Both are to be rejected because, however tempting that view might become once externalism is properly acknowledged, the fact remains that the god's-eye view is nothing *to us*—it is not a view which we can generally take of ourselves as we go about our business, Intentional and otherwise—and it thus simply cannot help us gain the sort of self-understanding which, as meaning-theorists, we set out to find (§ 12).

I conclude, then, that the Russellian mixed strategy towards names mentioned in §§ 77 and 83 is preferable to the KE alternative: although, of course, this latter treatment lives on as an important component of the Russellian approach. Descriptive names, and names as used by consumers, are to be given a Russellian treatment (§§ 76, 82): for the rest—names as used by producers—the KE treatment is to be preferred (§ 78).

Further Reading

The works by Kripke mentioned in this chapter are 'Naming and Necessity' and 'A Puzzle About Belief'. The first appeared in *Semantics of Natural Language*, ed. D. Davidson and G. Harman (Dordrecht, 1972), and was later issued as S. Kripke, *Naming and Necessity* (Oxford, 1980) (page refs. are to this version). The second is to be found in *Meaning and Use*, ed. A. Margalit (Jerusalem, 1979). Much work on natural names is distorted by a heavy involvement with a Kripkean equation of 'having sense' and 'abbreviating a description'. But in addition to the works cited in the Further Reading to chap. 4 see also G. Evans, *The Varieties of Reference*, ed. J. McDowell (Oxford, 1982), chaps. 2, 3, 11; M. Devitt, *Designation* (New York, 1981), chaps. 1, 2, 5; P. T. Geach, 'The Perils of Pauline', in id., *Logic Matters* (Oxford, 1972); and M. Davies, *Meaning, Quantification and Modality* (London, 1980), chap. 5. For the 'cluster' theory of names (§§ 76, 83) see J. Searle, 'Proper Names', *Mind*, 67 (1958); repr. in P. F. Strawson (ed.), *Philosophical Logic* (Oxford, 1967) to which page refs. apply.

Compare L. Wittgenstein, *Philosophical Investigations*, tr. G. E. M. Anscombe (Oxford, 1953), Pt. I, § 78. For Frege's remarks on the proliferation of *Sinne* for names see 'On Sense and Reference', in *Translations From the Philosophical Writings of Gottlob Frege*, ed. P. T. Geach and M. Black (Oxford, 1960), p. 58 n., and 'The Thought: A logical enquiry', tr. A. and M. Quinton, *Mind*, 65 (1956), pp. 24–5; repr. in P. F. Strawson (ed.), *Philosophical Logic* (Oxford, 1967) to which page refs. apply.

For descriptive names (§ 82) see Evans, chap. 2, M. Dummett, *The Interpretation of Frege's Philosophy* (London, 1981), App. 3, and G. McCulloch, 'A Variety of Reference?', *Mind*, 94 (1985).

NOTES

1. Here is another way of approaching the point. If it were true that speakers take their natural names to abbreviate the sorts of descriptions they would (if they could) offer in answer to the 'Who is N?' question, then certain propositions would come out as *analytically true*, that is as true by definition: whereas such propositions are not generally so regarded by competent speakers. For example, suppose S offers 'the G' as answers to the question 'Who is N?' If this established that S took 'N' to be an abbreviation of 'the G', then S surely should regard the proposition 'N is the G' as analytically true. But this is incompatible with the point in the text that S's understanding of 'N' allows for the possibility that 'N is the G' may actually be *false*.

2. Note too the danger of circularity (to be distinguished, of course, from that discussed in § 75). In trying to eliminate 'Nottingham', say, from the description alleged to abbreviate 'the river Trent', one could well end up appealing to a description containing 'the river Trent'.

3. Note that there appears to be some support here, which we could not find in the modal arguments considered in chap. 4, for Kripke's claims (i) that names and descriptions differ both in respect of modalization and in respect of the kind of access they give us to objects, and (ii) that these two matters are somehow related. In the first place if, as seems very likely, names are Proper Names at least when used by their introducers, then the Thoughts to which these names contribute in these uses are genuine singular Thoughts which contain the named object. Thus any situation, counterfactual or otherwise, which does not contain, say, the Moon, is not a situation where *our* Thought that the Moon is made of green cheese can even exist (although such a situation might be such that 'the Moon is made of green cheese', *as used in that situation*, expresses a Thought: recall the distinction in chap. 4 n. 5 between truth *at* and truth *in* a possible world). Thus, clearly, when we ask whether our Thought about the Moon might have been true, we ask something to which only possible worlds which contain the Moon can be relevant.

Note that there is no point, either, in a notion of *scope* for names. By contrast, if descriptions are quantificational, then the Thought, say, that the only satellite of the Earth is made of green cheese can certainly exist, and perhaps even be true, at a situation where the Moon does not exist.

If the Kripkean claims are supported in this way, however, it is better not to go along with the 'designator' classification, according to which names are rigid and descriptions need not be. For if names are treated as Proper Names and descriptions treated quantificationally, then there is no interesting semantic classification, in a Fregean framework anyway, according to which these expressions belong to the same semantic type. It is then mysterious, and confusing, to subsume names and descriptions alike under terms like 'designator', 'singular term', 'referring expression', and the other informal terms which tend to be introduced in this regard. For a related point see n. 9 below.

4. Evans remarks that in a literate tradition most new consumers actually 'short-circuit' the transmission-procedure for a name either by reading ancient documents, or by being only a few links away from someone who has (VR, p. 391). But I shall ignore this in what follows.

5. It is usual thus to distinguish here between different kinds of possibility (and necessity): the strong or *metaphysical* type of possibility, which is the sense in which Orwell could not possibly not have been Blair (given that he is), and the weaker of *epistemic* type of possibility, which is the sense in which Orwell's not being Blair is at least imaginable. See *NN*, pp. 34–9.

6. Kripke actually acknowledges this for once in an extraordinary footnote. He writes that '... according to Russell, what are ordinarily called "names" are not genuine, logically proper names, but disguised definite descriptions. Since Russell also regards definite descriptions as in turn disguised notation [for quantifier phrases], he does not associate any "senses" with descriptions, since they are not genuine singular terms' (PB, p. 271 n. 3). But Kripke then immediately goes on to say that he will ignore this point 'for convenience'! What convenience?—the only thought seems to be that 'the philosophical community has generally understood Fregean senses in terms of descriptions' (ibid.). But why base one's arguments on a known error, in a way practically guaranteed to perpetuate it?

7. Frege too believed that a name can have different *Sinne* for different speakers. Naturally such a view—which we have just seen to be more or less obligatory—undermines somewhat the Fregean idea mentioned in §42 that words have an invariant core of conventional meaning by virtue of belonging to a public language. In effect, what has to be made room for is the idea that the *Sinn* carried by a word in the mouth of a speaker is likely to be somewhat 'idiosyncratic': compare, for example, the account of demonstrative Thoughts given in §60. However, as we

saw in that discussion, such a fact neither makes one's Thoughts inaccessible to other speakers, nor, therefore, makes communication impossible: although, as we all know, it can be rather difficult at times. Thus Frege exaggerates when he says that speakers who attach different *Sinne* to the same name 'do not speak the same language' as far as that name is concerned ('The Thought', p. 25).

8. Note that even in cases of extreme irrationality, where someone does apparently both affirm and deny the very same claim, there will presumably be *some* explanation of this, even if we have to forsake psychology and turn to chemistry or physics in order to give it. And no doubt the same kind of chemical or physical explanation will be available of why Mary both affirms and denies the sentence 'John Smith is an extrovert' (and, indeed, of why an ignorant historian might affirm 'Cicero denounced Cataline' and deny 'Tully denounced Cataline'). But the principal point of the PB-type examples, as in the 'Cicero-Tully' cases, is that they concern subjects whose states of mind make complete sense. What needs to be explained, then, is not just how the subject manages to produce the different *sentences* under different circumstances, but rather how it can so much as *make sense* to produce these sentences in this way. This is clearly a very different type of explanatory project from that envisaged in the extreme irrationality case (and possible, as acknowledged, in the other cases too). Compare the account of rendering someone understandable from the Intentional point of view given in § 51.

9. In VR, chap. 2 Evans produces a curious 'hybrid' theory according to which (a) non-descriptive names are Proper Names in the sense described in § 78 above, (b) descriptive names are not, but instead mean the same as their introducing description (apart from scope behaviour: see pp. 50–1, 60–1), even though, (c) a descriptive name 'refers to [its bearer], and in exactly the same sense as that in which [an ordinary] name refers to its bearer' (p. 50). Such a theory falls foul of the general § 72 argument against the idea that outward-looking descriptions can enable us to name, in any meaningful sense (to us), the objects (if any) they describe. Neither are Evans's arguments for the position at all compelling: see McCULLOCH (1985).

10. It seems to me to be a significant defect of Evans's treatment of names that he was evidently perfectly happy with option (i): see VR, pp. 377–8, 400 ff.

11. This is not to deny, of course, that a study of such things as etymology and the history of ideas can improve one's self-understanding, and affect one's use of language: it would be foolish to deny this. The point, rather, is that it is pointless to build significant amounts of the above sort of knowledge into the requirements for ordinary linguistic competence, simply because doing so makes mere mouthpieces of too many ordinary

speakers. However tempted one may be to make this sort of claim when thinking in god's-eye terms (§ 72), it is plain, once the Intentional point of view of one's fellow speakers is taken, that it cannot be sustained: we standardly know each other as fellow-understanders (see §§ 50–4).

Bibliography

AYER, A. J. (1956). *The Problem of Knowledge*, Harmondsworth.

BLACKBURN, S. (1979). 'Thought and Things', *PAS*, supp. vol. 53.

—— (1984). *Spreading the Word*, Oxford.

BUTTERFIELD, J. (ed.) (1986). *Language, Mind and Logic*, Cambridge.

CARRUTHERS, P. (1986). *Introducing Persons*, Beckenham.

—— (1987). 'Russellian Thoughts', *Mind*, 96.

—— (1988). 'More Faith than Hope: Russellian Thoughts Attacked', *A* 48.

CHASTAIN, C. (1975). 'Reference and Context', in K. Gunderson (ed.), *Language, Mind and Knowledge*, Minnesota.

CHURCHLAND, P. (1979). *Scientific Realism and the Plasticity of Mind*, Cambridge.

DAVIDSON, D. (1969). 'On Saying That', *S* 19; repr. in DAVIDSON (1984).

—— (1980). *Essays on Actions and Events*, Oxford.

—— (1984). *Inquiries into Truth and Interpretation*, Oxford.

DAVIES, M. (1980). *Meaning, Quantification and Modality*, London.

DENNETT, D. C. (1987). *The Intentional Stance*, Cambridge, Mass.

DESCARTES, R. (1641). *Meditations on First Philosophy*, in DESCARTES (1985).

—— (1985). *The Philosophical Writings of Descartes*, vol. 2, tr. J. Cottingham *et al.*, Cambridge.

DEVITT, M. (1981). *Designation*, New York.

DONNELLAN, K. (1966). 'Reference and Definite Descriptions' (RDD), *PR* 75.

DUMMETT, M. (1973). *Frege: Philosophy of Language*, London.

—— (1978). *Truth and Other Enigmas*, London.

—— (1981). *The Interpretation of Frege's Philosophy*, London.

EVANS, G. (1979). 'Understanding Demonstratives', in H. Parret and J. Bouveresse (eds.), *Meaning and Understanding*, Berlin.

—— (1982). *The Varieties of Reference* (*VR*), ed. J. McDowell, Oxford.

—— and McDOWELL J. (eds.) (1976). *Truth and Meaning*, Oxford.

FODOR, J. (1976). *The Language of Thought*, Hassocks.

—— (1980). 'Methodological Solipsism Considered as a Research Strategy in Cognitive Psychology', *BBS* 3; repr. in FODOR (1981).

—— (1981). *Representations*, Brighton.

—— (1986). 'Individualism and Supervenience', *PAS*, suppl. vol. 60.

FORBES, G. (1985). *The Metaphysics of Modality*, Oxford.

FREGE, G. (1879). *Begriffsschrift*, in FREGE (1960) (to which page refs. apply) and FREGE (1972).

—— (1891). *Function and Concept*, in FREGE (1960).
—— (1892a). 'On Concept and Object', in FREGE (1960).
—— (1892b). 'On Sense and Reference', in FREGE (1960).
—— (1956). 'The Thought: A Logical Enquiry', tr. A. and M. Quinton, *Mind*, 65; repr. in STRAWSON (1967) (to which page refs. apply).
—— (1960). *Translations from the Philosophical Writings of Gottlob Frege*, eds. P. T. Geach and M. Black, Oxford.
—— (1964). *The Basic Laws of Arithmetic*, tr. M. Furth, Berkeley and Los Angeles.
—— (1972). *Conceptual Notation and Other Articles*, tr. T. W. Bynum, Oxford.
—— (1979). *Posthumous Writings*, tr. P. Long, *et al.*, Oxford.
GEACH, P. T. (1962). *Reference and Generality*, Ithaca.
—— (1972a). *Logic Matters*, Oxford.
—— (1972b). 'The Perils of Pauline', in GEACH (1972a).
HACKING, I. (1975). *Why Does Language Matter to Philosophy?* Cambridge.
HEAL, J. (1986). 'Replication and Functionalism', in BUTTERFIELD (1986).
HINTIKKA, J. (1962). *Knowledge and Belief*, Ithaca.
HORNSBY, J. (1977). 'Singular Terms in Contexts of Propositional Attitude', *Mind*, 86.
KAPLAN, D. (1969). 'Quantifying in', in D. Davidson and J. Hintikka (eds.), *Words and Objections: Essays on the Work of W. V. Quine*, Dordrecht; repr. in LINSKY (1971).
—— (1978). 'Dthat', in P. Cole (ed.), *Syntax and Semantics*, vol. ix, *Pragmatics*, New York.
KRIPKE, S. (1971), 'Identity and Necessity', in M. Munitz (ed.), *Identity and Individuation*, New York.
—— (1977). 'Speaker's Reference and Semantic Reference', in P. A. French *et al.* (eds.), *Midwest Studies in Philosophy*, ii, Univ. of Minnesota.
—— (1979). 'A Puzzle About Belief' (PB), in A. Margalit (ed.), *Meaning and Use*, Jerusalem.
—— (1980). *Naming and Necessity* (*NN*), Oxford (orig. pub. in D. Davidson and H. Harman (eds.), *Semantics of Natural Languages*, Dordrecht, 1972).
LEWIS, D. (1980). 'Index, Context and Content', in S. Kanger and S. Ohman (eds.), *Philosophy and Grammar*, Dordrecht.
—— (1986). *On the Plurality of Worlds*, Oxford.
LINSKY, L. (ed.) (1971). *Reference and Modality*, Oxford.
LOCKE, J. (1961). *An Essay Concerning Human Understanding*, ed. J. Yolton, vol. ii, New York.
LOUX, M. (ed.) (1979). *The Possible and the Actual*, Ithaca.
McCULLOCH, G. (1984). 'Frege, Sommers, Singular Reference', *PQ* 34; repr. in WRIGHT (1984).
—— (1985). 'A Variety of Reference?', *Mind*, 94.

—— (1986). 'Scientism, Mind, and Meaning', in PETTIT and McDowell (1986).

—— (1988a). 'Faith, Hope and Charity: Russellian Thoughts Defended', *A* 48.

—— (1988b). 'Carruthers Repulsed', *A* 48.

—— (1988c). 'What it is like', *PQ* 38.

MACDONALD, G. and PETTIT, P. (1981). *Semantics and Social Science*, London.

McDowell, J. (1977). 'On the Sense and Reference of a Proper Name', *Mind*, 86; repr. in M. Platts (ed.), *Reference, Truth and Reality*, London. 1980.

McGinn, C. (1983). *The Subjective View*, Oxford.

NAGEL, T. (1974). 'What is it like to be a bat?', *PR* 83; repr. in NAGEL (1979).

—— (1979). *Mortal Questions*, Cambridge.

NOONAN, H. (1980/1). 'Names and Belief', *PAS* 81.

—— (1984). 'Fregean Thoughts', in WRIGHT (1984).

—— (1986). 'Russellian Thoughts and Methodological Solipsism', in BUTTERFIELD (1986).

PERRY, J. (1977). 'Frege on Demonstratives', *PR* 86.

PETTIT, P. and McDowell, J. (eds.) (1986). *Subject, Thought, and Context*, Oxford.

PUTNAM, H. (1975). *Mind, Language and Reality*, Cambridge.

PLATTS, M. (1979). *Ways of Meaning*, London.

QUINE, W. V. (1940). *Mathematical Logic*, Cambridge, Mass.

—— (1953a). *From a Logical Point of View*, Cambridge, Mass.

—— (1953b). 'On What There Is', in QUINE (1953a).

—— (1953c). 'Reference and Modality', in QUINE (1953a); repr. in LINSKY (1971).

—— (1953d). 'Two Dogmas of Empiricism', in QUINE (1953a).

—— (1960). *World and Object*, Cambridge, Mass.

—— (1969a). 'Epistemology Naturalized', in QUINE (1969b).

—— (1969b). *Ontological Relativity and Other Essays*, New York.

RUSSELL, B. (1903). *The Principles of Mathematics*, London.

—— (1905). 'On Denoting' (OD), *Mind*, 14; repr. in RUSSELL (1956) (to which page refs. apply).

—— (1910). 'Knowledge by Acquaintance and Knowledge by Description', in RUSSELL (1918a).

—— (1912). *The Problems of Philosophy*, London.

—— (1914). 'The Nature of Acquaintance', in RUSSELL (1956).

—— (1918a). *Mysticism and Logic*, New York.

—— (1918b). 'The Philosophy of Logical Atomism' (PLA), in RUSSELL (1956).

—— (1956). *Logic and Knowledge*, ed. R. Marsh, London.

—— and WHITEHEAD, A. N. (1910). *Principia Mathematica*, vol. i, Cambridge.

SAINSBURY, R. M. (1979). *Russell*, London.

—— (1986). 'Russell on Acquaintance', in G. Vesey (ed.), *Philosophers Ancient and Modern*, Cambridge.

SEARLE, J. (1958). 'Proper Names', *Mind*, 67; repr. in STRAWSON (1967) (to which page refs. apply).

SOMMERS, F. (1982). *The Logic of Natural Language*, Oxford.

STITCH, S. (1983). *From Folk Psychology to Cognitive Science*, Cambridge, Mass.

STRAWSON, P. F. (1950). 'On Referring' (OR), *Mind*, 59; repr. in STRAWSON (1971) (to which page refs. apply).

—— (1952). *Introduction to Logical Theory*, London.

—— (ed.) (1967). *Philosophical Logic*, Oxford.

—— (1971). *Logico-Linguistic Papers*, London.

WITTGENSTEIN, L. (1953). *Philosophical Investigations*, tr. G. E. M. Anscombe, Oxford.

—— (1958). *The Blue and Brown Books*, Oxford.

WOODFIELD, A. (ed.) (1982). *Thought and Object*, Oxford.

WRIGHT, C. (1983). *Frege's Conception of Numbers as Objects*, Aberdeen.

—— (ed.) (1984). *Frege: Tradition and Influence*, Oxford.

Index